PSYCHIC POWER NANAKI™

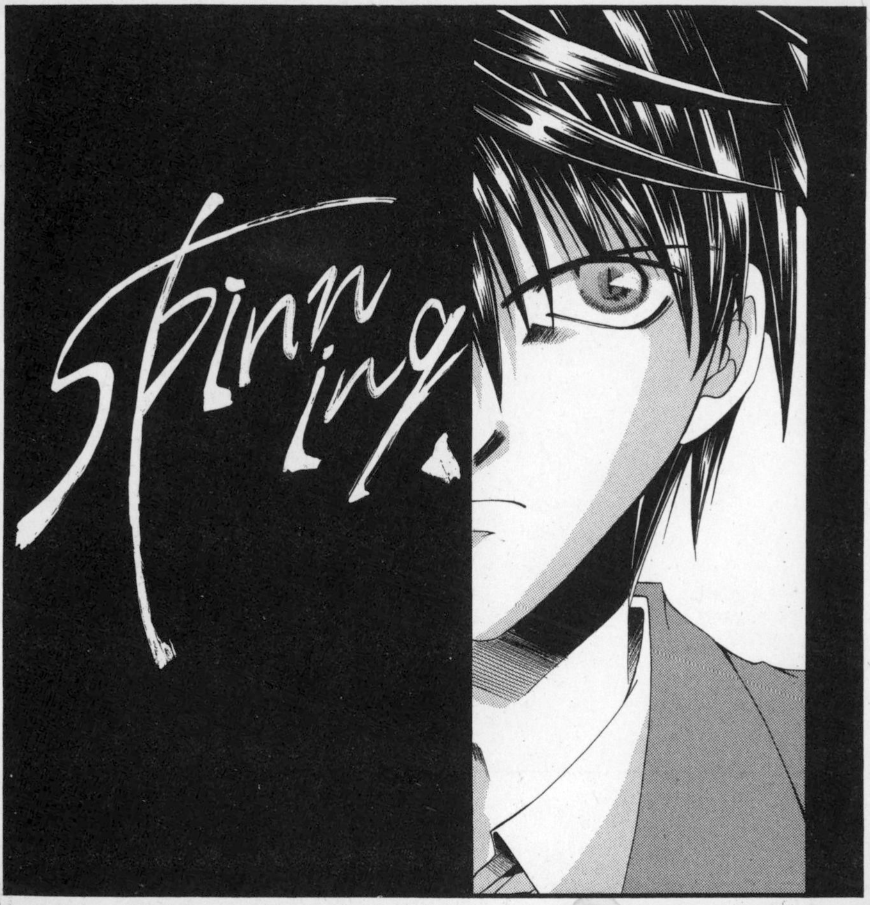
Spinning

Psychic Power Nanaki Vol. 1
Created by Ryo Saenagi

Translation - Elina Ishikawa
English Adaptation - Alex de Campi
Retouch and Lettering - Star Print Brokers
Production Artist - Michael Paolilli
Graphic Designer - James Lee

Editor - Peter Ahlstrom
Digital Imaging Manager - Chris Buford
Pre-Production Supervisor - Erika Terriquez
Production Manager - Elisabeth Brizzi
Managing Editor - Vy Nguyen
Art Director - Anne Marie Horne
Editor-in-Chief - Rob Tokar
Publisher - Mike Kiley
President and C.O.O. - John Parker
C.E.O. and Chief Creative Officer - Stuart Levy

A 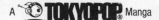 Manga

TOKYOPOP and 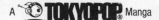 are trademarks or registered trademarks of TOKYOPOP Inc.

TOKYOPOP Inc.
5900 Wilshire Blvd. Suite 2000
Los Angeles, CA 90036

E-mail: info@TOKYOPOP.com
Come visit us online at www.TOKYOPOP.com

CHOU SHINRIGENSHOU NOURYOKUSHA NANAKI by Ryo Saenagi © 2003 Ryo Saenagi All rights reserved. First published in Japan in 2004 by HAKUSENSHA, INC., Tokyo English language translation rights in the United States of America and Canada arranged with HAKUSENSHA, INC., Tokyo through Tuttle-Mori Agency Inc., Tokyo English text copyright © 2007 TOKYOPOP Inc.

ISBN: 978-1-4278-0304-7

First TOKYOPOP printing: November 2007
10 9 8 7 6 5 4 3 2 1
Printed in the USA

PSYCHIC POWER NANAKI™

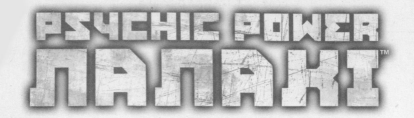

Volume 1

by
Ryo Saenagi

TOKYOPOP®

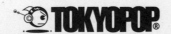

HAMBURG // LONDON // LOS ANGELES // TOKYO

PSYCHIC POWER NANAKI™

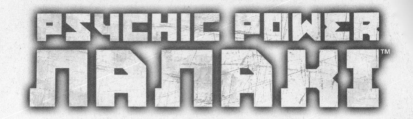

CONTENTS

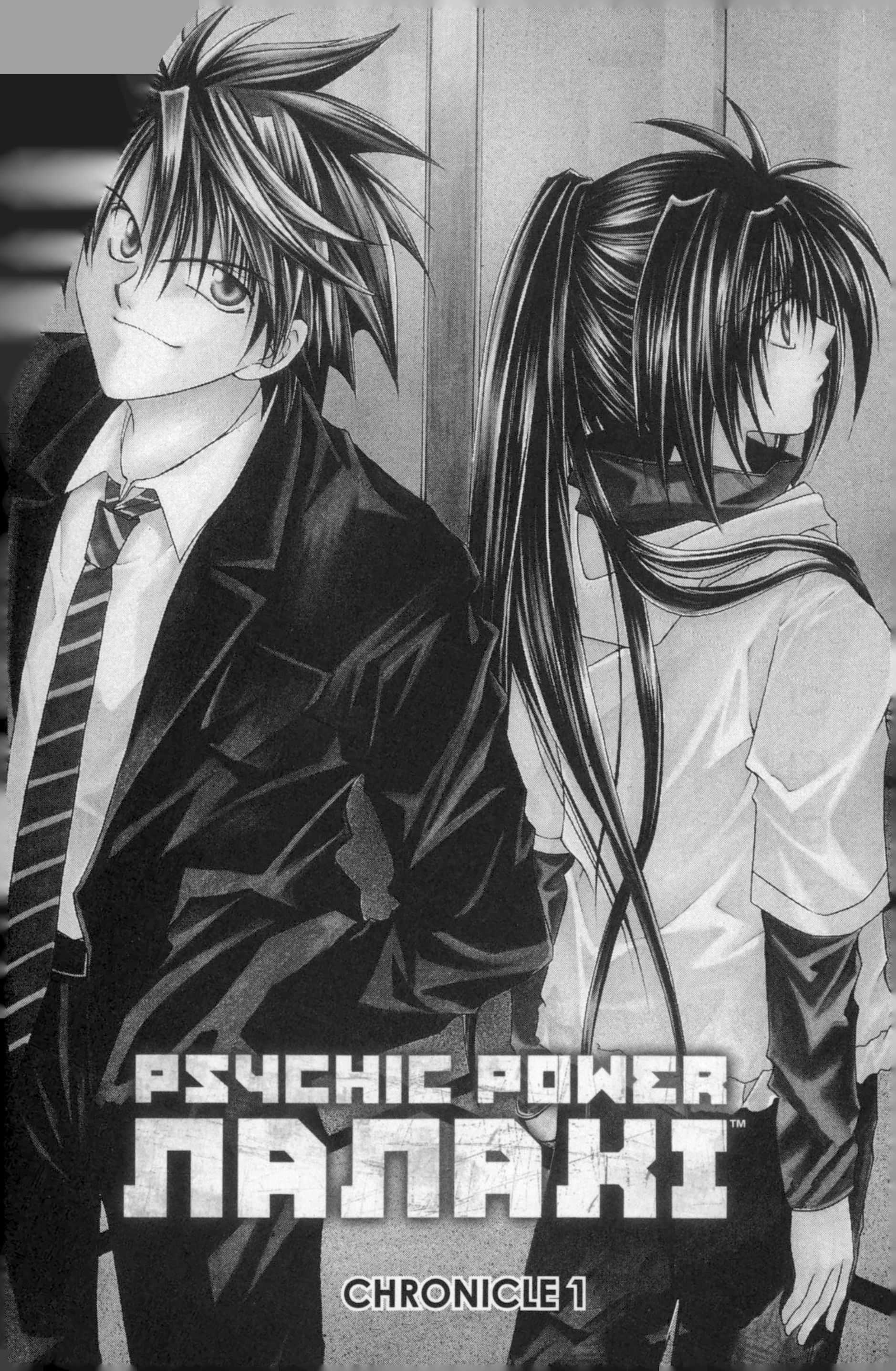
PSYCHIC POWER
NANAKI™
CHRONICLE 1

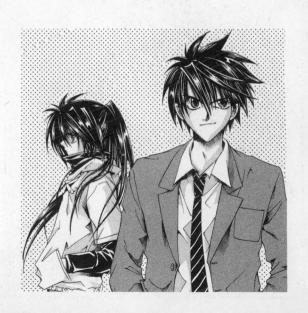

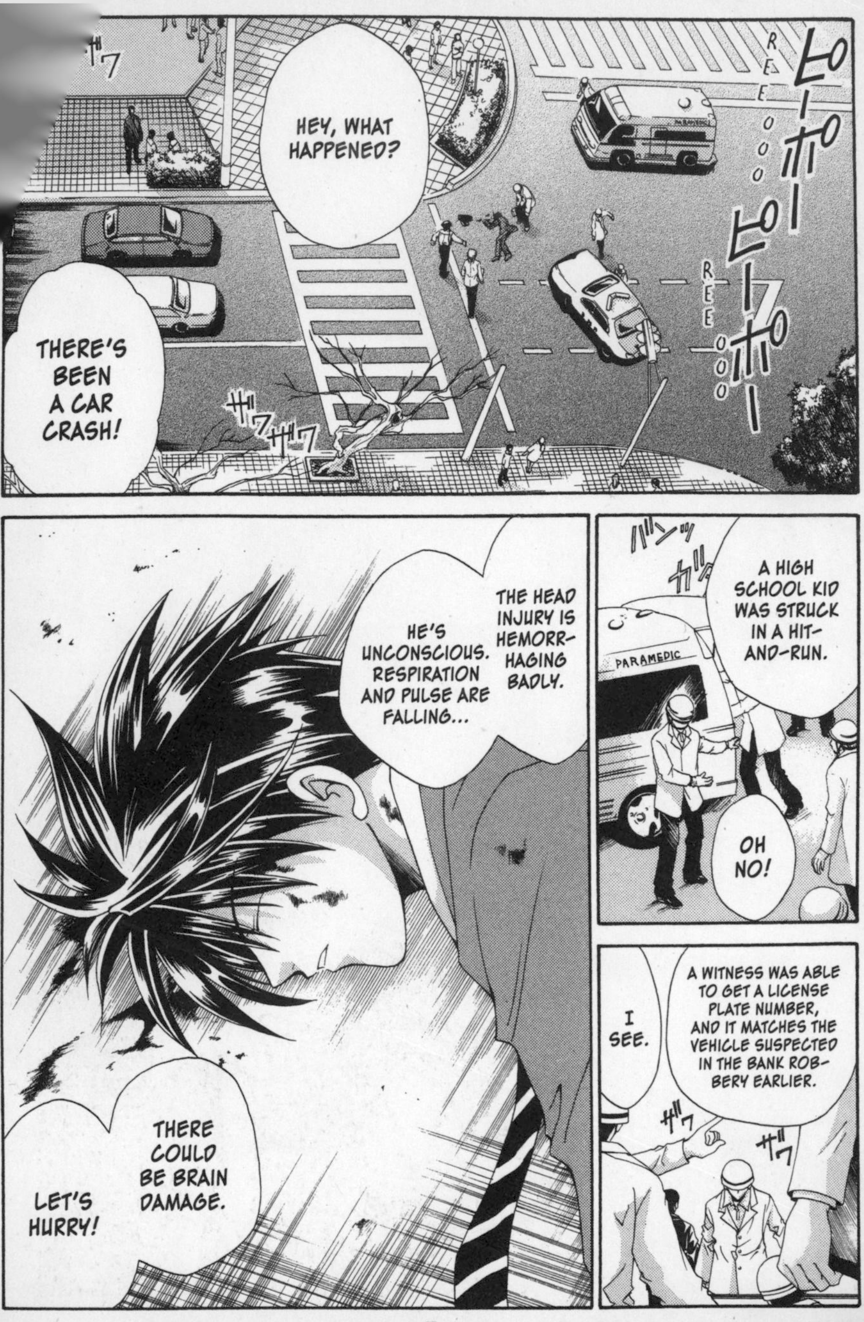
REEOOO REEOOO
HEY, WHAT HAPPENED?
THERE'S BEEN A CAR CRASH!
A HIGH SCHOOL KID WAS STRUCK IN A HIT-AND-RUN.
PARAMEDIC
OH NO!
A WITNESS WAS ABLE TO GET A LICENSE PLATE NUMBER, AND IT MATCHES THE VEHICLE SUSPECTED IN THE BANK ROBBERY EARLIER.
I SEE.
THE HEAD INJURY IS HEMORRHAGING BADLY.
HE'S UNCONSCIOUS. RESPIRATION AND PULSE ARE FALLING...
THERE COULD BE BRAIN DAMAGE.
LET'S HURRY!

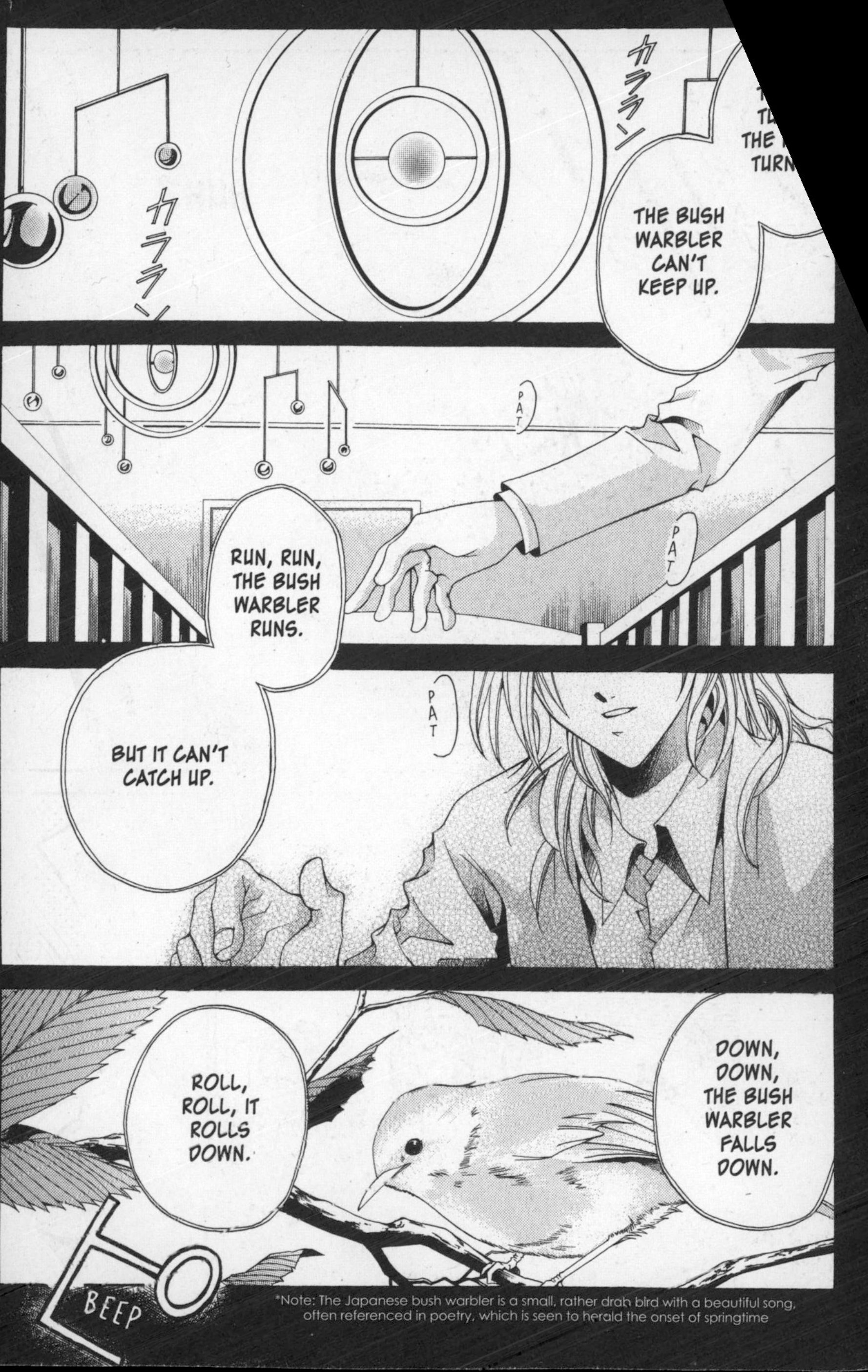
カララン
THE BUSH WARBLER CAN'T KEEP UP.
カララン
PAT
PAT
RUN, RUN, THE BUSH WARBLER RUNS.
PAT
BUT IT CAN'T CATCH UP.
DOWN, DOWN, THE BUSH WARBLER FALLS DOWN.
ROLL, ROLL, IT ROLLS DOWN.
BEEP

*Note: The Japanese bush warbler is a small, rather drab bird with a beautiful song, often referenced in poetry, which is seen to herald the onset of springtime

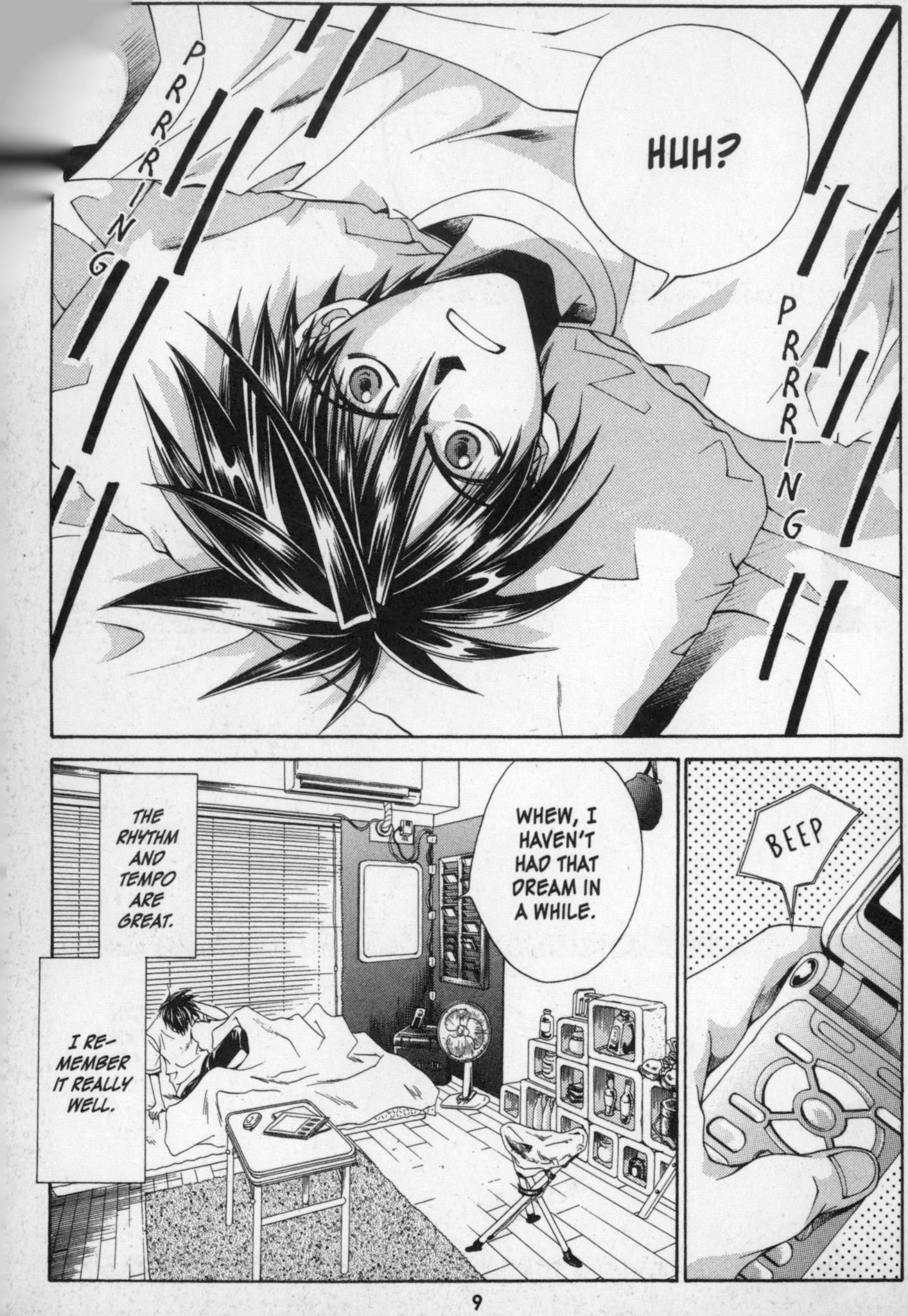
HUH?
PRRRING
PRRRING
BEEP
WHEW, I HAVEN'T HAD THAT DREAM IN A WHILE.
THE RHYTHM AND TEMPO ARE GREAT.
I RE-MEMBER IT REALLY WELL.

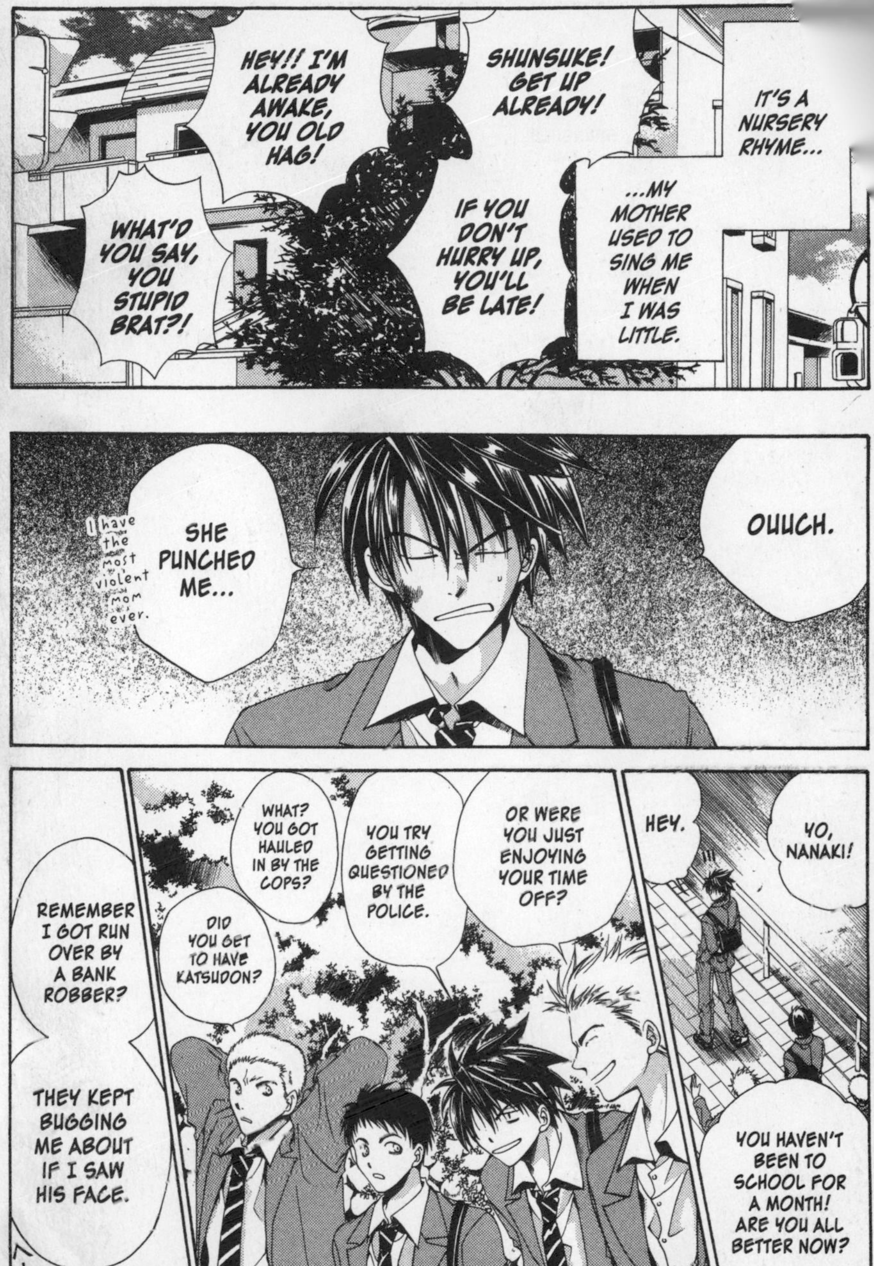
IT'S A NURSERY RHYME...
...MY MOTHER USED TO SING ME WHEN I WAS LITTLE.
SHUNSUKE! GET UP ALREADY!
IF YOU DON'T HURRY UP, YOU'LL BE LATE!
HEY!! I'M ALREADY AWAKE, YOU OLD HAG!
WHAT'D YOU SAY, YOU STUPID BRAT?!
OUUCH.
SHE PUNCHED ME...
I have the most violent mom ever.
YO, NANAKI!
HEY.
YOU HAVEN'T BEEN TO SCHOOL FOR A MONTH! ARE YOU ALL BETTER NOW?
OR WERE YOU JUST ENJOYING YOUR TIME OFF?
YOU TRY GETTING QUESTIONED BY THE POLICE.
WHAT? YOU GOT HAULED IN BY THE COPS?
DID YOU GET TO HAVE KATSUDON?
REMEMBER I GOT RUN OVER BY A BANK ROBBER?
THEY KEPT BUGGING ME ABOUT IF I SAW HIS FACE.

*Note: Katsudon (deep-fried pork cutlet on rice) is known to be served at police stations.

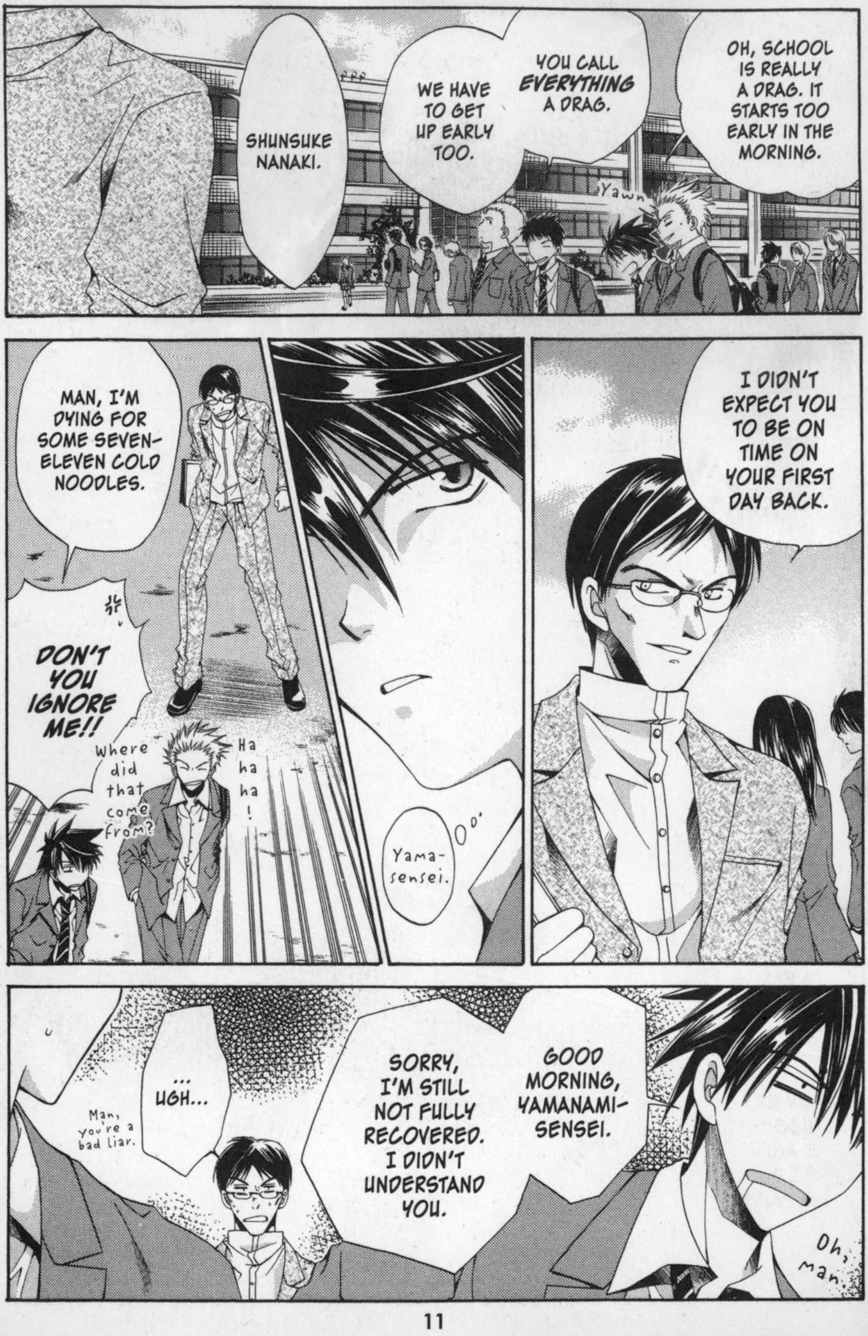
OH, SCHOOL IS REALLY A DRAG. IT STARTS TOO EARLY IN THE MORNING.
Yawn
YOU CALL EVERYTHING A DRAG.
WE HAVE TO GET UP EARLY TOO.
SHUNSUKE NANAKI.
I DIDN'T EXPECT YOU TO BE ON TIME ON YOUR FIRST DAY BACK.
Yama-sensei.
MAN, I'M DYING FOR SOME SEVEN-ELEVEN COLD NOODLES.
DON'T YOU IGNORE ME!!
Ha ha ha!
Where did that come from?
GOOD MORNING, YAMANAMI-SENSEI.
Oh, man.
SORRY, I'M STILL NOT FULLY RECOVERED. I DIDN'T UNDERSTAND YOU.
... UGH...
Man, you're a bad liar.

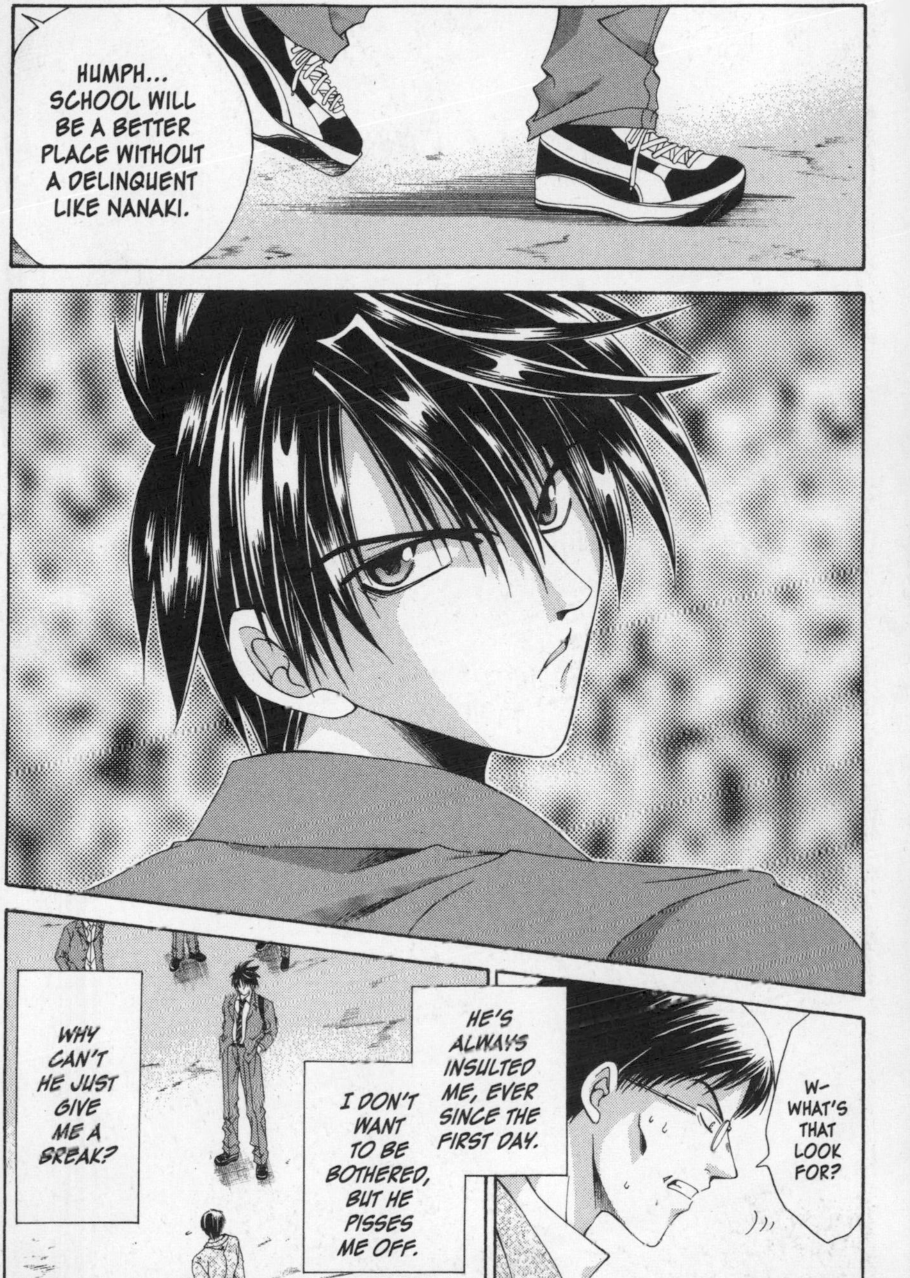
HUMPH... SCHOOL WILL BE A BETTER PLACE WITHOUT A DELINQUENT LIKE NANAKI.
W-WHAT'S THAT LOOK FOR?
HE'S ALWAYS INSULTED ME, EVER SINCE THE FIRST DAY.
I DON'T WANT TO BE BOTHERED, BUT HE PISSES ME OFF.
WHY CAN'T HE JUST GIVE ME A BREAK?

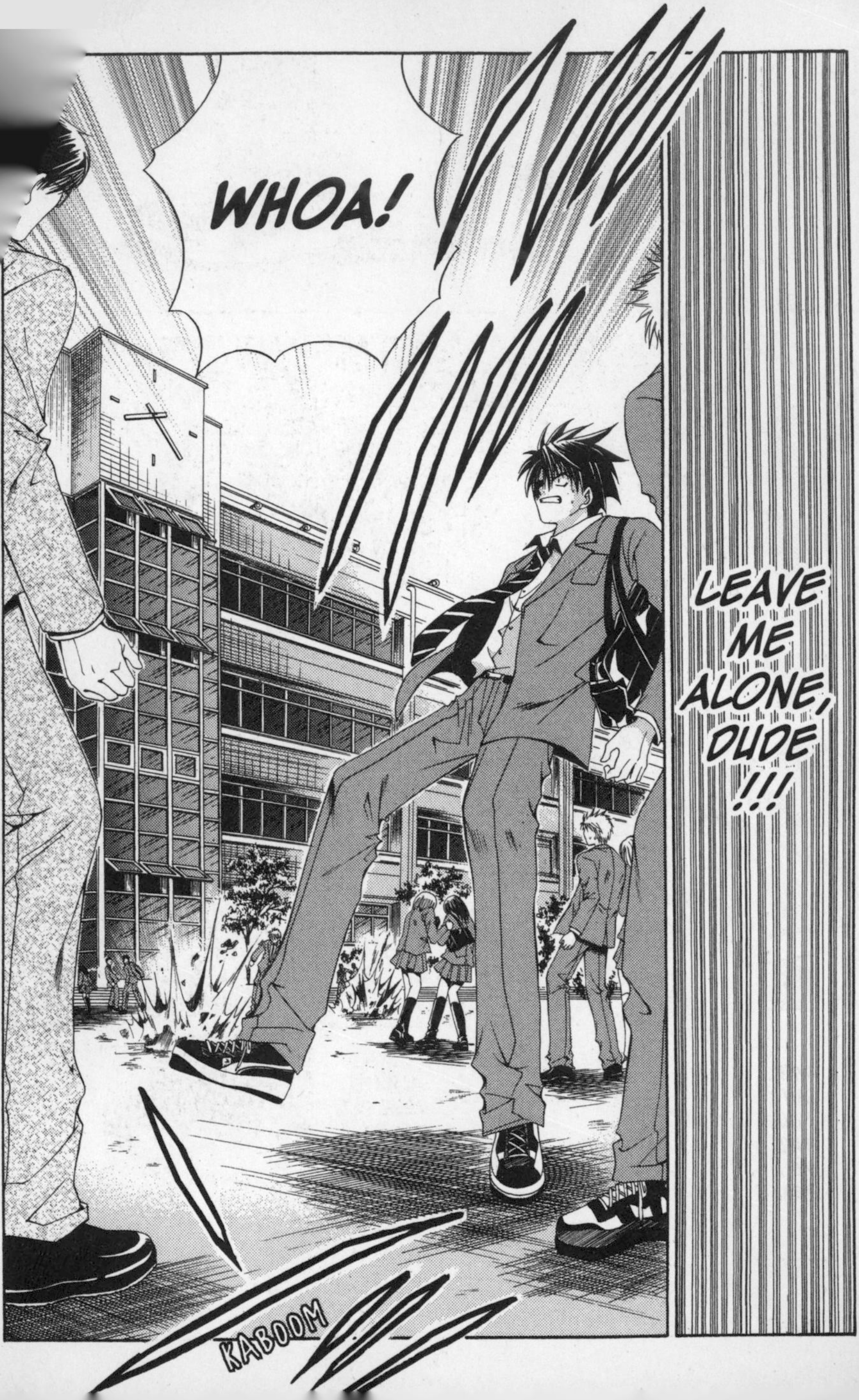
LEAVE ME ALONE, DUDE!!!
WHOA!
KABOOM

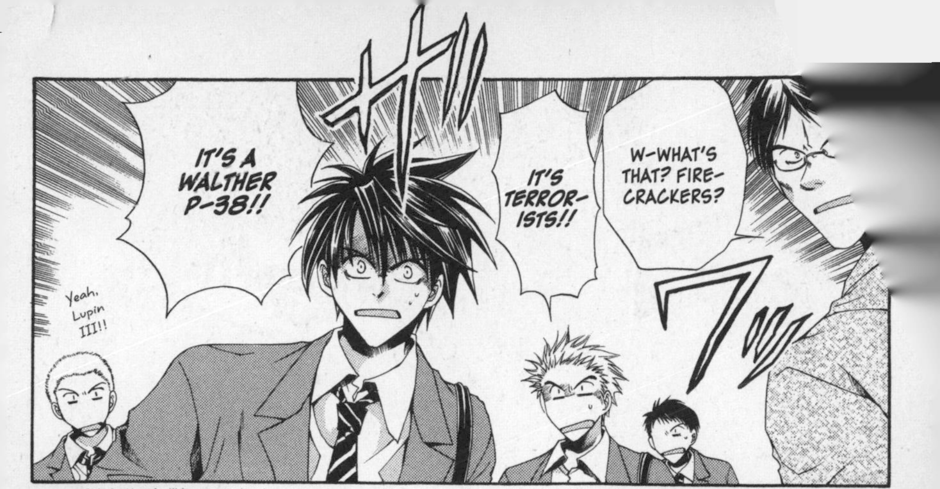
W-WHAT'S THAT? FIRE-CRACKERS?
IT'S TERROR-ISTS!!
IT'S A WALTHER P-38!!
Yeah, Lupin III!!

*Note: Lupin III is a popular Japanese manga thief who carries a Walther P-38 handgun.

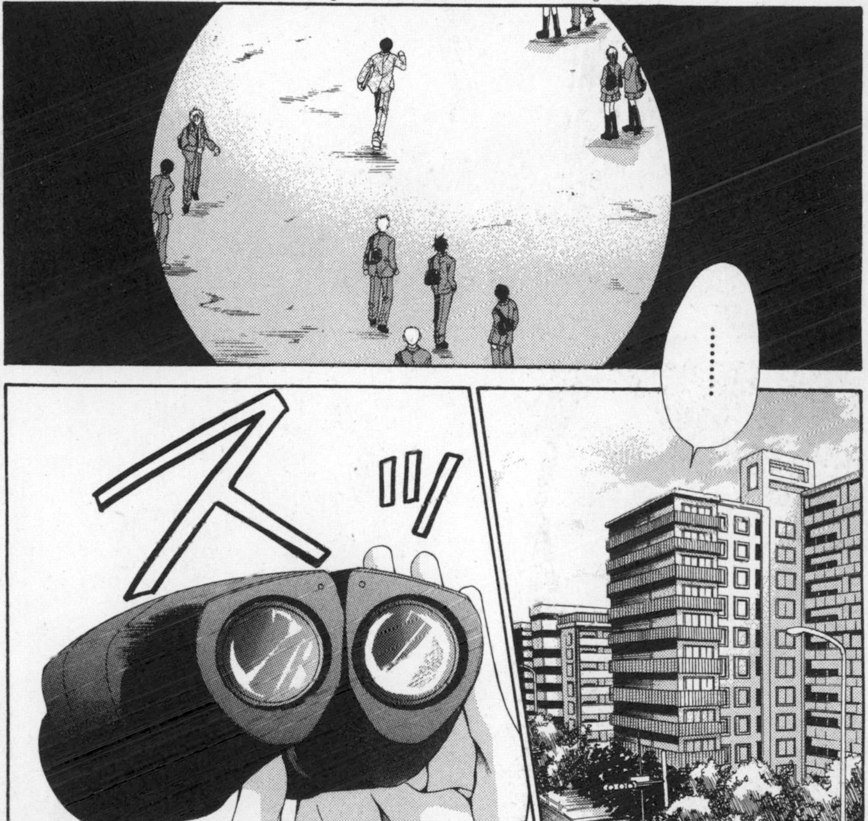
......

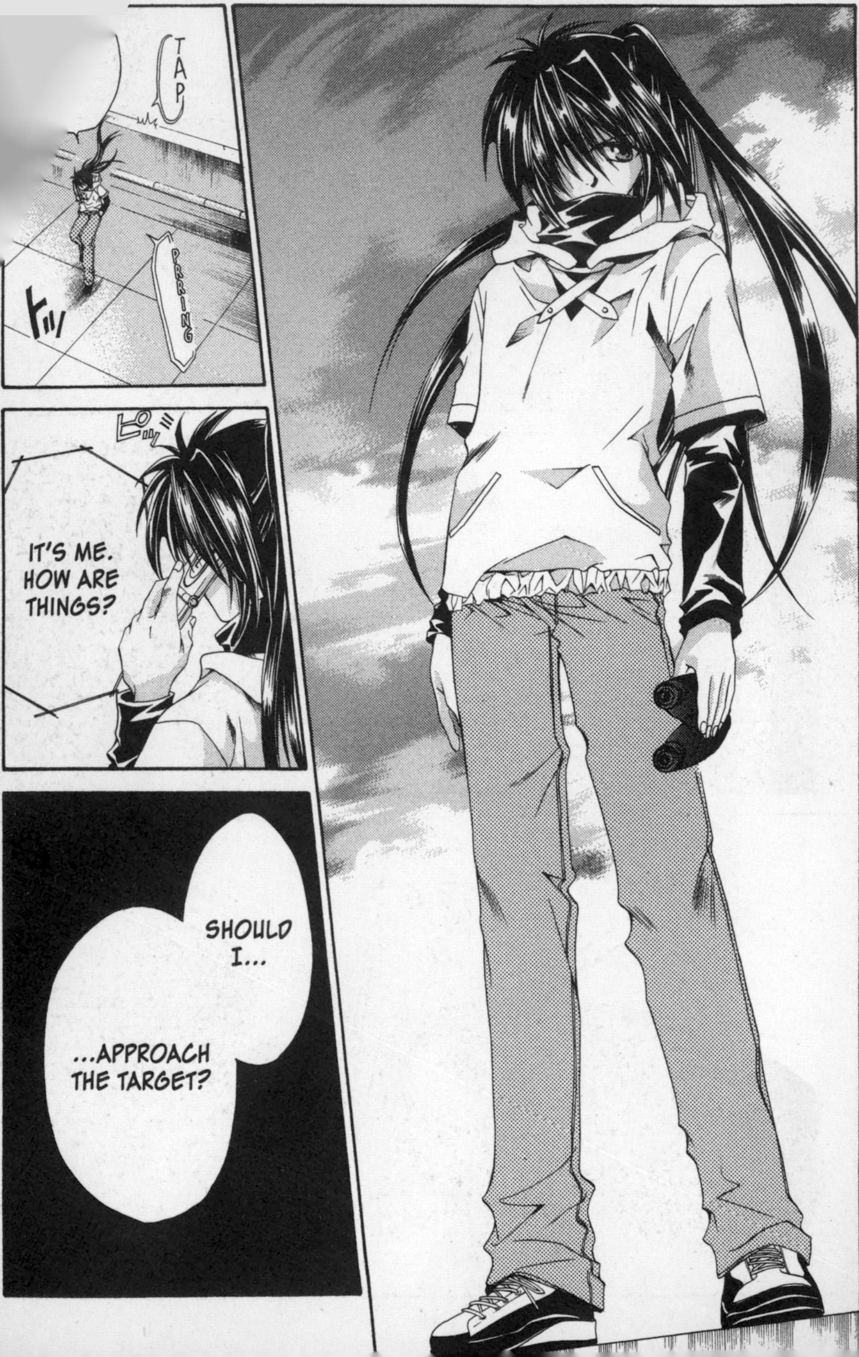

TAP
PRRING
IT'S ME. HOW ARE THINGS?
SHOULD I...
...APPROACH THE TARGET?

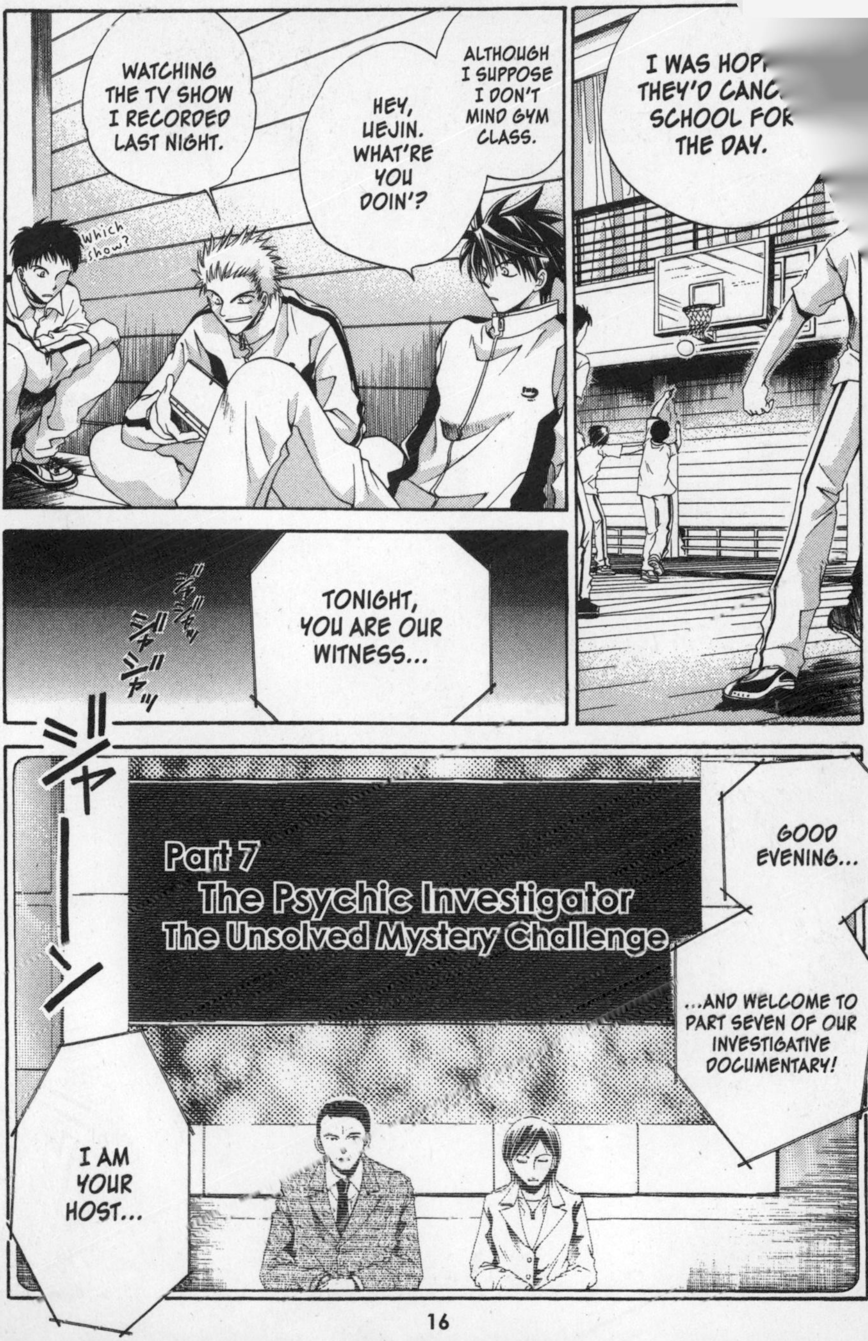
I WAS HOP
THEY'D CANC
SCHOOL FOR
THE DAY.
ALTHOUGH I SUPPOSE I DON'T MIND GYM CLASS.
HEY, UEJIN. WHAT'RE YOU DOIN'?
WATCHING THE TV SHOW I RECORDED LAST NIGHT.
Which show?
TONIGHT, YOU ARE OUR WITNESS...
ジャーン
GOOD EVENING...
Part 7
The Psychic Investigator
The Unsolved Mystery Challenge
...AND WELCOME TO PART SEVEN OF OUR INVESTIGATIVE DOCUMENTARY!
I AM YOUR HOST...

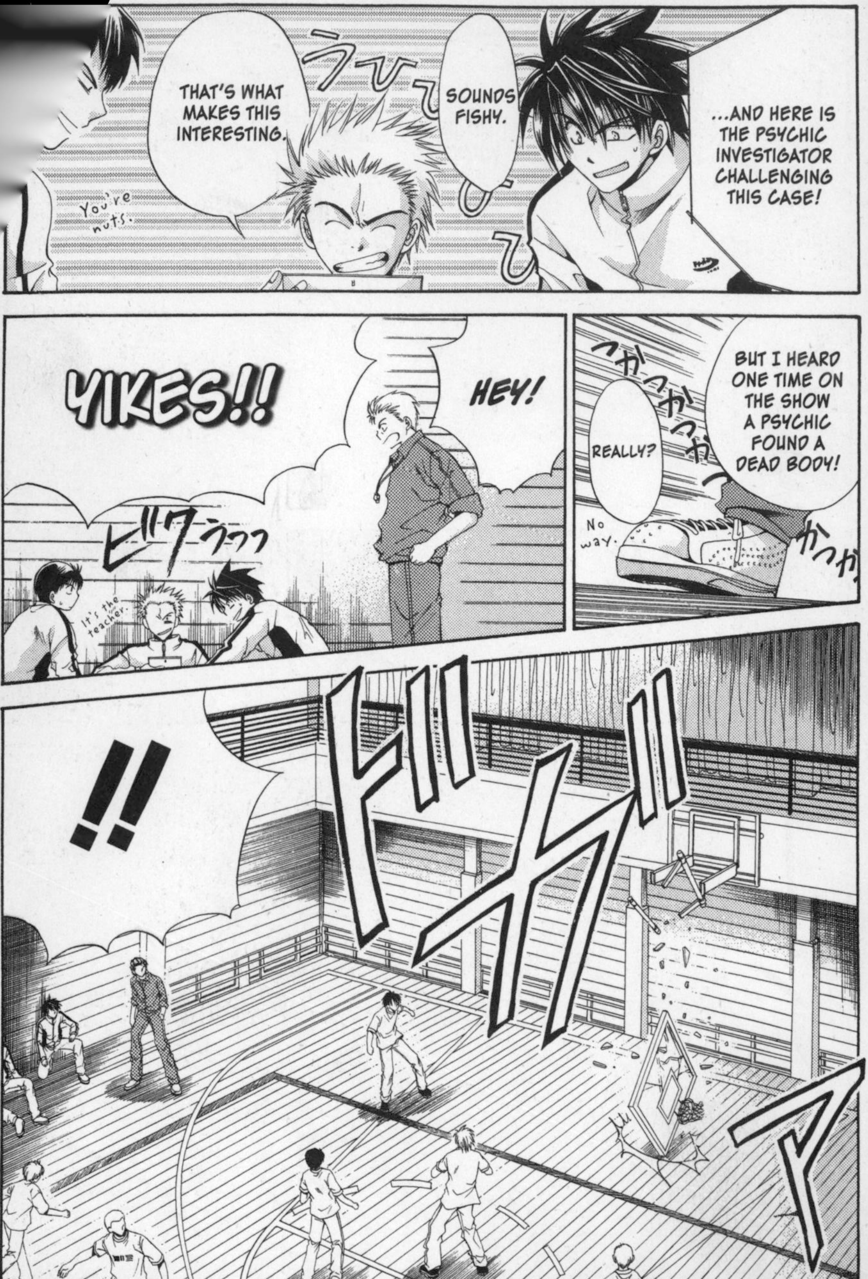
...AND HERE IS THE PSYCHIC INVESTIGATOR CHALLENGING THIS CASE!
SOUNDS FISHY.
THAT'S WHAT MAKES THIS INTERESTING.
You're nuts.
BUT I HEARD ONE TIME ON THE SHOW A PSYCHIC FOUND A DEAD BODY!
REALLY?
No way.
HEY!
YIKES!!
It's the teacher.
!!

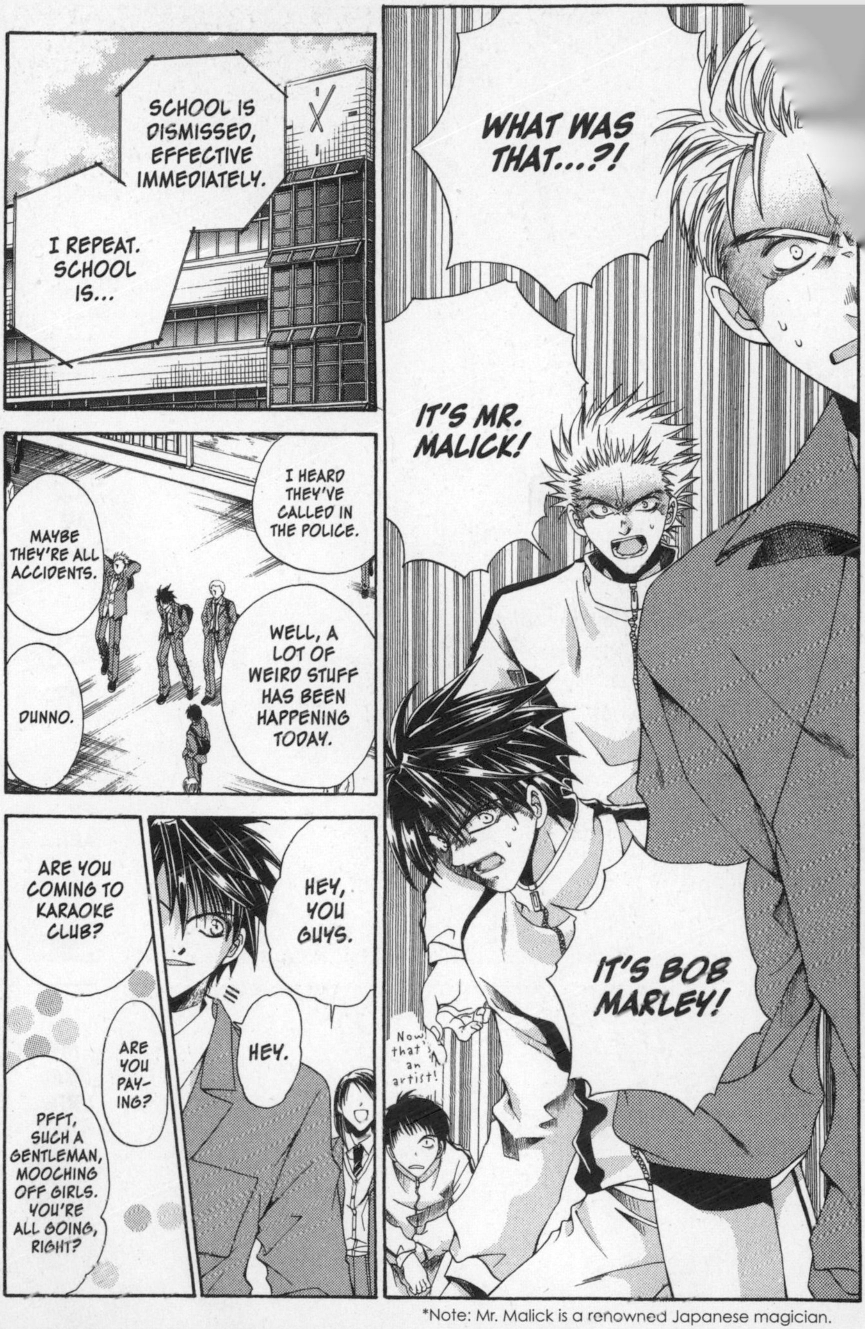
WHAT WAS THAT...?!
IT'S MR. MALICK!
IT'S BOB MARLEY!
Now that's an artist!
SCHOOL IS DISMISSED, EFFECTIVE IMMEDIATELY.
I REPEAT. SCHOOL IS...
I HEARD THEY'VE CALLED IN THE POLICE.
MAYBE THEY'RE ALL ACCIDENTS.
WELL, A LOT OF WEIRD STUFF HAS BEEN HAPPENING TODAY.
DUNNO.
HEY, YOU GUYS.
ARE YOU COMING TO KARAOKE CLUB?
HEY.
ARE YOU PAY-ING?
PFFT, SUCH A GENTLEMAN, MOOCHING OFF GIRLS. YOU'RE ALL GOING, RIGHT?

*Note: Mr. Malick is a renowned Japanese magician.

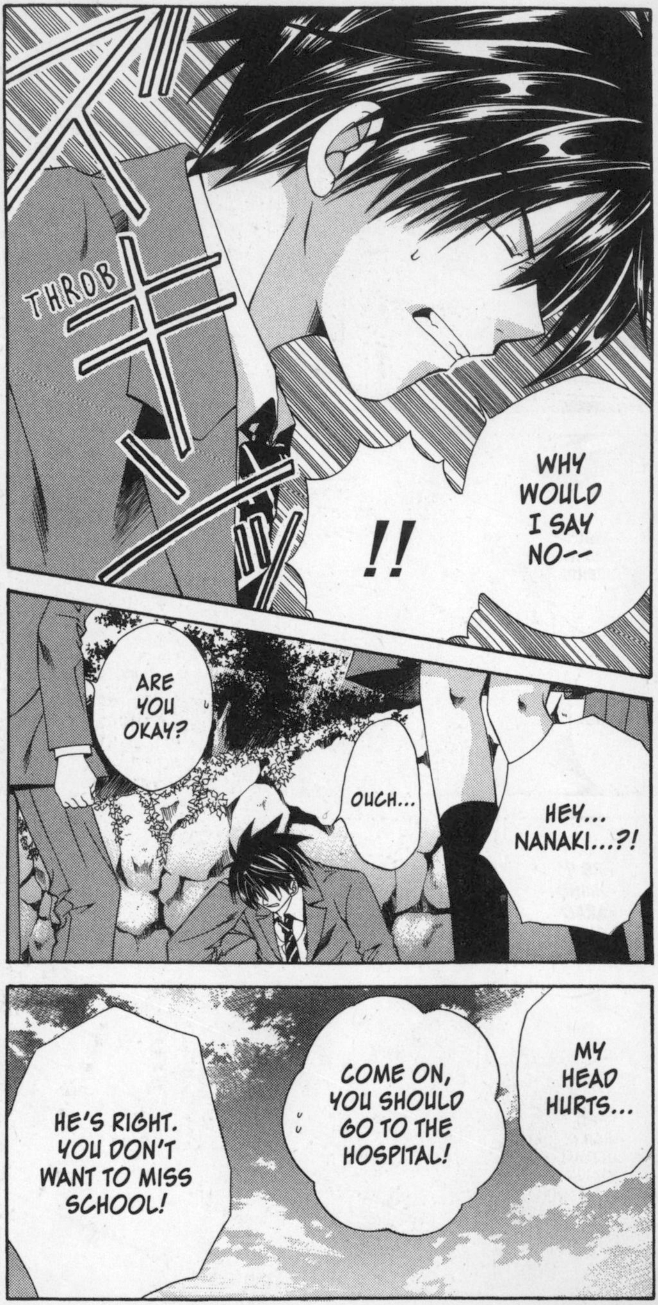
THROB
WHY WOULD I SAY NO--
!!
HEY... NANAKI...?!
OUCH...
ARE YOU OKAY?
MY HEAD HURTS...
COME ON, YOU SHOULD GO TO THE HOSPITAL!
HE'S RIGHT. YOU DON'T WANT TO MISS SCHOOL!

•ALPHA•

Hello, nice to meet you all. Ryo Saenagi, here. This is the first volume of *Psychic Power Nanaki*. ...Actually, I'm sorry for having such a long title. (Nervous giggle.) It was a real struggle to come up with this title. I had several other ideas, but this one gave me the best impression of all.

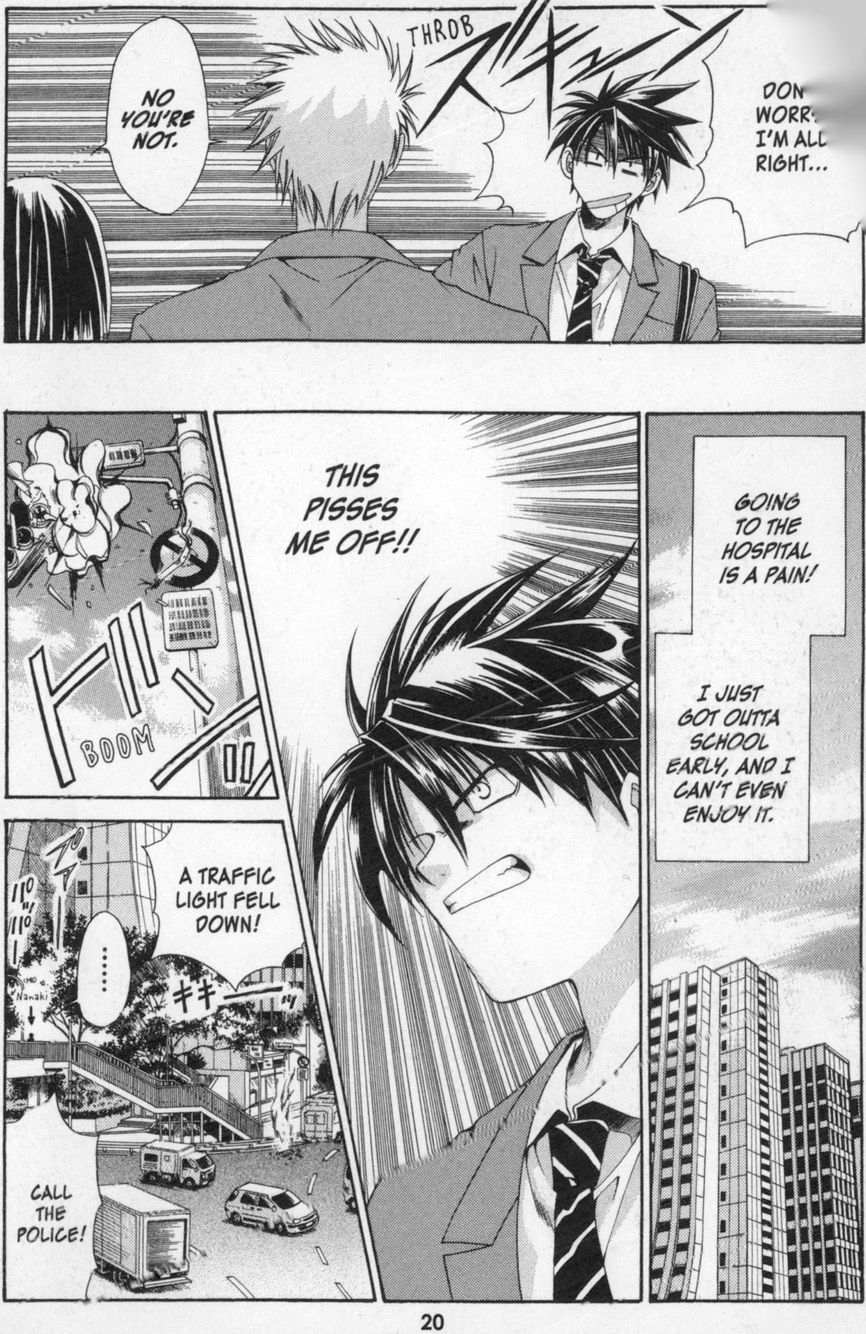
DON
WORR
I'M ALL
RIGHT...
THROB
NO YOU'RE NOT.
GOING TO THE HOSPITAL IS A PAIN!
I JUST GOT OUTTA SCHOOL EARLY, AND I CAN'T EVEN ENJOY IT.
THIS PISSES ME OFF!!
BOOM
A TRAFFIC LIGHT FELL DOWN!
......
Nanaki
CALL THE POLICE!

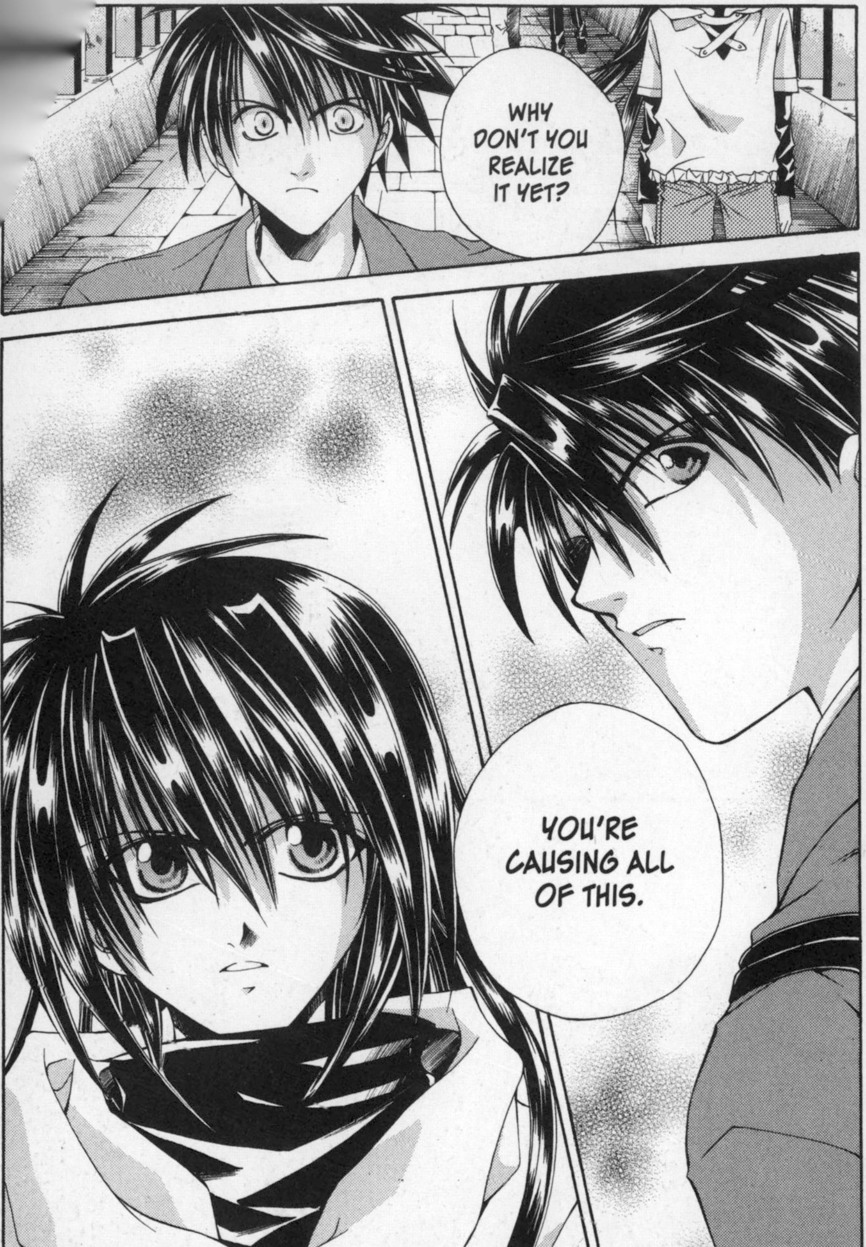
WHY DON'T YOU REALIZE IT YET?
YOU'RE CAUSING ALL OF THIS.

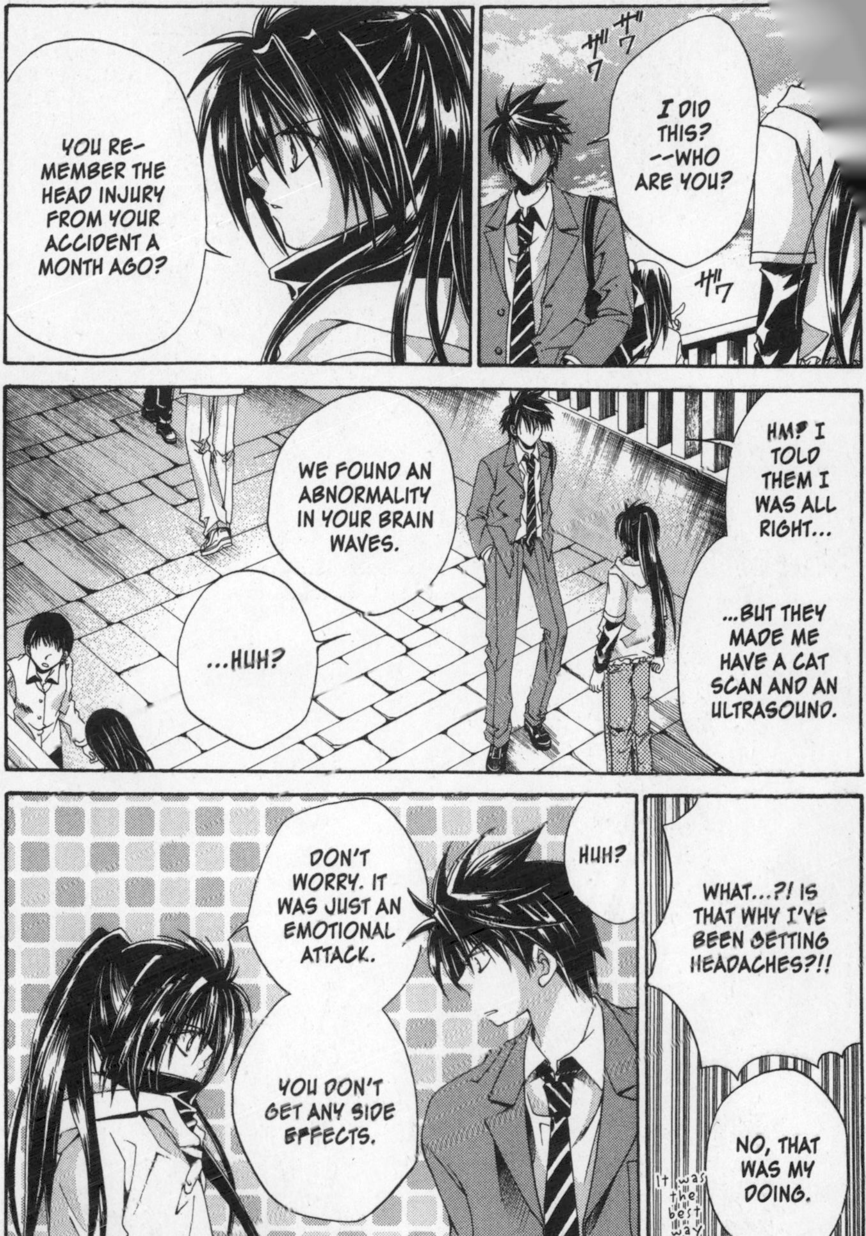
ザワ ザワ
I DID THIS? --WHO ARE YOU?
ザワ
YOU RE-MEMBER THE HEAD INJURY FROM YOUR ACCIDENT A MONTH AGO?
HM? I TOLD THEM I WAS ALL RIGHT...
...BUT THEY MADE ME HAVE A CAT SCAN AND AN ULTRASOUND.
WE FOUND AN ABNORMALITY IN YOUR BRAIN WAVES.
...HUH?
WHAT...?! IS THAT WHY I'VE BEEN GETTING HEADACHES?!!
NO, THAT WAS MY DOING.
It was the best way to stop you.
HUH?
DON'T WORRY. IT WAS JUST AN EMOTIONAL ATTACK.
YOU DON'T GET ANY SIDE EFFECTS.

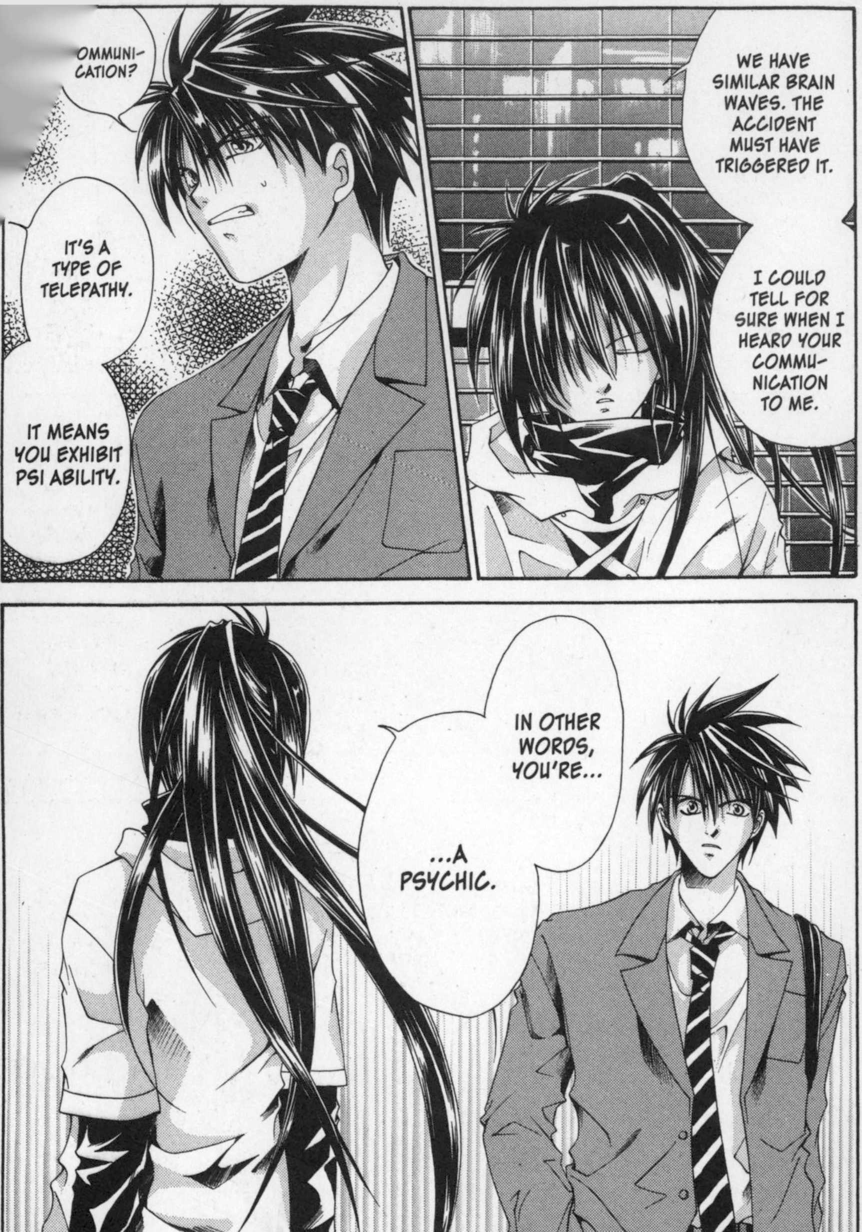

WE HAVE SIMILAR BRAIN WAVES. THE ACCIDENT MUST HAVE TRIGGERED IT.
I COULD TELL FOR SURE WHEN I HEARD YOUR COMMUNICATION TO ME.
OMMUNICATION?
IT'S A TYPE OF TELEPATHY.
IT MEANS YOU EXHIBIT PSI ABILITY.
IN OTHER WORDS, YOU'RE...
...A PSYCHIC.

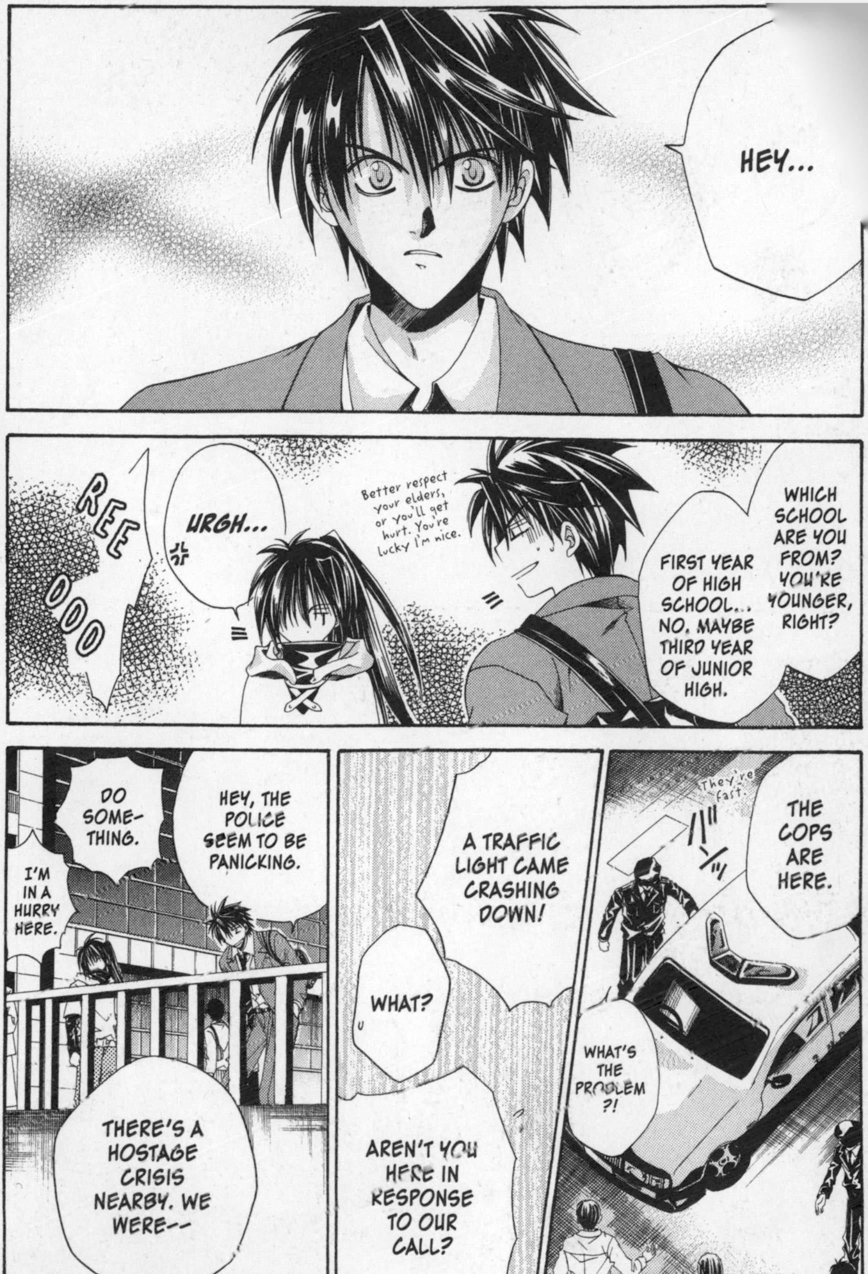
HEY...
WHICH SCHOOL ARE YOU FROM? YOU'RE YOUNGER, RIGHT?
FIRST YEAR OF HIGH SCHOOL... NO. MAYBE THIRD YEAR OF JUNIOR HIGH.
Better respect your elders, or you'll get hurt. You're lucky I'm nice.
URGH...
REEOOO
They're fast.
THE COPS ARE HERE.
WHAT'S THE PROBLEM ?!
A TRAFFIC LIGHT CAME CRASHING DOWN!
WHAT?
AREN'T YOU HERE IN RESPONSE TO OUR CALL?
HEY, THE POLICE SEEM TO BE PANICKING.
DO SOME- THING.
I'M IN A HURRY HERE.
THERE'S A HOSTAGE CRISIS NEARBY. WE WERE--

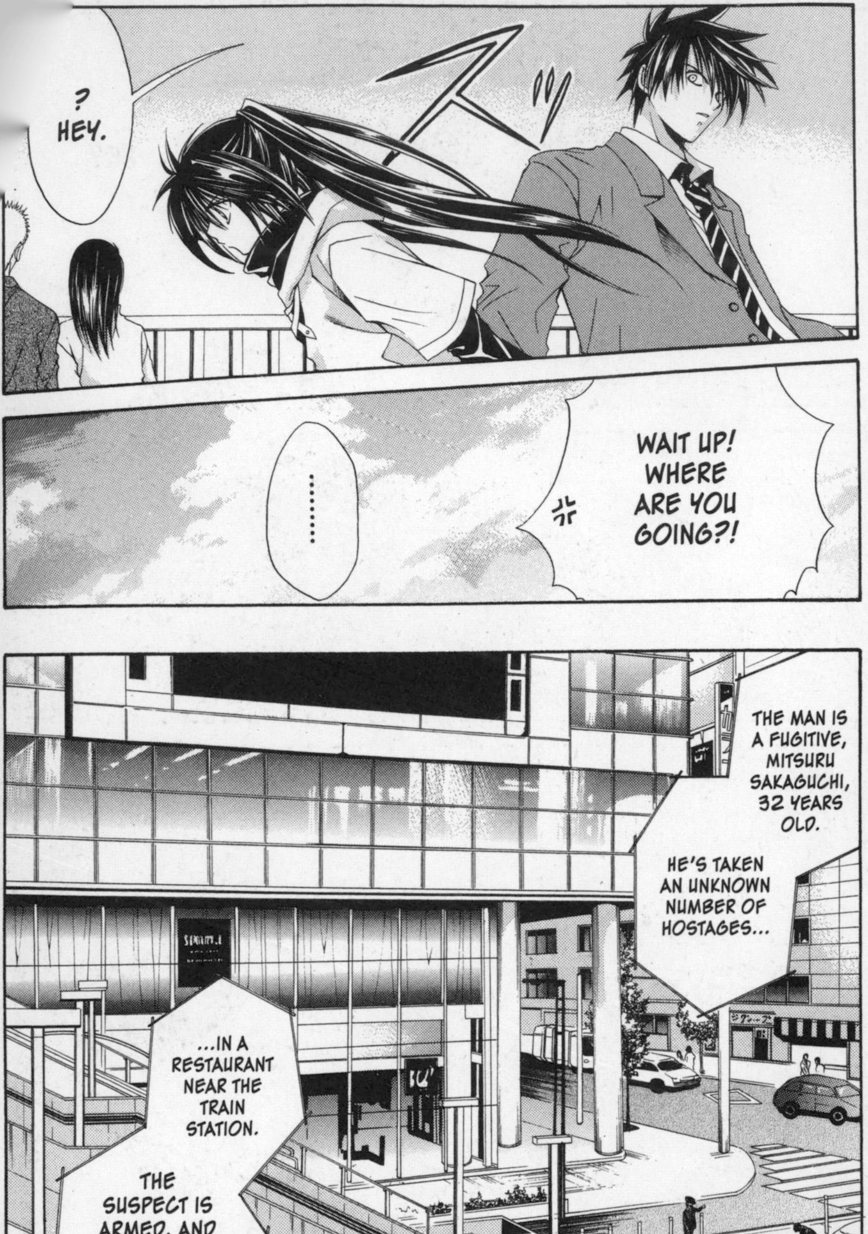
スッ
? HEY.
WAIT UP! WHERE ARE YOU GOING?!
......
THE MAN IS A FUGITIVE, MITSURU SAKAGUCHI, 32 YEARS OLD.
HE'S TAKEN AN UNKNOWN NUMBER OF HOSTAGES...
...IN A RESTAURANT NEAR THE TRAIN STATION.
THE SUSPECT IS ARMED, AND WE NEED BACKUP.

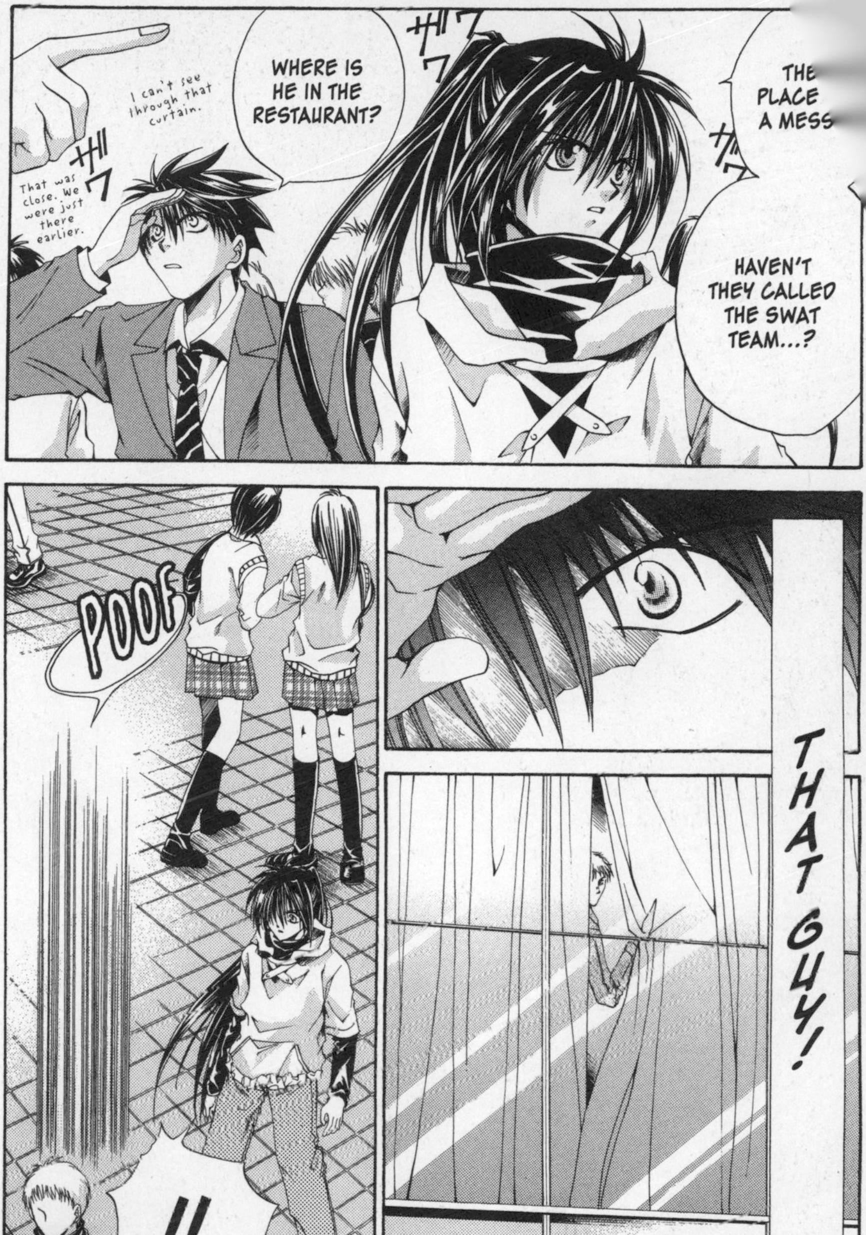
THE PLACE A MESS
HAVEN'T THEY CALLED THE SWAT TEAM...?
WHERE IS HE IN THE RESTAURANT?
I can't see through that curtain.
That was close. We were just there earlier.
THAT GUY!
POOF
!!

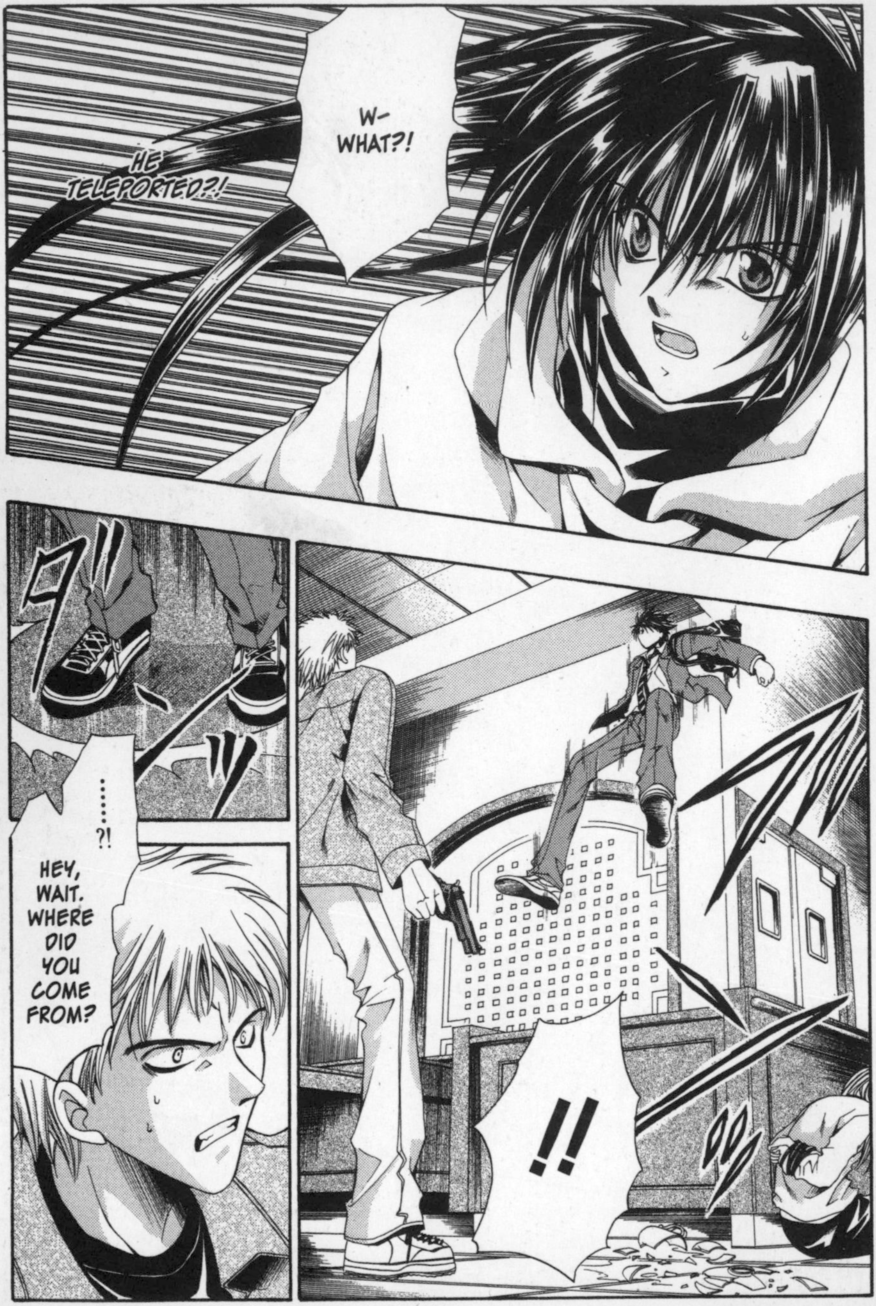
W-
WHAT?!
HE TELEPORTED?!
!!
......?!
HEY, WAIT. WHERE DID YOU COME FROM?

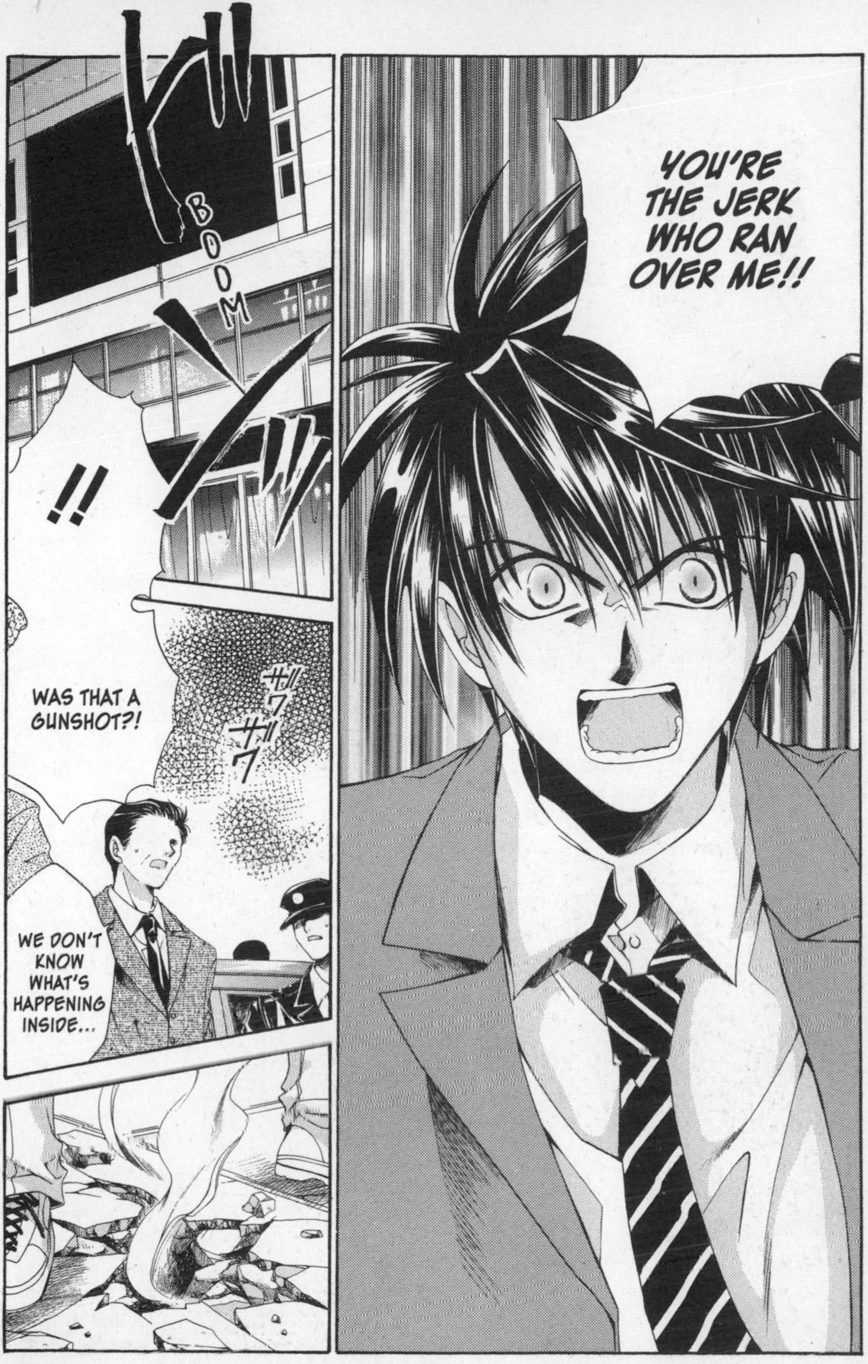
YOU'RE THE JERK WHO RAN OVER ME!!
BOOM
!!
WAS THAT A GUNSHOT?!
ザワザワ
WE DON'T KNOW WHAT'S HAPPENING INSIDE...

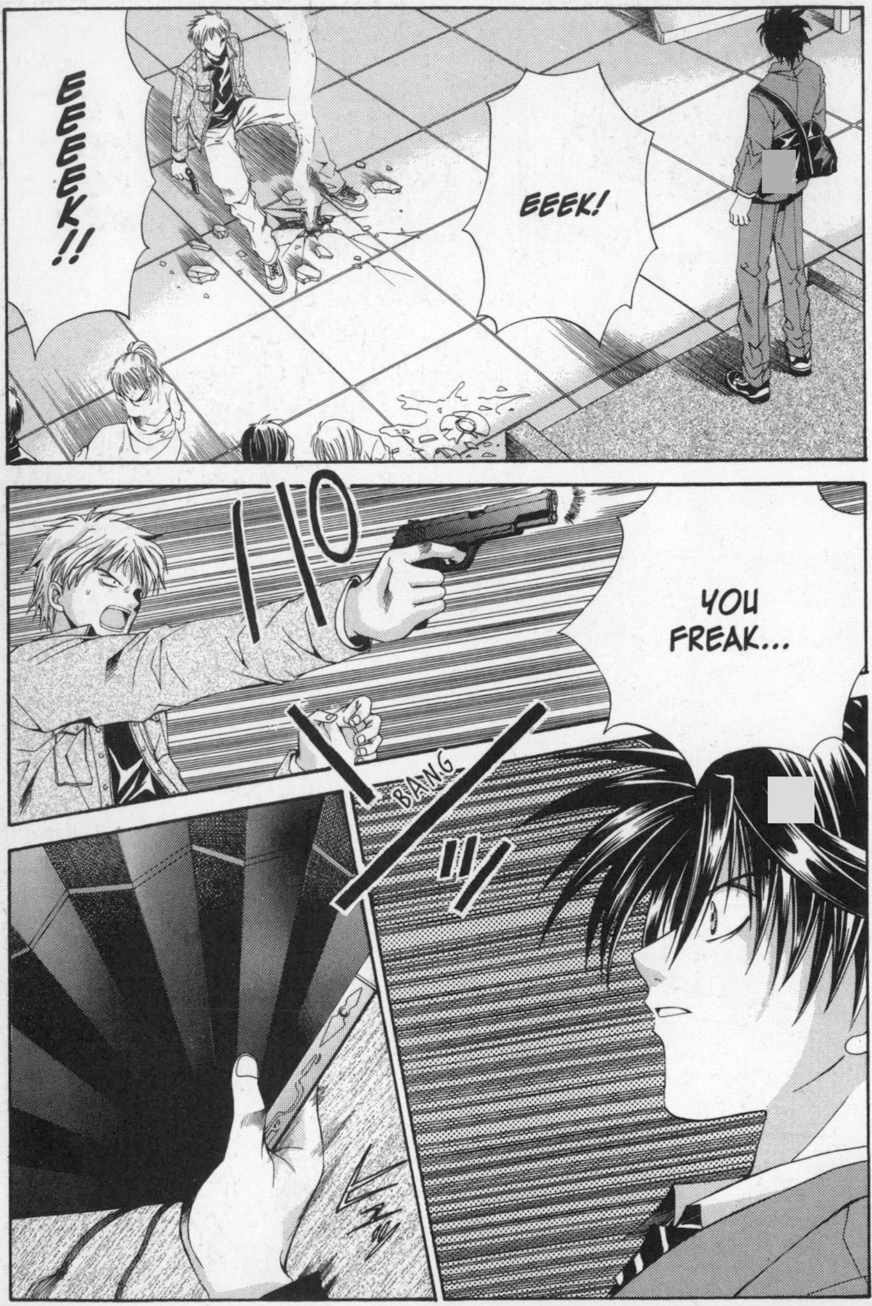
EEEK!
EEEEK!!
YOU FREAK...
BANG

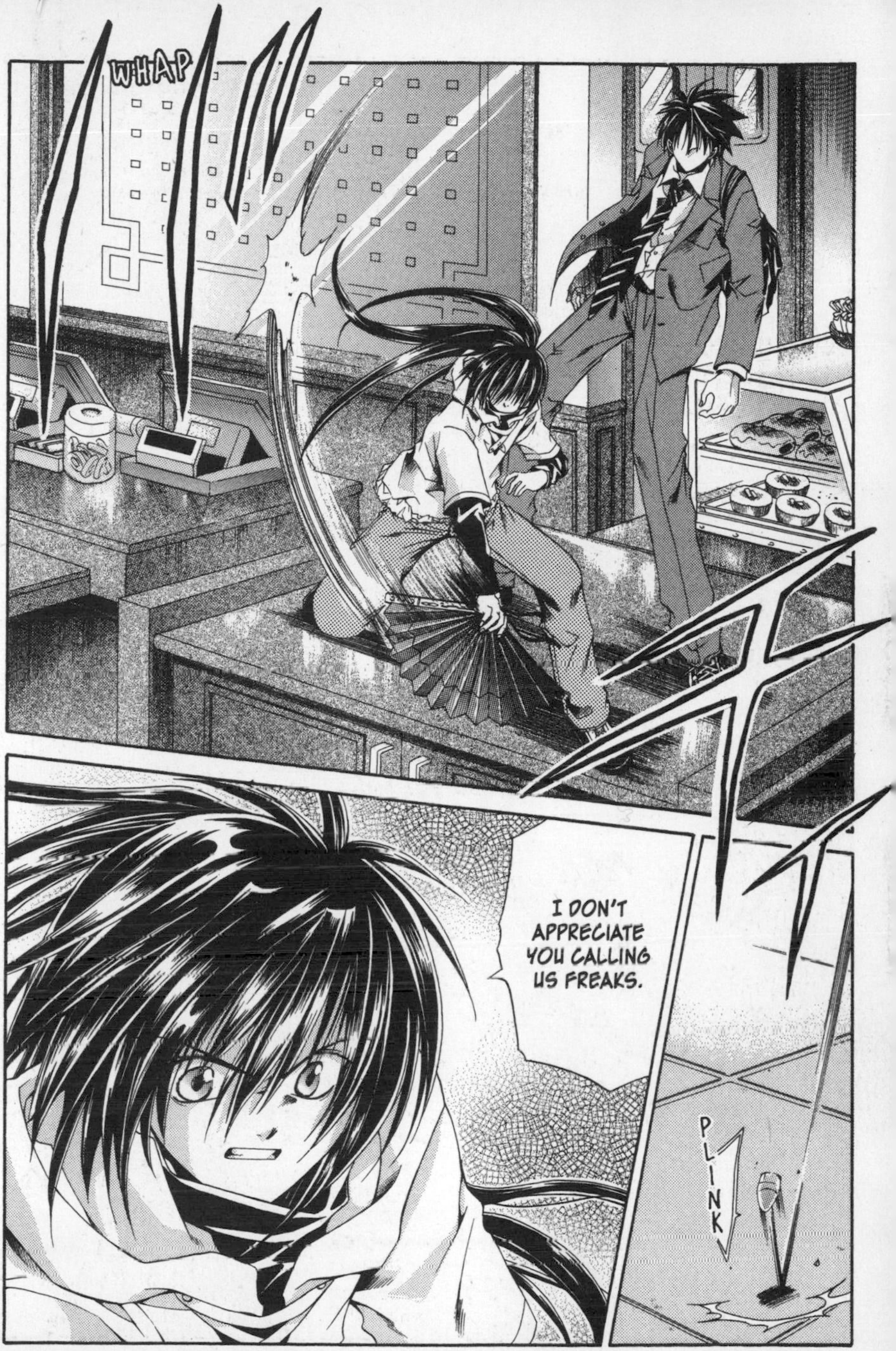
WHAP
I DON'T APPRECIATE YOU CALLING US FREAKS.
PLINK

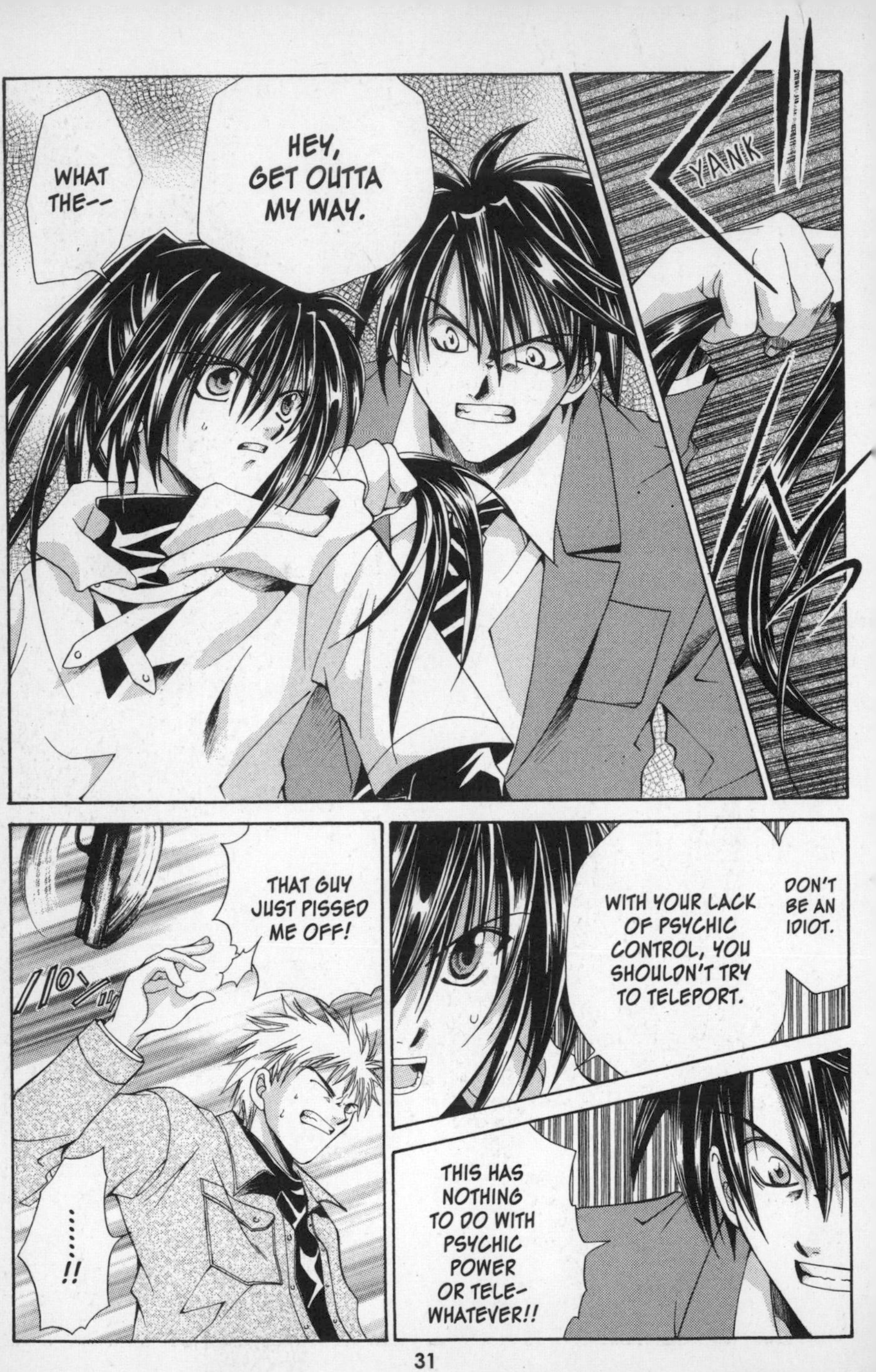
YANK
HEY, GET OUTTA MY WAY.
WHAT THE--
DON'T BE AN IDIOT.
WITH YOUR LACK OF PSYCHIC CONTROL, YOU SHOULDN'T TRY TO TELEPORT.
THIS HAS NOTHING TO DO WITH PSYCHIC POWER OR TELE-WHATEVER!!
THAT GUY JUST PISSED ME OFF!
......!!

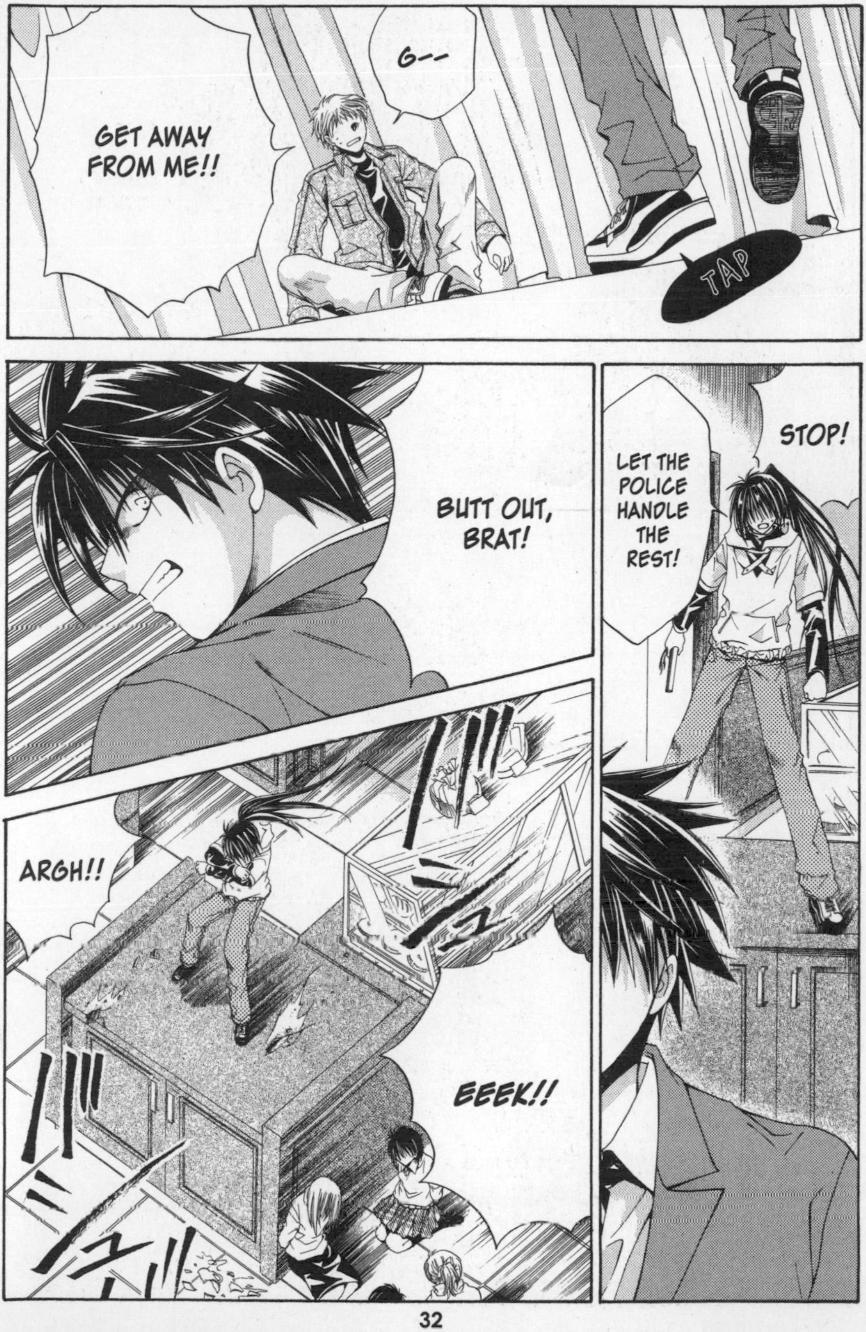
G--
GET AWAY FROM ME!!
TAP
STOP!
LET THE POLICE HANDLE THE REST!
BUTT OUT, BRAT!
ARGH!!
EEEK!!

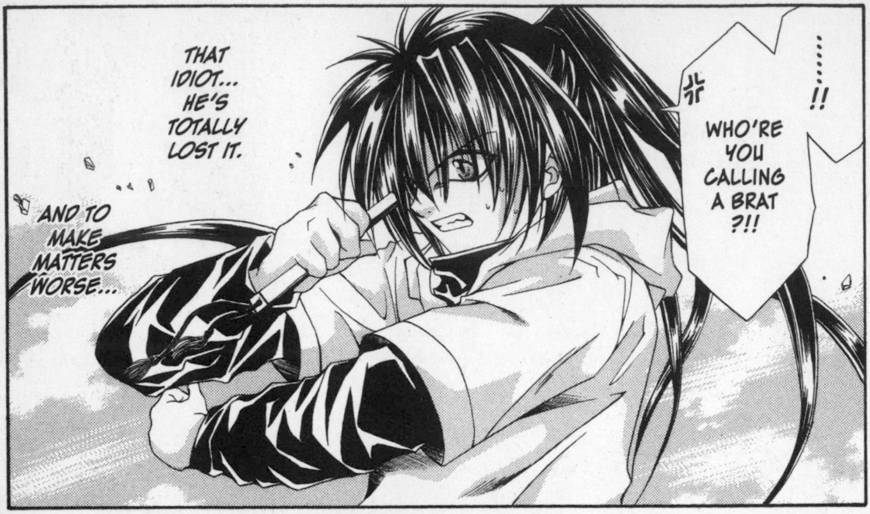
......!!
WHO'RE YOU CALLING A BRAT ?!!
THAT IDIOT... HE'S TOTALLY LOST IT.
AND TO MAKE MATTERS WORSE...

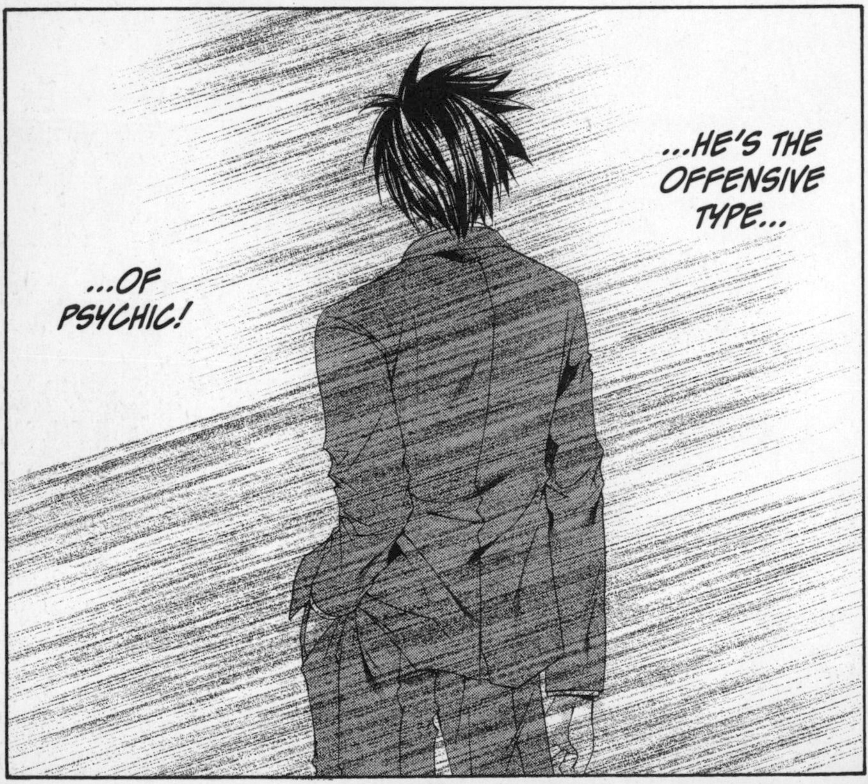
...HE'S THE OFFENSIVE TYPE...
...OF PSYCHIC!

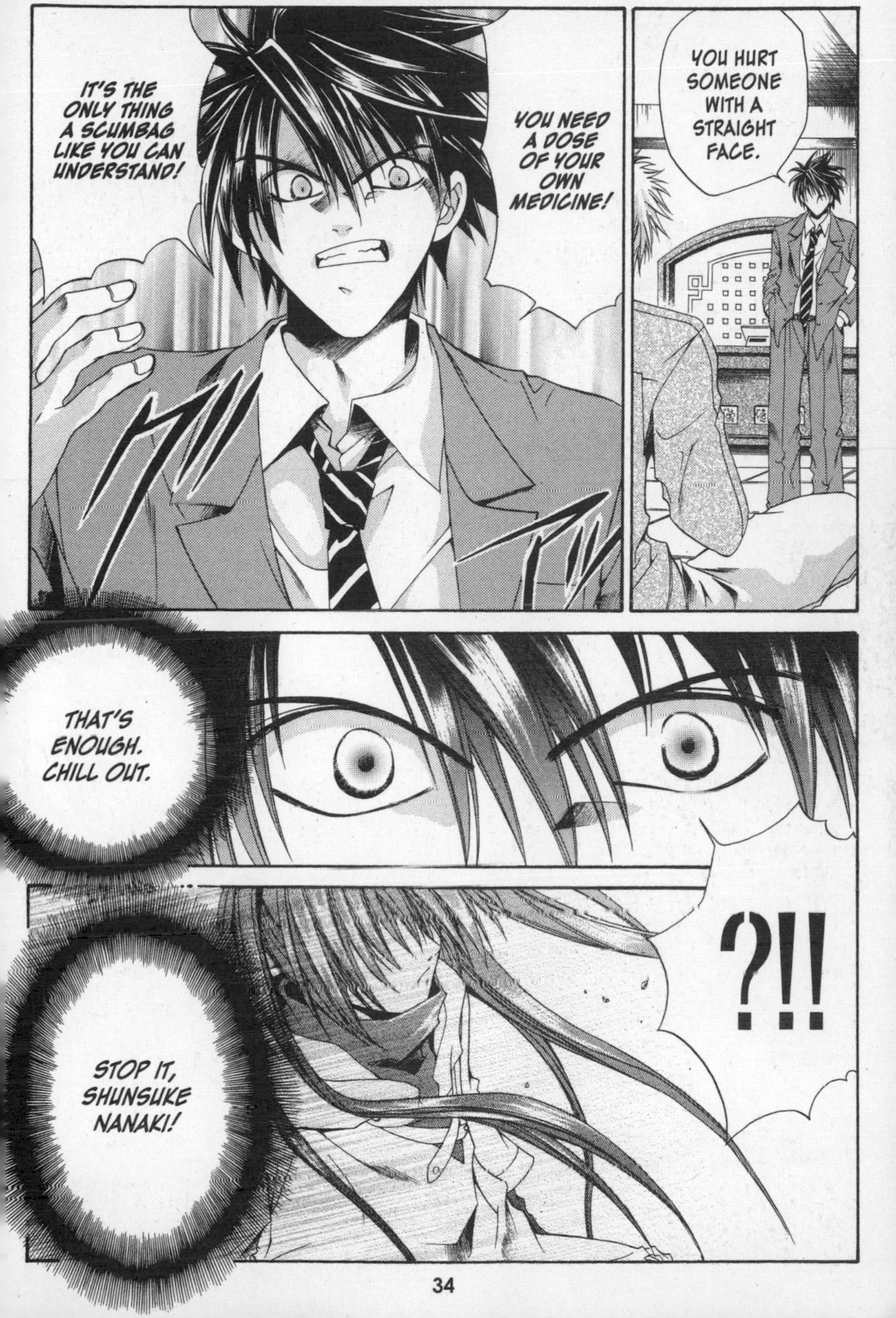
YOU HURT SOMEONE WITH A STRAIGHT FACE.
YOU NEED A DOSE OF YOUR OWN MEDICINE!
IT'S THE ONLY THING A SCUMBAG LIKE YOU CAN UNDERSTAND!
THAT'S ENOUGH. CHILL OUT.
?!!
STOP IT, SHUNSUKE NANAKI!

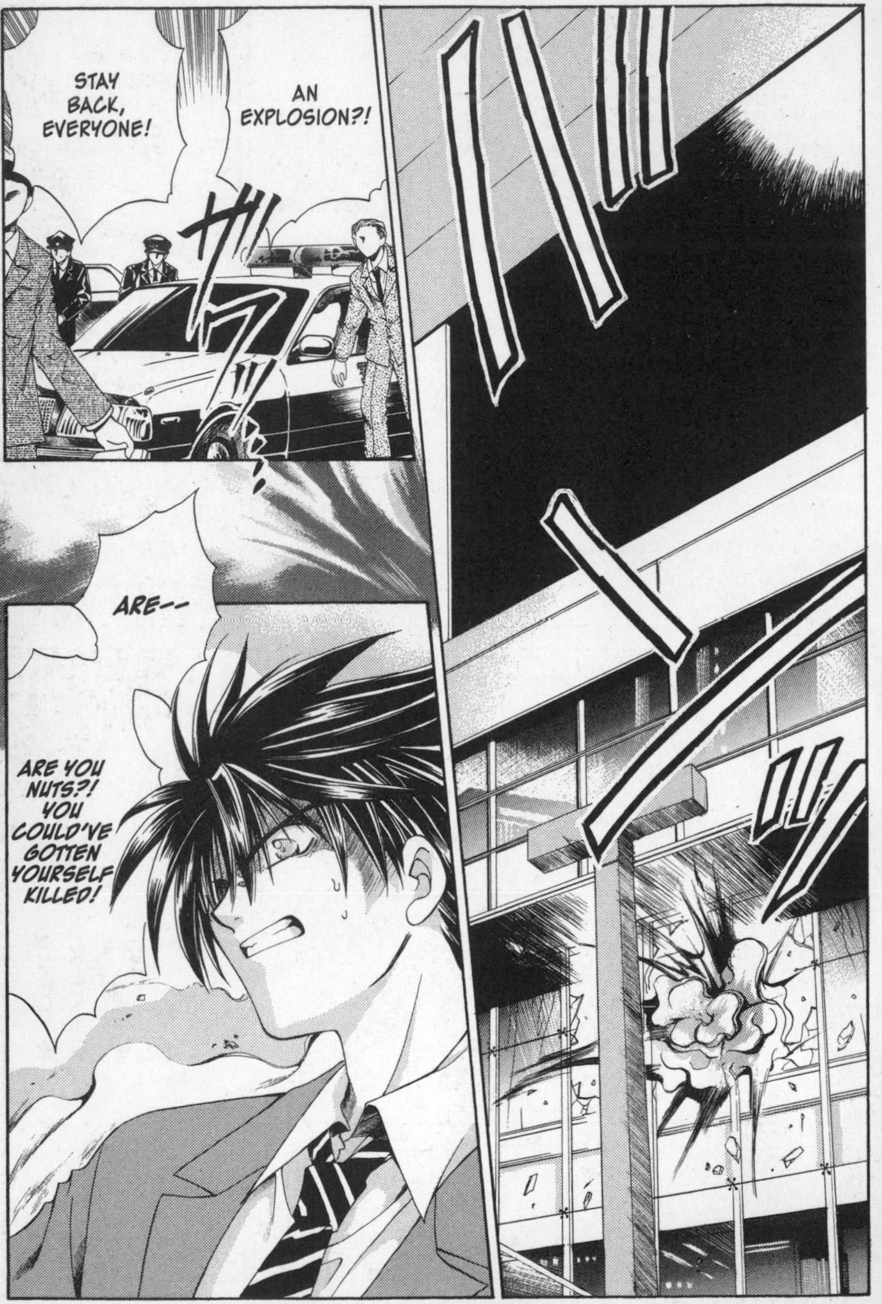
AN EXPLOSION?!
STAY BACK, EVERYONE!
ARE--
ARE YOU NUTS?! YOU COULD'VE GOTTEN YOURSELF KILLED!

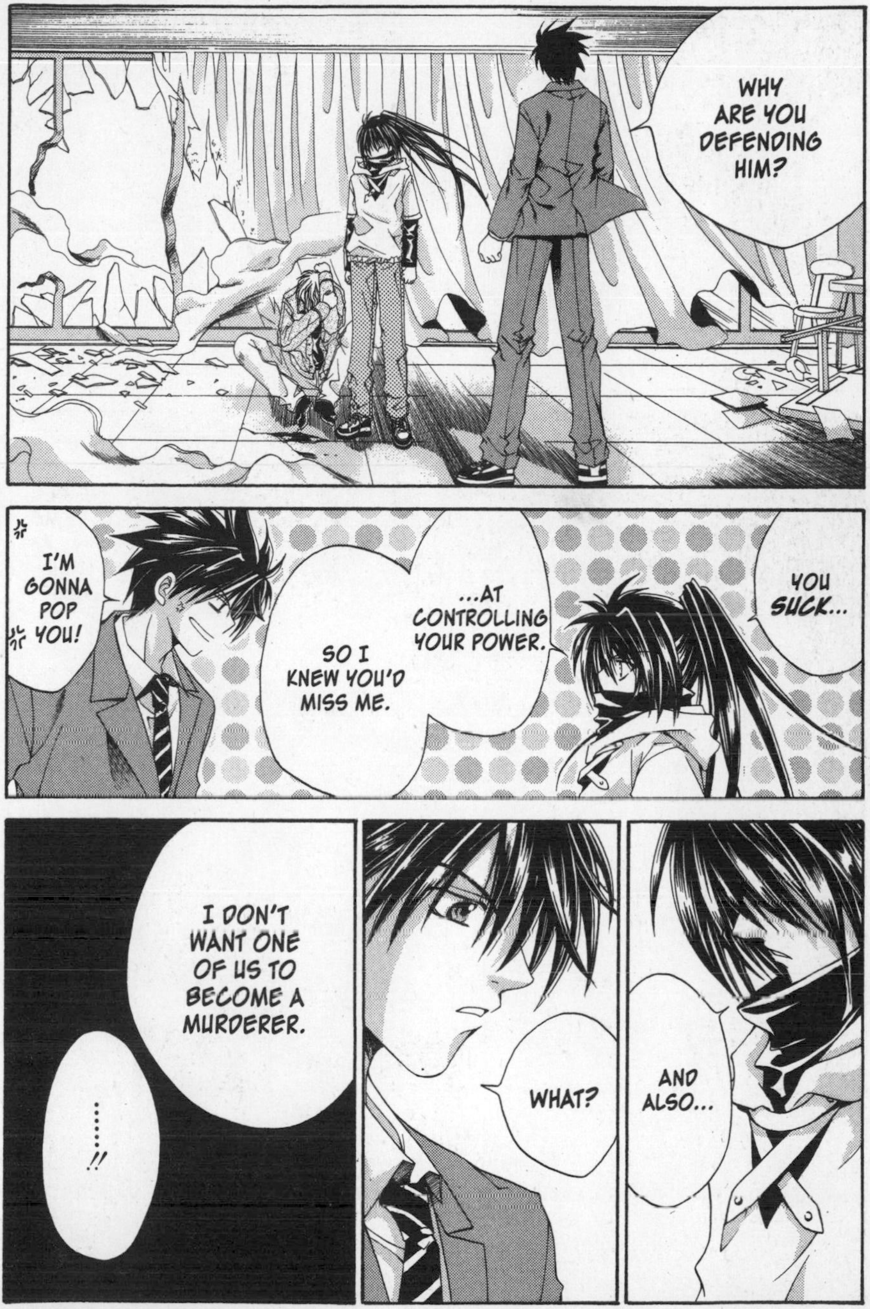
WHY ARE YOU DEFENDING HIM?
YOU SUCK...
...AT CONTROLLING YOUR POWER.
SO I KNEW YOU'D MISS ME.
I'M GONNA POP YOU!
AND ALSO...
WHAT?
I DON'T WANT ONE OF US TO BECOME A MURDERER.
......!!

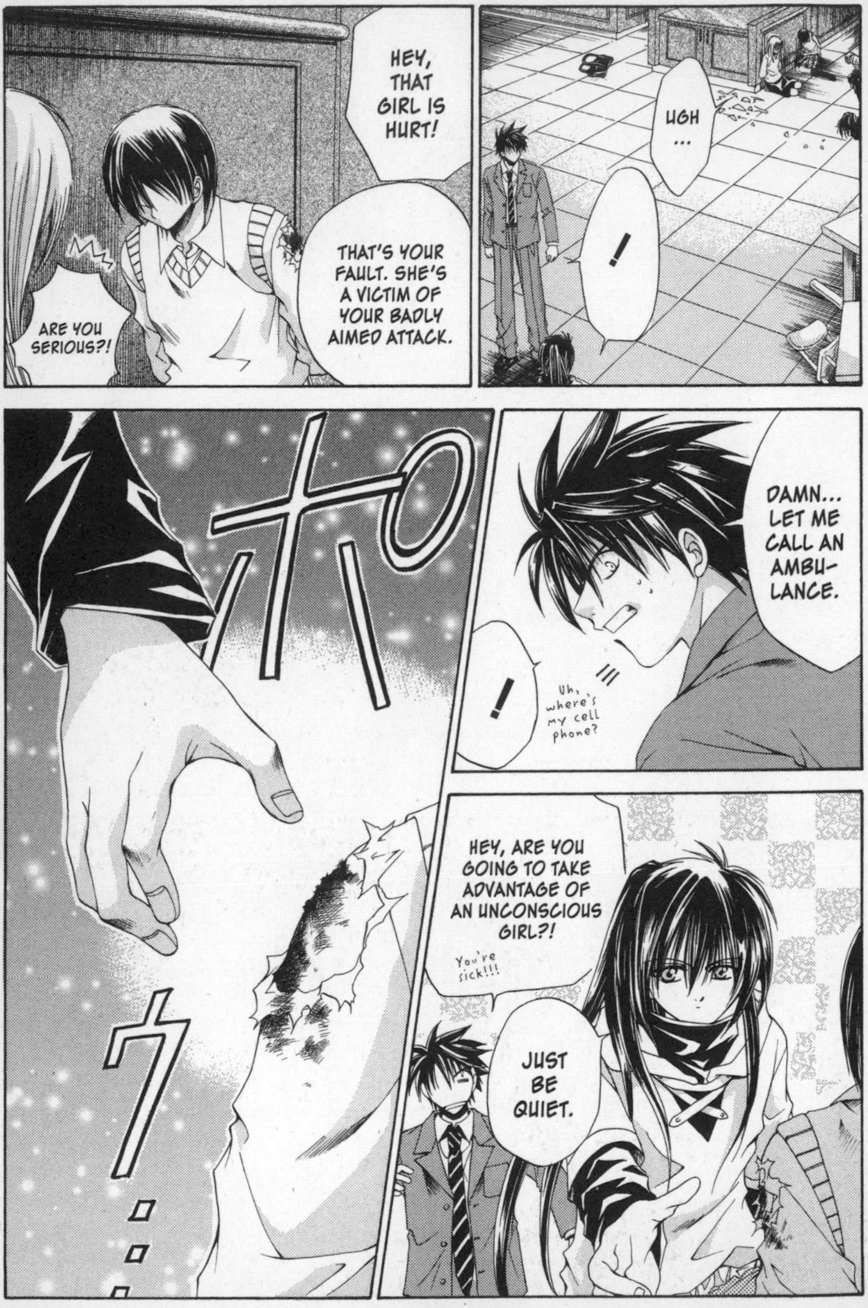
UGH...
!
HEY, THAT GIRL IS HURT!
THAT'S YOUR FAULT. SHE'S A VICTIM OF YOUR BADLY AIMED ATTACK.
ARE YOU SERIOUS?!
DAMN... LET ME CALL AN AMBU-LANCE.
!
Uh, where's my cell phone?
HEY, ARE YOU GOING TO TAKE ADVANTAGE OF AN UNCONSCIOUS GIRL?!
You're sick!!!
JUST BE QUIET.

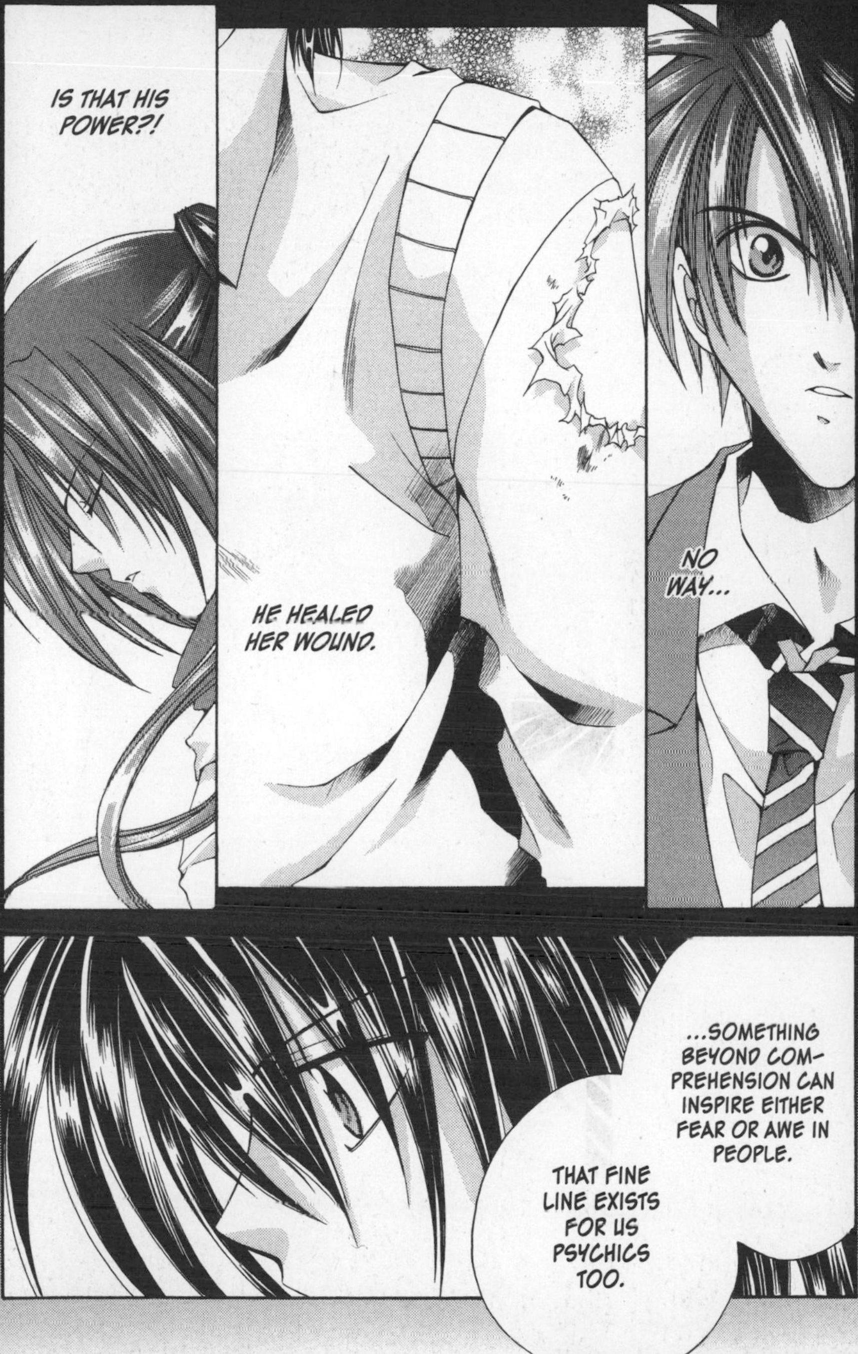
NO WAY...
HE HEALED HER WOUND.
IS THAT HIS POWER?!
...SOMETHING BEYOND COM-PREHENSION CAN INSPIRE EITHER FEAR OR AWE IN PEOPLE.
THAT FINE LINE EXISTS FOR US PSYCHICS TOO.

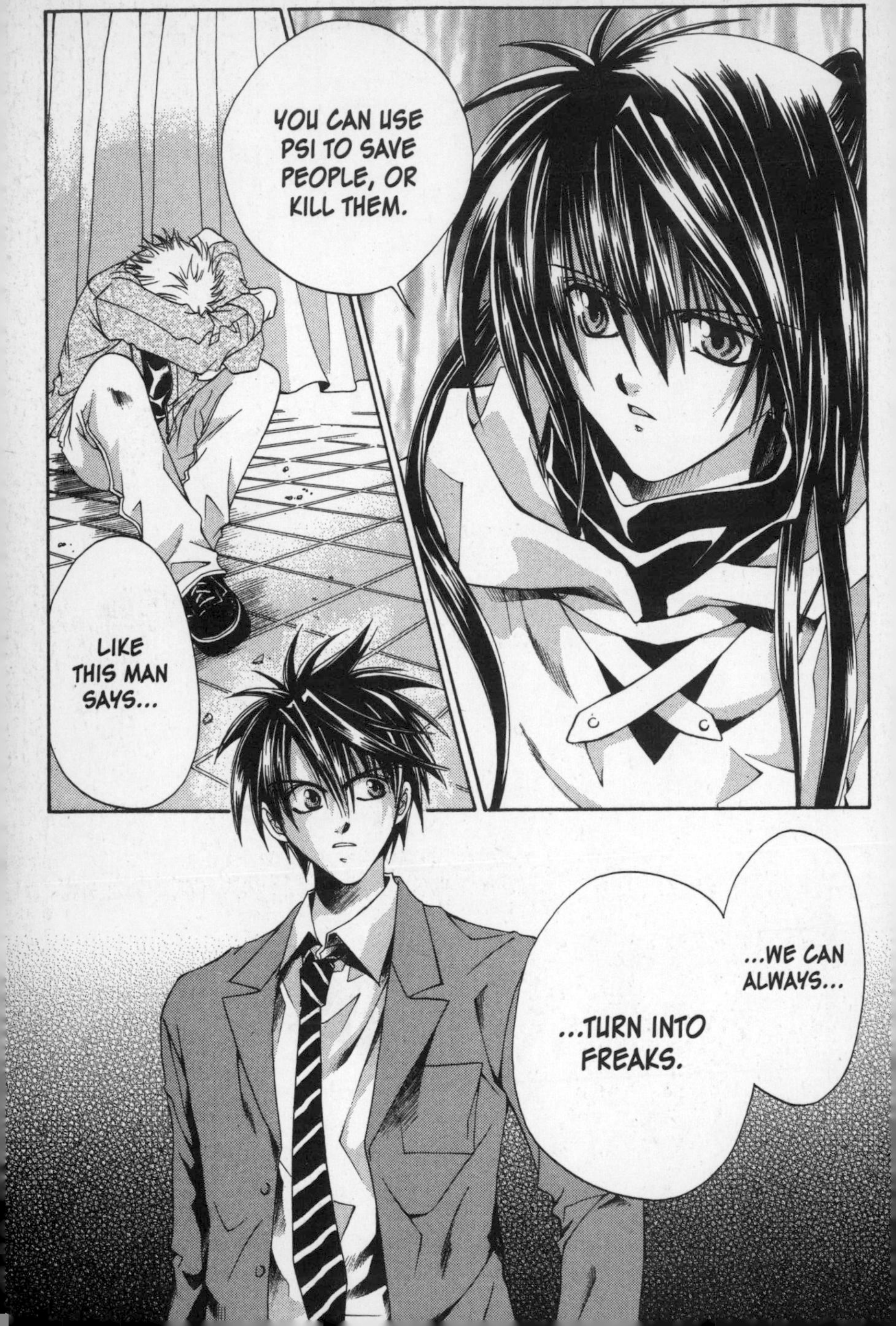
YOU CAN USE PSI TO SAVE PEOPLE, OR KILL THEM.
LIKE THIS MAN SAYS...
...WE CAN ALWAYS...
...TURN INTO FREAKS.

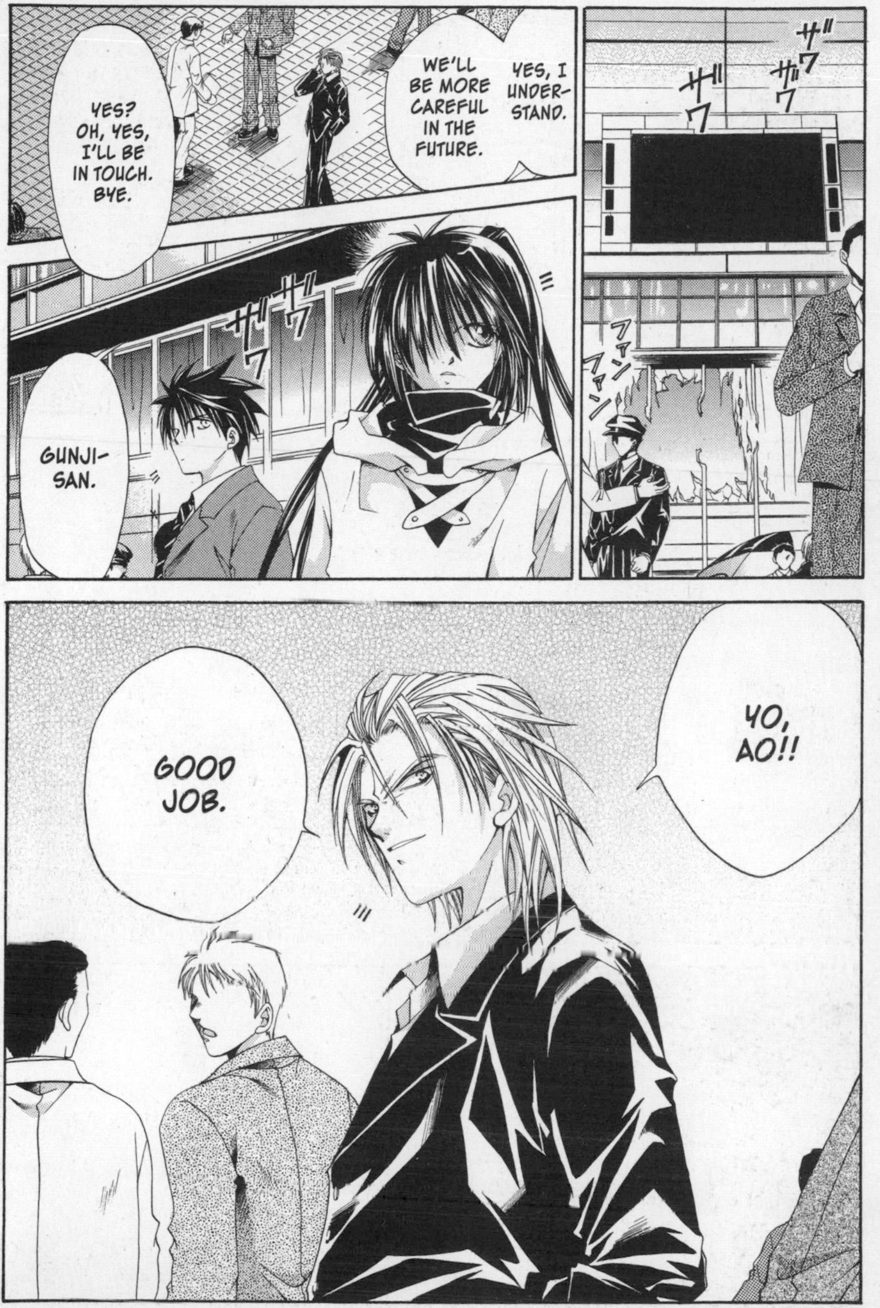
ザワ ザワ ザワ
ファン ファン
YES, I UNDER-STAND.
WE'LL BE MORE CAREFUL IN THE FUTURE.
YES? OH, YES, I'LL BE IN TOUCH. BYE.
ザワ ザワ
GUNJI-SAN.
YO, AO!!
GOOD JOB.

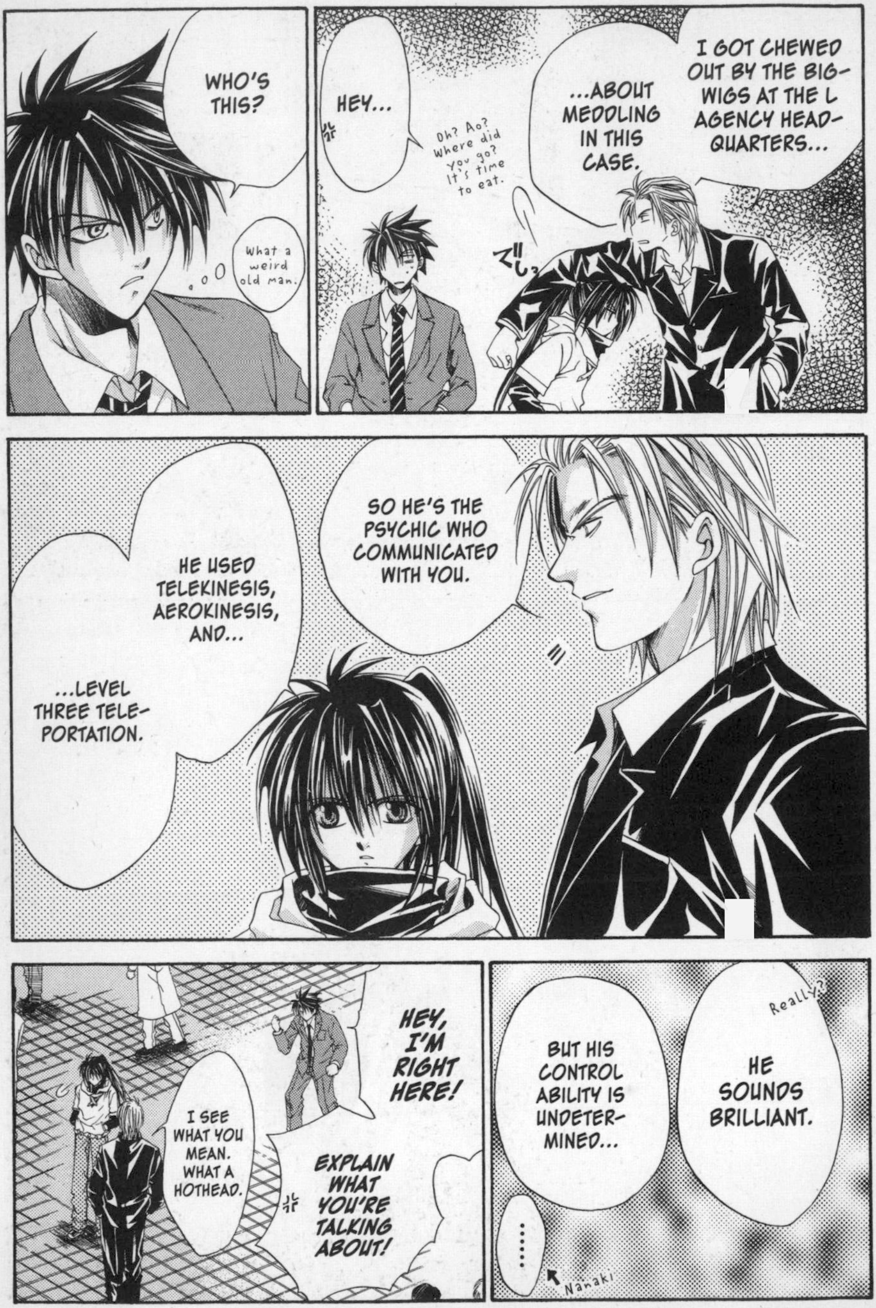
I GOT CHEWED OUT BY THE BIG-WIGS AT THE L AGENCY HEAD-QUARTERS...
...ABOUT MEDDLING IN THIS CASE.
Oh? Ao? Where did you go? It's time to eat.
HEY...
WHO'S THIS?
What a weird old man.
SO HE'S THE PSYCHIC WHO COMMUNICATED WITH YOU.
HE USED TELEKINESIS, AEROKINESIS, AND...
...LEVEL THREE TELE-PORTATION.
Really?
HE SOUNDS BRILLIANT.
BUT HIS CONTROL ABILITY IS UNDETER-MINED...
......
Nanaki
HEY, I'M RIGHT HERE!
I SEE WHAT YOU MEAN. WHAT A HOTHEAD.
EXPLAIN WHAT YOU'RE TALKING ABOUT!

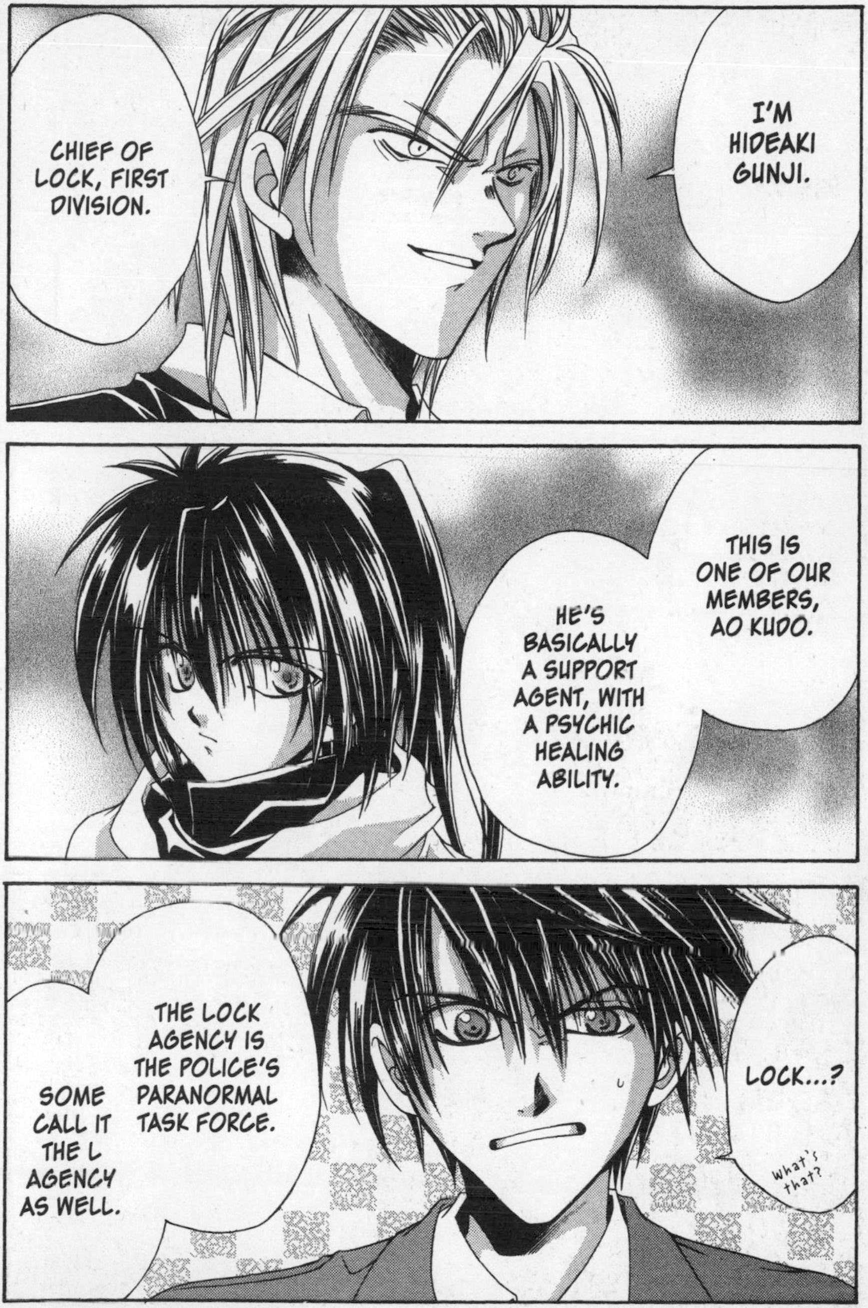
I'M HIDEAKI GUNJI.
CHIEF OF LOCK, FIRST DIVISION.
THIS IS ONE OF OUR MEMBERS, AO KUDO.
HE'S BASICALLY A SUPPORT AGENT, WITH A PSYCHIC HEALING ABILITY.
LOCK...?
what's that?
THE LOCK AGENCY IS THE POLICE'S PARANORMAL TASK FORCE.
SOME CALL IT THE L AGENCY AS WELL.

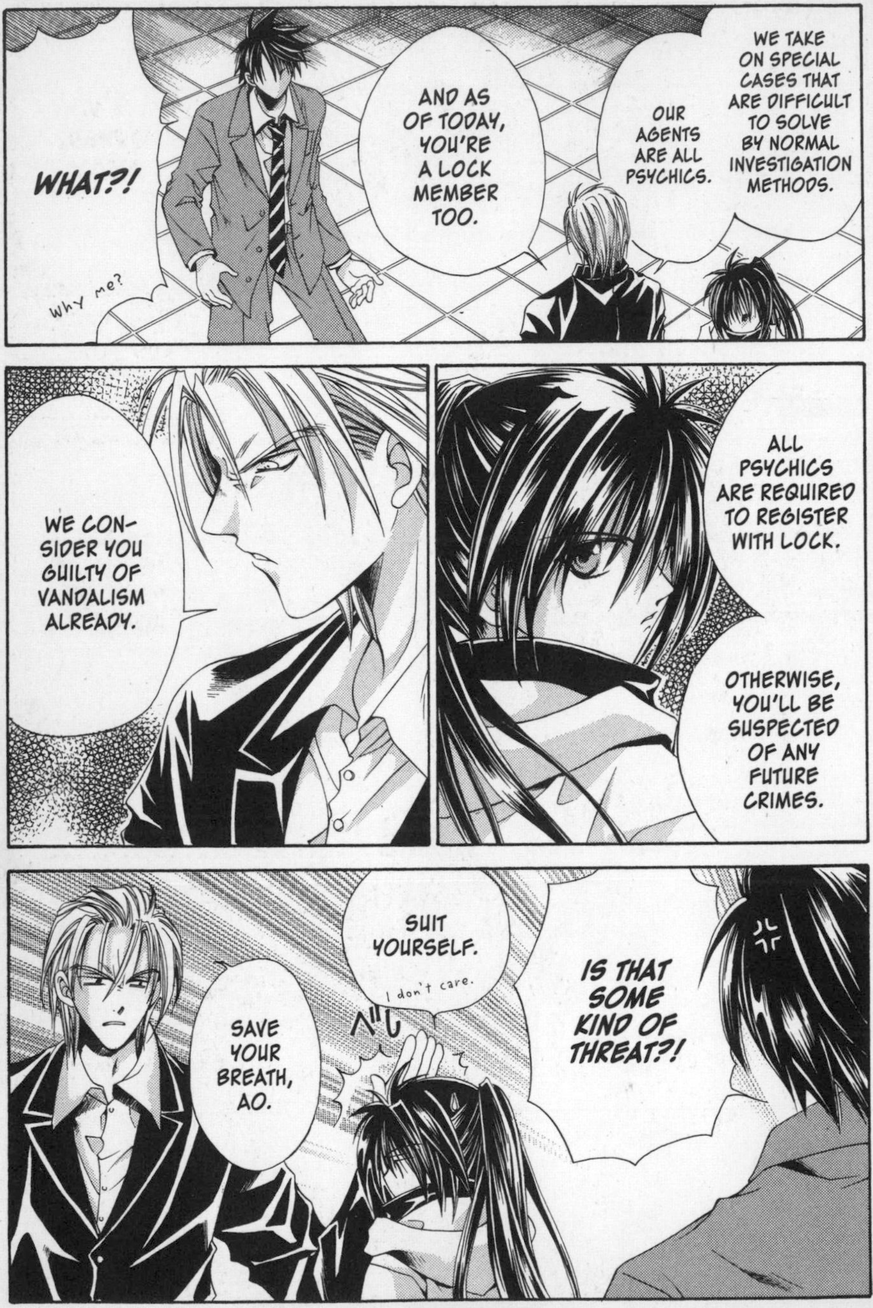

WE TAKE ON SPECIAL CASES THAT ARE DIFFICULT TO SOLVE BY NORMAL INVESTIGATION METHODS.
OUR AGENTS ARE ALL PSYCHICS.
AND AS OF TODAY, YOU'RE A LOCK MEMBER TOO.
WHAT?!
Why me?
ALL PSYCHICS ARE REQUIRED TO REGISTER WITH LOCK.
OTHERWISE, YOU'LL BE SUSPECTED OF ANY FUTURE CRIMES.
WE CONSIDER YOU GUILTY OF VANDALISM ALREADY.
IS THAT SOME KIND OF THREAT?!
SUIT YOURSELF.
I don't care.
SAVE YOUR BREATH, AO.

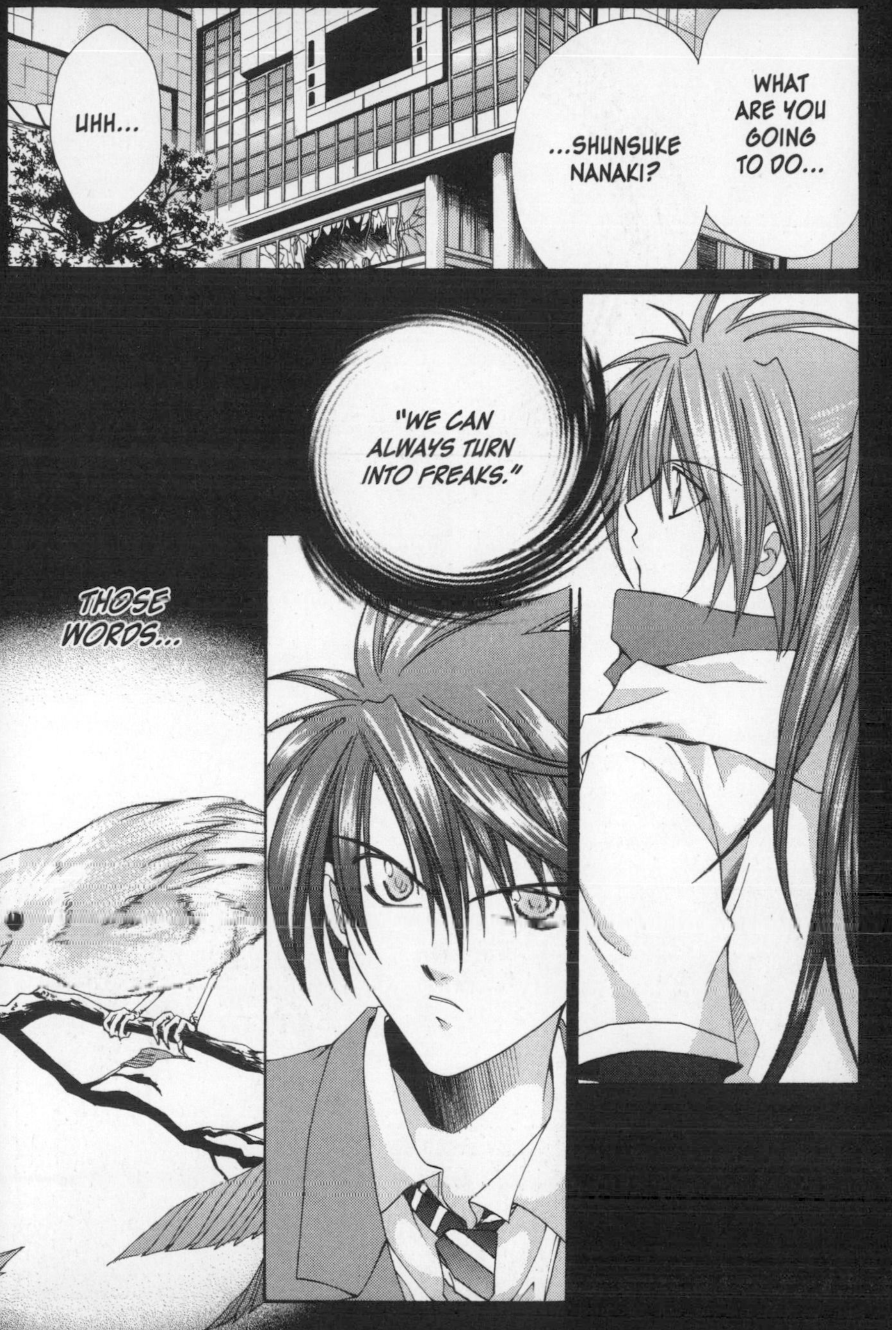
WHAT ARE YOU GOING TO DO...
...SHUNSUKE NANAKI?
UHH...
"WE CAN ALWAYS TURN INTO FREAKS."
THOSE WORDS...

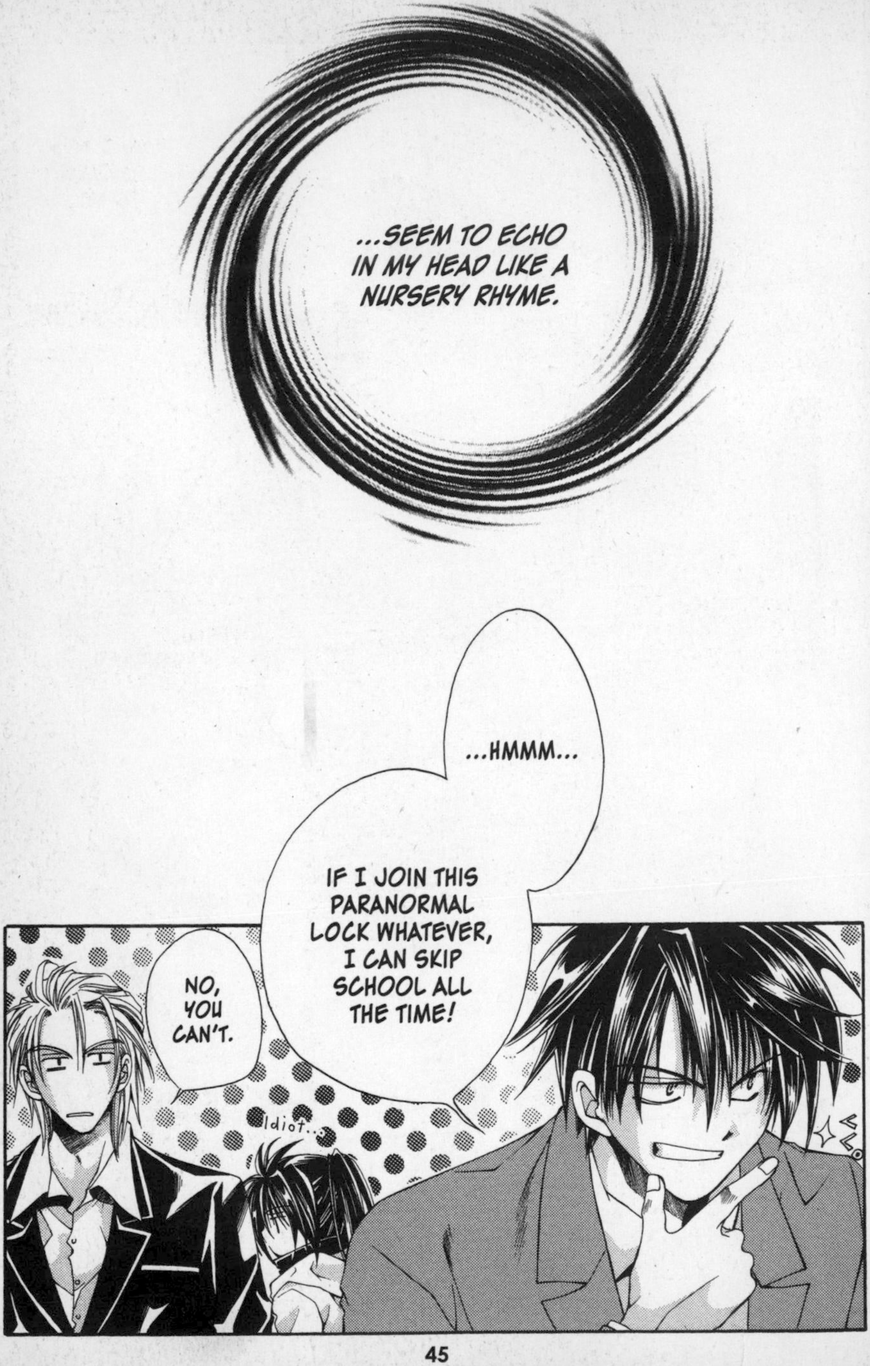
...SEEM TO ECHO IN MY HEAD LIKE A NURSERY RHYME.
...HMMM...
IF I JOIN THIS PARANORMAL LOCK WHATEVER, I CAN SKIP SCHOOL ALL THE TIME!
NO, YOU CAN'T.
Idiot...

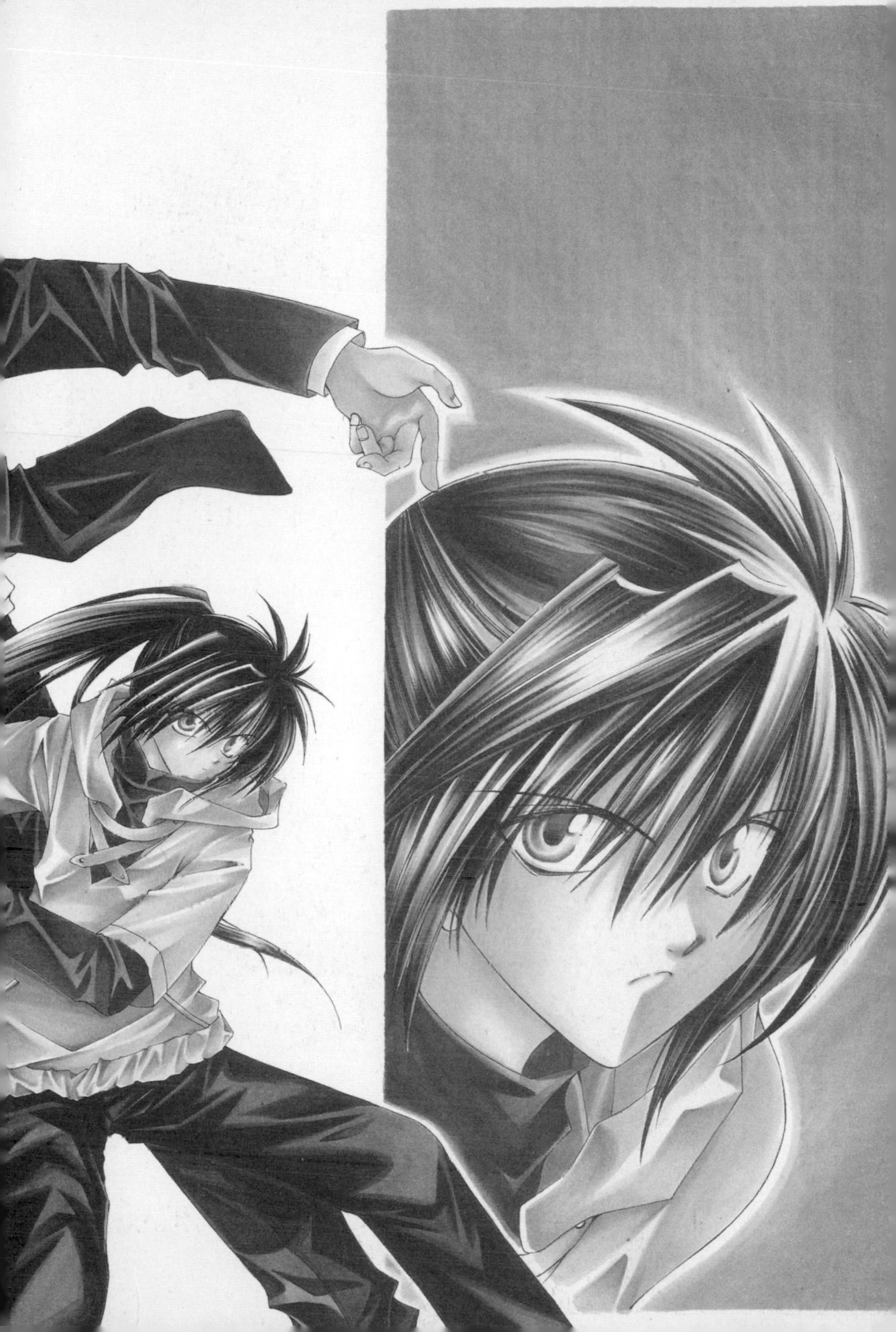

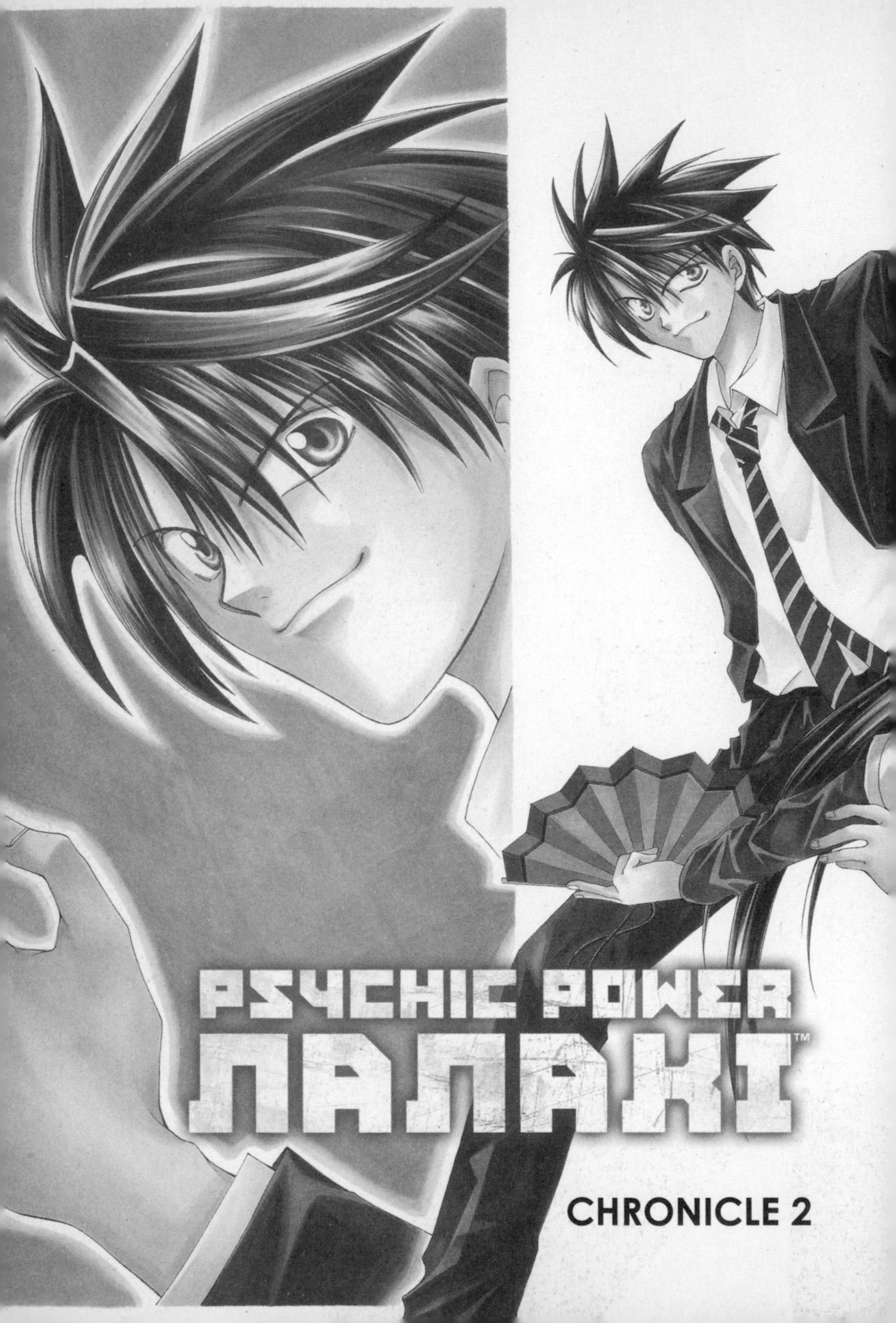
PSYCHIC POWER
NANAKI™
CHRONICLE 2

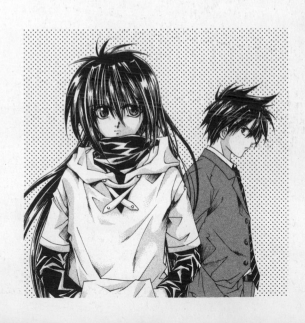

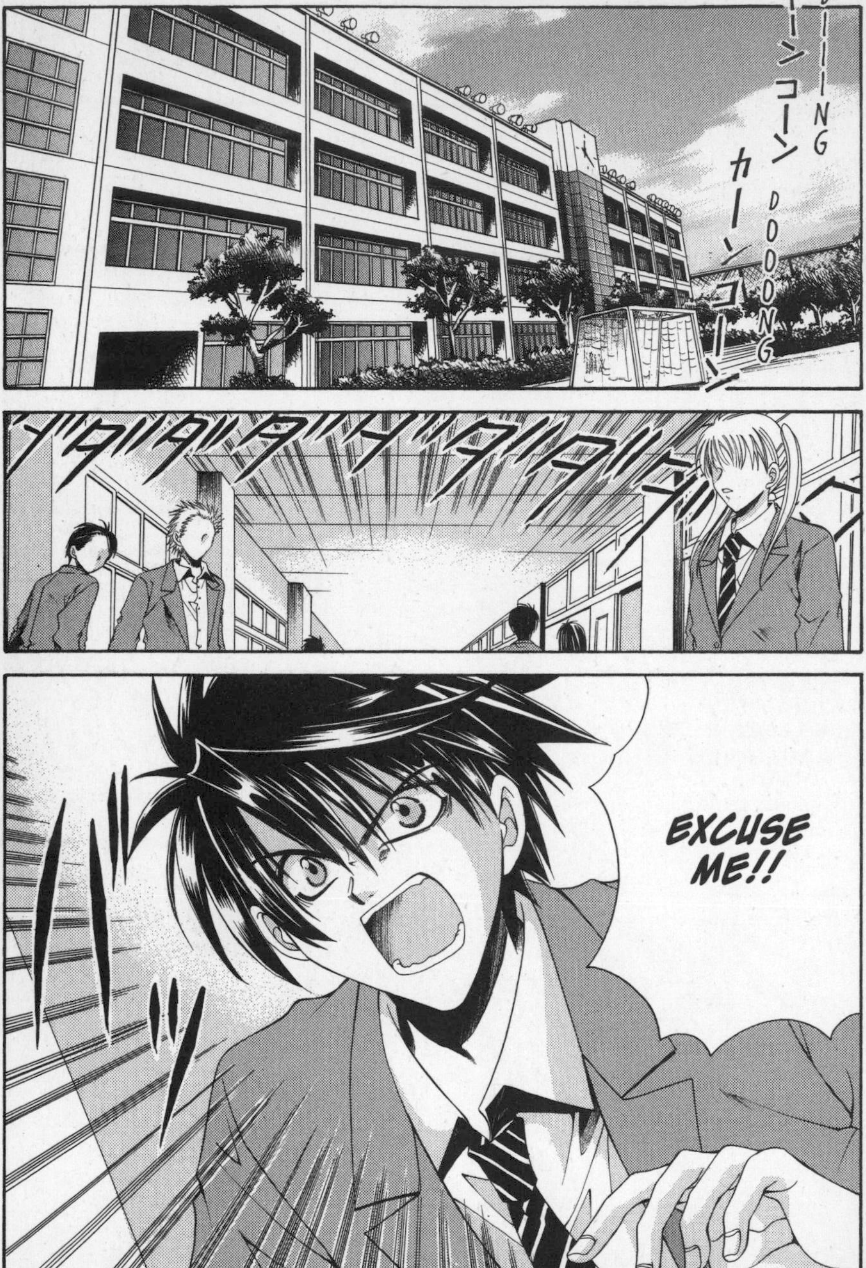
キーンコーン
DIIING
カーンコーン
DOOOONG
EXCUSE ME!!

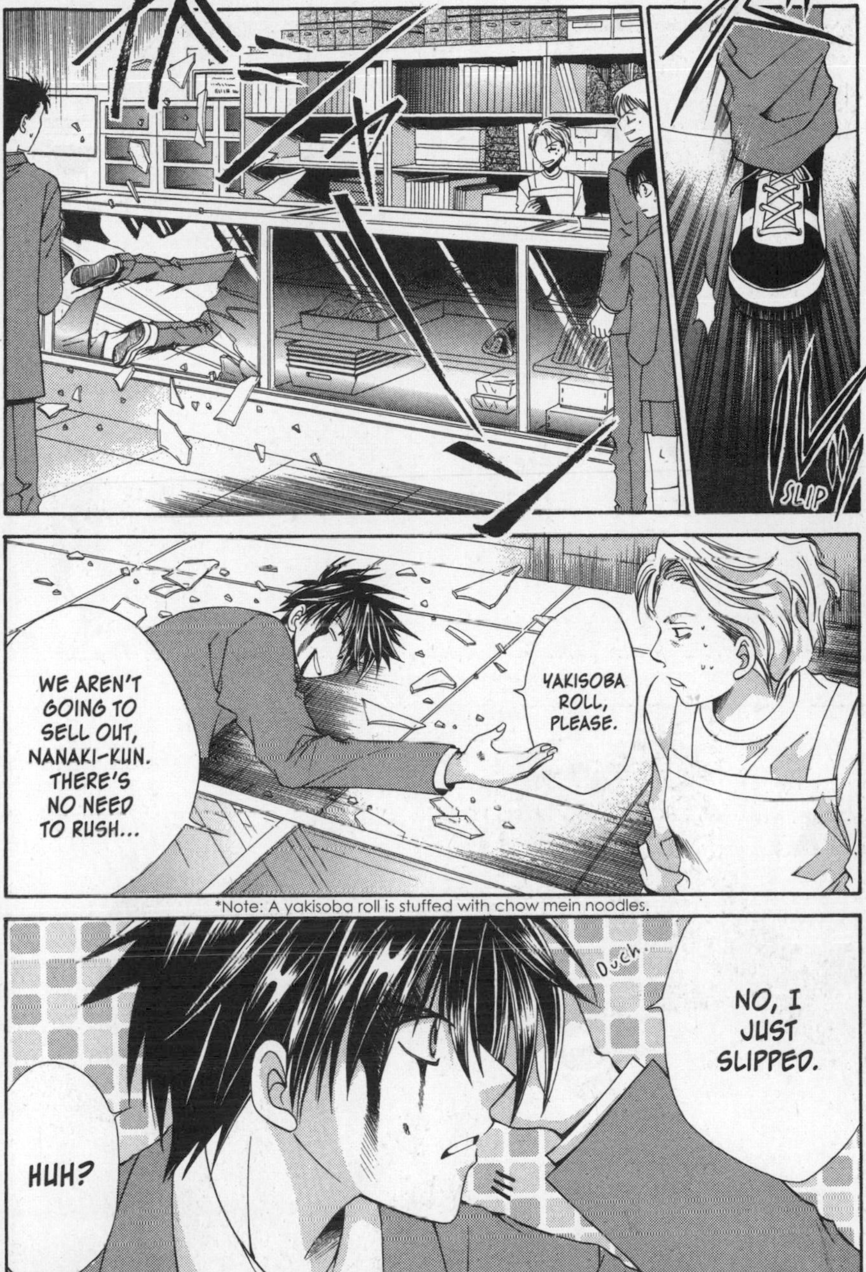
SLIP
YAKISOBA ROLL, PLEASE.
WE AREN'T GOING TO SELL OUT, NANAKI-KUN. THERE'S NO NEED TO RUSH...
*Note: A yakisoba roll is stuffed with chow mein noodles.
NO, I JUST SLIPPED.
Ouch.
HUH?

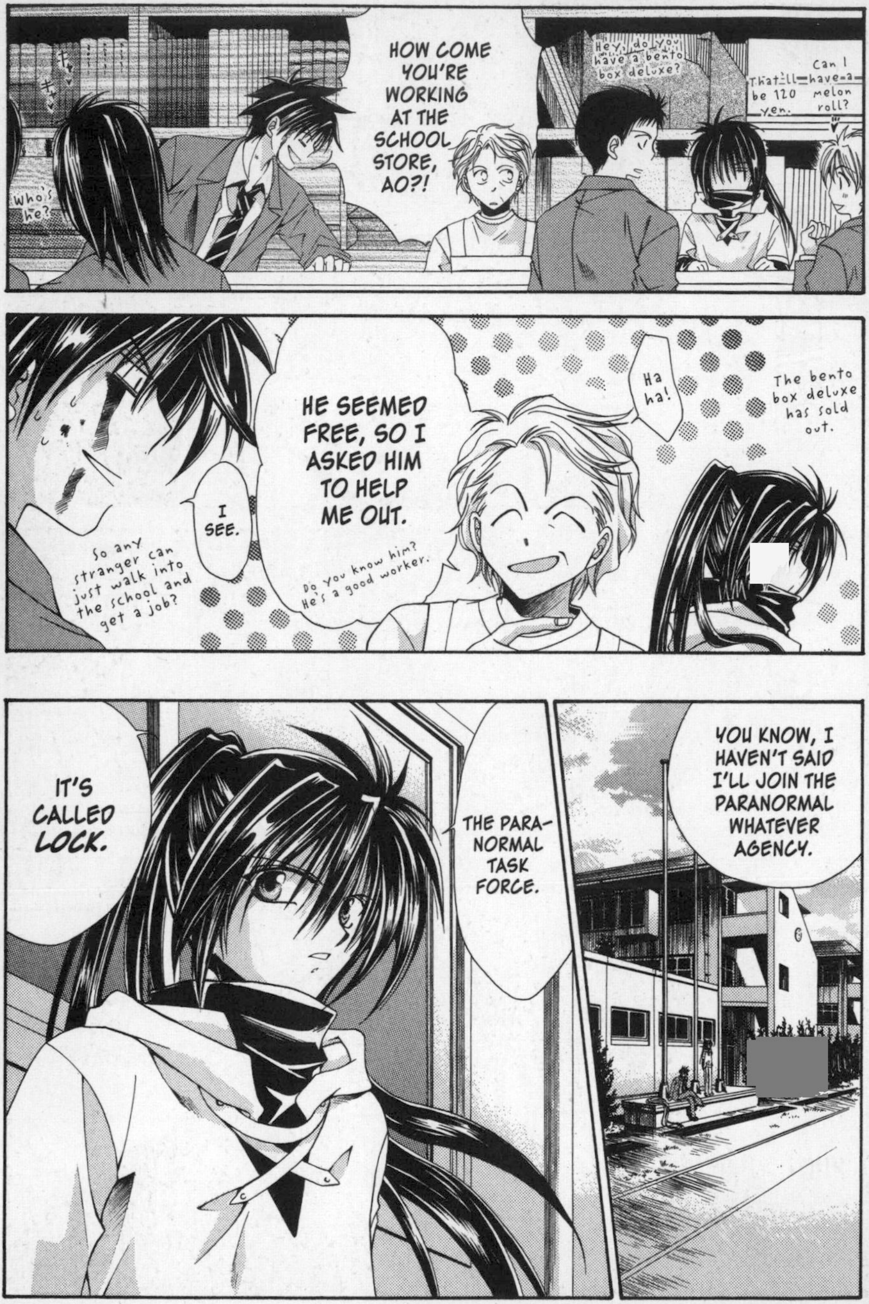
Can I have a melon roll?
That'll be 120 yen.
Hey, do you have a bento box deluxe?
HOW COME YOU'RE WORKING AT THE SCHOOL STORE, AO?!
Who's he?
The bento box deluxe has sold out.
Ha ha!
HE SEEMED FREE, SO I ASKED HIM TO HELP ME OUT.
Do you know him? He's a good worker.
I SEE.
So any stranger can just walk into the school and get a job?
YOU KNOW, I HAVEN'T SAID I'LL JOIN THE PARANORMAL WHATEVER AGENCY.
THE PARA-NORMAL TASK FORCE.
IT'S CALLED LOCK.

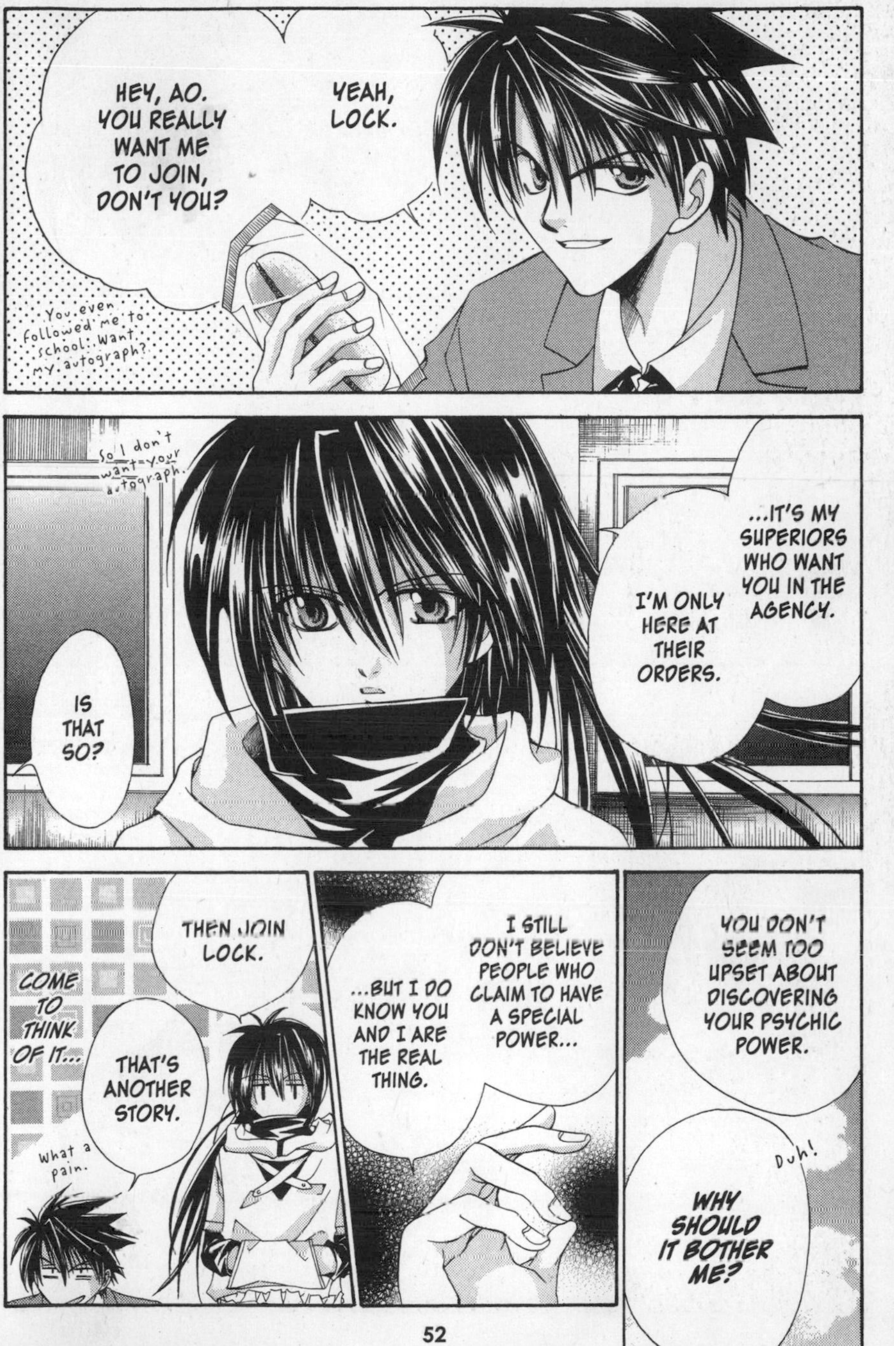
HEY, AO. YOU REALLY WANT ME TO JOIN, DON'T YOU?
YEAH, LOCK.
You even followed me to school. Want my autograph?
...IT'S MY SUPERIORS WHO WANT YOU IN THE AGENCY.
I'M ONLY HERE AT THEIR ORDERS.
So I don't want your autograph.
IS THAT SO?
YOU DON'T SEEM TOO UPSET ABOUT DISCOVERING YOUR PSYCHIC POWER.
Duh!
WHY SHOULD IT BOTHER ME?
I STILL DON'T BELIEVE PEOPLE WHO CLAIM TO HAVE A SPECIAL POWER...
...BUT I DO KNOW YOU AND I ARE THE REAL THING.
THEN JOIN LOCK.
COME TO THINK OF IT...
THAT'S ANOTHER STORY.
What a pain.

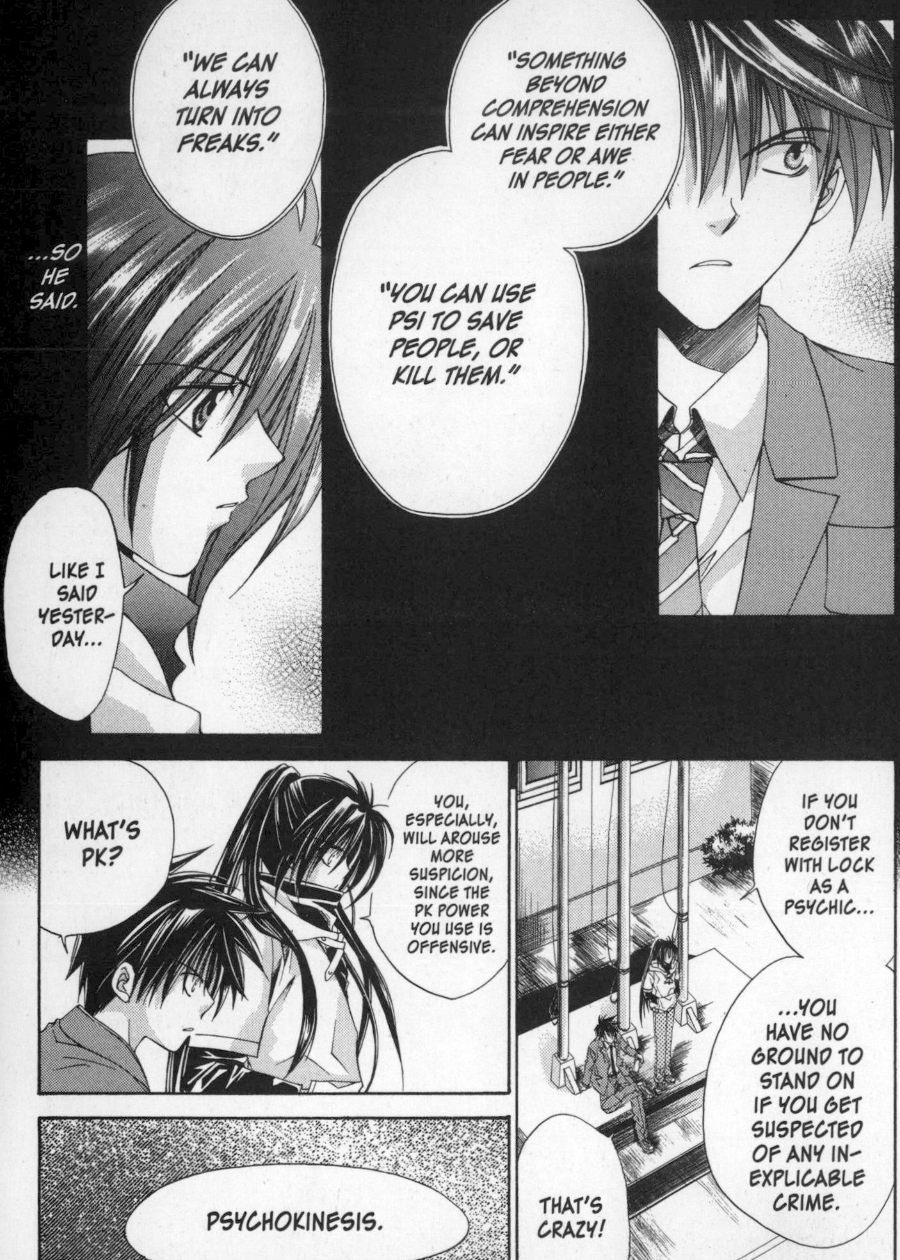
"SOMETHING BEYOND COMPREHENSION CAN INSPIRE EITHER FEAR OR AWE IN PEOPLE."
"YOU CAN USE PSI TO SAVE PEOPLE, OR KILL THEM."
"WE CAN ALWAYS TURN INTO FREAKS."
...SO HE SAID.
LIKE I SAID YESTER-DAY...
IF YOU DON'T REGISTER WITH LOCK AS A PSYCHIC...
...YOU HAVE NO GROUND TO STAND ON IF YOU GET SUSPECTED OF ANY IN-EXPLICABLE CRIME.
THAT'S CRAZY!
YOU, ESPECIALLY, WILL AROUSE MORE SUSPICION, SINCE THE PK POWER YOU USE IS OFFENSIVE.
WHAT'S PK?
PSYCHOKINESIS.

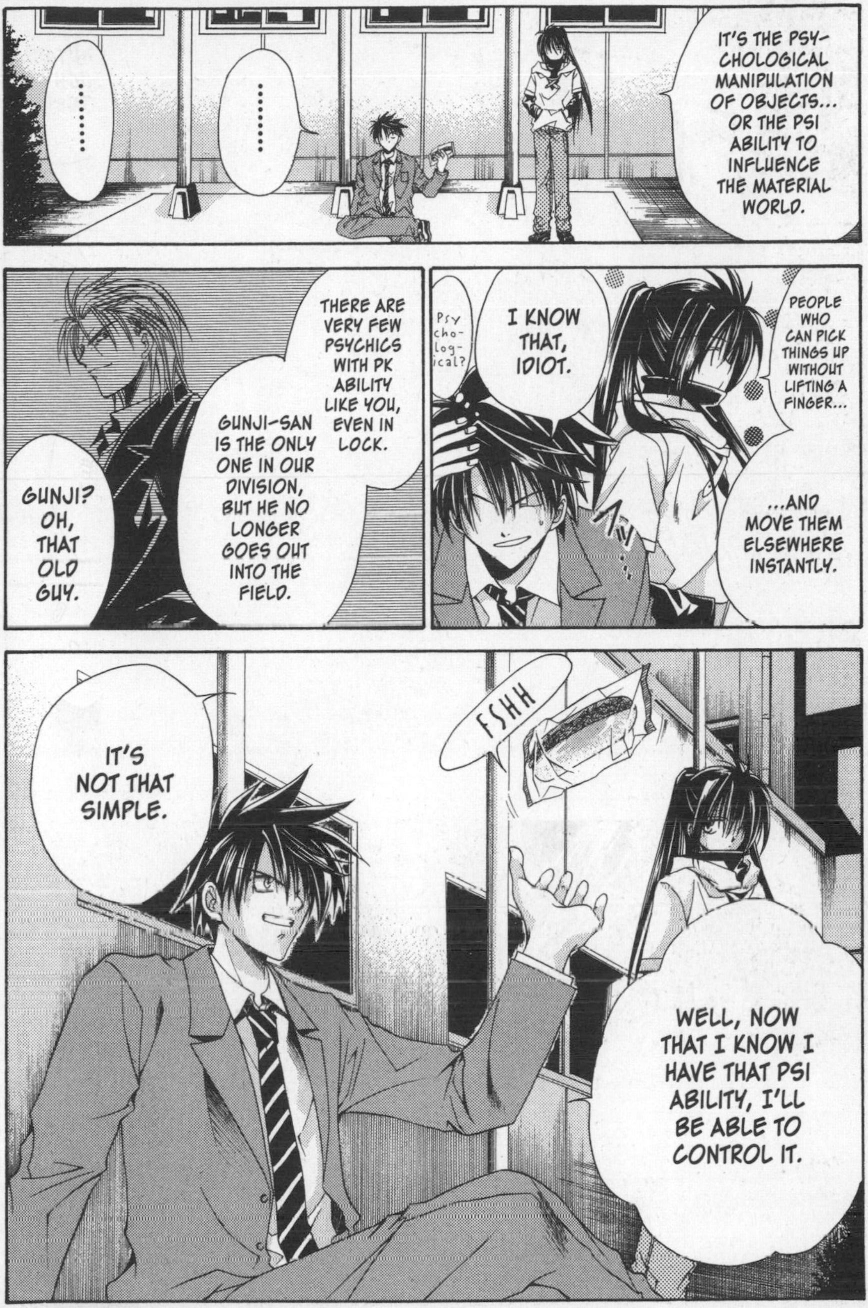
IT'S THE PSYCHOLOGICAL MANIPULATION OF OBJECTS... OR THE PSI ABILITY TO INFLUENCE THE MATERIAL WORLD.
......
......
PEOPLE WHO CAN PICK THINGS UP WITHOUT LIFTING A FINGER...
I KNOW THAT, IDIOT.
Psy-cho-log-ical?
...AND MOVE THEM ELSEWHERE INSTANTLY.
THERE ARE VERY FEW PSYCHICS WITH PK ABILITY LIKE YOU, EVEN IN LOCK.
GUNJI-SAN IS THE ONLY ONE IN OUR DIVISION, BUT HE NO LONGER GOES OUT INTO THE FIELD.
GUNJI? OH, THAT OLD GUY.
FSHH
WELL, NOW THAT I KNOW I HAVE THAT PSI ABILITY, I'LL BE ABLE TO CONTROL IT.
IT'S NOT THAT SIMPLE.

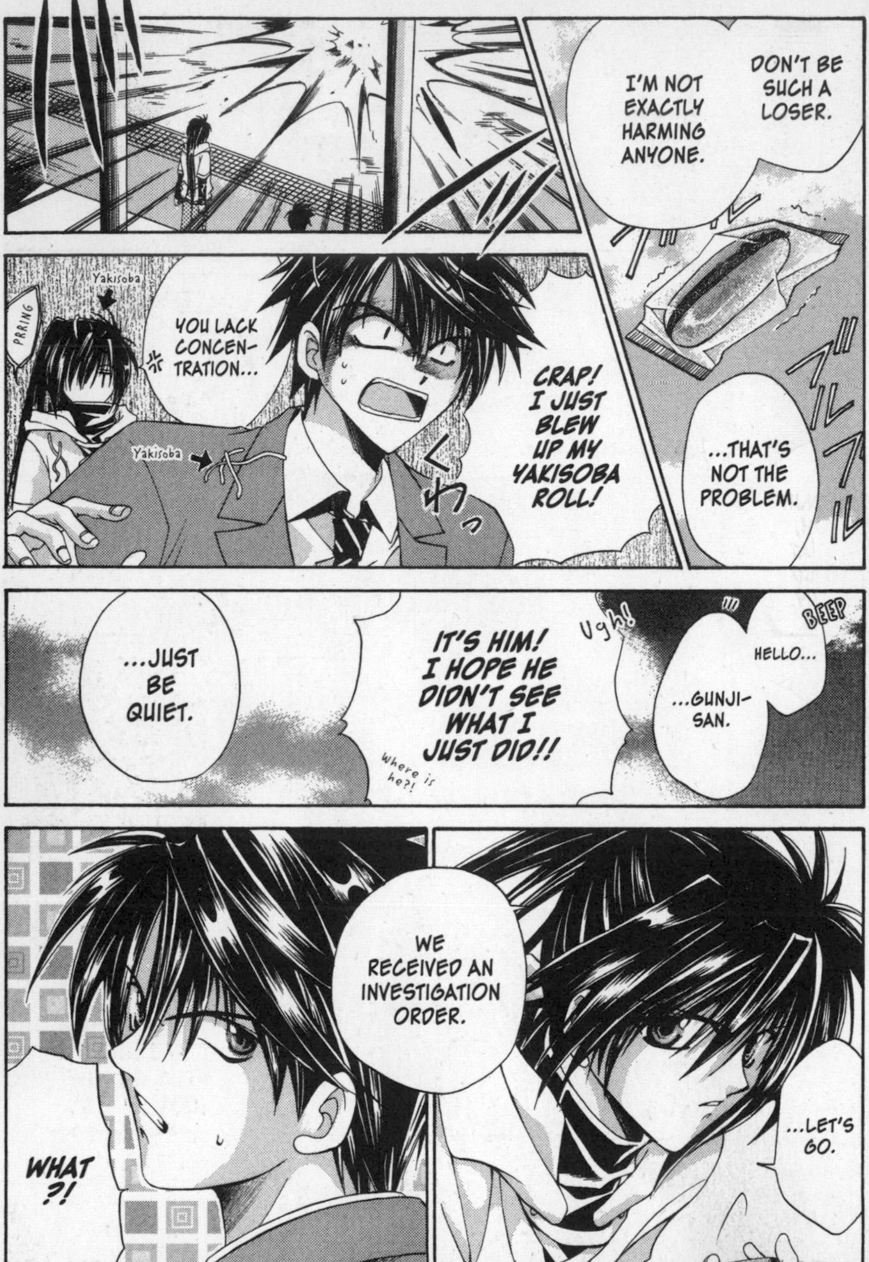
DON'T BE SUCH A LOSER.
I'M NOT EXACTLY HARMING ANYONE.
...THAT'S NOT THE PROBLEM.
CRAP! I JUST BLEW UP MY YAKISOBA ROLL!
YOU LACK CONCENTRATION...
Yakisoba
PRRING
Yakisoba
BEEP
HELLO...
...GUNJI-SAN.
Ugh!
IT'S HIM! I HOPE HE DIDN'T SEE WHAT I JUST DID!!
Where is he?!
...JUST BE QUIET.
...LET'S GO.
WE RECEIVED AN INVESTIGATION ORDER.
CLACK
WHAT?!

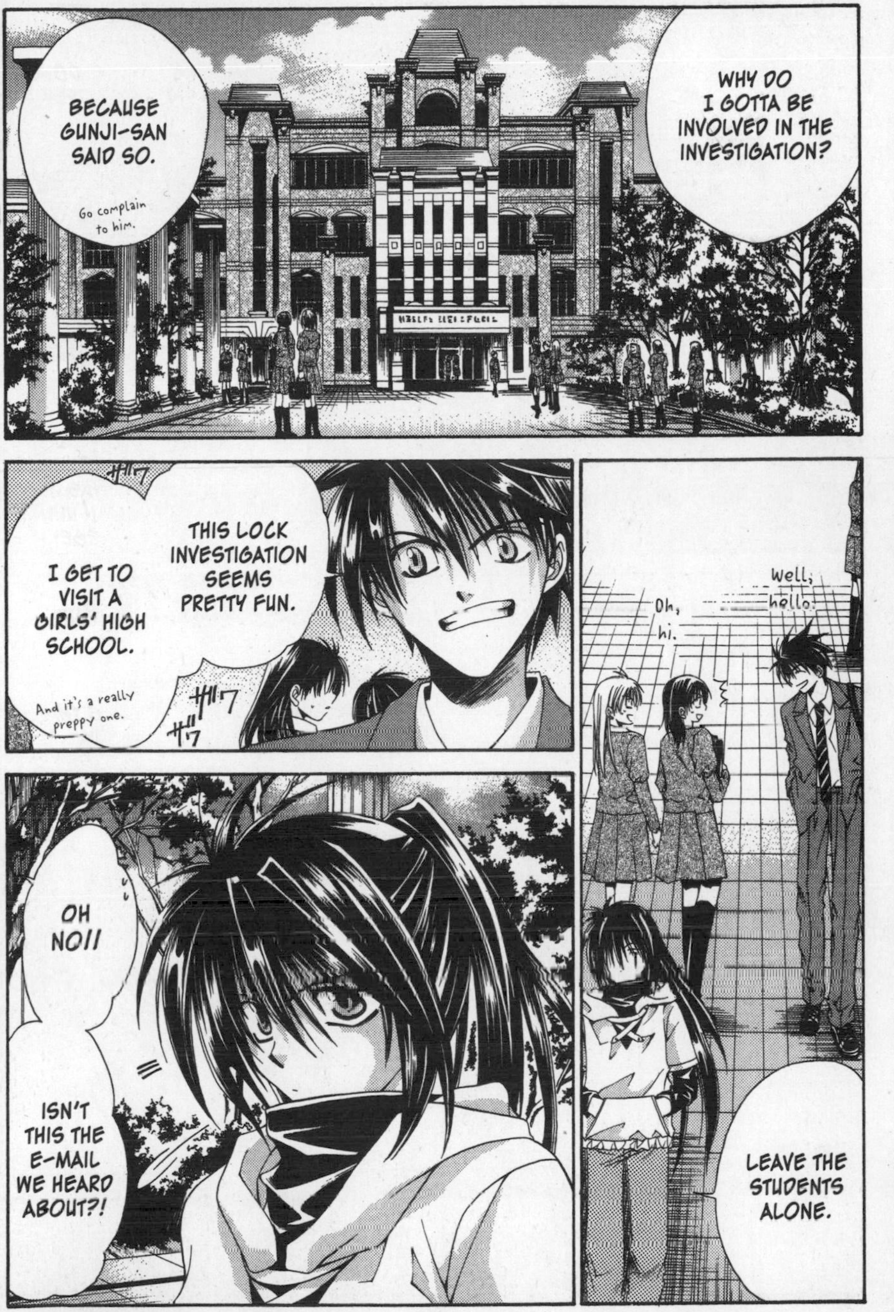
WHY DO I GOTTA BE INVOLVED IN THE INVESTIGATION?
BECAUSE GUNJI-SAN SAID SO.
Go complain to him.
Well, hello.
Oh, hi.
LEAVE THE STUDENTS ALONE.
THIS LOCK INVESTIGATION SEEMS PRETTY FUN.
I GET TO VISIT A GIRLS' HIGH SCHOOL.
And it's a really preppy one.
OH NO!!
ISN'T THIS THE E-MAIL WE HEARD ABOUT?!

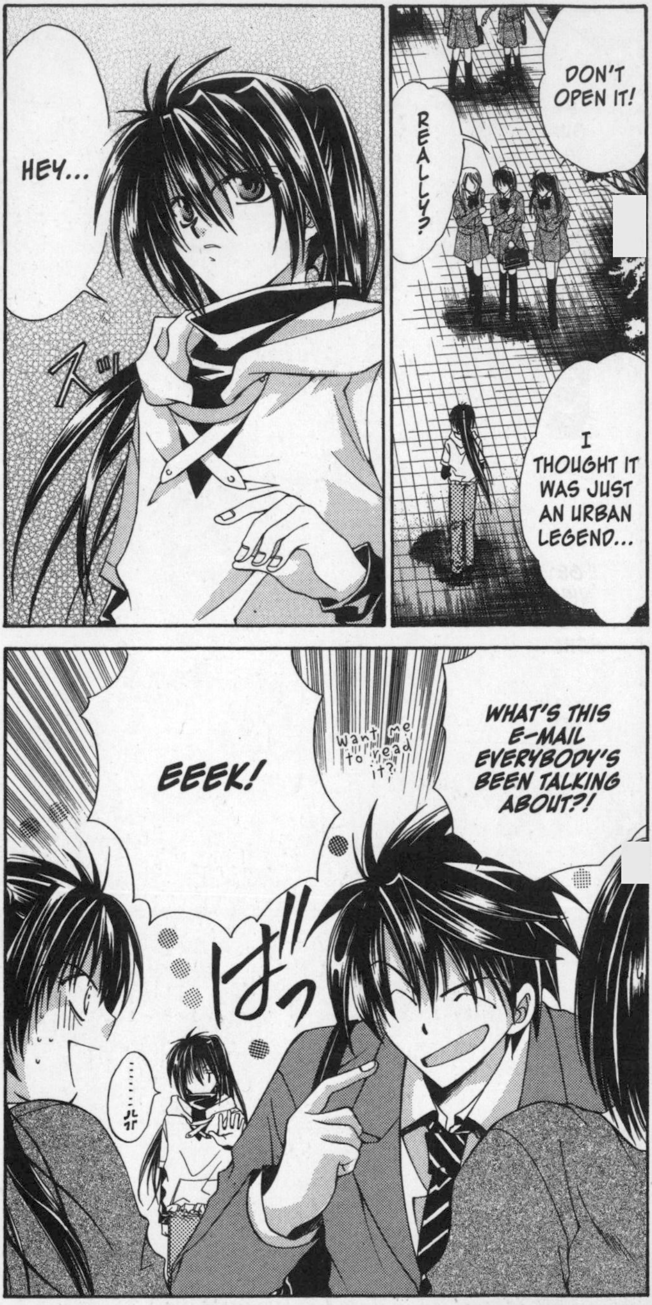
DON'T OPEN IT!
REALLY?
I THOUGHT IT WAS JUST AN URBAN LEGEND...
HEY...
WHAT'S THIS E-MAIL EVERYBODY'S BEEN TALKING ABOUT?!
Want me to read it?
EEEK!

▪BETA▪

I was hoping to insert a bonus manga in this book, but I ran out of time and had to give it up. Argh! Dammit. You may be aware of it from my other books in the past, but I also do pretty silly, funny manga. (Laughs.) I'd like to insert it when I get a chance next time, since I've got some ideas.

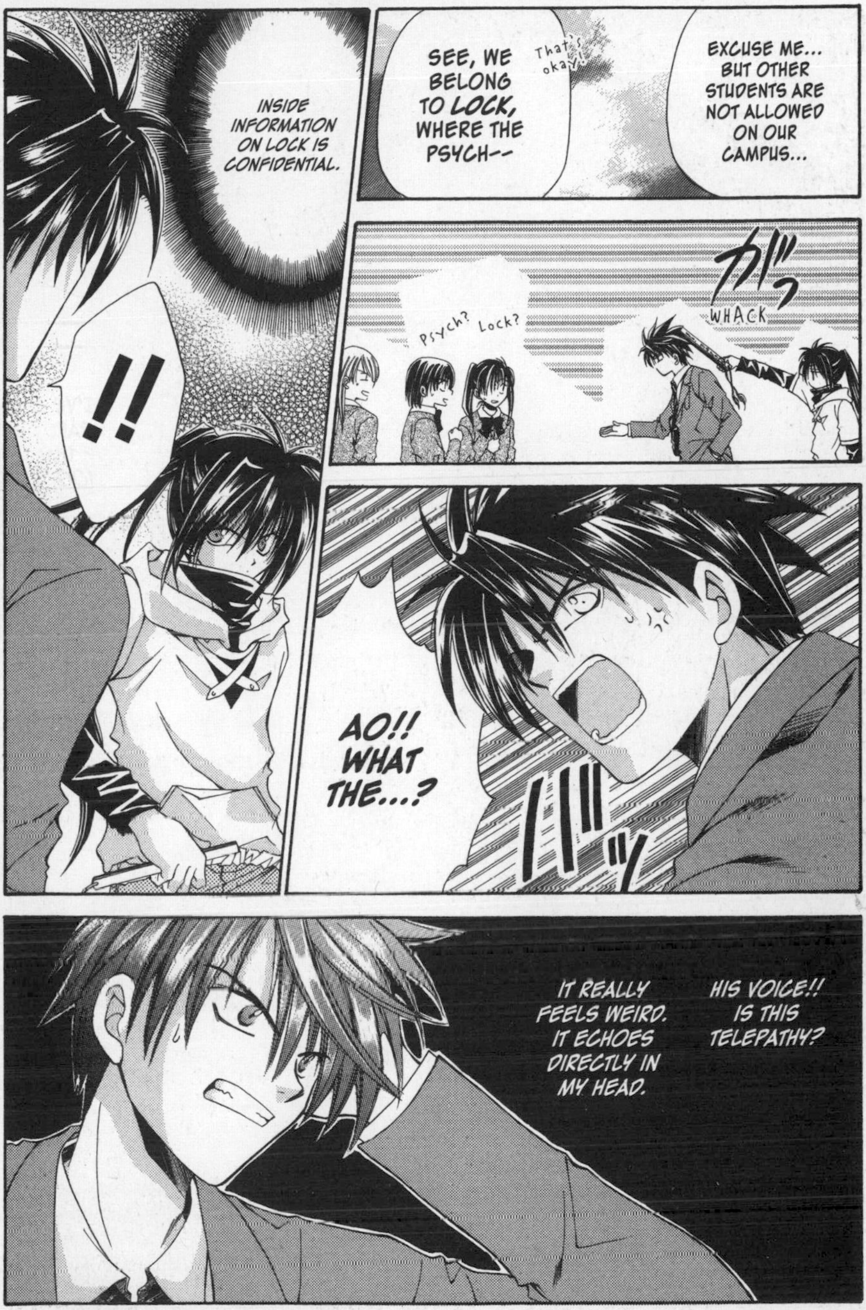
EXCUSE ME... BUT OTHER STUDENTS ARE NOT ALLOWED ON OUR CAMPUS...
That's okay!
SEE, WE BELONG TO LOCK, WHERE THE PSYCH--
WHACK
Lock?
Psych?
AO!! WHAT THE...?
INSIDE INFORMATION ON LOCK IS CONFIDENTIAL.
!!
HIS VOICE!! IS THIS TELEPATHY?
IT REALLY FEELS WEIRD. IT ECHOES DIRECTLY IN MY HEAD.

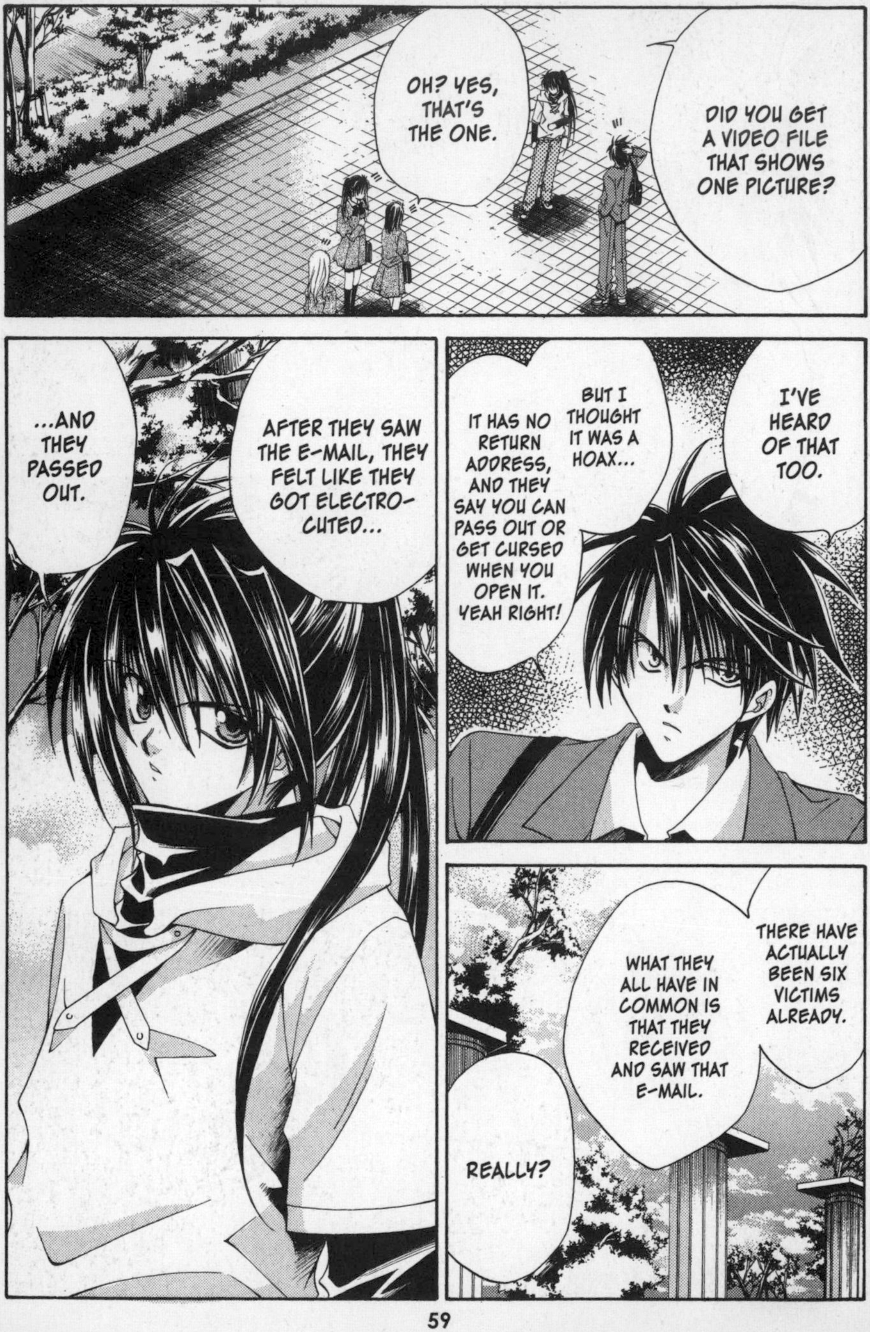
DID YOU GET A VIDEO FILE THAT SHOWS ONE PICTURE?
OH? YES, THAT'S THE ONE.
I'VE HEARD OF THAT TOO.
BUT I THOUGHT IT WAS A HOAX...
IT HAS NO RETURN ADDRESS, AND THEY SAY YOU CAN PASS OUT OR GET CURSED WHEN YOU OPEN IT. YEAH RIGHT!
THERE HAVE ACTUALLY BEEN SIX VICTIMS ALREADY.
WHAT THEY ALL HAVE IN COMMON IS THAT THEY RECEIVED AND SAW THAT E-MAIL.
REALLY?
AFTER THEY SAW THE E-MAIL, THEY FELT LIKE THEY GOT ELECTRO-CUTED...
...AND THEY PASSED OUT.

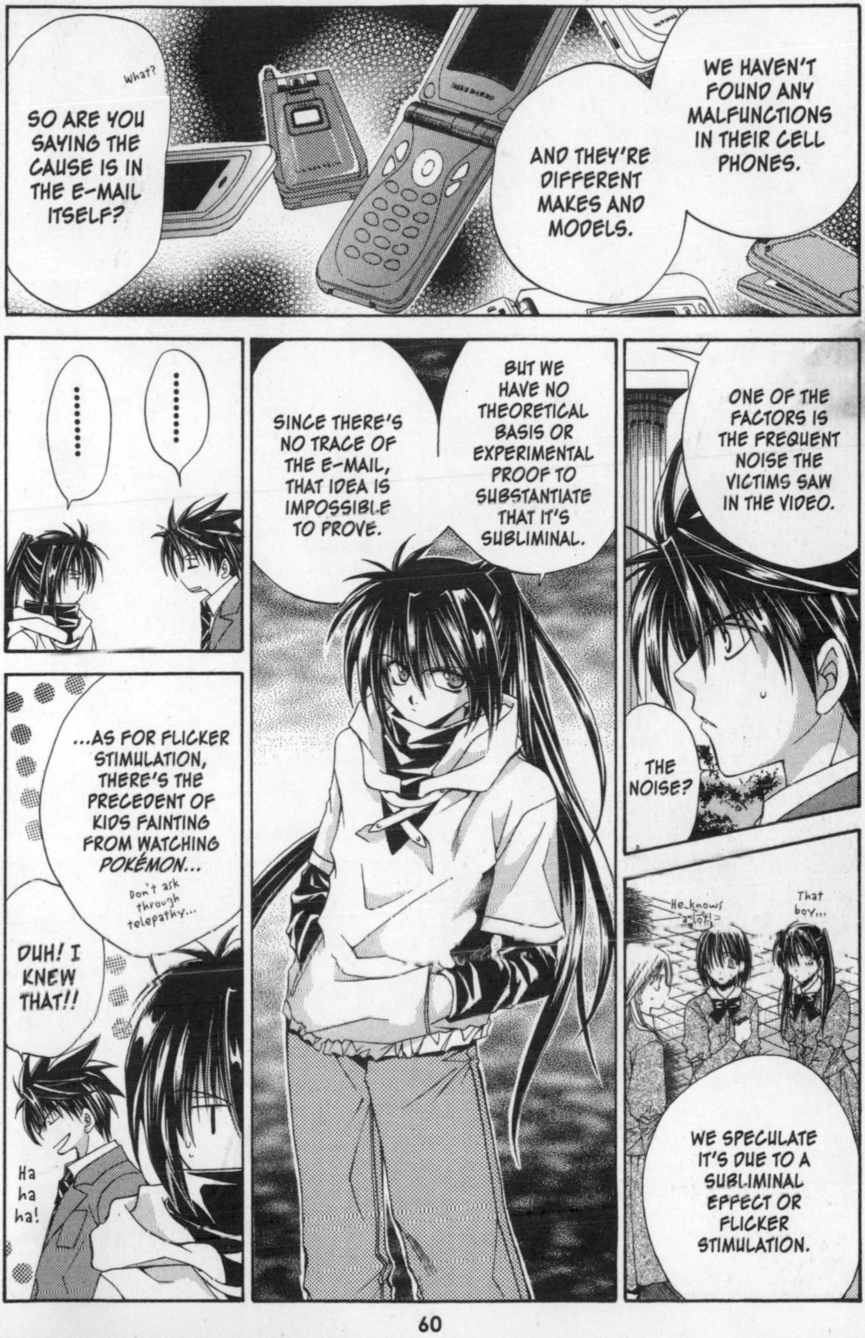

WE HAVEN'T FOUND ANY MALFUNCTIONS IN THEIR CELL PHONES.
AND THEY'RE DIFFERENT MAKES AND MODELS.
What?
SO ARE YOU SAYING THE CAUSE IS IN THE E-MAIL ITSELF?
ONE OF THE FACTORS IS THE FREQUENT NOISE THE VICTIMS SAW IN THE VIDEO.
THE NOISE?
That boy...
He knows a lot!
WE SPECULATE IT'S DUE TO A SUBLIMINAL EFFECT OR FLICKER STIMULATION.
BUT WE HAVE NO THEORETICAL BASIS OR EXPERIMENTAL PROOF TO SUBSTANTIATE THAT IT'S SUBLIMINAL.
SINCE THERE'S NO TRACE OF THE E-MAIL, THAT IDEA IS IMPOSSIBLE TO PROVE.
....
....
...AS FOR FLICKER STIMULATION, THERE'S THE PRECEDENT OF KIDS FAINTING FROM WATCHING *POKÉMON*...
Don't ask through telepathy...
DUH! I KNEW THAT!!
Ha ha ha!

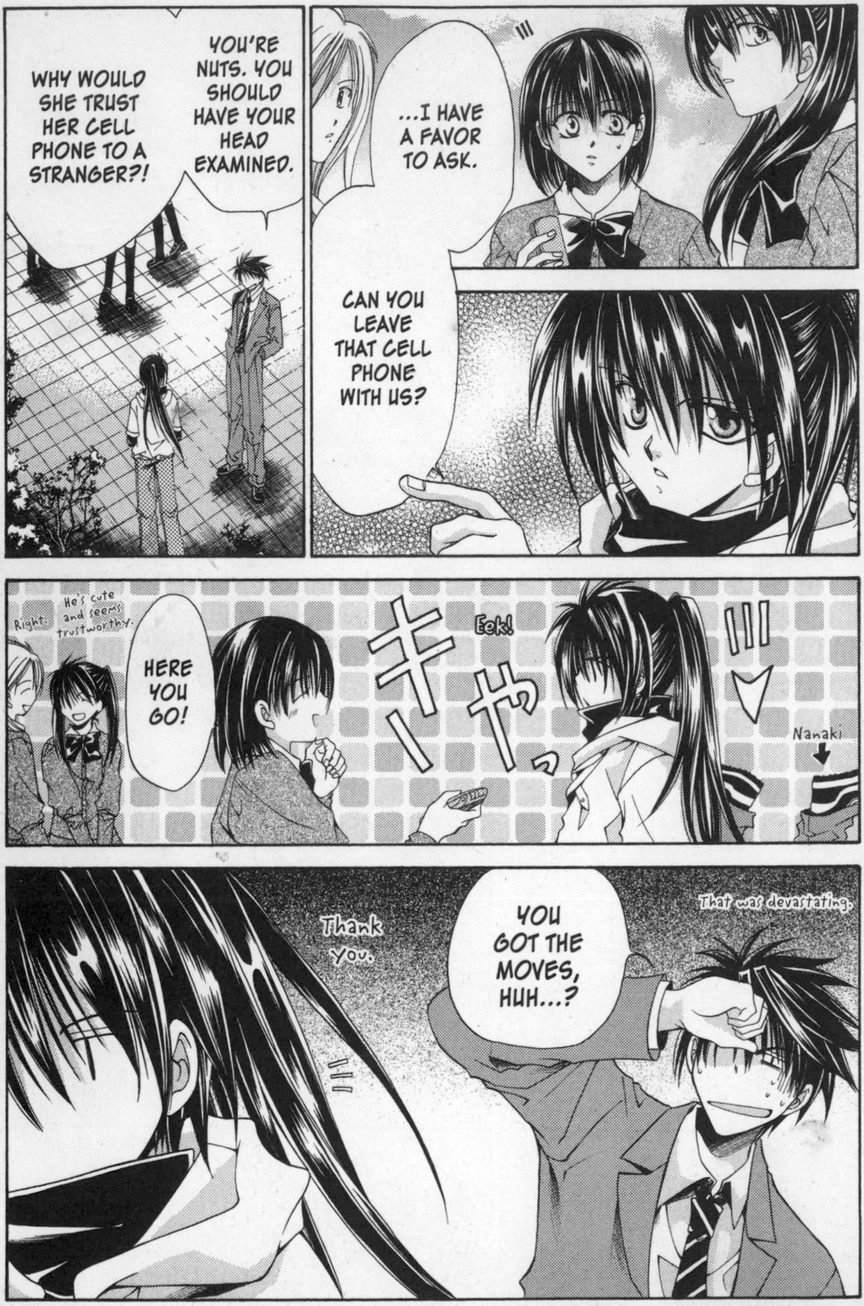

...I HAVE A FAVOR TO ASK.
CAN YOU LEAVE THAT CELL PHONE WITH US?
YOU'RE NUTS. YOU SHOULD HAVE YOUR HEAD EXAMINED.
WHY WOULD SHE TRUST HER CELL PHONE TO A STRANGER?!
Nanaki
キャッ
Eek!
HERE YOU GO!
He's cute and seems trustworthy.
Right.
That was devastating.
YOU GOT THE MOVES, HUH...?
Thank you.

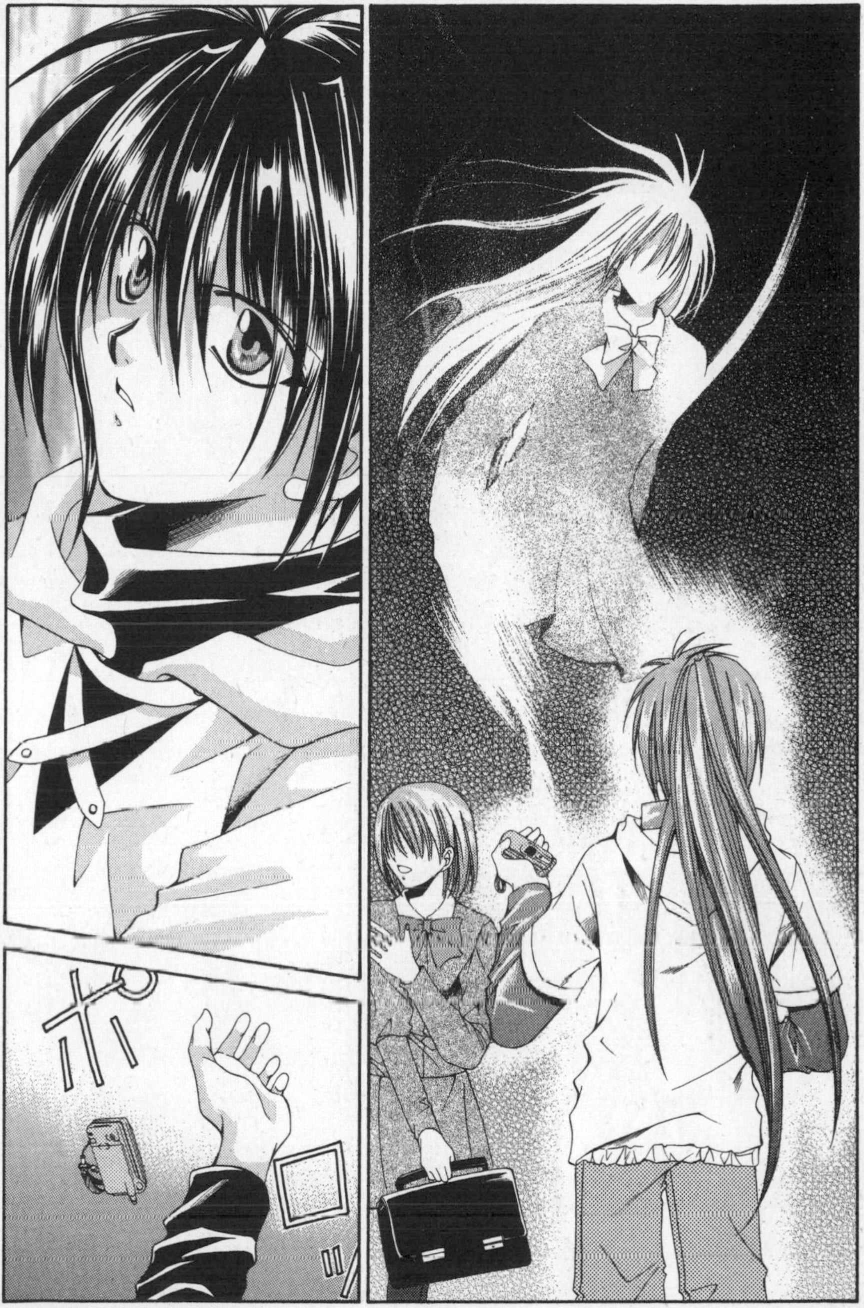

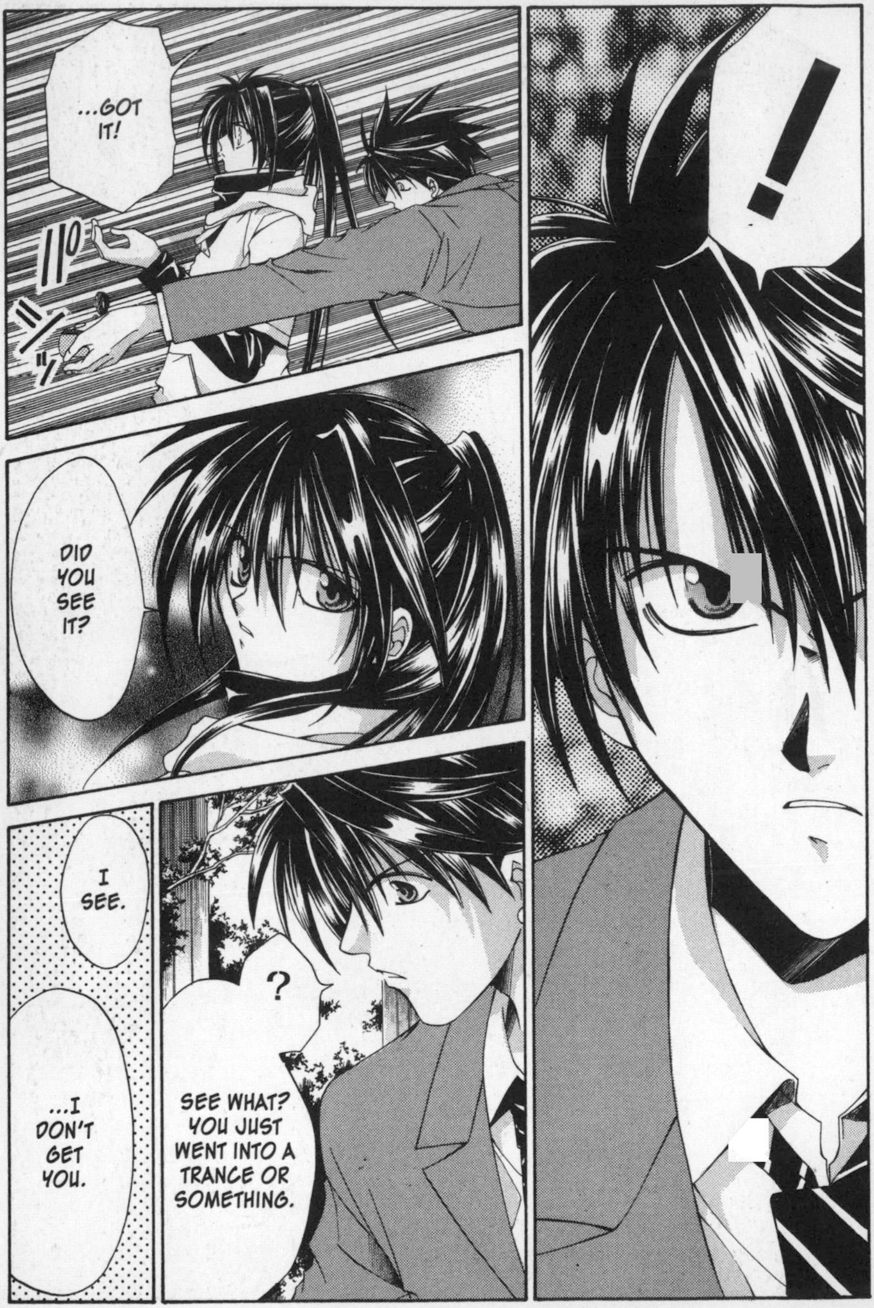
!
...GOT IT!
DID YOU SEE IT?
?
SEE WHAT? YOU JUST WENT INTO A TRANCE OR SOMETHING.
I SEE.
...I DON'T GET YOU.

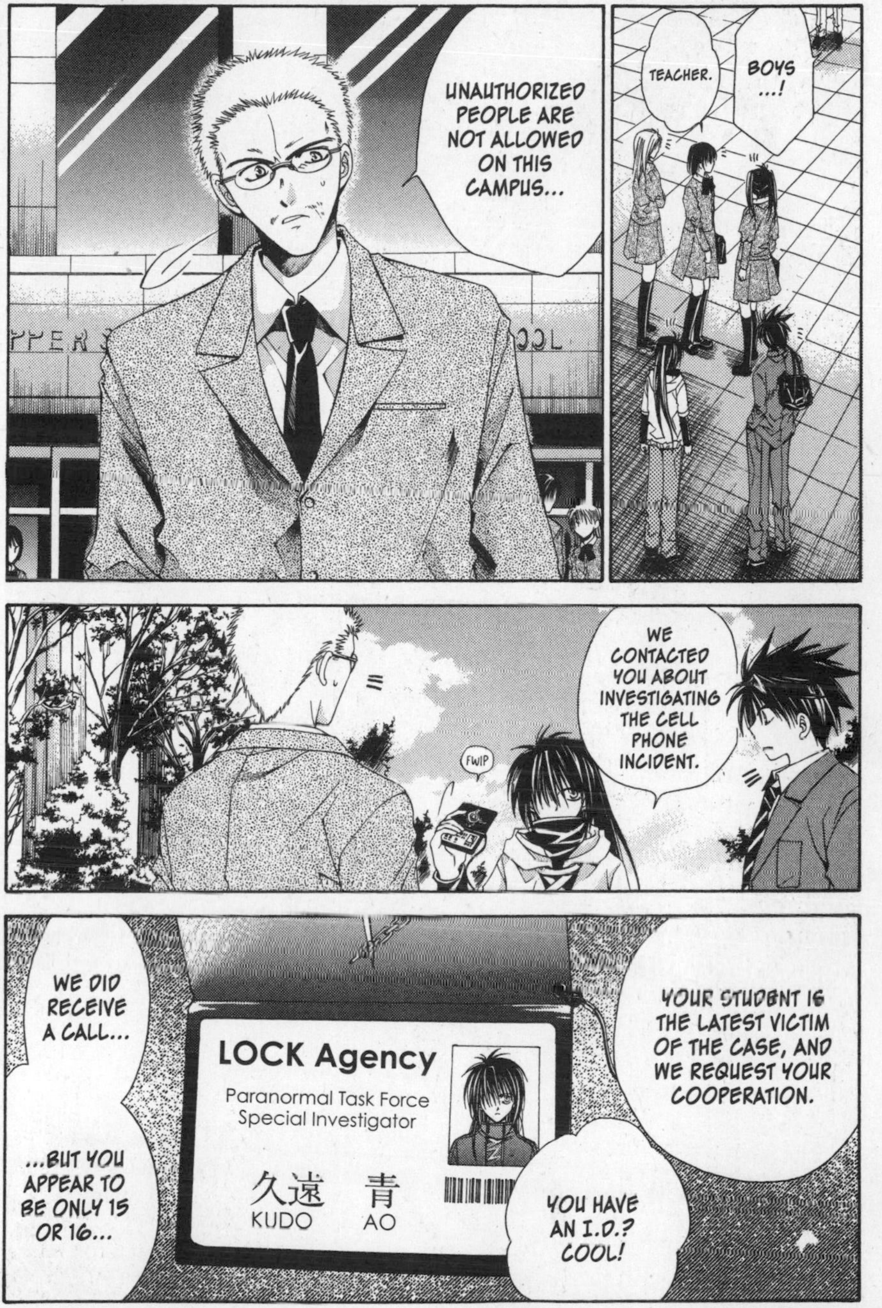
BOYS ...!
TEACHER.
UNAUTHORIZED PEOPLE ARE NOT ALLOWED ON THIS CAMPUS...
WE CONTACTED YOU ABOUT INVESTIGATING THE CELL PHONE INCIDENT.
FWIP
YOUR STUDENT IS THE LATEST VICTIM OF THE CASE, AND WE REQUEST YOUR COOPERATION.
YOU HAVE AN I.D.? COOL!
LOCK Agency
Paranormal Task Force Special Investigator
久遠 青
KUDO AO
WE DID RECEIVE A CALL...
...BUT YOU APPEAR TO BE ONLY 15 OR 16...

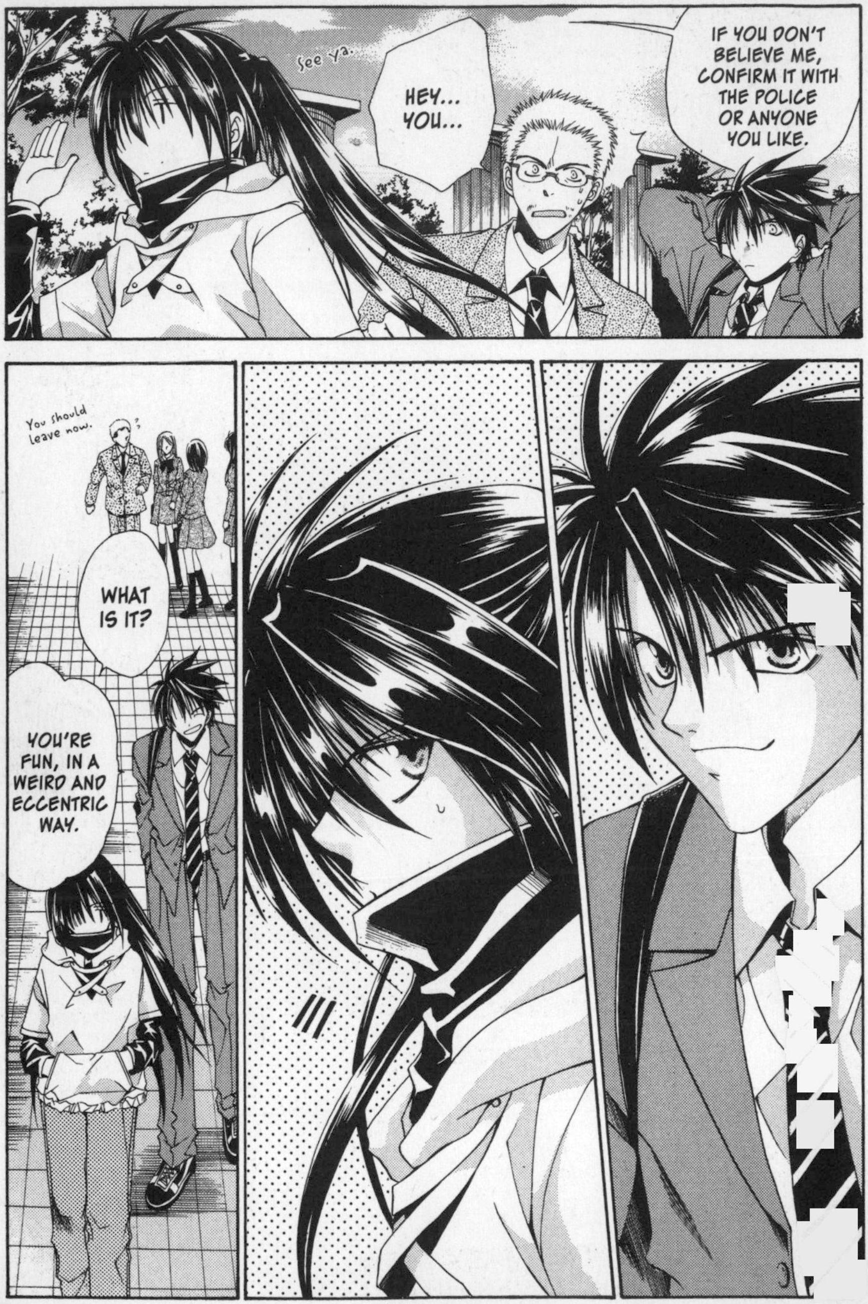
IF YOU DON'T BELIEVE ME, CONFIRM IT WITH THE POLICE OR ANYONE YOU LIKE.
HEY... YOU...
See ya.
You should leave now.
WHAT IS IT?
YOU'RE FUN, IN A WEIRD AND ECCENTRIC WAY.

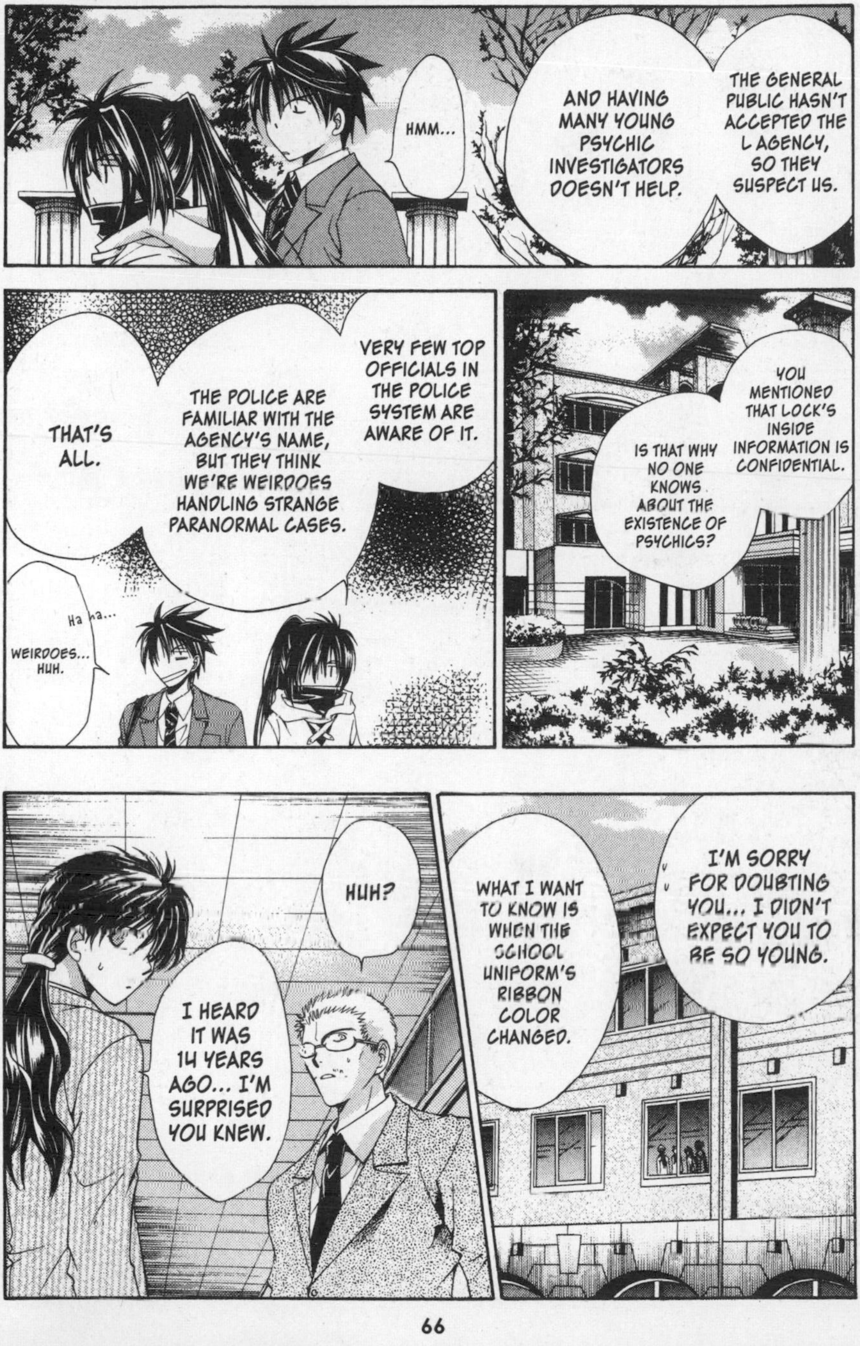
THE GENERAL PUBLIC HASN'T ACCEPTED THE L AGENCY, SO THEY SUSPECT US.
AND HAVING MANY YOUNG PSYCHIC INVESTIGATORS DOESN'T HELP.
HMM...
YOU MENTIONED THAT LOCK'S INSIDE INFORMATION IS CONFIDENTIAL.
IS THAT WHY NO ONE KNOWS ABOUT THE EXISTENCE OF PSYCHICS?
VERY FEW TOP OFFICIALS IN THE POLICE SYSTEM ARE AWARE OF IT.
THE POLICE ARE FAMILIAR WITH THE AGENCY'S NAME, BUT THEY THINK WE'RE WEIRDOES HANDLING STRANGE PARANORMAL CASES.
THAT'S ALL.
Ha ha...
WEIRDOES... HUH.
I'M SORRY FOR DOUBTING YOU... I DIDN'T EXPECT YOU TO BE SO YOUNG.
WHAT I WANT TO KNOW IS WHEN THE SCHOOL UNIFORM'S RIBBON COLOR CHANGED.
HUH?
I HEARD IT WAS 14 YEARS AGO... I'M SURPRISED YOU KNEW.

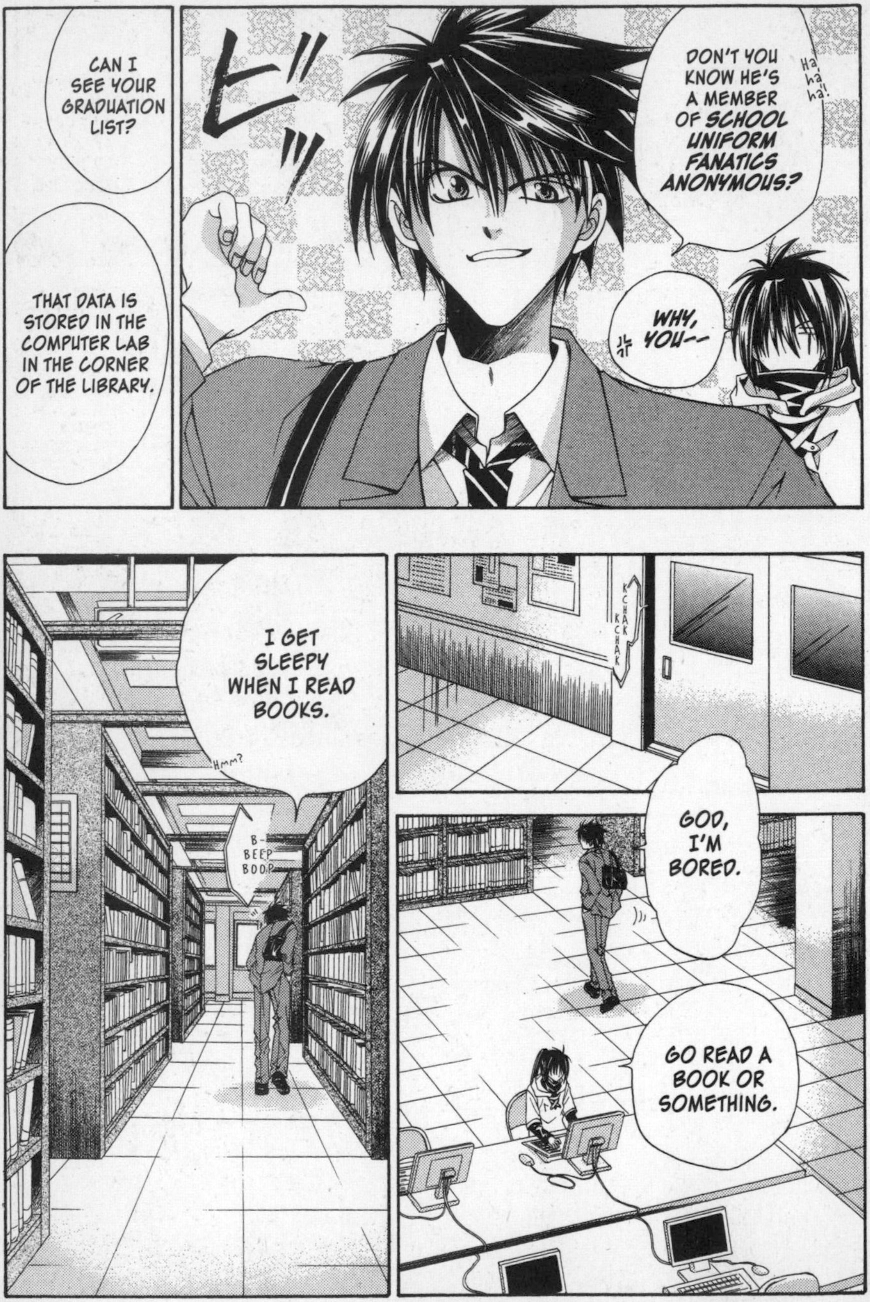
ビッ
DON'T YOU KNOW HE'S A MEMBER OF SCHOOL UNIFORM FANATICS ANONYMOUS?
Ha ha ha!
WHY, YOU--
CAN I SEE YOUR GRADUATION LIST?
THAT DATA IS STORED IN THE COMPUTER LAB IN THE CORNER OF THE LIBRARY.
KCHAK KCHAK
GOD, I'M BORED.
GO READ A BOOK OR SOMETHING.
I GET SLEEPY WHEN I READ BOOKS.
Hmm?
B-BEEP BOOP

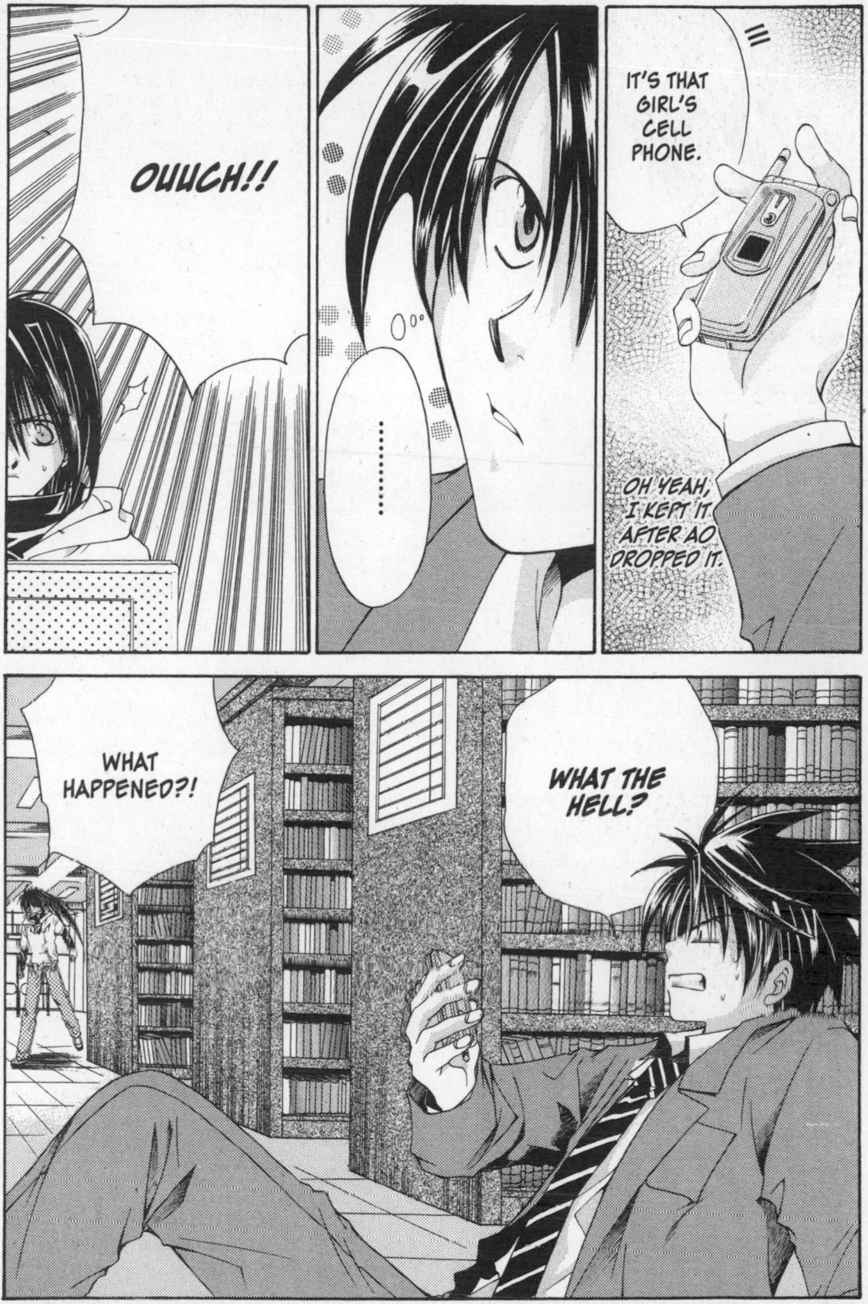
IT'S THAT GIRL'S CELL PHONE.
OH YEAH, I KEPT IT AFTER AO DROPPED IT.
....
OUUCH!!
WHAT THE HELL?
WHAT HAPPENED?!

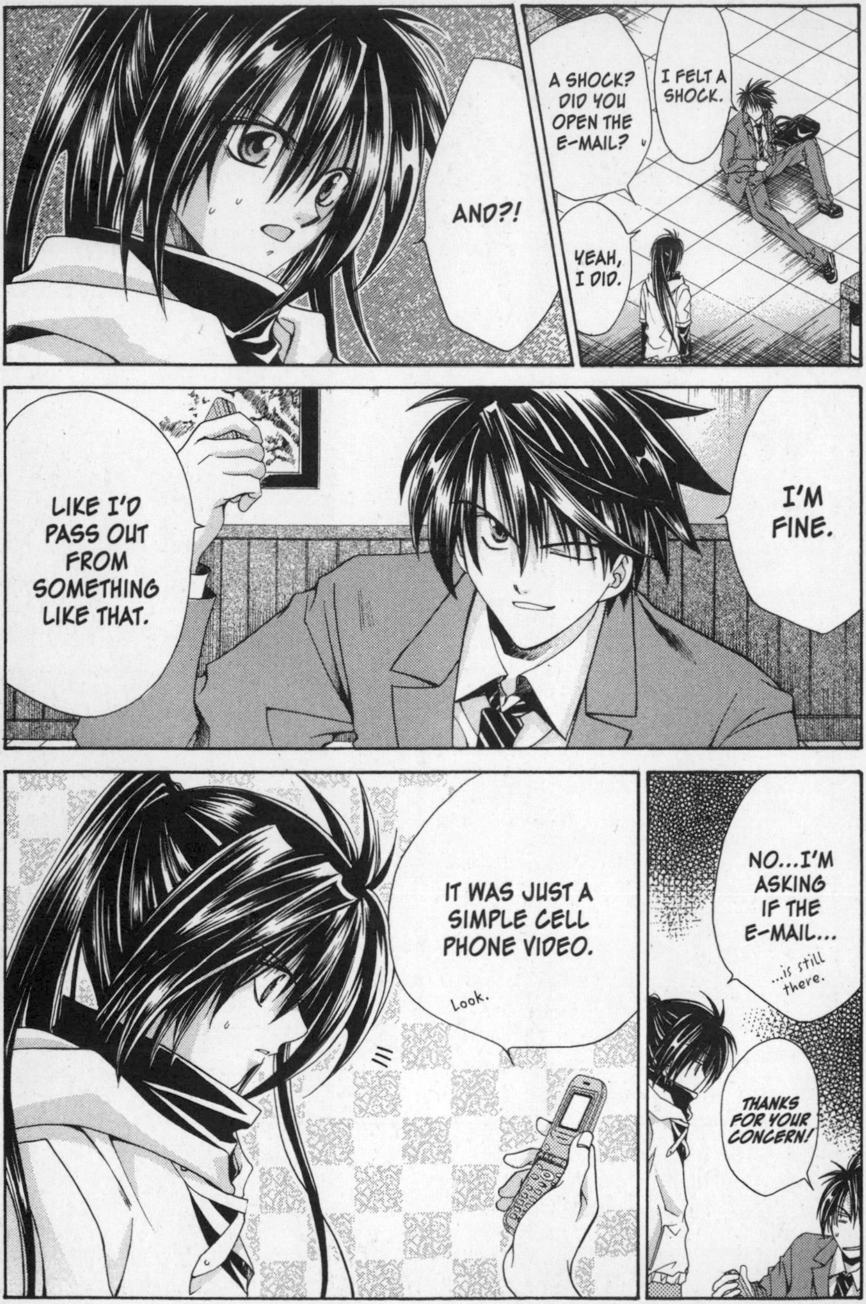
I FELT A SHOCK.
A SHOCK? DID YOU OPEN THE E-MAIL?
YEAH, I DID.
AND?!
I'M FINE.
LIKE I'D PASS OUT FROM SOMETHING LIKE THAT.
NO...I'M ASKING IF THE E-MAIL...
...is still there.
THANKS FOR YOUR CONCERN!
IT WAS JUST A SIMPLE CELL PHONE VIDEO.
Look.

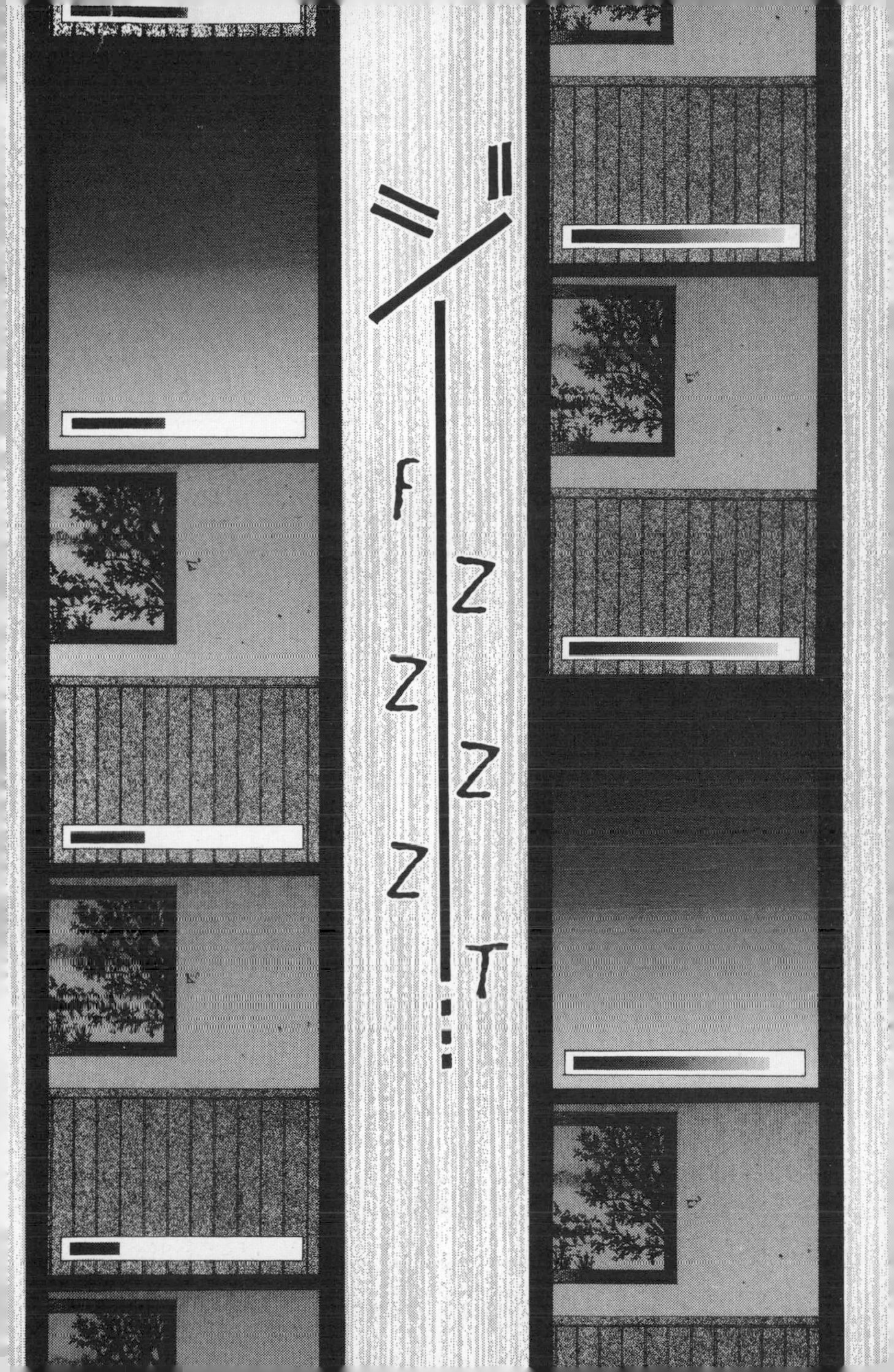
ジー…
FZZZZT

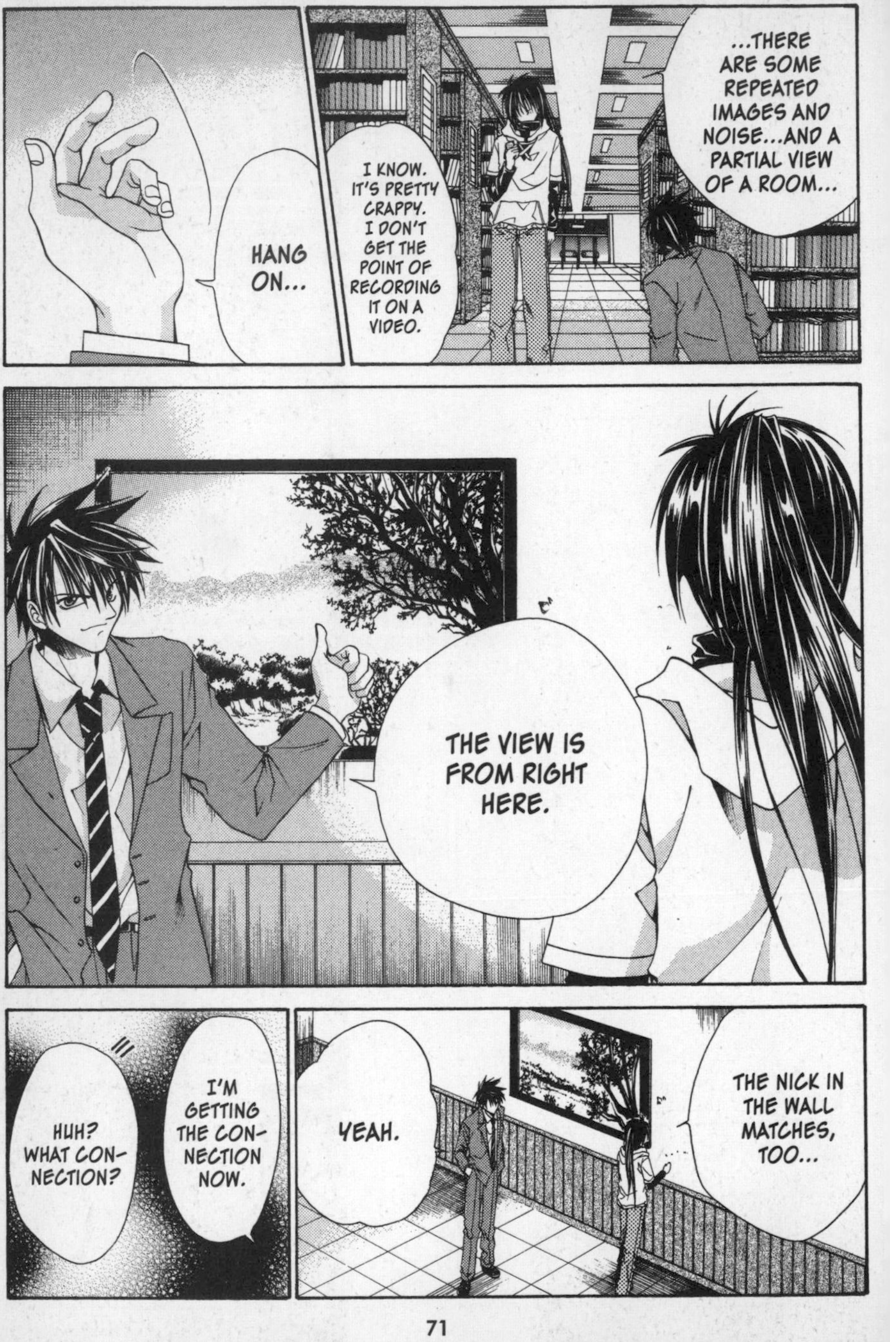
...THERE ARE SOME REPEATED IMAGES AND NOISE...AND A PARTIAL VIEW OF A ROOM...
I KNOW. IT'S PRETTY CRAPPY. I DON'T GET THE POINT OF RECORDING IT ON A VIDEO.
HANG ON...
THE VIEW IS FROM RIGHT HERE.
THE NICK IN THE WALL MATCHES, TOO...
YEAH.
I'M GETTING THE CON-NECTION NOW.
HUH? WHAT CON-NECTION?

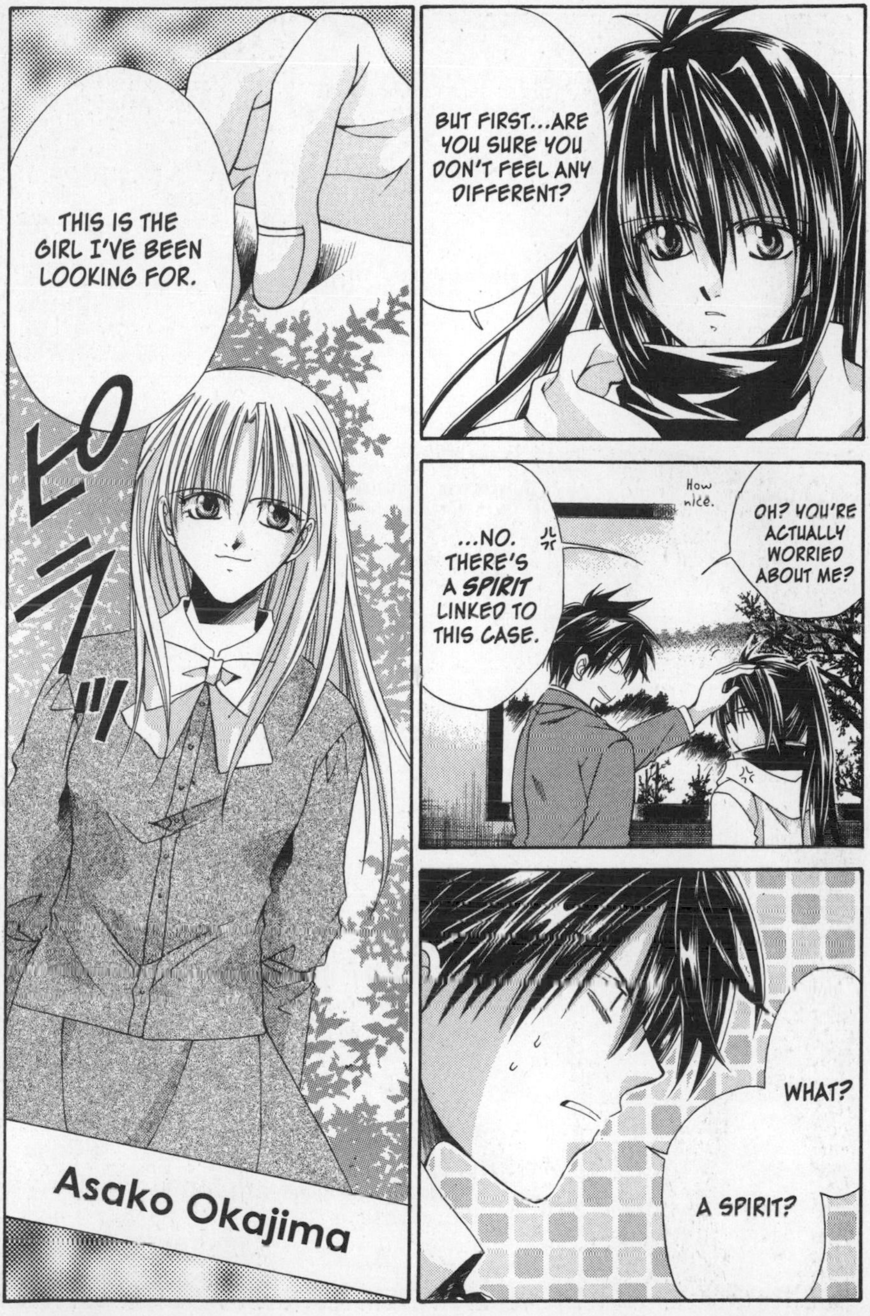
BUT FIRST...ARE YOU SURE YOU DON'T FEEL ANY DIFFERENT?
OH? YOU'RE ACTUALLY WORRIED ABOUT ME?
How nice.
...NO. THERE'S A *SPIRIT* LINKED TO THIS CASE.
WHAT?
A SPIRIT?
THIS IS THE GIRL I'VE BEEN LOOKING FOR.
Asako Okajima

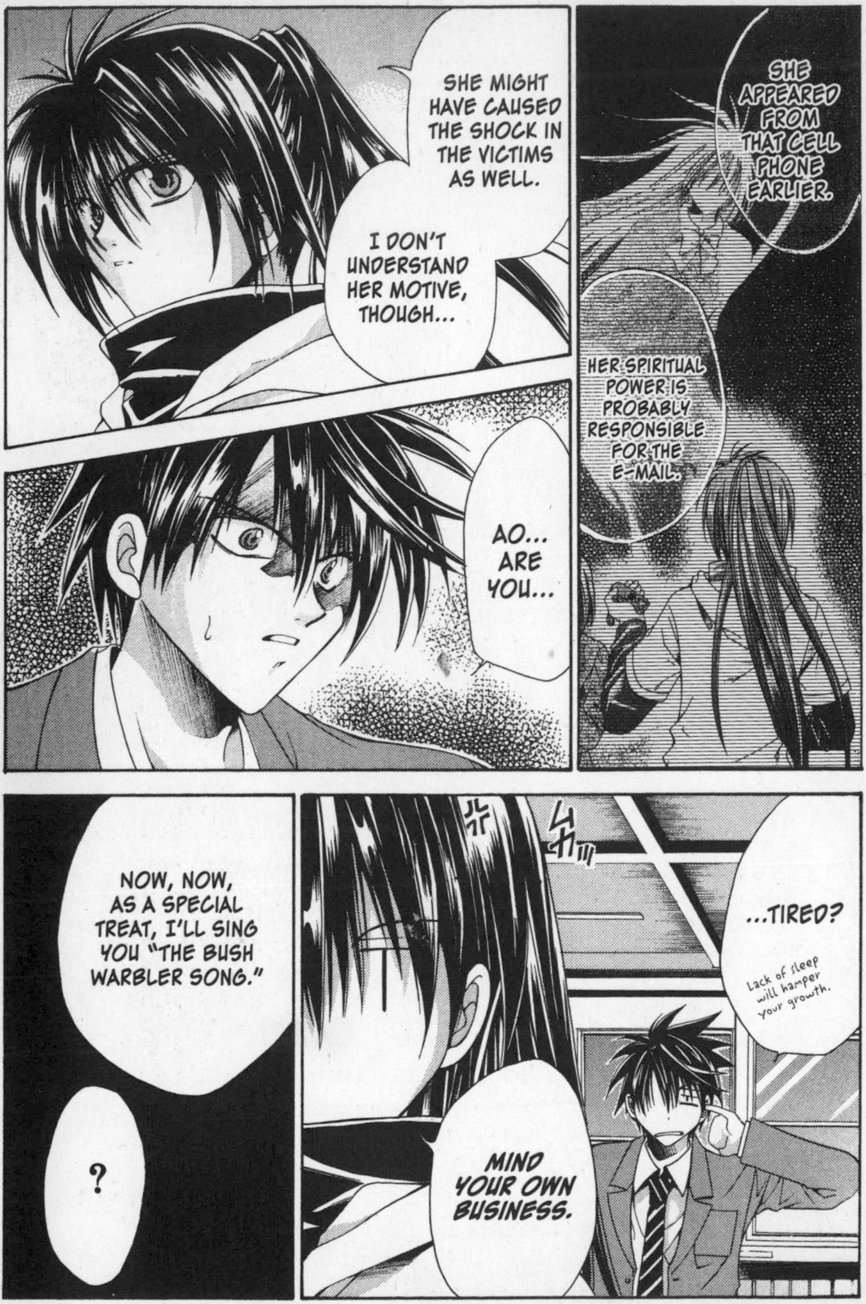
SHE APPEARED FROM THAT CELL PHONE EARLIER.
HER SPIRITUAL POWER IS PROBABLY RESPONSIBLE FOR THE E-MAIL.
SHE MIGHT HAVE CAUSED THE SHOCK IN THE VICTIMS AS WELL.
I DON'T UNDERSTAND HER MOTIVE, THOUGH...
AO... ARE YOU...
...TIRED?
Lack of sleep will hamper your growth.
MIND YOUR OWN BUSINESS.
NOW, NOW, AS A SPECIAL TREAT, I'LL SING YOU "THE BUSH WARBLER SONG."
?

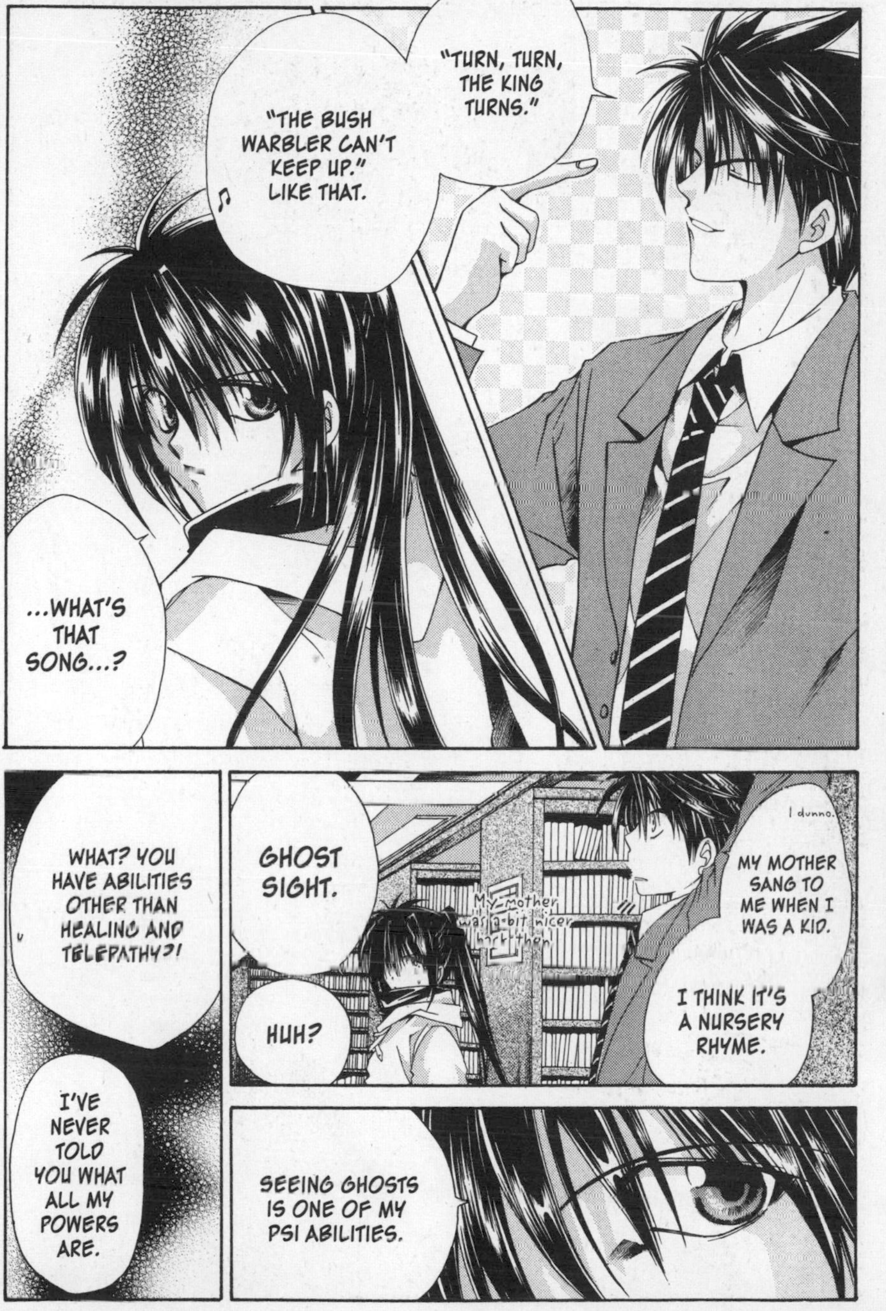
"TURN, TURN, THE KING TURNS."
"THE BUSH WARBLER CAN'T KEEP UP." LIKE THAT.
...WHAT'S THAT SONG...?
I dunno.
MY MOTHER SANG TO ME WHEN I WAS A KID.
I THINK IT'S A NURSERY RHYME.
My mother was a bit nicer back then.
GHOST SIGHT.
HUH?
SEEING GHOSTS IS ONE OF MY PSI ABILITIES.
WHAT? YOU HAVE ABILITIES OTHER THAN HEALING AND TELEPATHY?!
I'VE NEVER TOLD YOU WHAT ALL MY POWERS ARE.

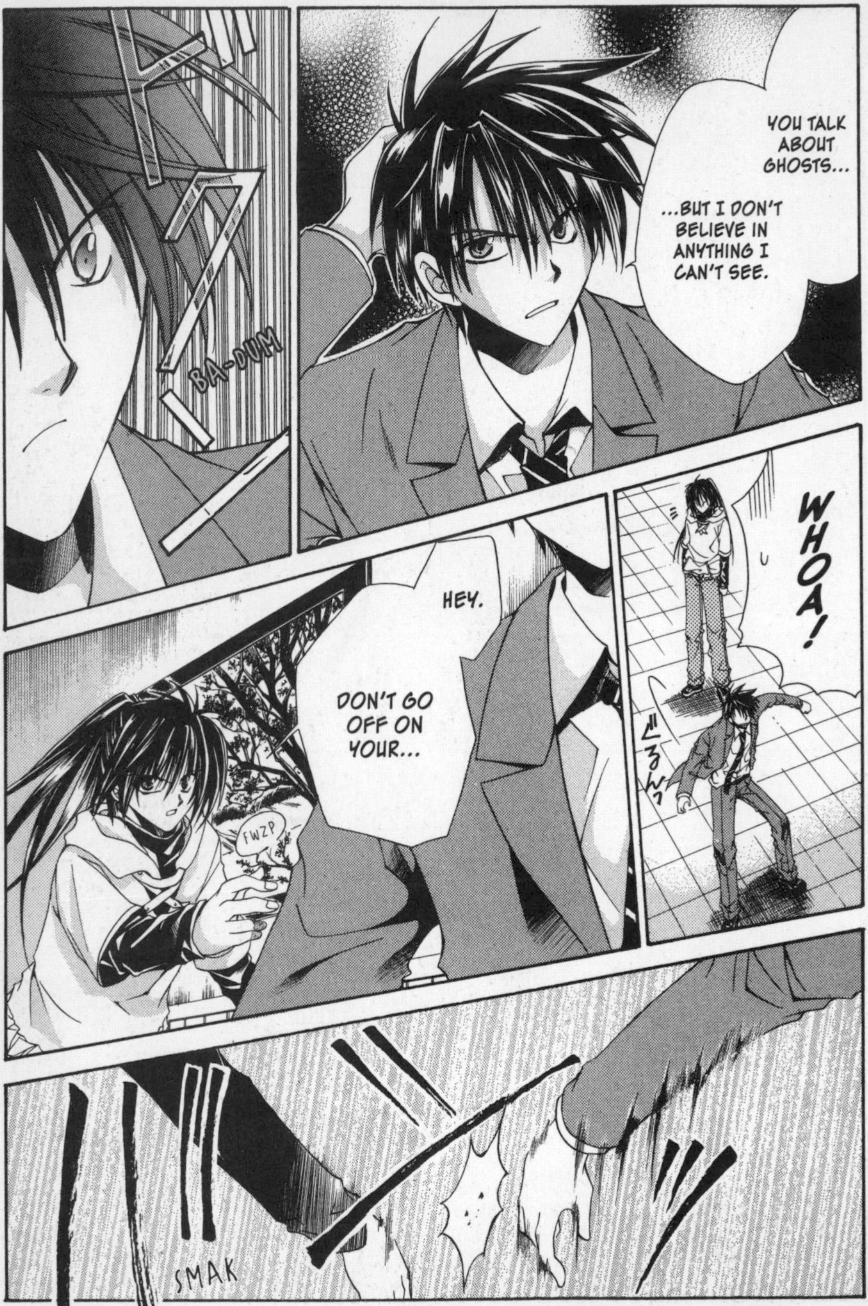
YOU TALK ABOUT GHOSTS...
...BUT I DON'T BELIEVE IN ANYTHING I CAN'T SEE.
BA-DUM
WHOA!
ぐるんっ
HEY.
DON'T GO OFF ON YOUR...
FWZP
SMAK

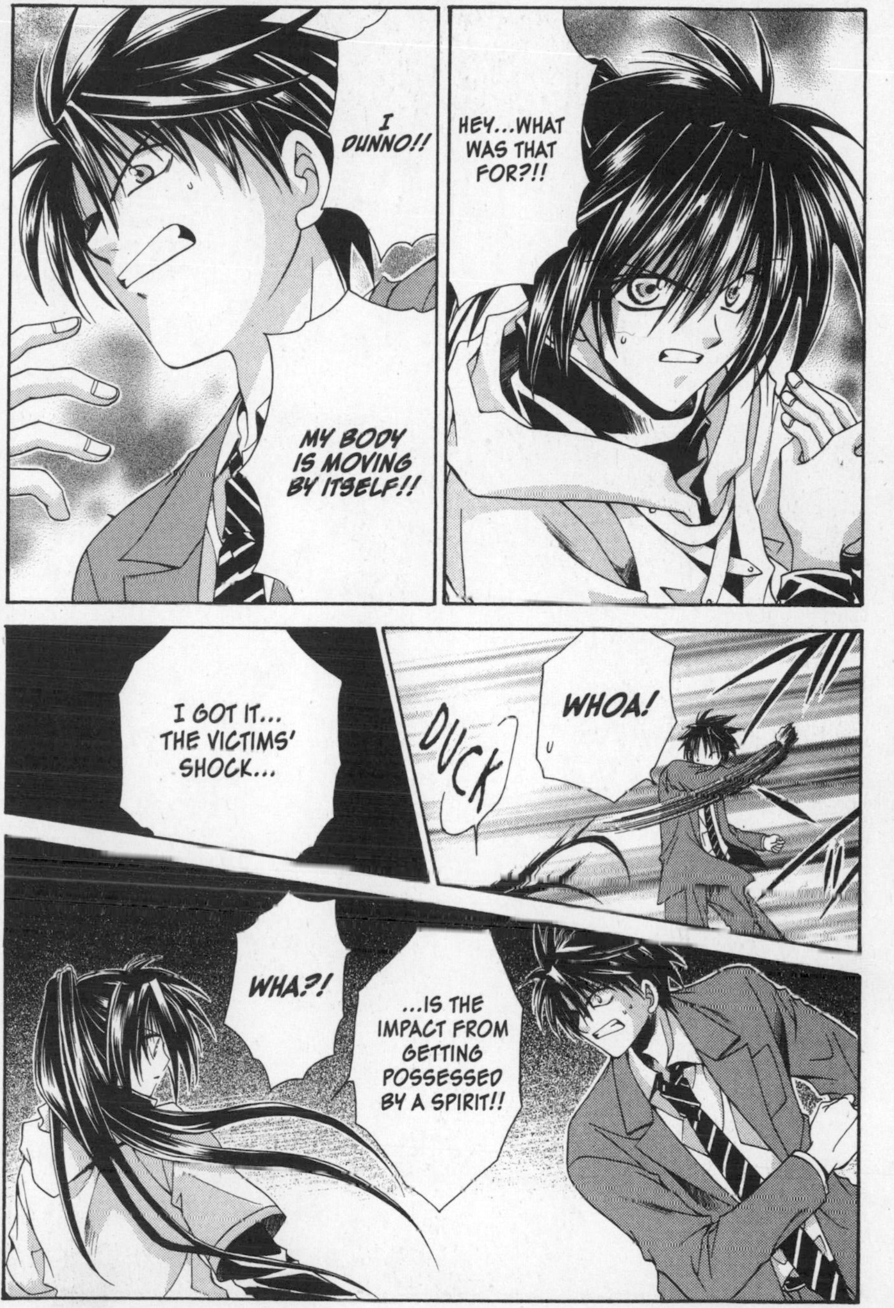
HEY...WHAT WAS THAT FOR?!!
I DUNNO!!
MY BODY IS MOVING BY ITSELF!!
WHOA!
DUCK
I GOT IT... THE VICTIMS' SHOCK...
...IS THE IMPACT FROM GETTING POSSESSED BY A SPIRIT!!
WHA?!

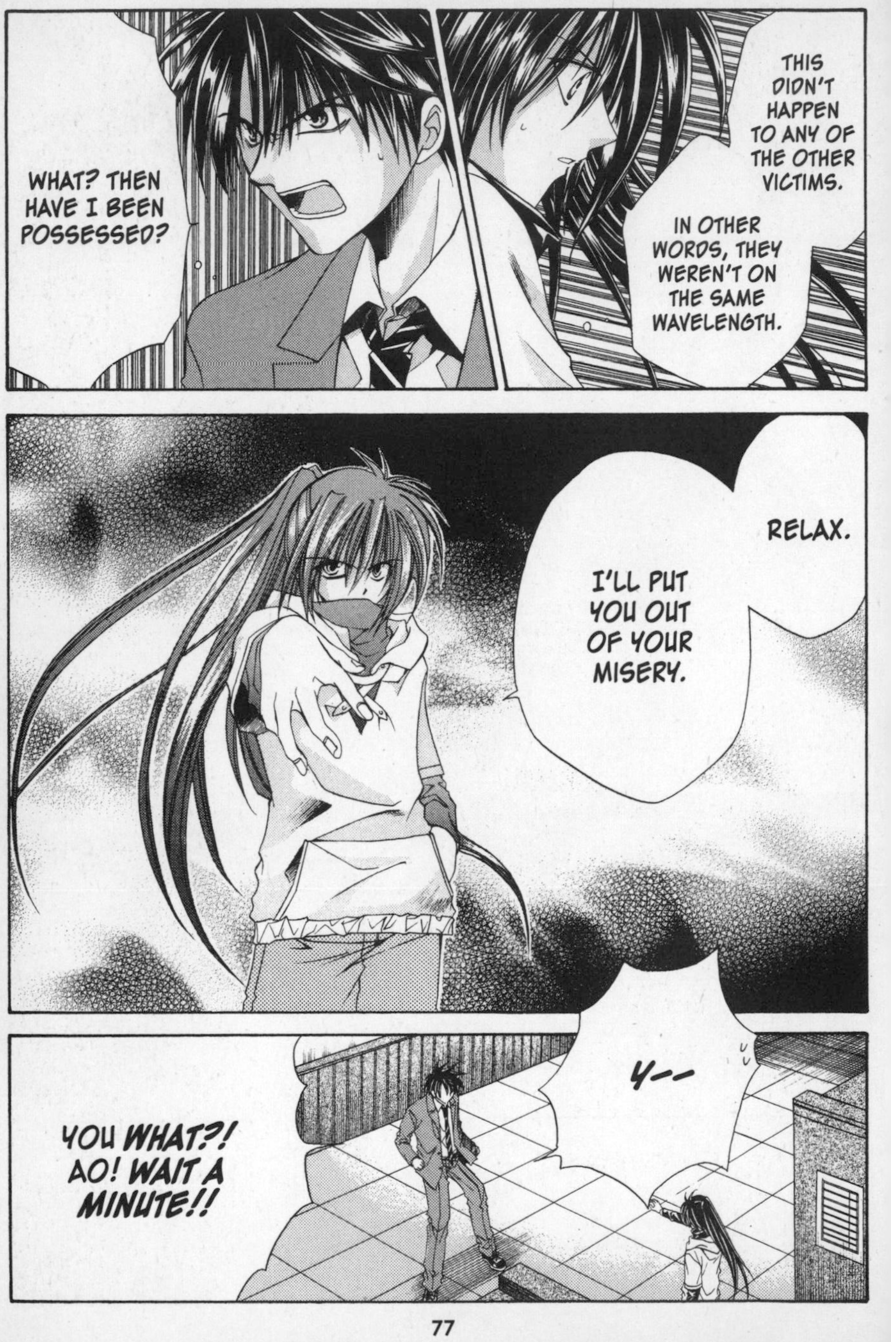
THIS DIDN'T HAPPEN TO ANY OF THE OTHER VICTIMS.
IN OTHER WORDS, THEY WEREN'T ON THE SAME WAVELENGTH.
WHAT? THEN HAVE I BEEN POSSESSED?
RELAX.
I'LL PUT YOU OUT OF YOUR MISERY.
Y--
YOU WHAT?! AO! WAIT A MINUTE!!

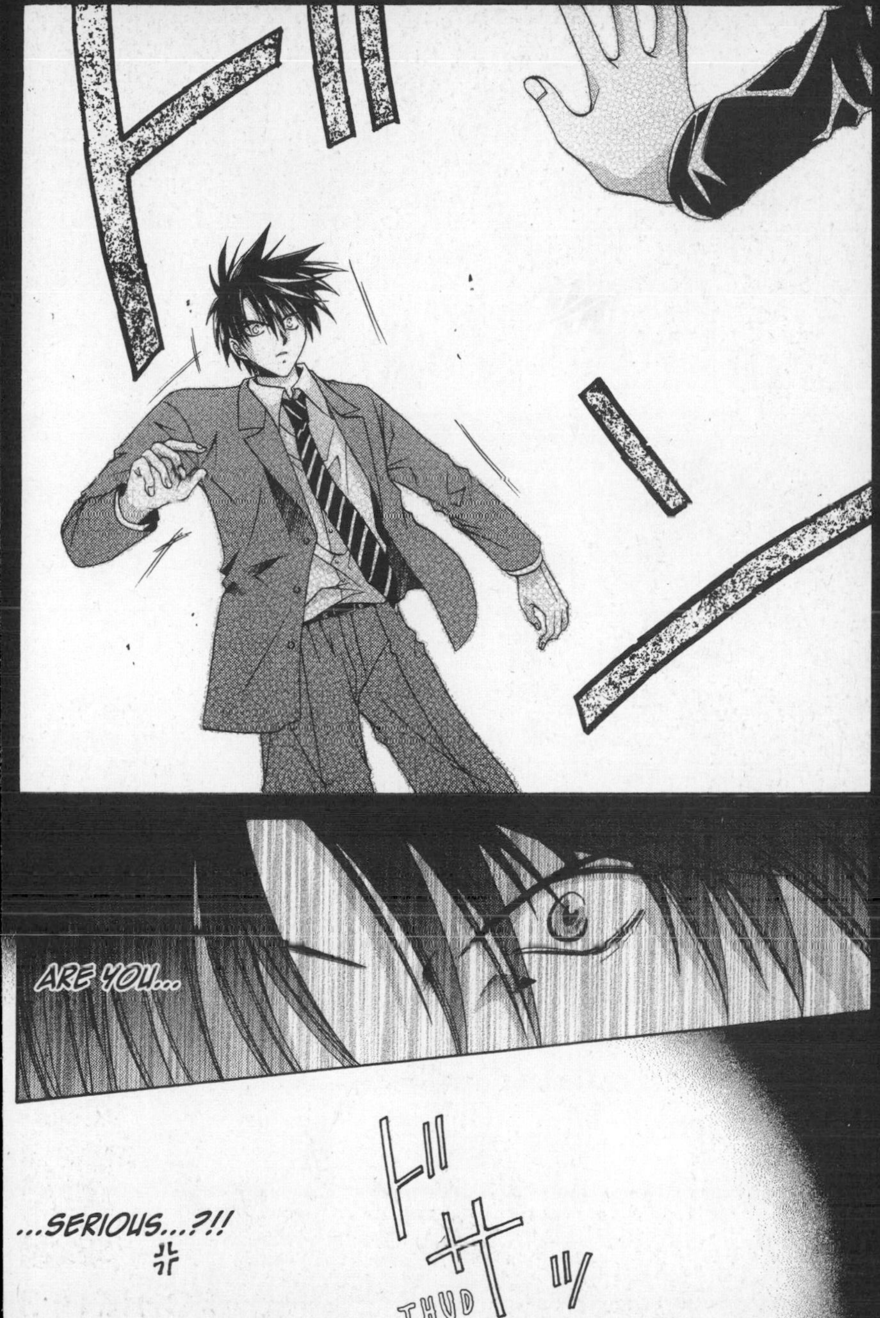
ARE YOU...
...SERIOUS...?!!
THUD

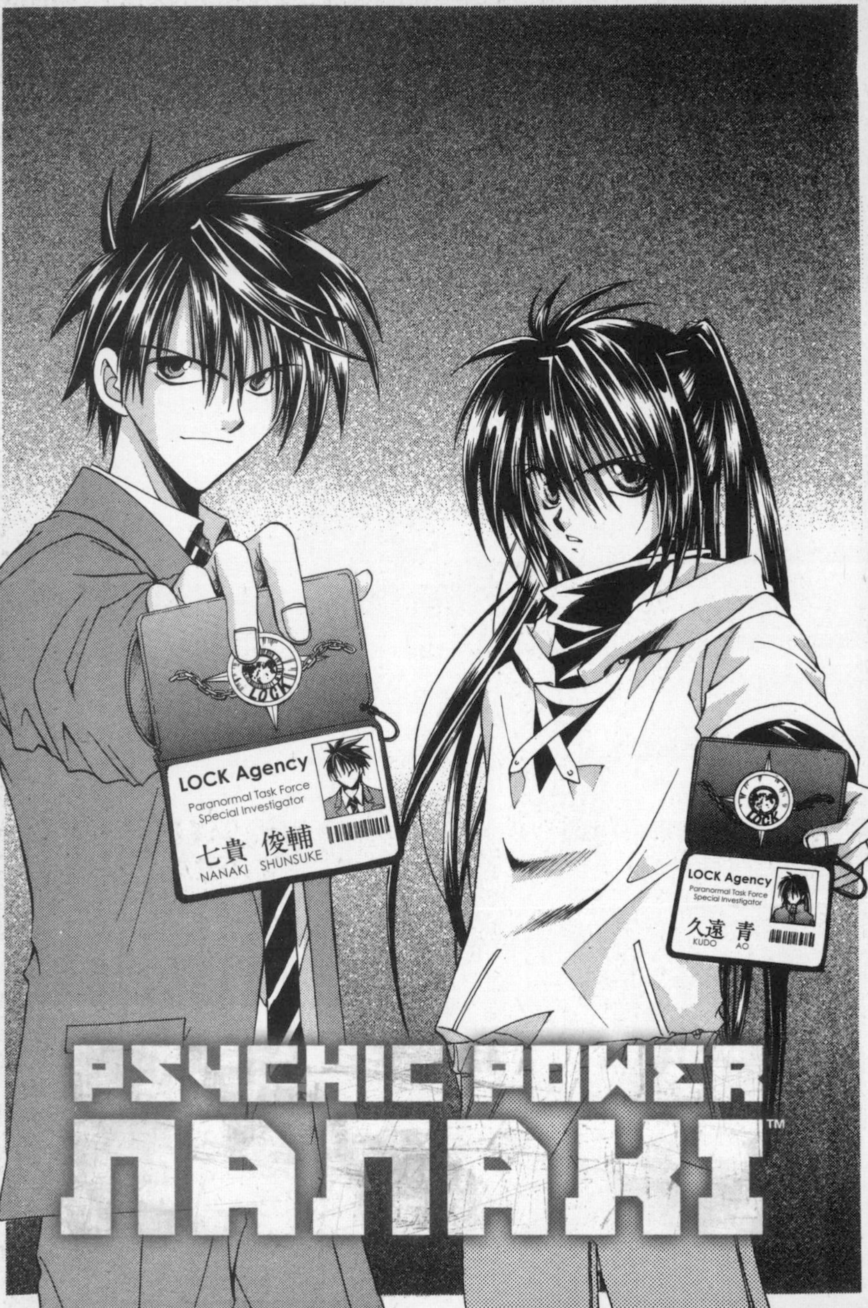
LOCK
LOCK Agency
Paranormal Task Force
Special Investigator
七貴 俊輔
NANAKI SHUNSUKE
LOCK
LOCK Agency
Paranormal Task Force
Special Investigator
久遠 青
KUDO AO
PSYCHIC POWER
NANAKI™

CHRONICLE 3

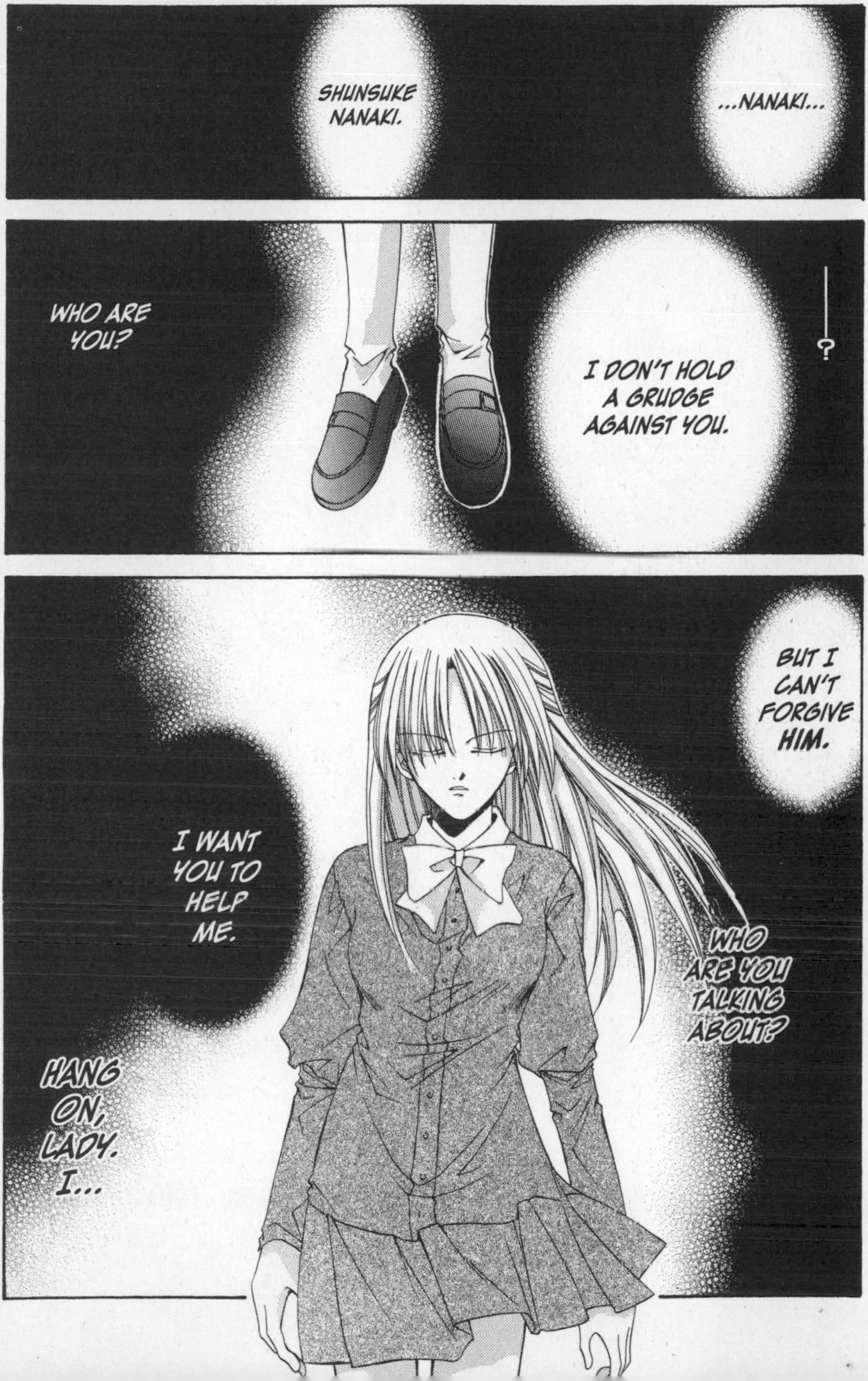
...NANAKI...
SHUNSUKE NANAKI.
——?
I DON'T HOLD A GRUDGE AGAINST YOU.
WHO ARE YOU?
BUT I CAN'T FORGIVE HIM.
I WANT YOU TO HELP ME.
WHO ARE YOU TALKING ABOUT?
HANG ON, LADY. I...

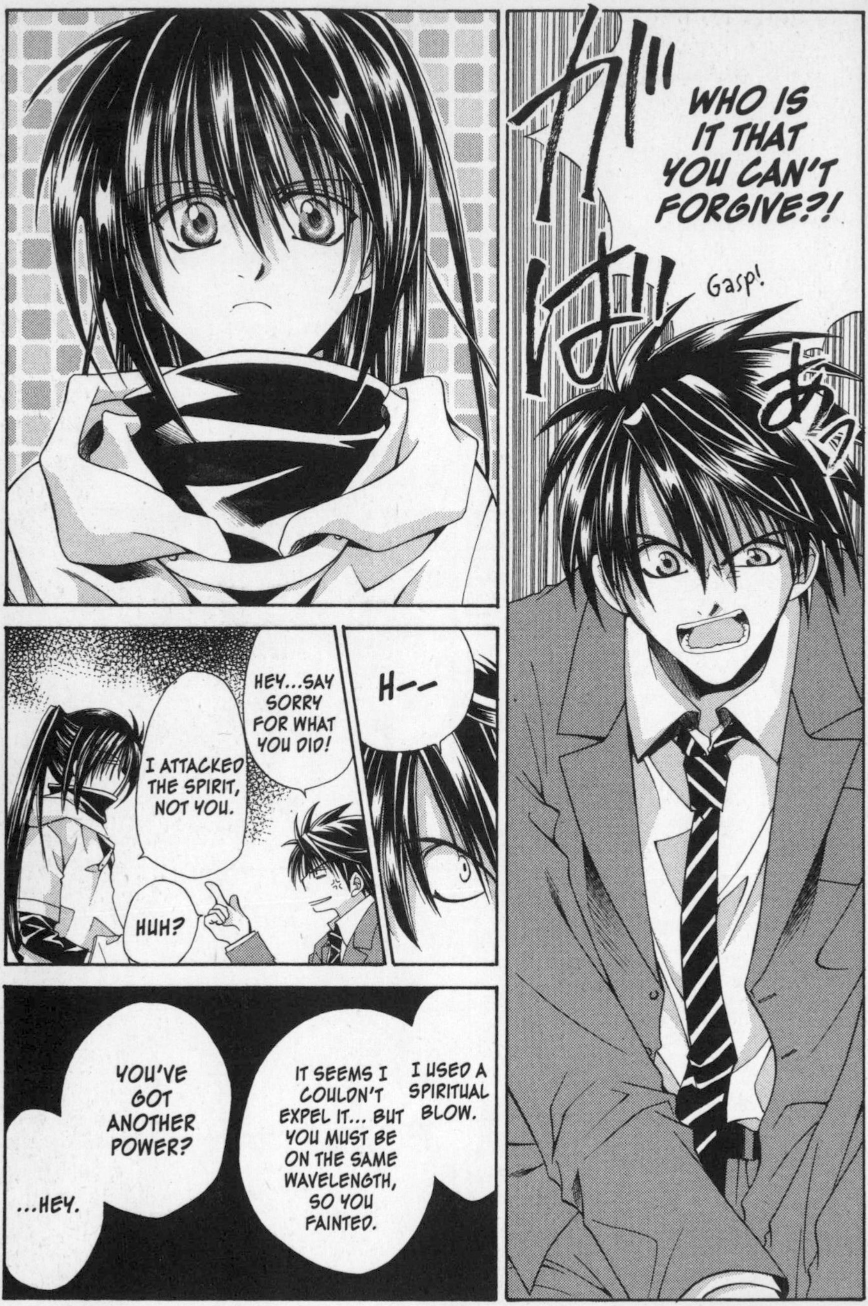
WHO IS IT THAT YOU CAN'T FORGIVE?!
Gasp!
H--
HEY...SAY SORRY FOR WHAT YOU DID!
I ATTACKED THE SPIRIT, NOT YOU.
HUH?
I USED A SPIRITUAL BLOW.
IT SEEMS I COULDN'T EXPEL IT... BUT YOU MUST BE ON THE SAME WAVELENGTH, SO YOU FAINTED.
YOU'VE GOT ANOTHER POWER?
...HEY.

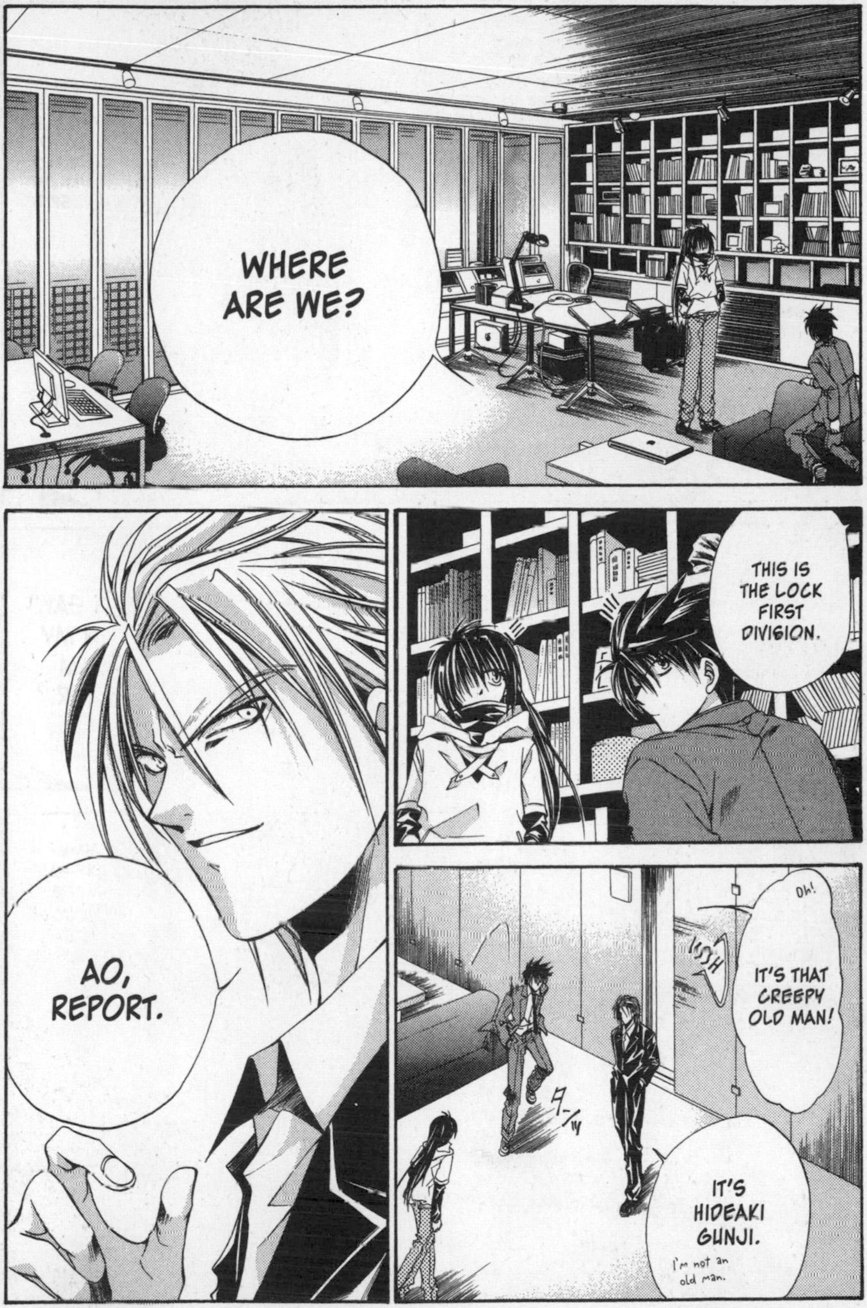
WHERE ARE WE?
THIS IS THE LOCK FIRST DIVISION.
Oh!
IT'S THAT CREEPY OLD MAN!
IT'S HIDEAKI GUNJI.
I'm not an old man.
AO, REPORT.

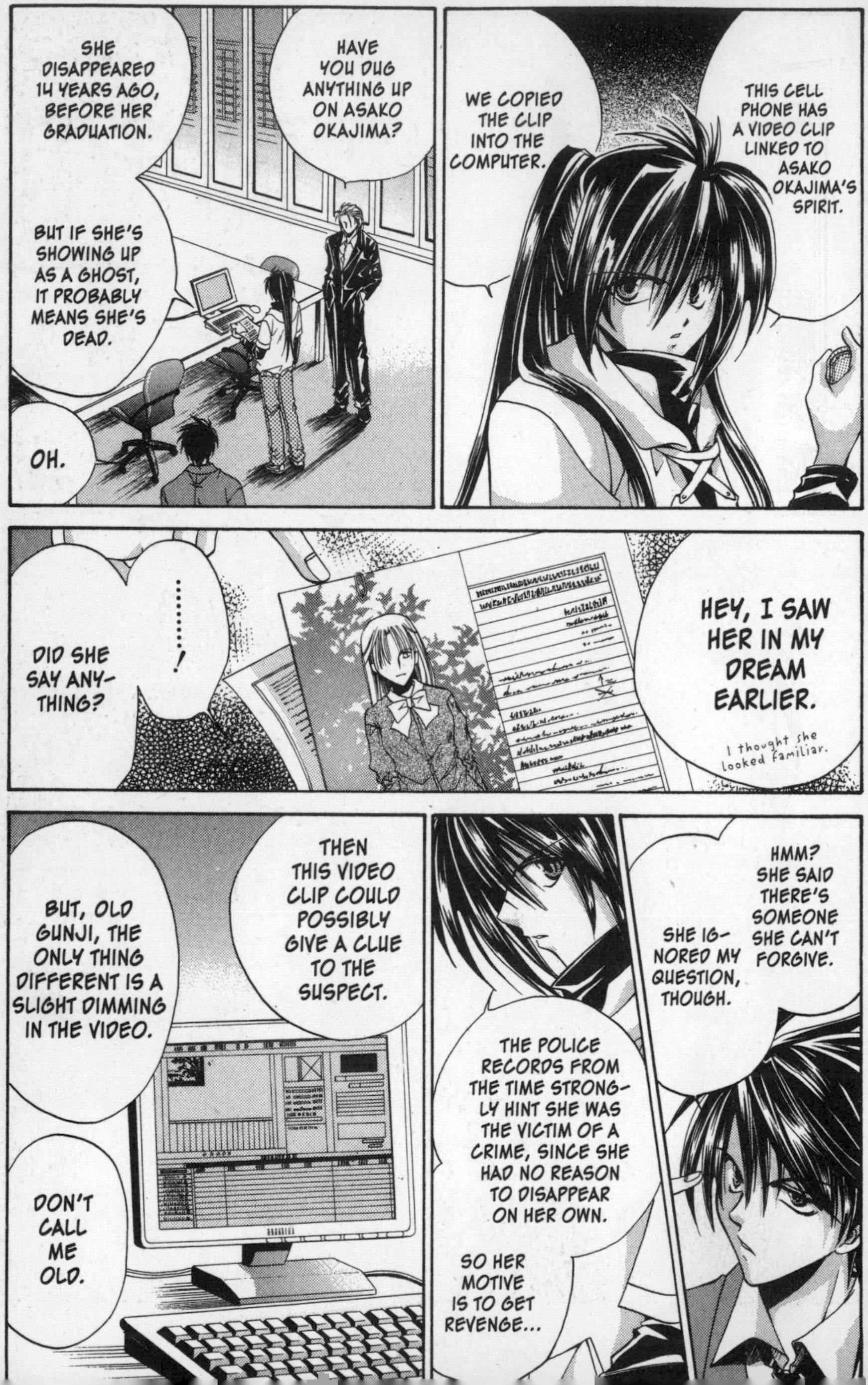
THIS CELL PHONE HAS A VIDEO CLIP LINKED TO ASAKO OKAJIMA'S SPIRIT.
WE COPIED THE CLIP INTO THE COMPUTER.
HAVE YOU DUG ANYTHING UP ON ASAKO OKAJIMA?
SHE DISAPPEARED 14 YEARS AGO, BEFORE HER GRADUATION.
BUT IF SHE'S SHOWING UP AS A GHOST, IT PROBABLY MEANS SHE'S DEAD.
OH.
HEY, I SAW HER IN MY DREAM EARLIER.
I thought she looked familiar.
......!
DID SHE SAY ANY-THING?
HMM? SHE SAID THERE'S SOMEONE SHE CAN'T FORGIVE.
SHE IG-NORED MY QUESTION, THOUGH.
THE POLICE RECORDS FROM THE TIME STRONG-LY HINT SHE WAS THE VICTIM OF A CRIME, SINCE SHE HAD NO REASON TO DISAPPEAR ON HER OWN.
SO HER MOTIVE IS TO GET REVENGE...
THEN THIS VIDEO CLIP COULD POSSIBLY GIVE A CLUE TO THE SUSPECT.
BUT, OLD GUNJI, THE ONLY THING DIFFERENT IS A SLIGHT DIMMING IN THE VIDEO.
DON'T CALL ME OLD.

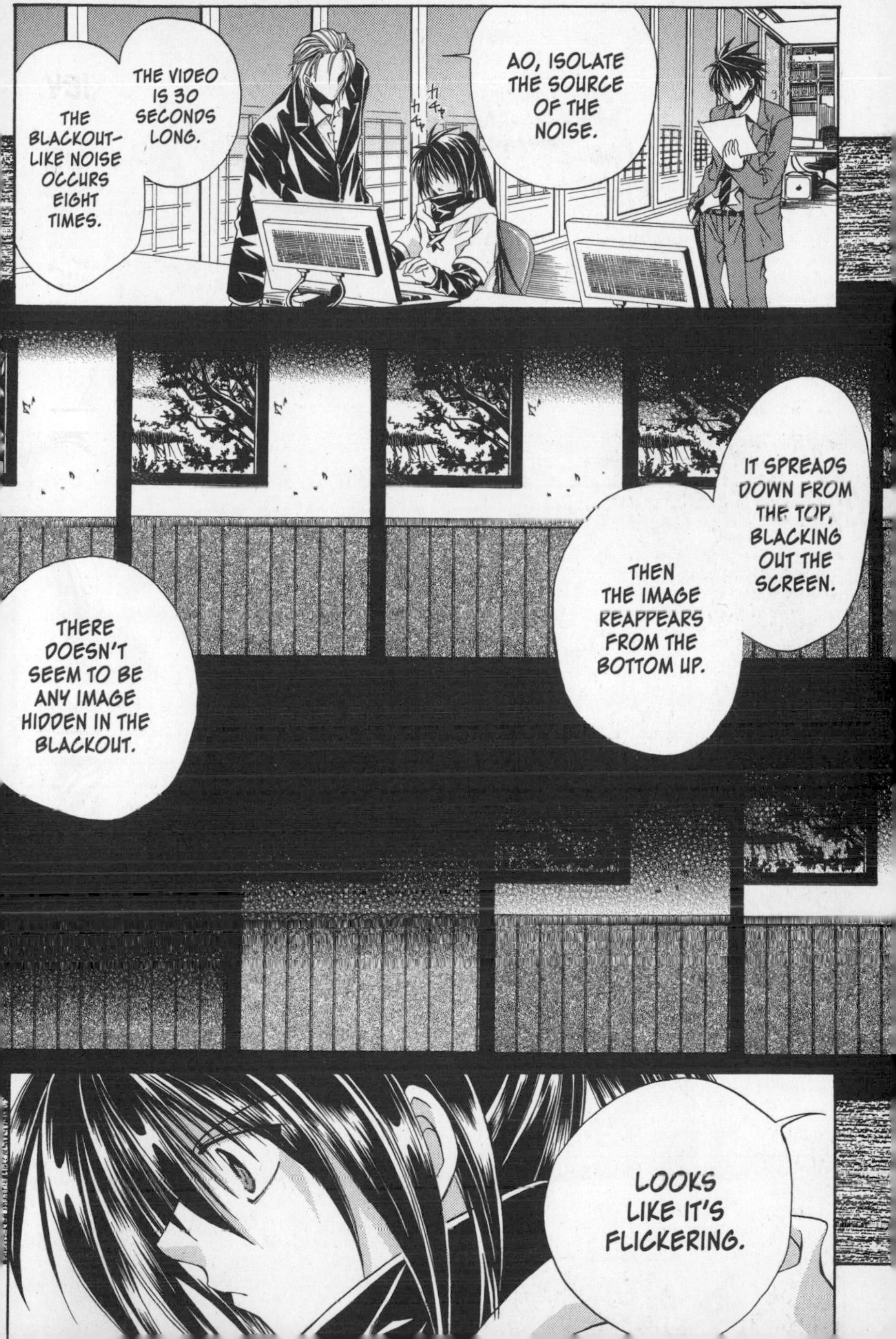
AO, ISOLATE THE SOURCE OF THE NOISE.
THE VIDEO IS 30 SECONDS LONG.
THE BLACKOUT-LIKE NOISE OCCURS EIGHT TIMES.
IT SPREADS DOWN FROM THE TOP, BLACKING OUT THE SCREEN.
THEN THE IMAGE REAPPEARS FROM THE BOTTOM UP.
THERE DOESN'T SEEM TO BE ANY IMAGE HIDDEN IN THE BLACKOUT.
LOOKS LIKE IT'S FLICKERING.

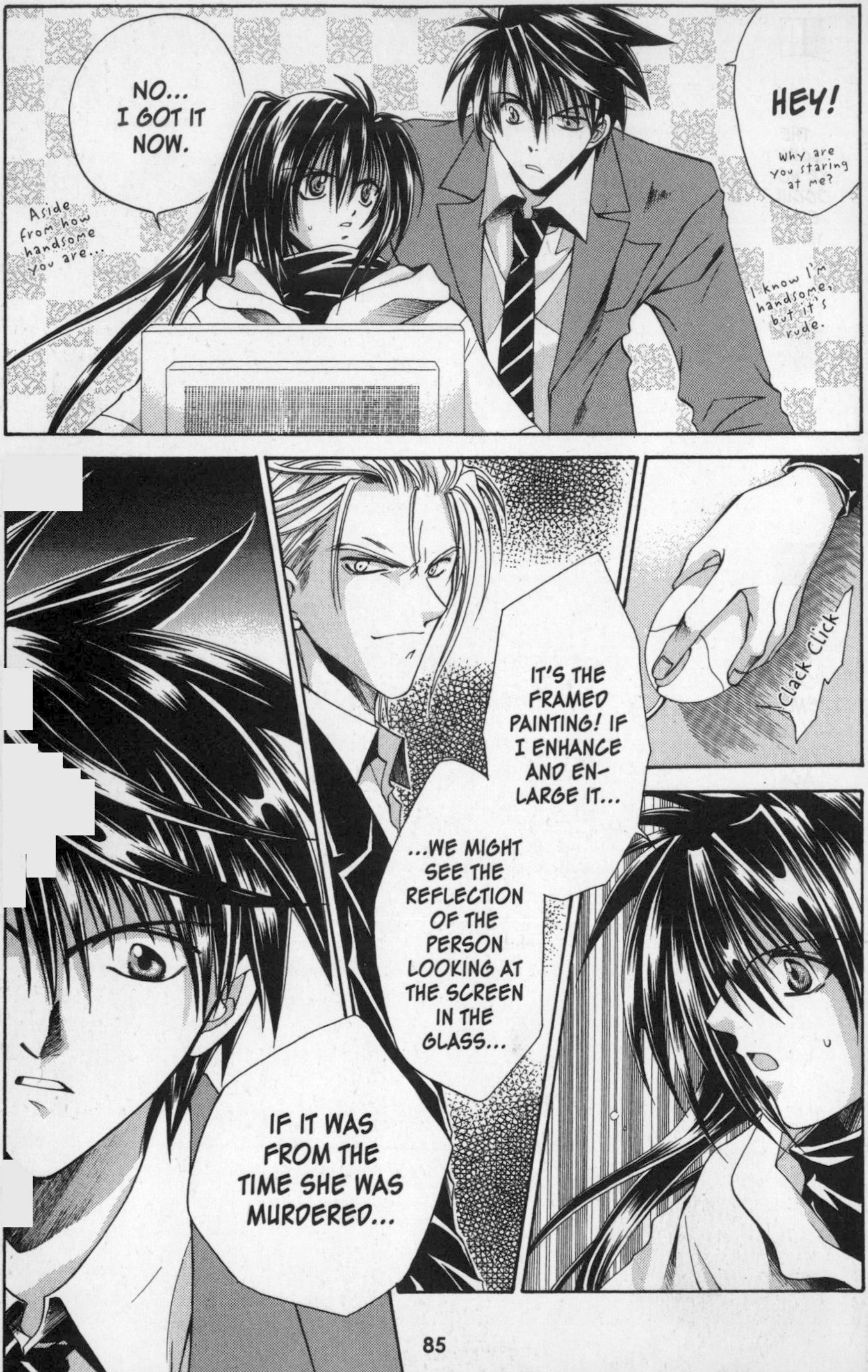
HEY!
Why are you staring at me?
I know I'm handsome, but it's rude.
NO... I GOT IT NOW.
Aside from how handsome you are...
Clack Click
IT'S THE FRAMED PAINTING! IF I ENHANCE AND EN-LARGE IT...
...WE MIGHT SEE THE REFLECTION OF THE PERSON LOOKING AT THE SCREEN IN THE GLASS...
IF IT WAS FROM THE TIME SHE WAS MURDERED...

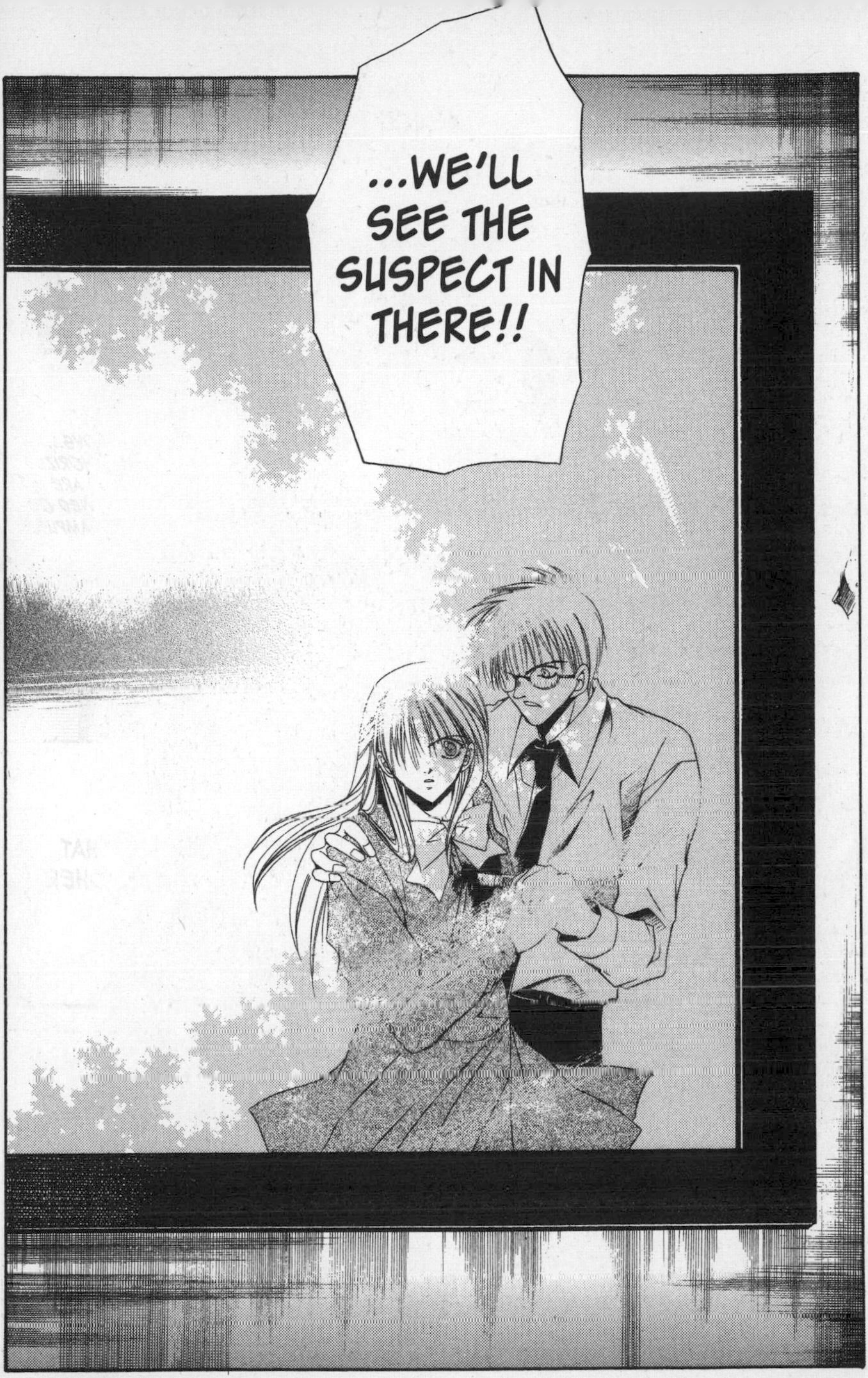
...WE'LL SEE THE SUSPECT IN THERE!!

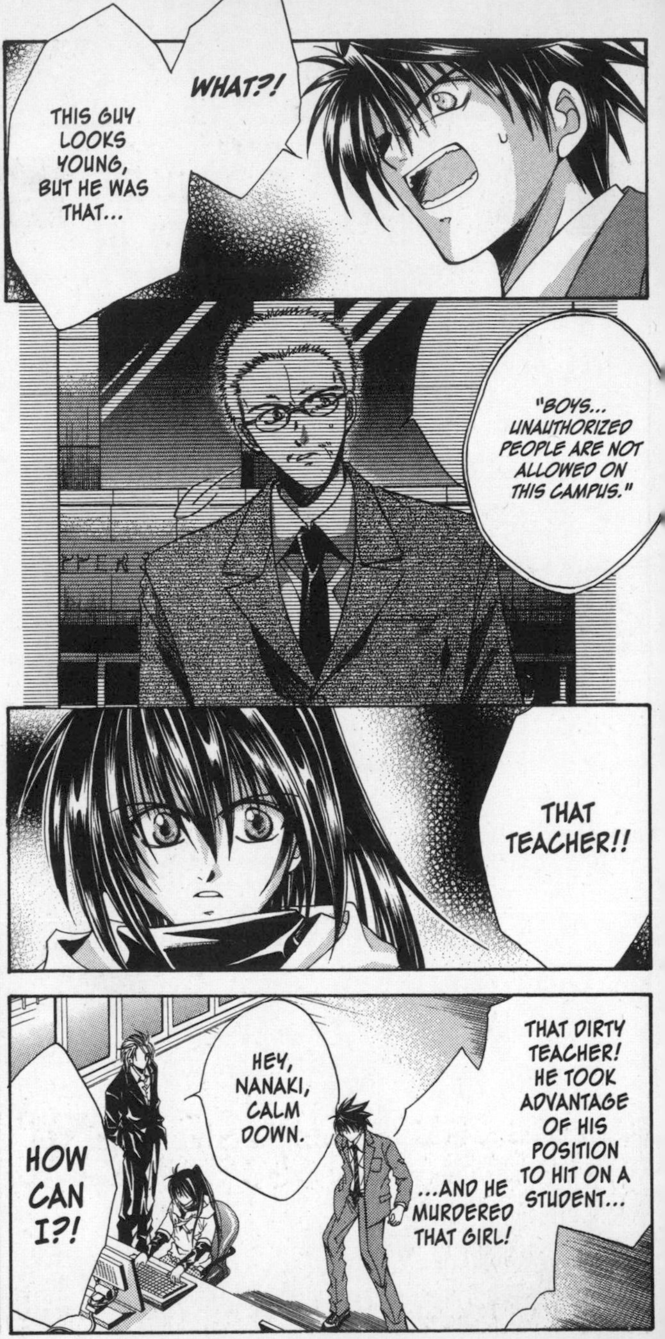
WHAT?!
THIS GUY LOOKS YOUNG, BUT HE WAS THAT...
"BOYS... UNAUTHORIZED PEOPLE ARE NOT ALLOWED ON THIS CAMPUS."
THAT TEACHER!!
THAT DIRTY TEACHER! HE TOOK ADVANTAGE OF HIS POSITION TO HIT ON A STUDENT...
...AND HE MURDERED THAT GIRL!
HEY, NANAKI, CALM DOWN.
HOW CAN I?!

•GAMMA•

- Ghosts and spirits appear in *Nanaki*, but I've never seen one myself. I have some friends and acquaintances who claim they have. They say they've experienced it once, but that hasn't happened to me at all. (Laughs.) Though I did see a strange creature when I was little...but it's hard to say if that really happened, since there were no other witnesses... (Nervous laugh.)

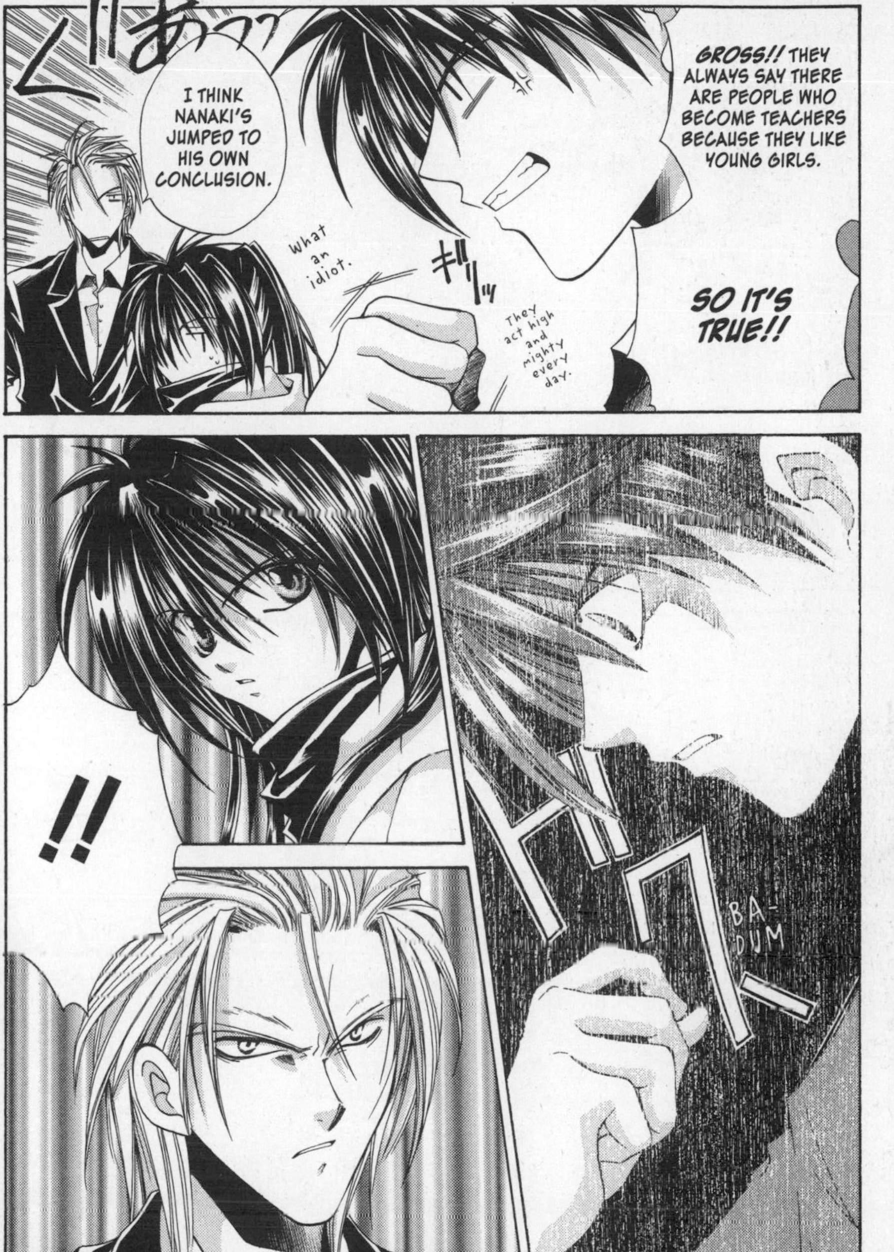
GROSS!! THEY ALWAYS SAY THERE ARE PEOPLE WHO BECOME TEACHERS BECAUSE THEY LIKE YOUNG GIRLS.
SO IT'S TRUE!!
They act high and mighty every day.
I THINK NANAKI'S JUMPED TO HIS OWN CONCLUSION.
what an idiot.
BA-DUM
!!

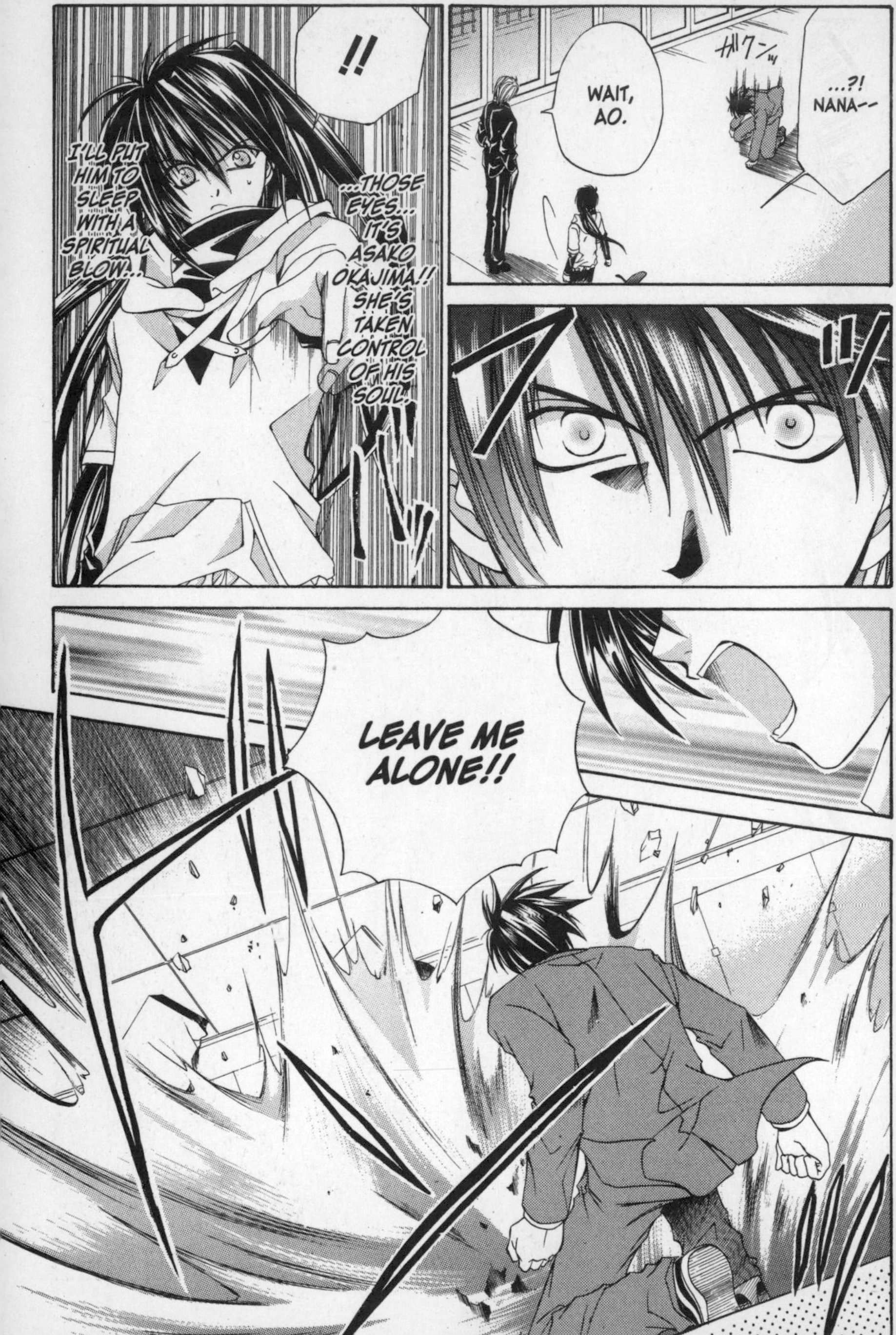
...?! NANA--
ガクン
WAIT, AO.
!!
...THOSE EYES... IT'S ASAKO OKAJIMA!! SHE'S TAKEN CONTROL OF HIS SOUL.
I'LL PUT HIM TO SLEEP WITH A SPIRITUAL BLOW...
LEAVE ME ALONE!!

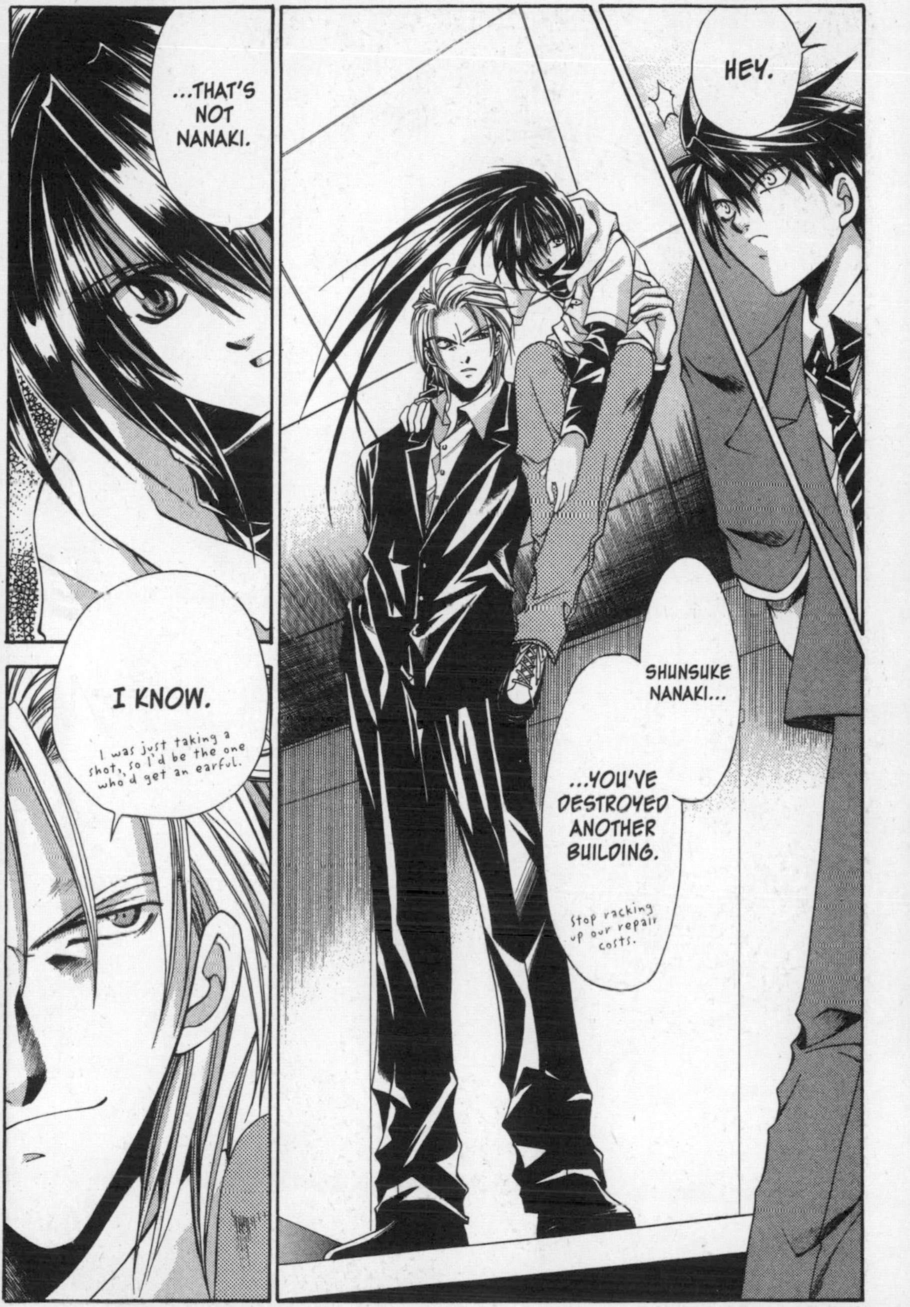
HEY.
SHUNSUKE NANAKI...
...YOU'VE DESTROYED ANOTHER BUILDING.
Stop racking up our repair costs.
...THAT'S NOT NANAKI.
I KNOW.
I was just taking a shot, so I'd be the one who'd get an earful.

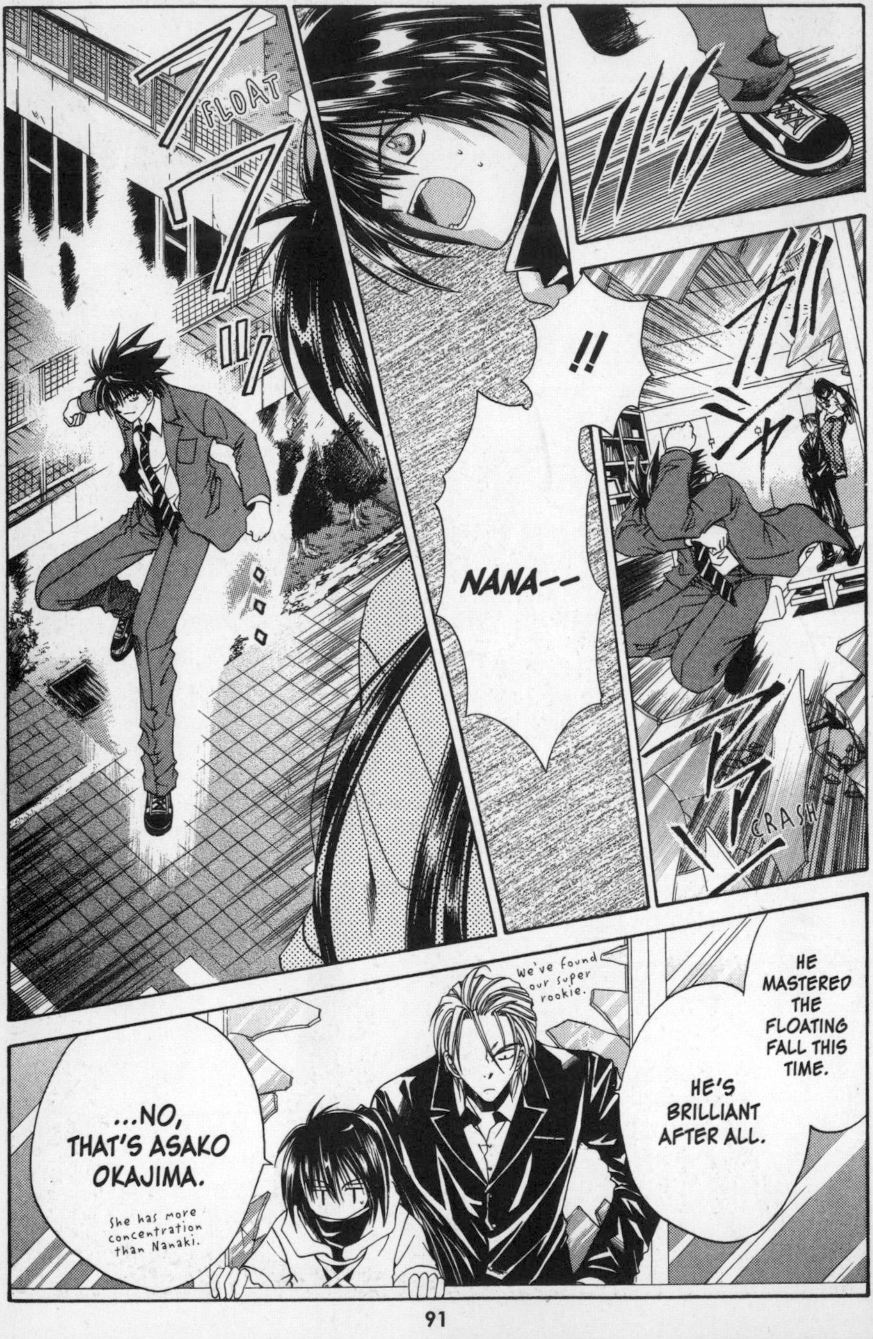
CRASH
!!
NANA--
FLOAT
HE MASTERED THE FLOATING FALL THIS TIME.
HE'S BRILLIANT AFTER ALL.
We've found our super rookie.
...NO, THAT'S ASAKO OKAJIMA.
She has more concentration than Nanaki.

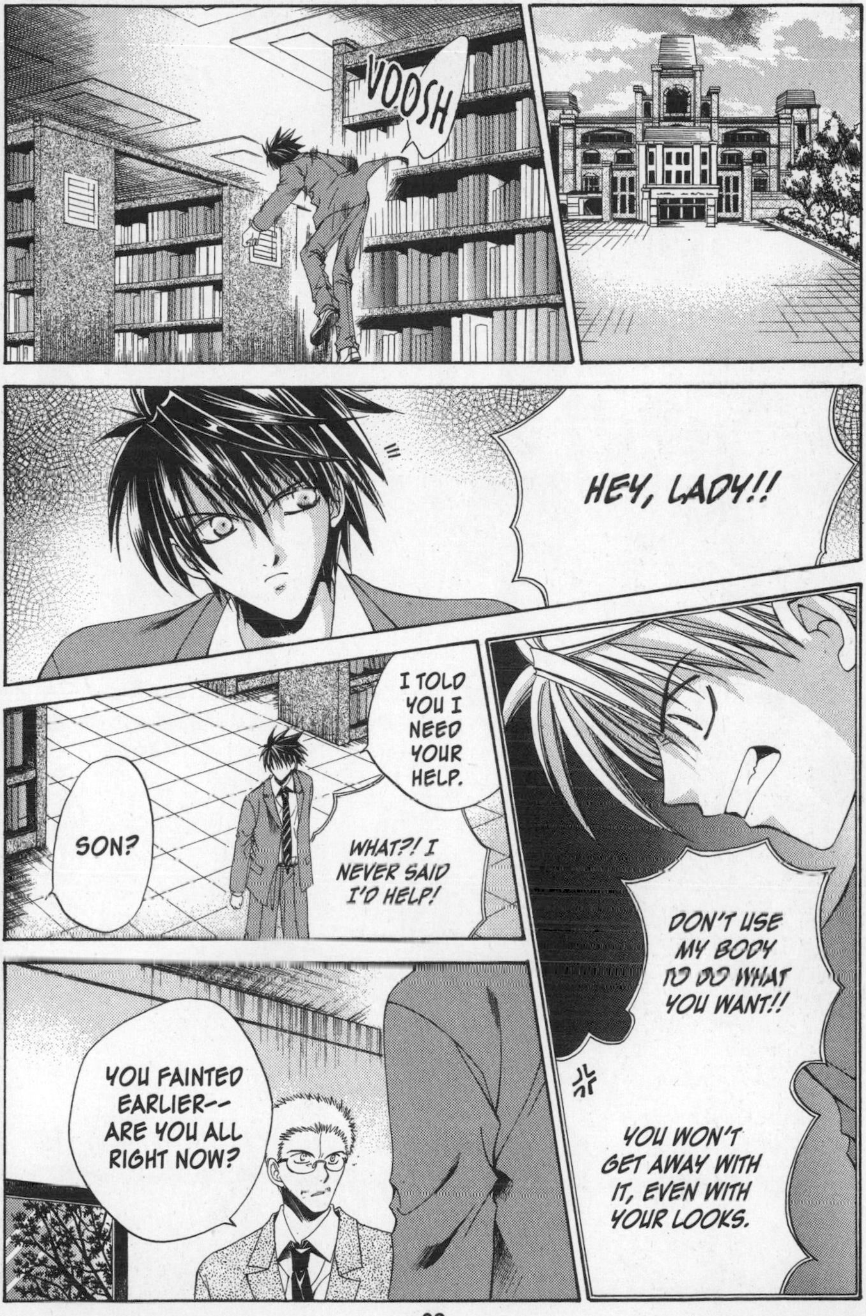
VOOSH
HEY, LADY!!
DON'T USE MY BODY TO DO WHAT YOU WANT!!
YOU WON'T GET AWAY WITH IT, EVEN WITH YOUR LOOKS.
I TOLD YOU I NEED YOUR HELP.
WHAT?! I NEVER SAID I'D HELP!
SON?
YOU FAINTED EARLIER-- ARE YOU ALL RIGHT NOW?

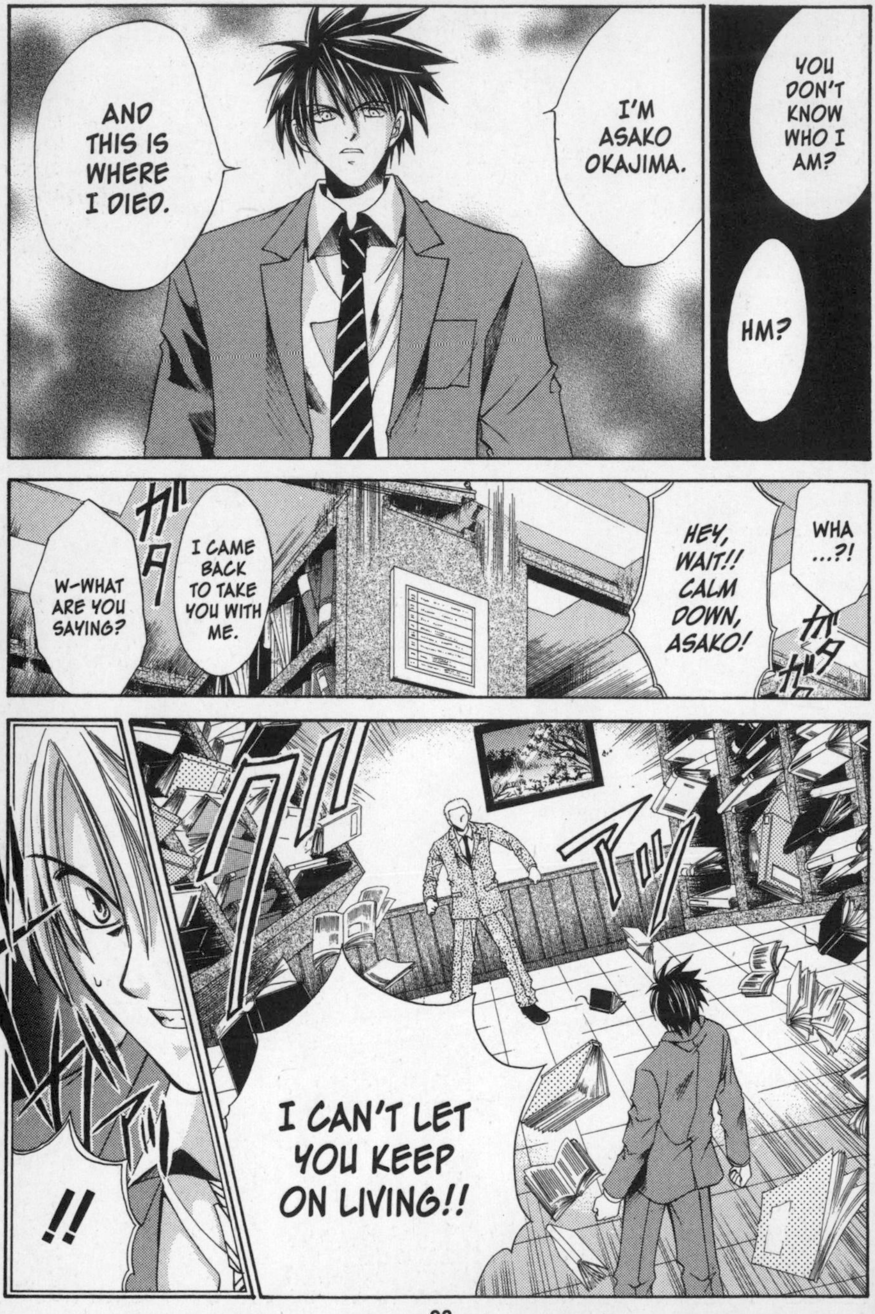
YOU DON'T KNOW WHO I AM?
HM?
I'M ASAKO OKAJIMA.
AND THIS IS WHERE I DIED.
WHA ...?!
HEY, WAIT!! CALM DOWN, ASAKO!
I CAME BACK TO TAKE YOU WITH ME.
W-WHAT ARE YOU SAYING?
I CAN'T LET YOU KEEP ON LIVING!!
!!

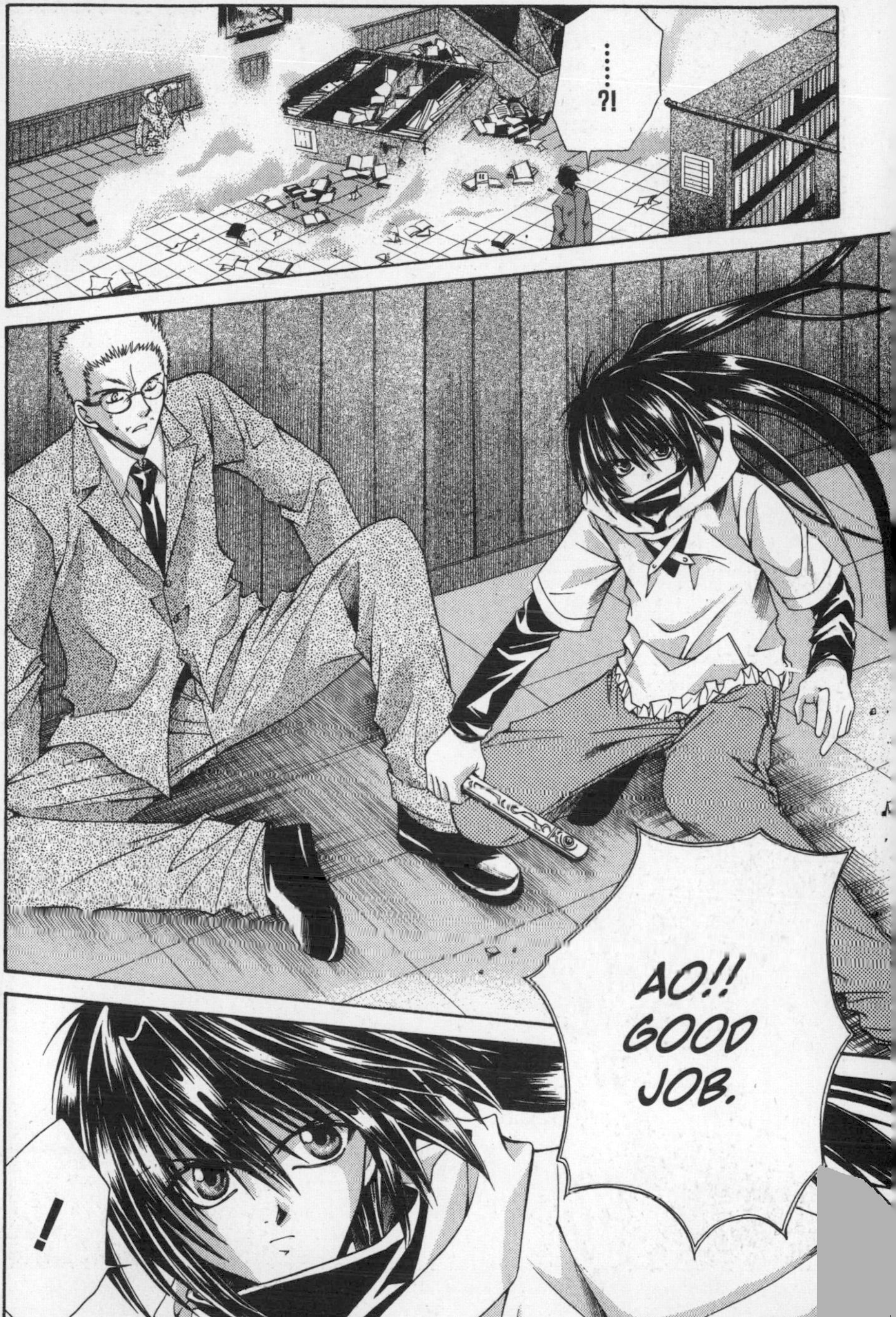
......?!
AO!! GOOD JOB.
!

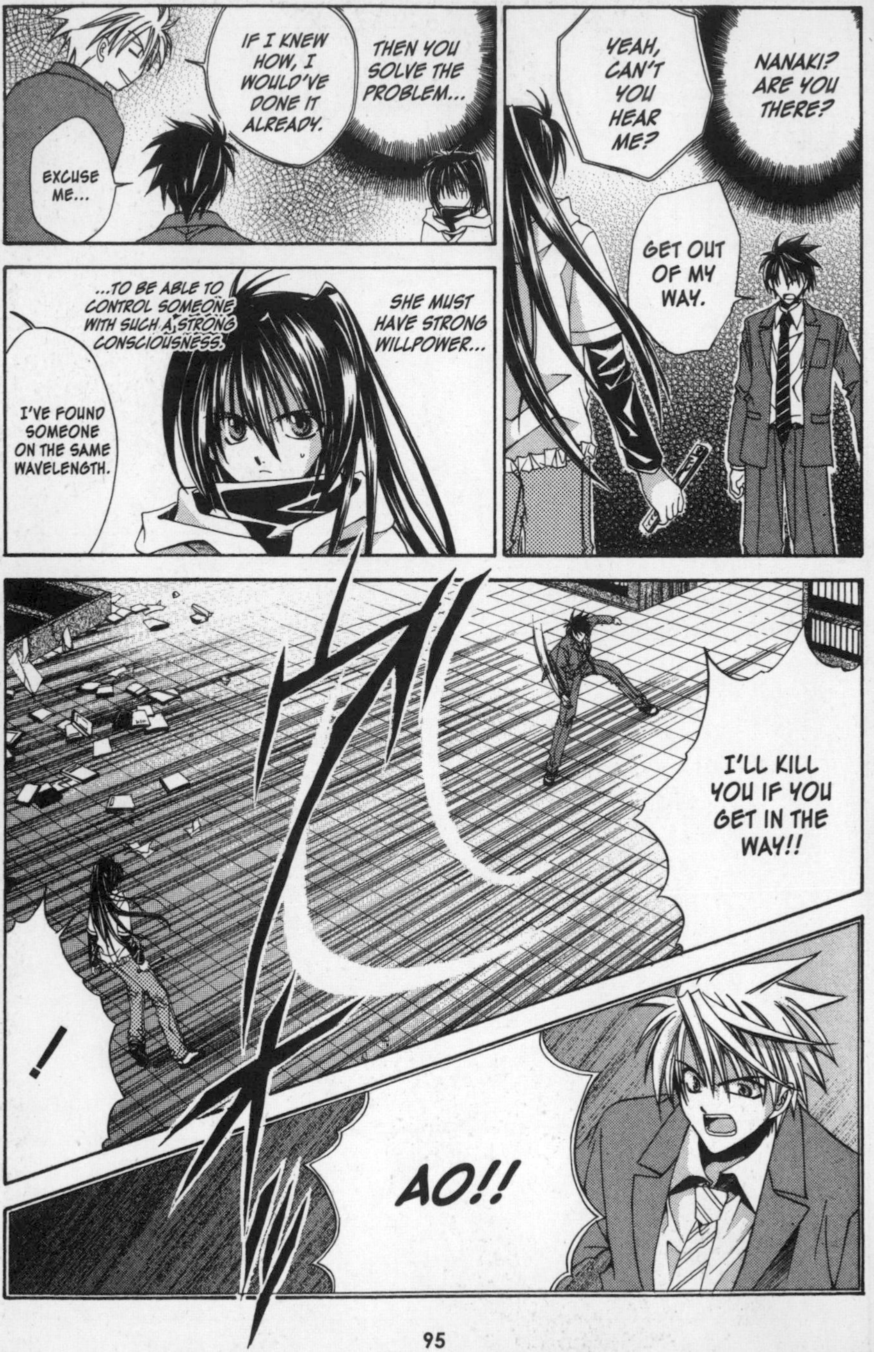
NANAKI? ARE YOU THERE?
YEAH, CAN'T YOU HEAR ME?
GET OUT OF MY WAY.
THEN YOU SOLVE THE PROBLEM...
IF I KNEW HOW, I WOULD'VE DONE IT ALREADY.
EXCUSE ME...
SHE MUST HAVE STRONG WILLPOWER...
...TO BE ABLE TO CONTROL SOMEONE WITH SUCH A STRONG CONSCIOUSNESS.
I'VE FOUND SOMEONE ON THE SAME WAVELENGTH.
I'LL KILL YOU IF YOU GET IN THE WAY!!
!
AO!!

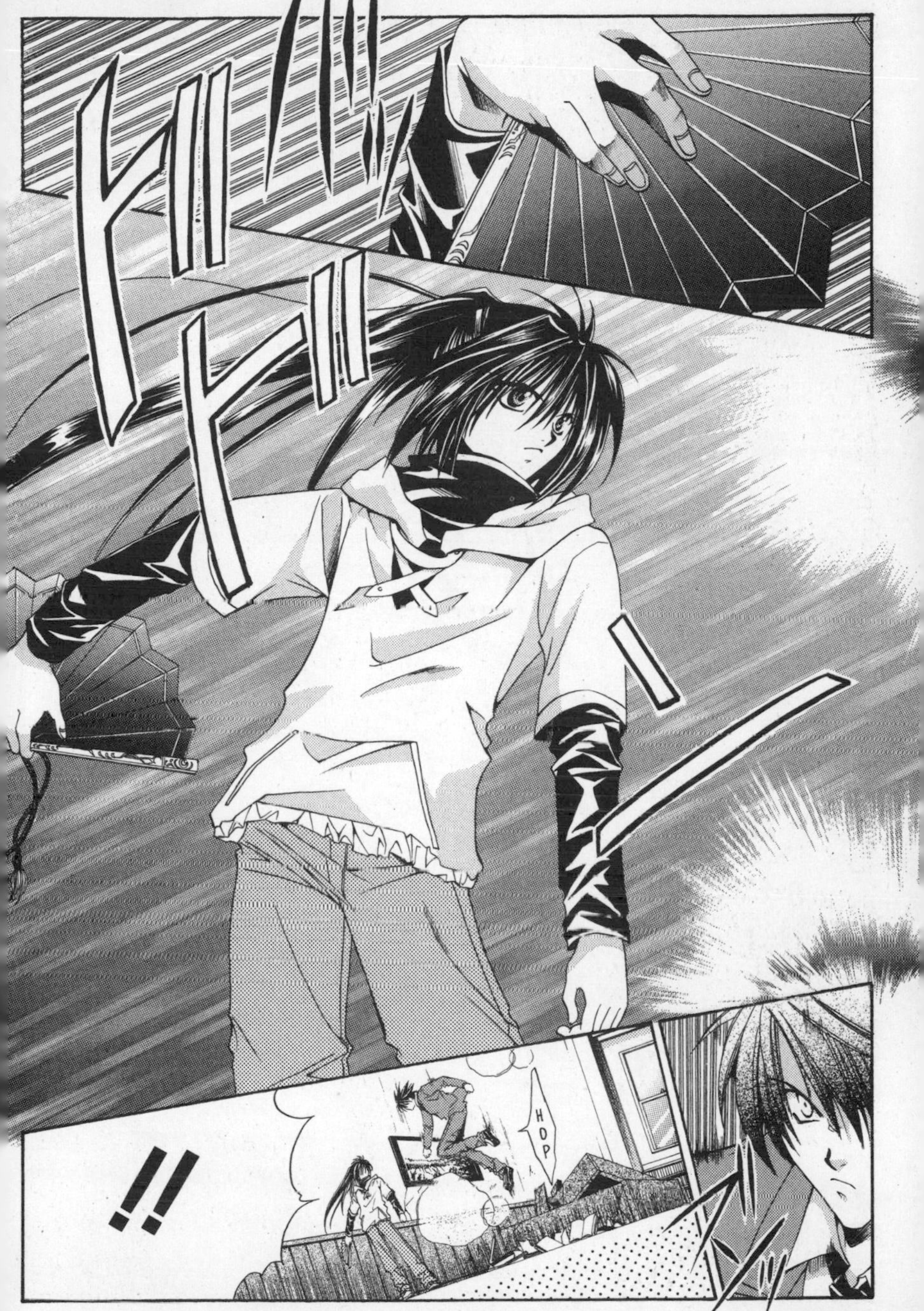
HOP
!!

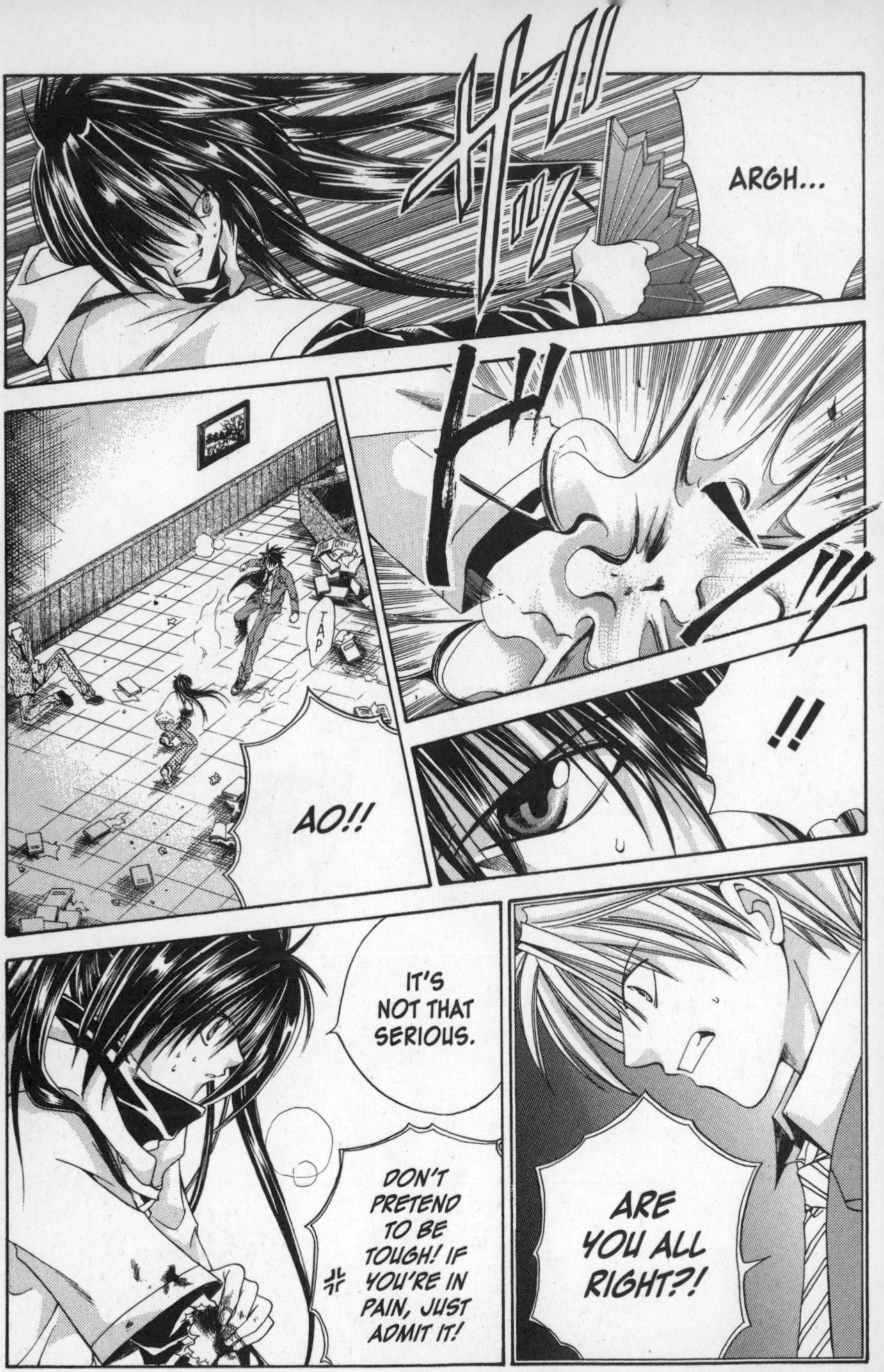
ARGH...
!!
TAP
AO!!
ARE YOU ALL RIGHT?!
IT'S NOT THAT SERIOUS.
DON'T PRETEND TO BE TOUGH! IF YOU'RE IN PAIN, JUST ADMIT IT!

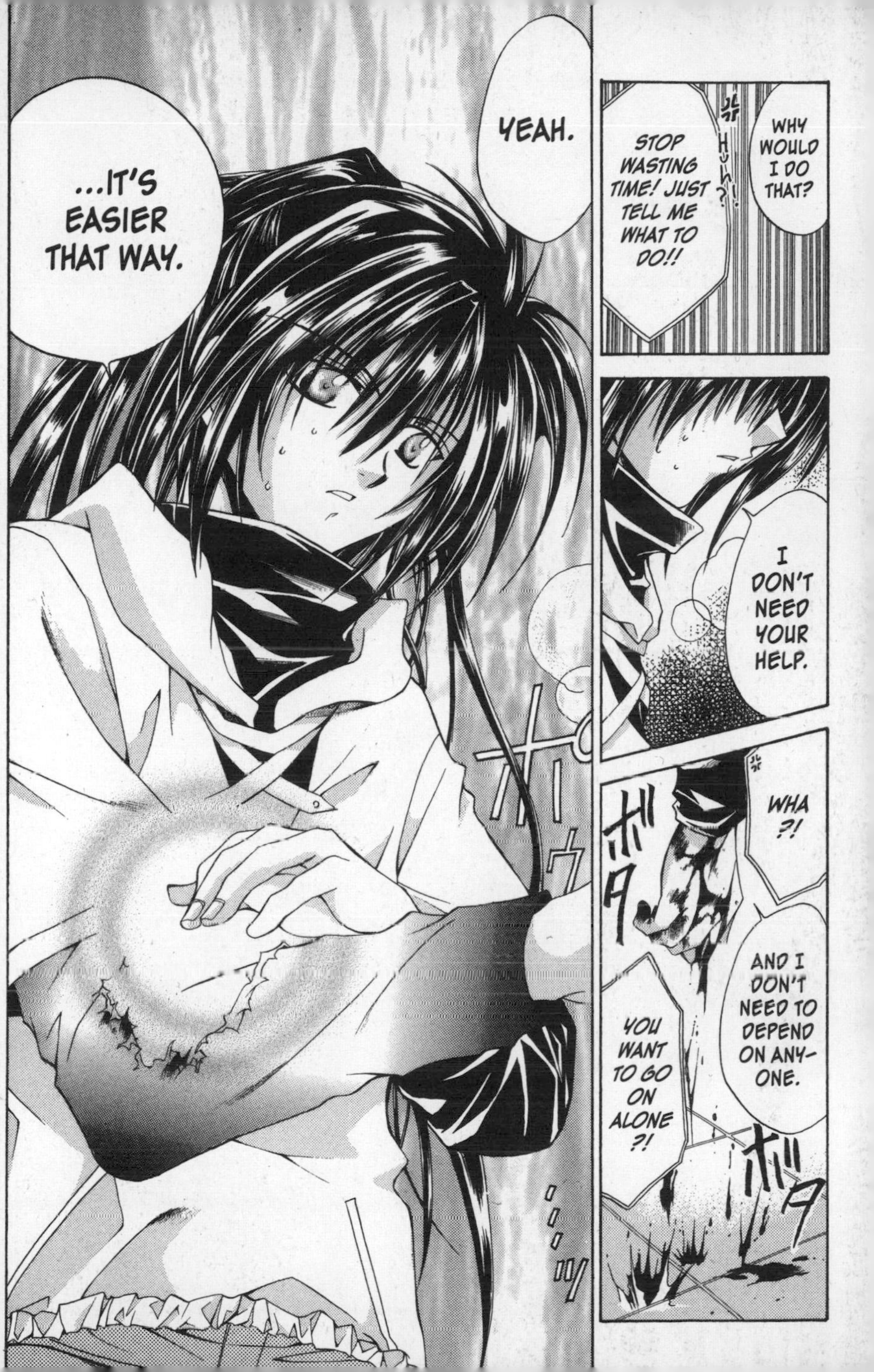
WHY WOULD I DO THAT?
HUH?!
STOP WASTING TIME! JUST TELL ME WHAT TO DO!!
I DON'T NEED YOUR HELP.
WHA?!
AND I DON'T NEED TO DEPEND ON ANY-ONE.
YOU WANT TO GO ON ALONE?!
YEAH.
...IT'S EASIER THAT WAY.

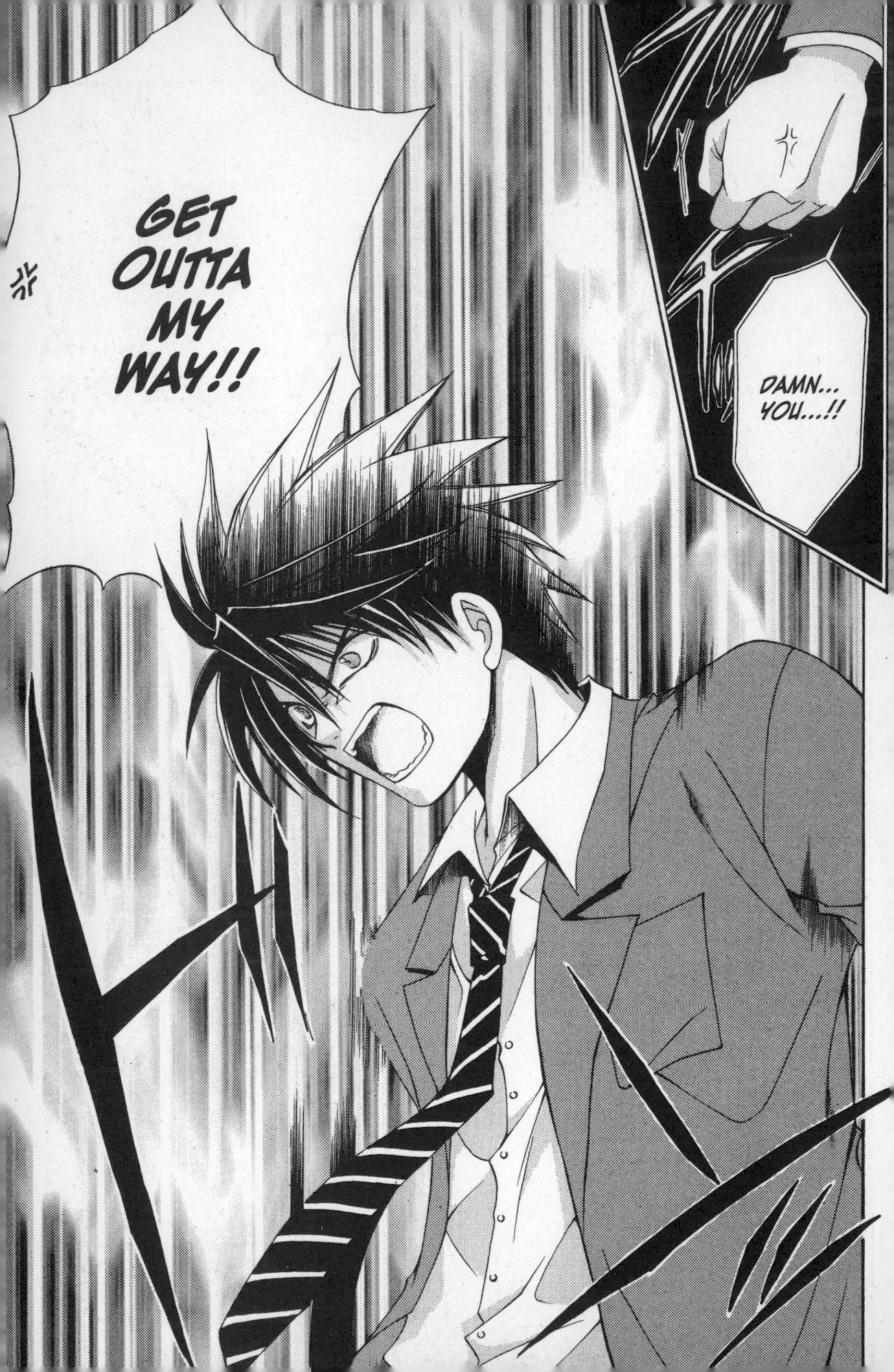
DAMN... YOU...!!
GET OUTTA MY WAY!!

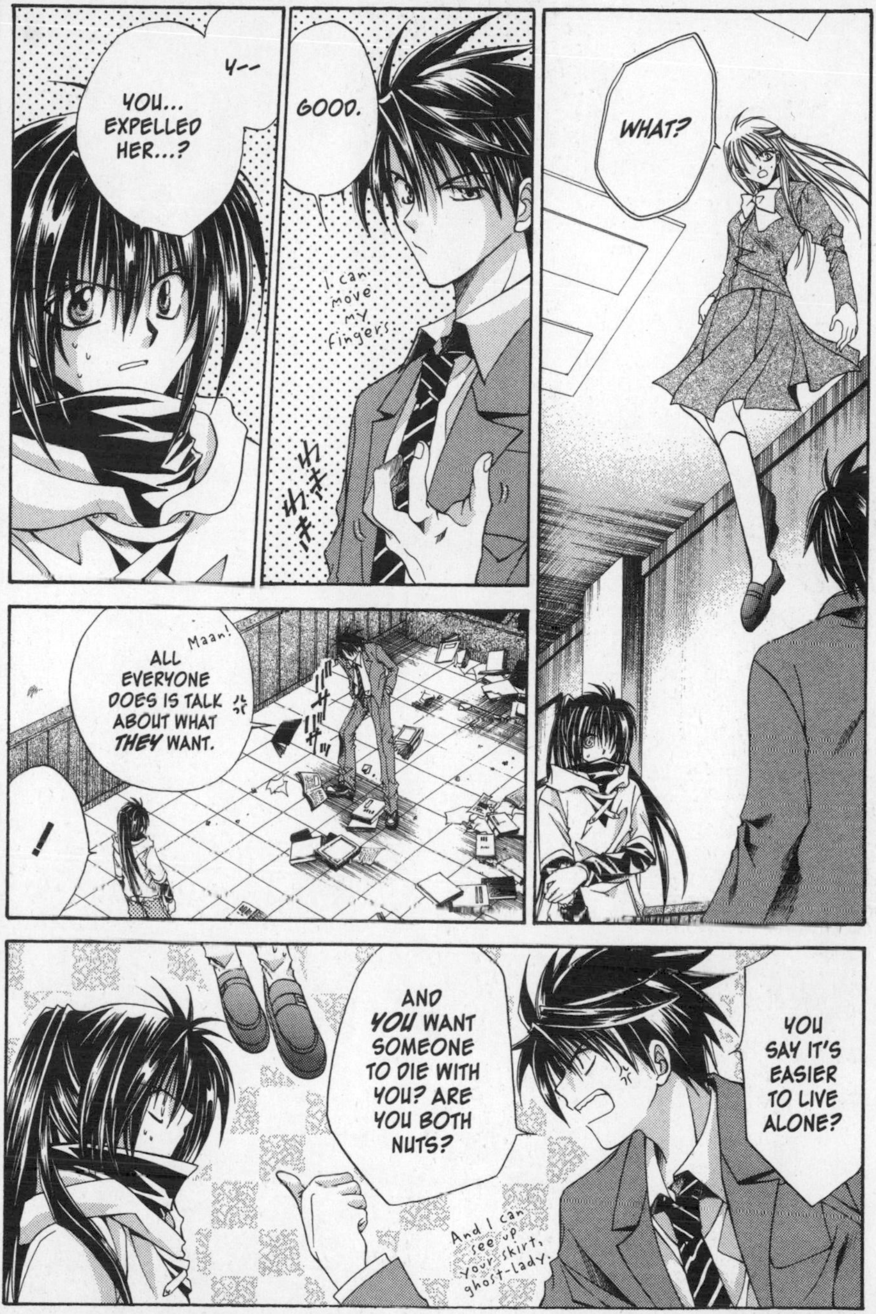
WHAT?
GOOD.
I can move my fingers.
Y--
YOU... EXPELLED HER...?
Maan!
ALL EVERYONE DOES IS TALK ABOUT WHAT THEY WANT.
!
YOU SAY IT'S EASIER TO LIVE ALONE?
AND YOU WANT SOMEONE TO DIE WITH YOU? ARE YOU BOTH NUTS?
And I can see up your skirt, ghost-lady.

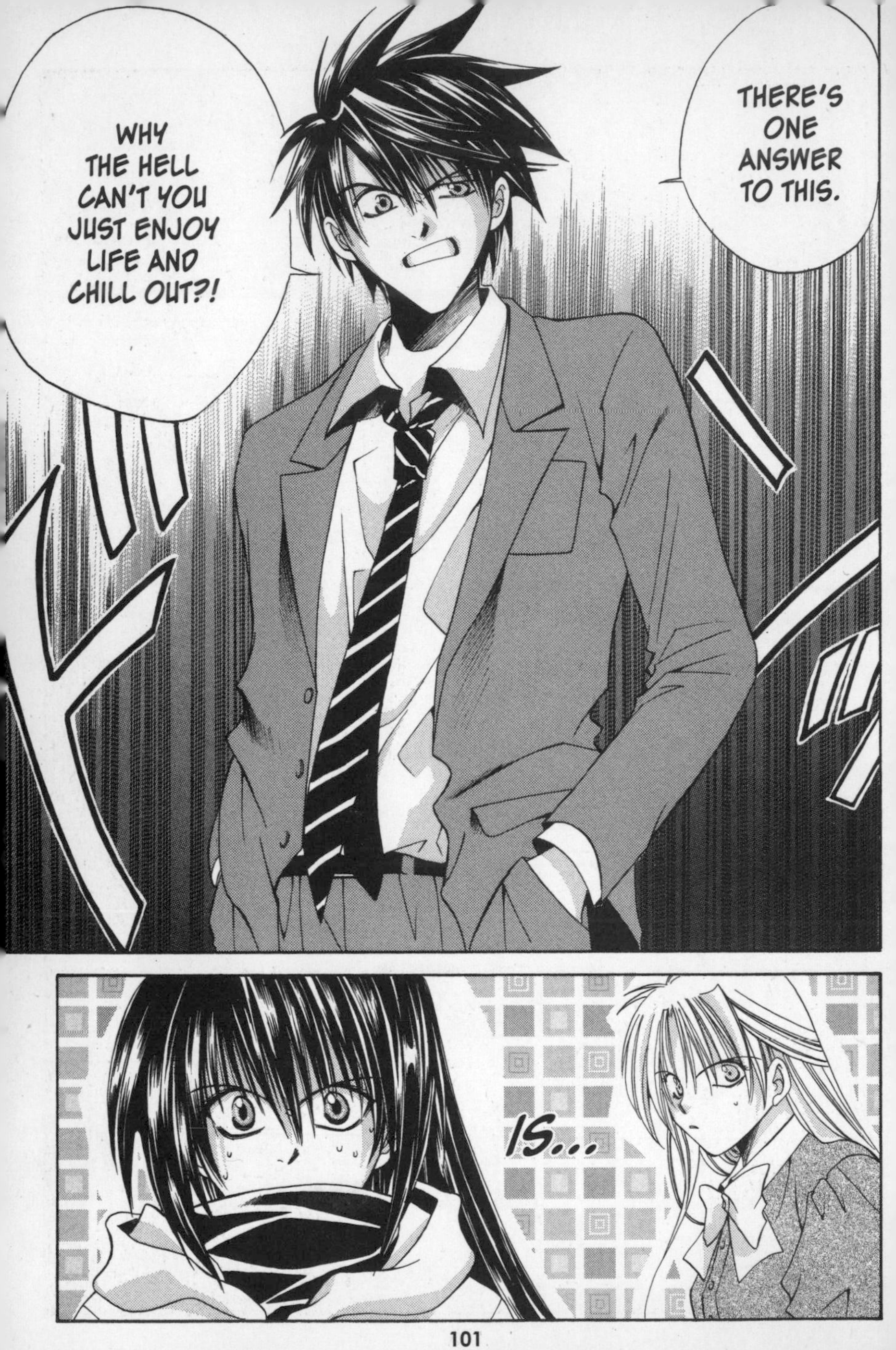
THERE'S ONE ANSWER TO THIS.
WHY THE HELL CAN'T YOU JUST ENJOY LIFE AND CHILL OUT?!
IS...

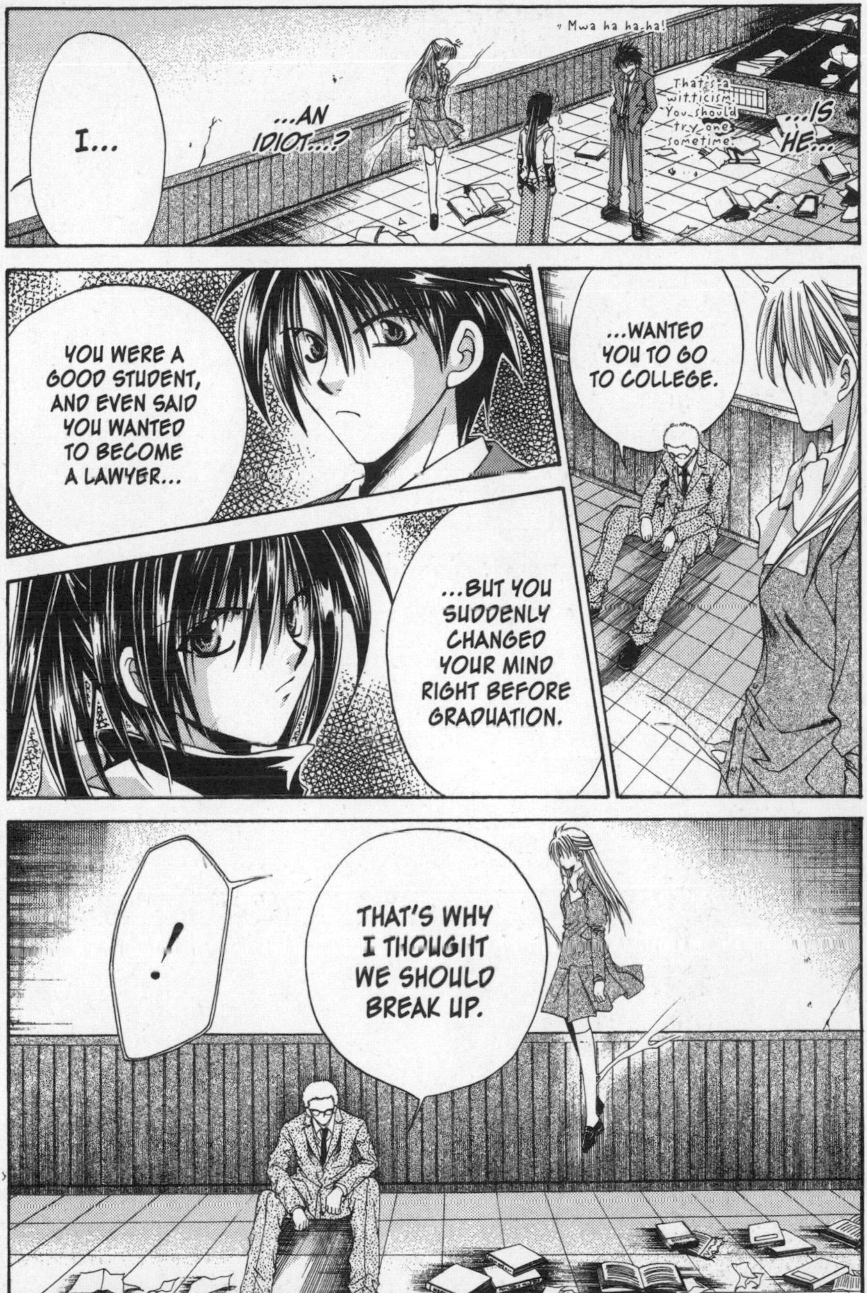

...IS HE...
Mwa ha ha-ha!
That's a witticism. You should try one sometime.
...AN IDIOT...?
I...
...WANTED YOU TO GO TO COLLEGE.
YOU WERE A GOOD STUDENT, AND EVEN SAID YOU WANTED TO BECOME A LAWYER...
...BUT YOU SUDDENLY CHANGED YOUR MIND RIGHT BEFORE GRADUATION.
THAT'S WHY I THOUGHT WE SHOULD BREAK UP.
!

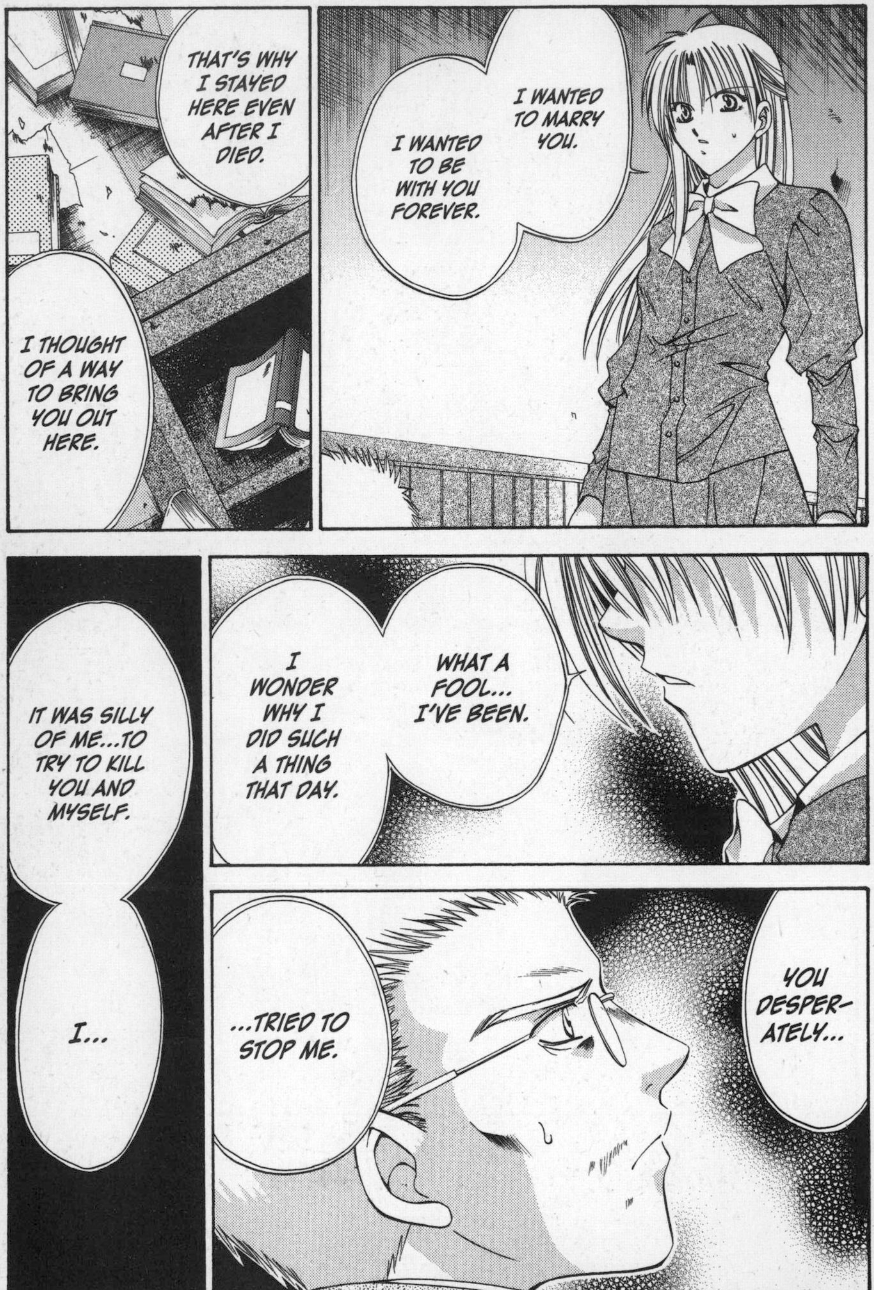
I WANTED TO MARRY YOU.
I WANTED TO BE WITH YOU FOREVER.
THAT'S WHY I STAYED HERE EVEN AFTER I DIED.
I THOUGHT OF A WAY TO BRING YOU OUT HERE.
WHAT A FOOL... I'VE BEEN.
I WONDER WHY I DID SUCH A THING THAT DAY.
YOU DESPERATELY...
...TRIED TO STOP ME.
IT WAS SILLY OF ME...TO TRY TO KILL YOU AND MYSELF.
I...

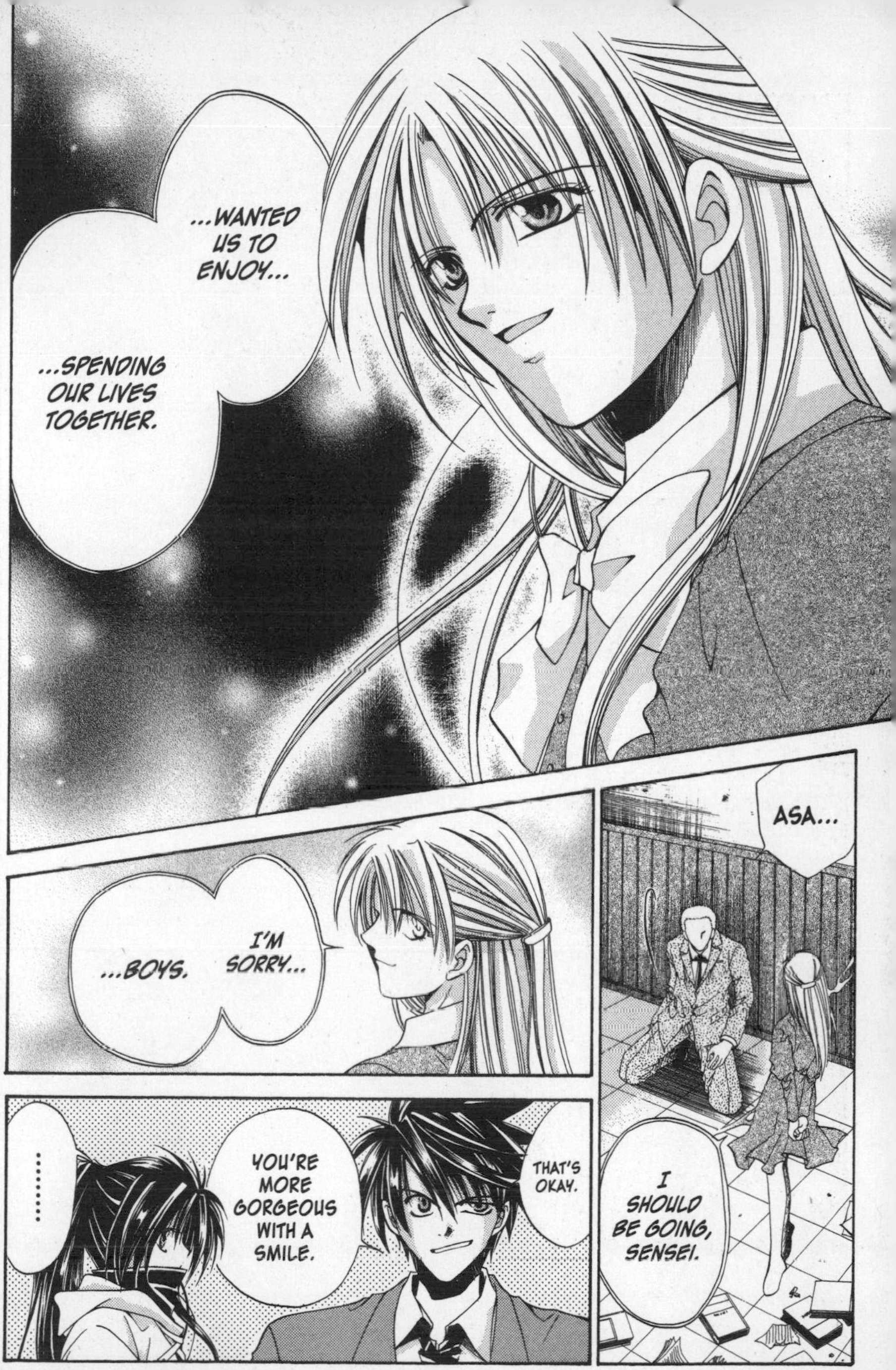
...WANTED US TO ENJOY...
...SPENDING OUR LIVES TOGETHER.
ASA...
I SHOULD BE GOING, SENSEI.
I'M SORRY...
...BOYS.
THAT'S OKAY.
YOU'RE MORE GORGEOUS WITH A SMILE.
......

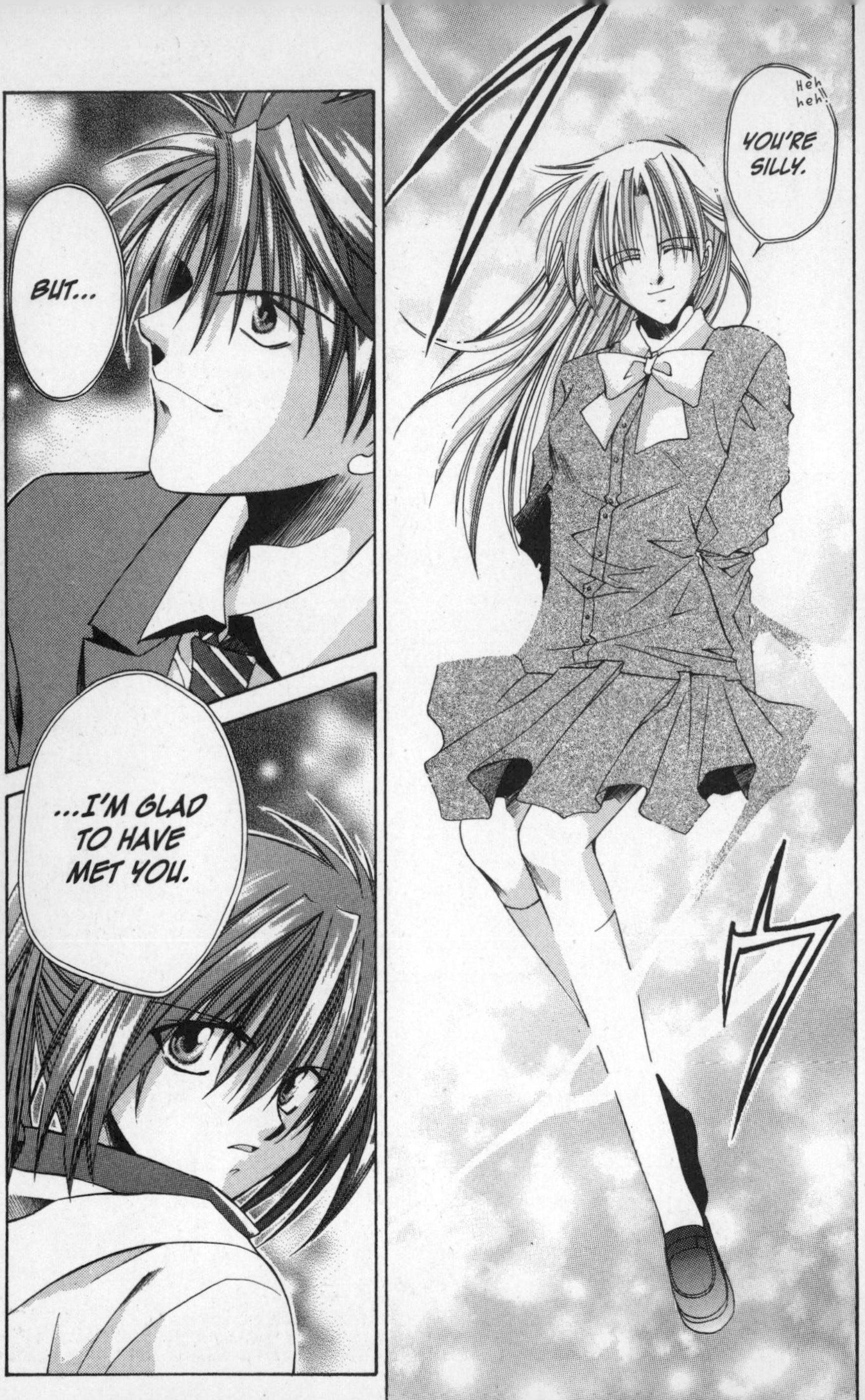
Heh heh!!
YOU'RE SILLY.
BUT...
...I'M GLAD TO HAVE MET YOU.

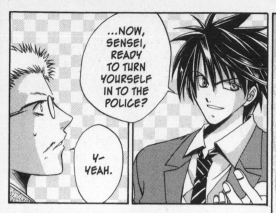

...NOW, SENSEI, READY TO TURN YOURSELF IN TO THE POLICE?

Y-YEAH.

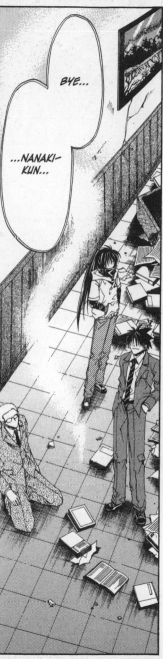

BYE...

...NANAKI-KUN...

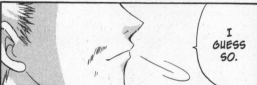

I GUESS SO.

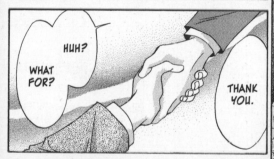

HUH?

WHAT FOR?

THANK YOU.

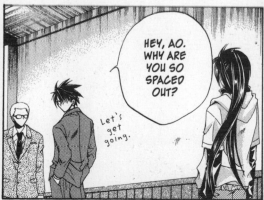

HEY, AO. WHY ARE YOU SO SPACED OUT?

Let's get going.

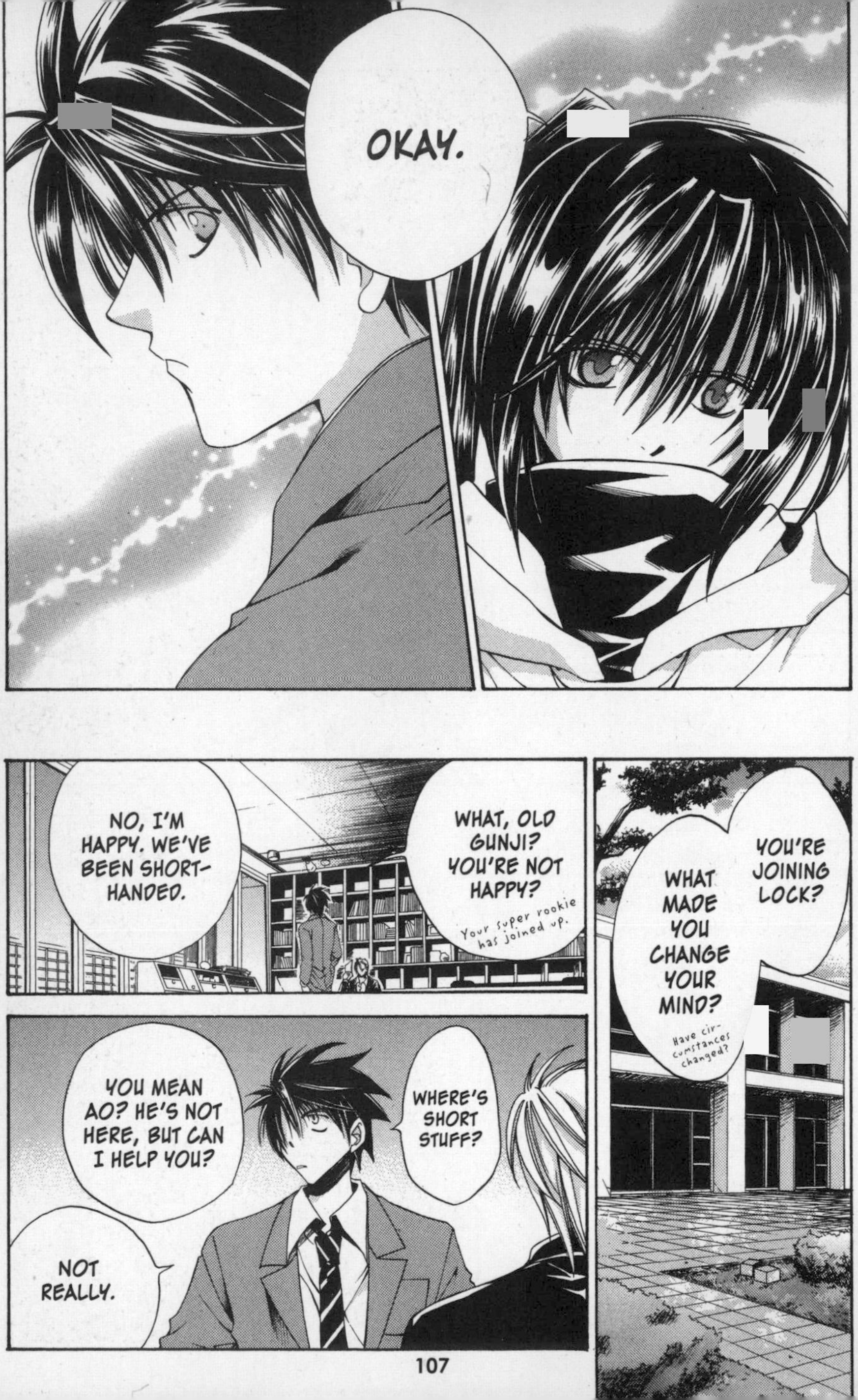
OKAY.
YOU'RE JOINING LOCK?
WHAT MADE YOU CHANGE YOUR MIND?
Have circumstances changed?
WHAT, OLD GUNJI? YOU'RE NOT HAPPY?
Your super rookie has joined up.
NO, I'M HAPPY. WE'VE BEEN SHORT-HANDED.
WHERE'S SHORT STUFF?
YOU MEAN AO? HE'S NOT HERE, BUT CAN I HELP YOU?
NOT REALLY.

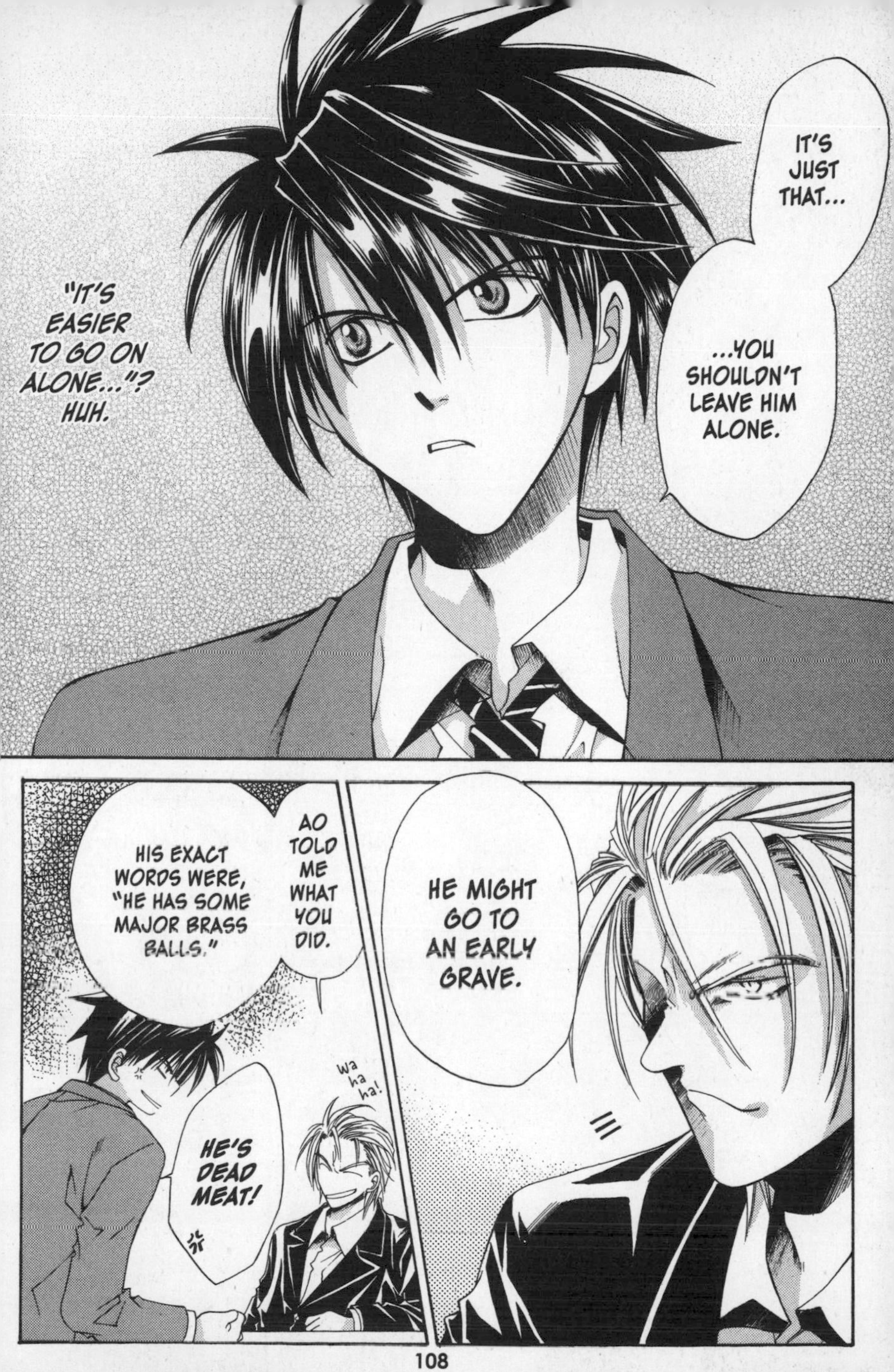
IT'S JUST THAT...
...YOU SHOULDN'T LEAVE HIM ALONE.
"IT'S EASIER TO GO ON ALONE..."? HUH.
HE MIGHT GO TO AN EARLY GRAVE.
AO TOLD ME WHAT YOU DID.
HIS EXACT WORDS WERE, "HE HAS SOME MAJOR BRASS BALLS."
Wa ha ha!
HE'S DEAD MEAT!

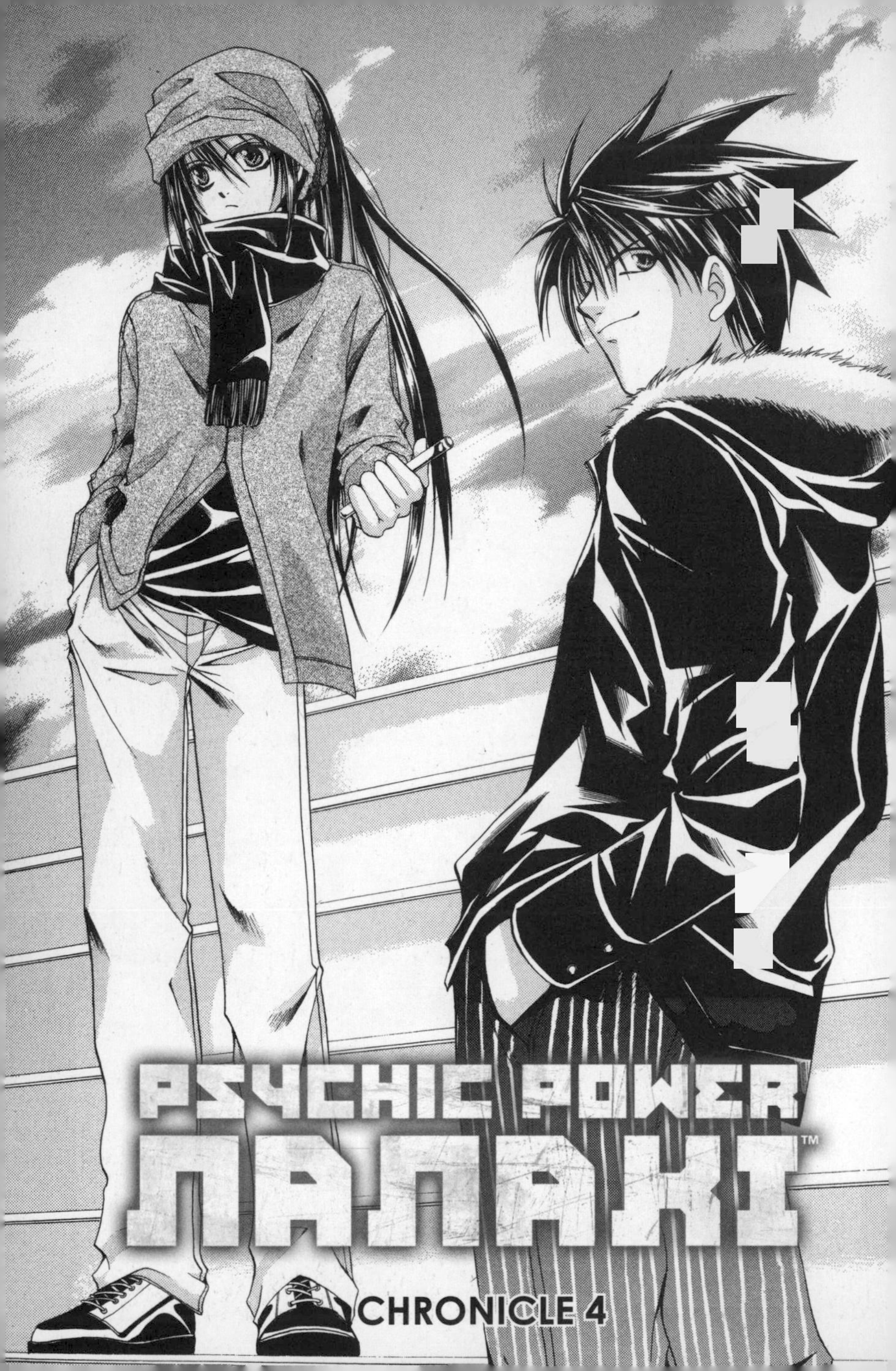
PSYCHIC POWER
NANAKI™
CHRONICLE 4

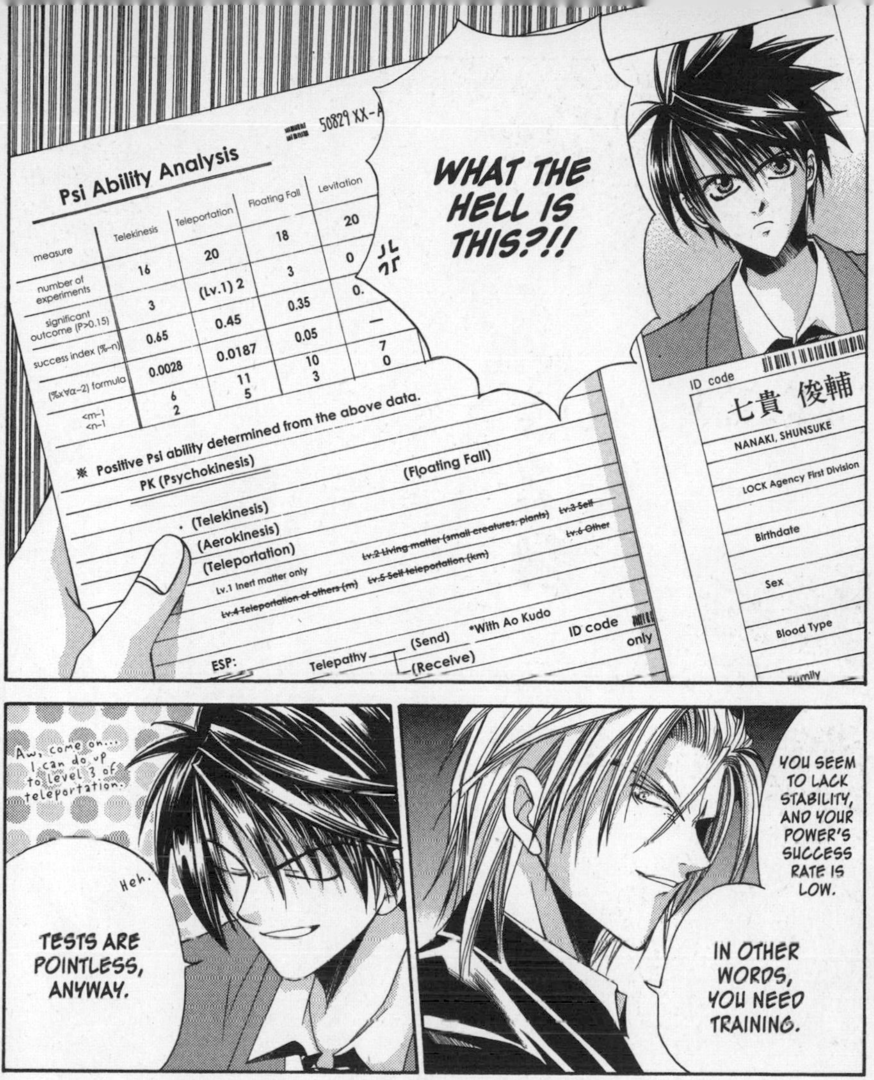
50829 XX-A
Psi Ability Analysis
measure
Telekinesis
Teleportation
Floating Fall
Levitation
number of experiments
significant outcome (P>0.15)
success index (%–n)
(%×∀α–2) formula
<m–1
<n–1
16
3
0.65
0.0028
6
2
20
(Lv.1) 2
0.45
0.0187
11
5
18
3
0.35
0.05
10
3
20
0
0.
—
7
0
※ Positive Psi ability determined from the above data.
PK (Psychokinesis)
(Floating Fall)
• (Telekinesis)
(Aerokinesis)
(Teleportation)
Lv.1 Inert matter only
Lv.2 Living matter (small creatures, plants)
Lv.3 Self
Lv.4 Teleportation of others (m)
Lv.5 Self teleportation (km)
Lv.6 Other
*With Ao Kudo only
ESP:
Telepathy
(Send)
(Receive)
ID code
ID code
七貴 俊輔
NANAKI, SHUNSUKE
LOCK Agency First Division
Birthdate
Sex
Blood Type
Family
WHAT THE HELL IS THIS?!!
YOU SEEM TO LACK STABILITY, AND YOUR POWER'S SUCCESS RATE IS LOW.
IN OTHER WORDS, YOU NEED TRAINING.
Aw, come on... I can do up to level 3 of teleportation.
Heh.
TESTS ARE POINTLESS, ANYWAY.

INNER CHANGE

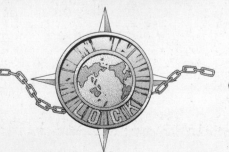

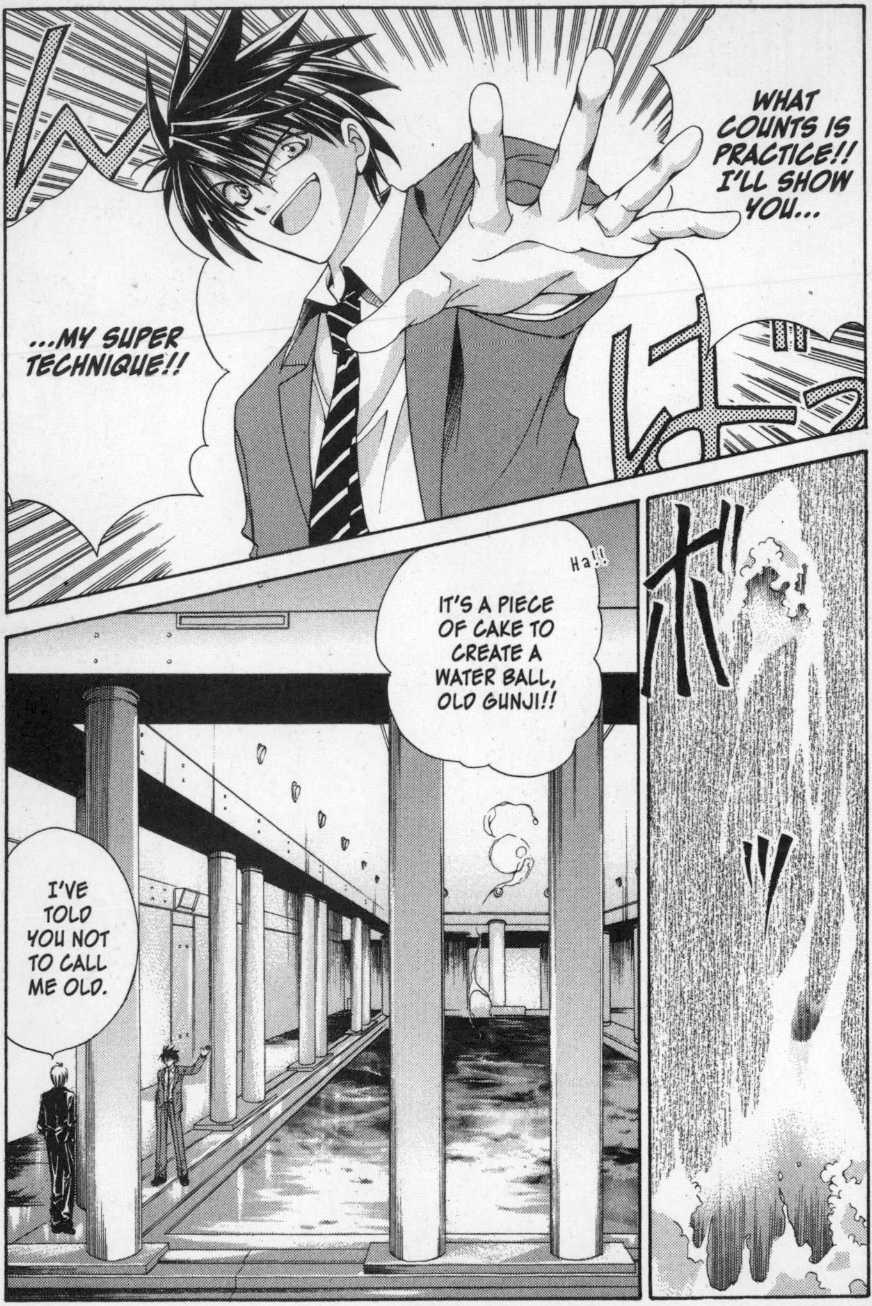
WHAT COUNTS IS PRACTICE!! I'LL SHOW YOU...
...MY SUPER TECHNIQUE!!
Ha!!
IT'S A PIECE OF CAKE TO CREATE A WATER BALL, OLD GUNJI!!
I'VE TOLD YOU NOT TO CALL ME OLD.

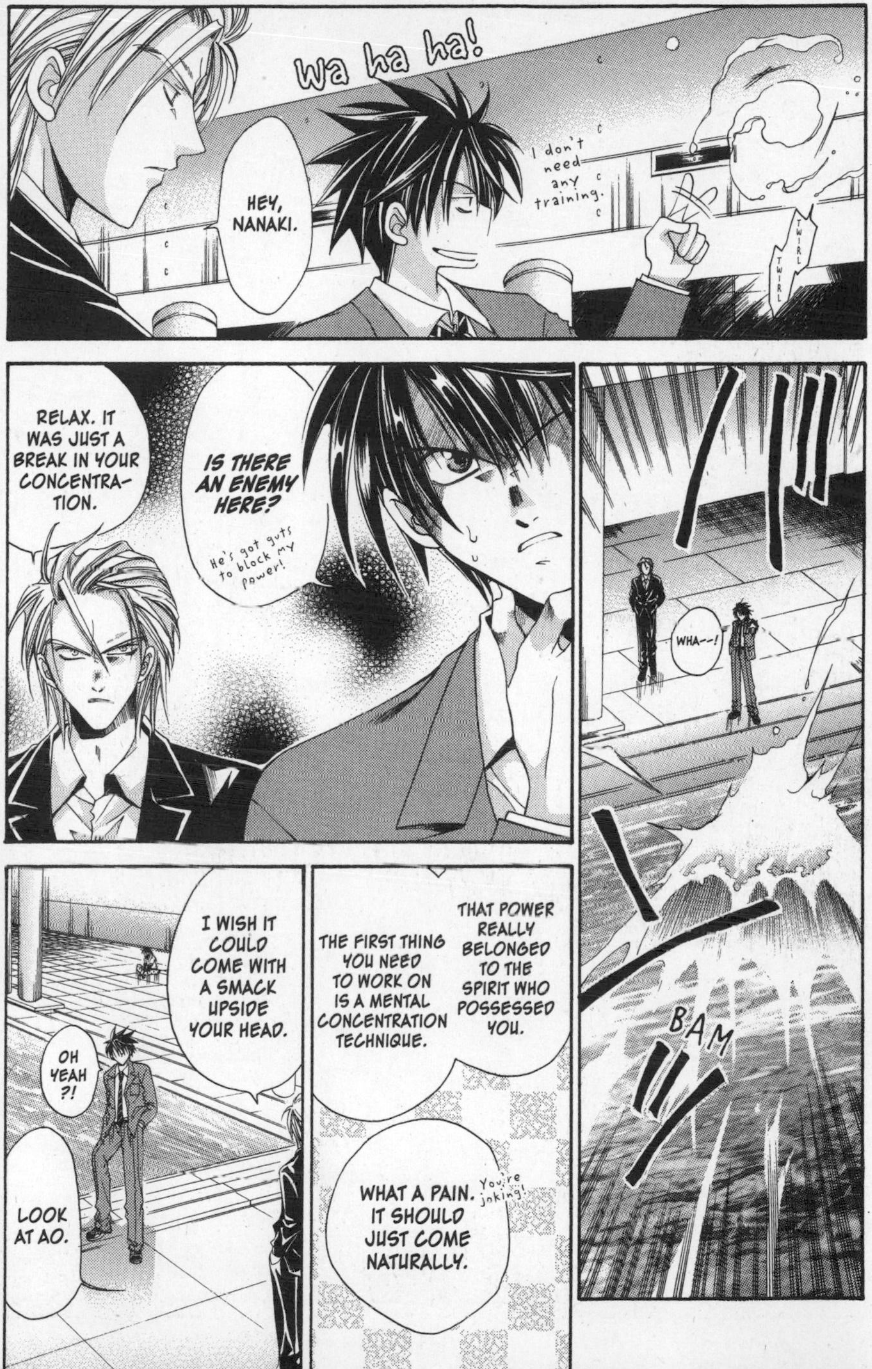
Wa ha ha!
I don't need any training.
TWIRL TWIRL
HEY, NANAKI.
WHA--!
BAM
IS THERE AN ENEMY HERE?
He's got guts to block my power!
RELAX. IT WAS JUST A BREAK IN YOUR CONCENTRATION.
THAT POWER REALLY BELONGED TO THE SPIRIT WHO POSSESSED YOU.
THE FIRST THING YOU NEED TO WORK ON IS A MENTAL CONCENTRATION TECHNIQUE.
WHAT A PAIN. IT SHOULD JUST COME NATURALLY.
You're joking!
I WISH IT COULD COME WITH A SMACK UPSIDE YOUR HEAD.
OH YEAH?!
LOOK AT AO.

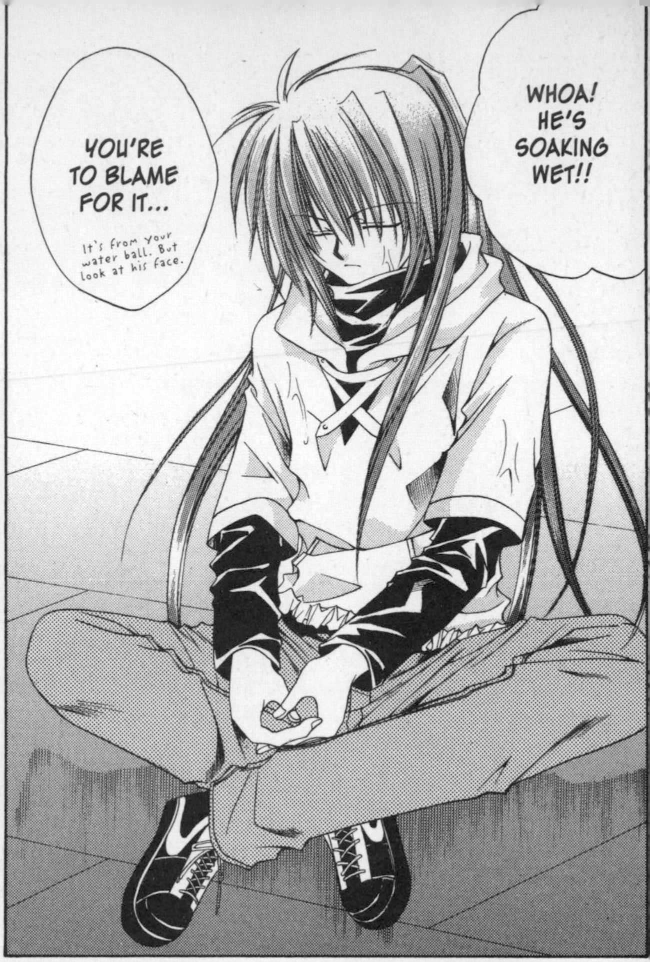
WHOA! HE'S SOAKING WET!!
YOU'RE TO BLAME FOR IT...
It's from your water ball. But look at his face.

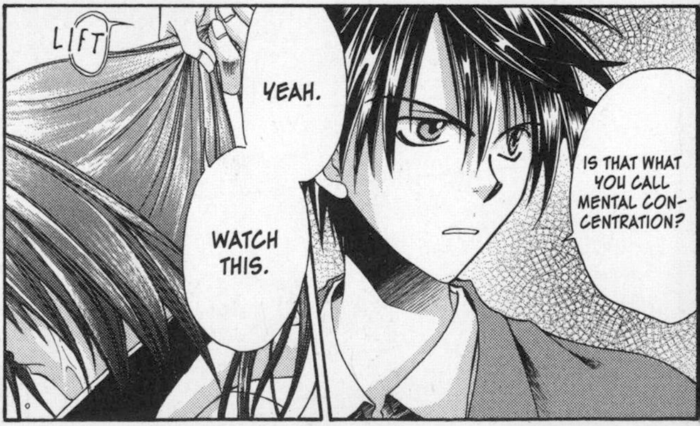
IS THAT WHAT YOU CALL MENTAL CON-CENTRATION?
YEAH.
WATCH THIS.
LIFT

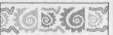

七貴 俊輔

NANAKI, SHUNSUKE

- High school jr., age 17
- A member of the Paranormal Task Force (LOCK) First Division

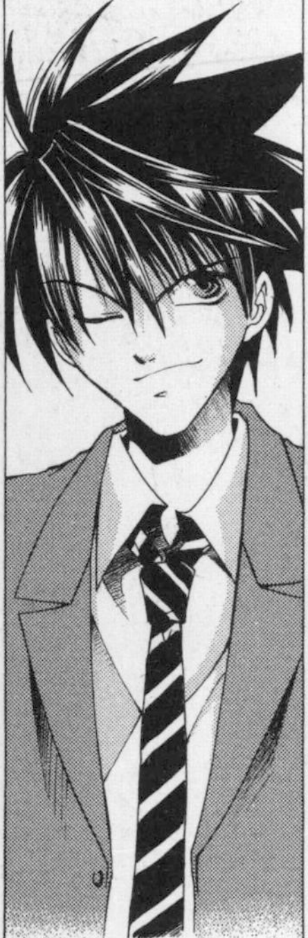

■Psi Abilities■

- Telekinesis
- Floating Fall
- Aerokinesis
- Teleportation (Lv.1-3)
- Telepathy
  - Send (with Ao only)
  - Receive

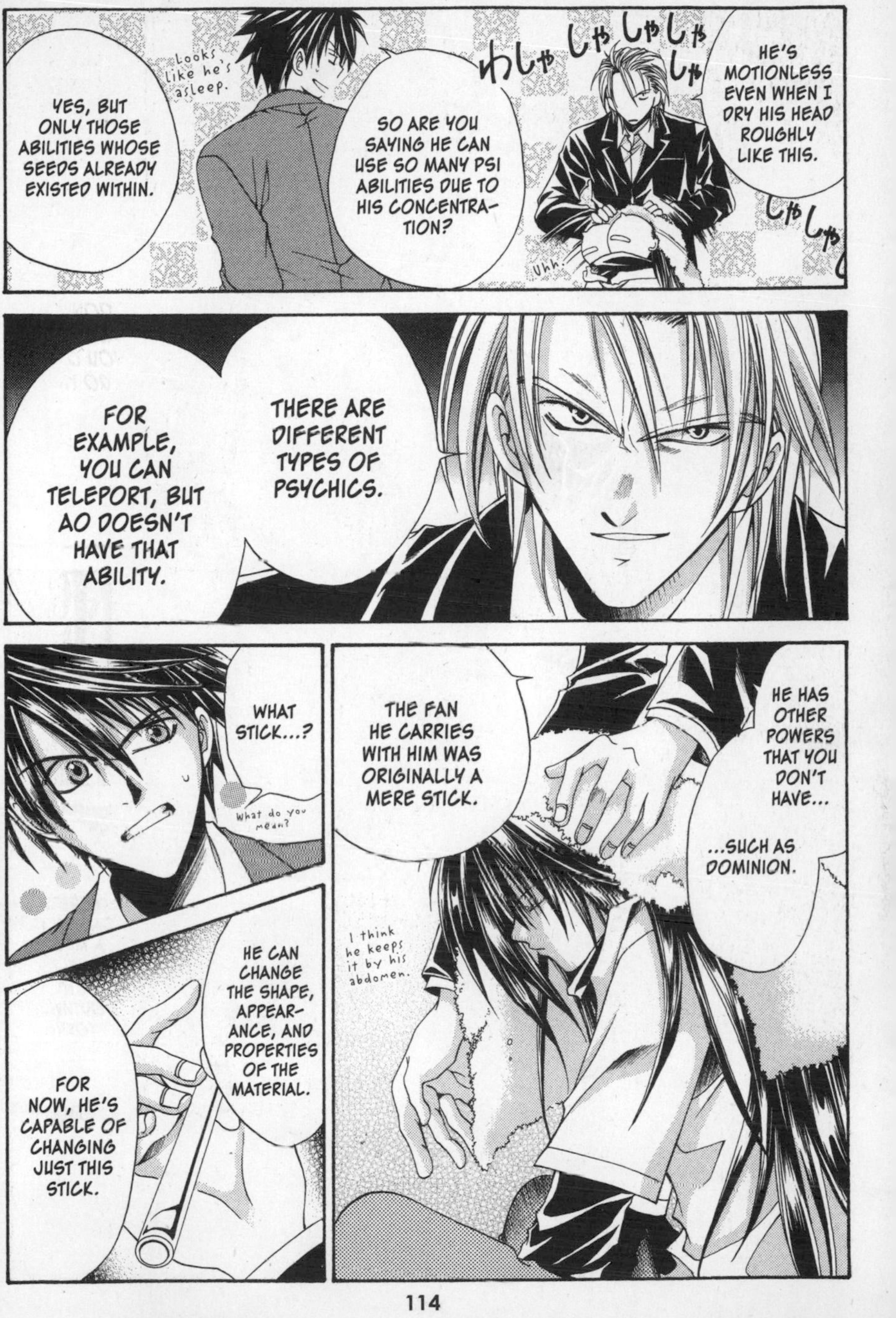
わしゃ しゃ しゃしゃ しゃ
HE'S MOTIONLESS EVEN WHEN I DRY HIS HEAD ROUGHLY LIKE THIS.
しゃしゃ
Uhh...
SO ARE YOU SAYING HE CAN USE SO MANY PSI ABILITIES DUE TO HIS CONCENTRATION?
Looks like he's asleep.
YES, BUT ONLY THOSE ABILITIES WHOSE SEEDS ALREADY EXISTED WITHIN.
THERE ARE DIFFERENT TYPES OF PSYCHICS.
FOR EXAMPLE, YOU CAN TELEPORT, BUT AO DOESN'T HAVE THAT ABILITY.
HE HAS OTHER POWERS THAT YOU DON'T HAVE...
...SUCH AS DOMINION.
THE FAN HE CARRIES WITH HIM WAS ORIGINALLY A MERE STICK.
I think he keeps it by his abdomen.
WHAT STICK...?
What do you mean?
HE CAN CHANGE THE SHAPE, APPEARANCE, AND PROPERTIES OF THE MATERIAL.
FOR NOW, HE'S CAPABLE OF CHANGING JUST THIS STICK.

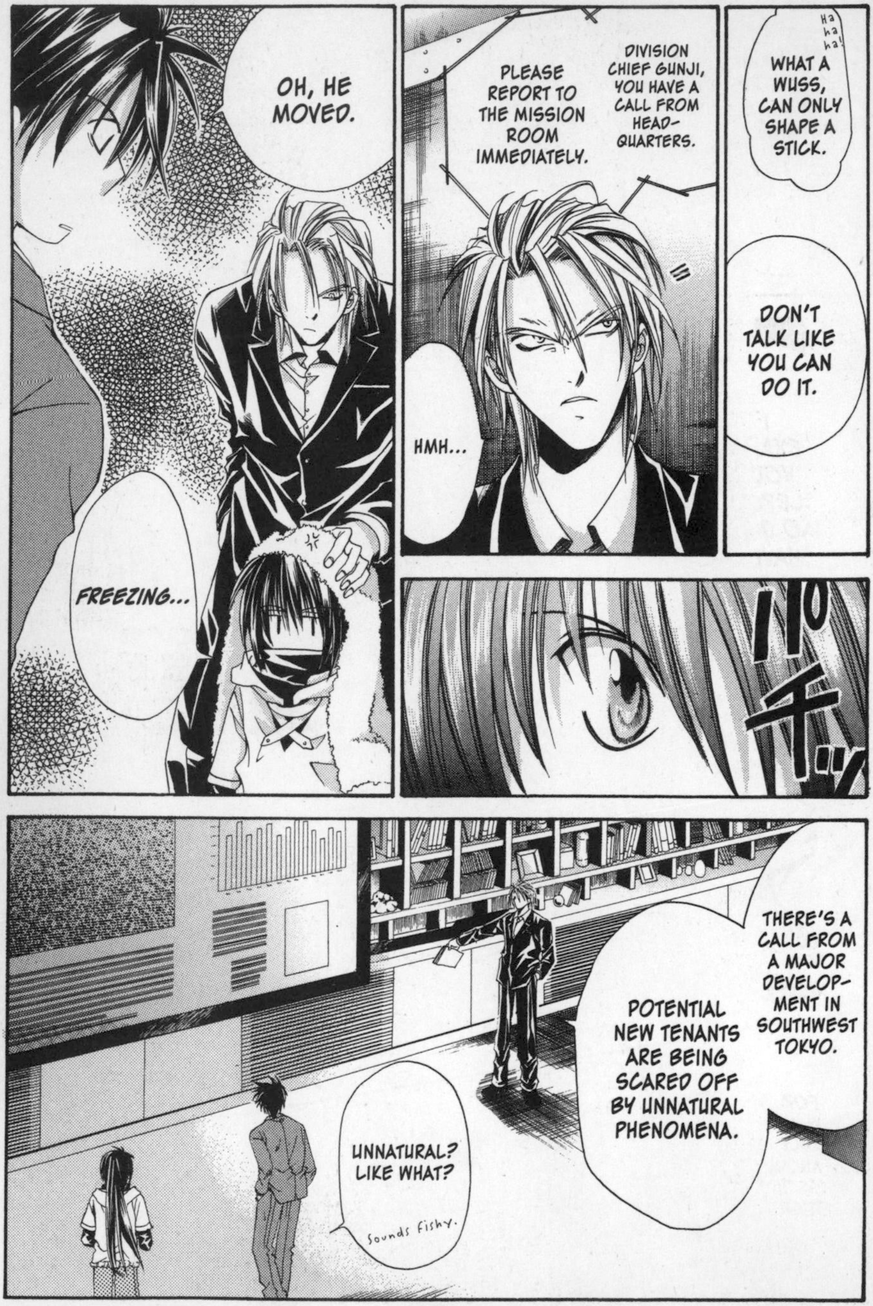
Ha ha ha!
WHAT A WUSS, CAN ONLY SHAPE A STICK.
DON'T TALK LIKE YOU CAN DO IT.
DIVISION CHIEF GUNJI, YOU HAVE A CALL FROM HEAD-QUARTERS.
PLEASE REPORT TO THE MISSION ROOM IMMEDIATELY.
HMH...
OH, HE MOVED.
FREEZING...
THERE'S A CALL FROM A MAJOR DEVELOP-MENT IN SOUTHWEST TOKYO.
POTENTIAL NEW TENANTS ARE BEING SCARED OFF BY UNNATURAL PHENOMENA.
UNNATURAL? LIKE WHAT?
Sounds fishy.

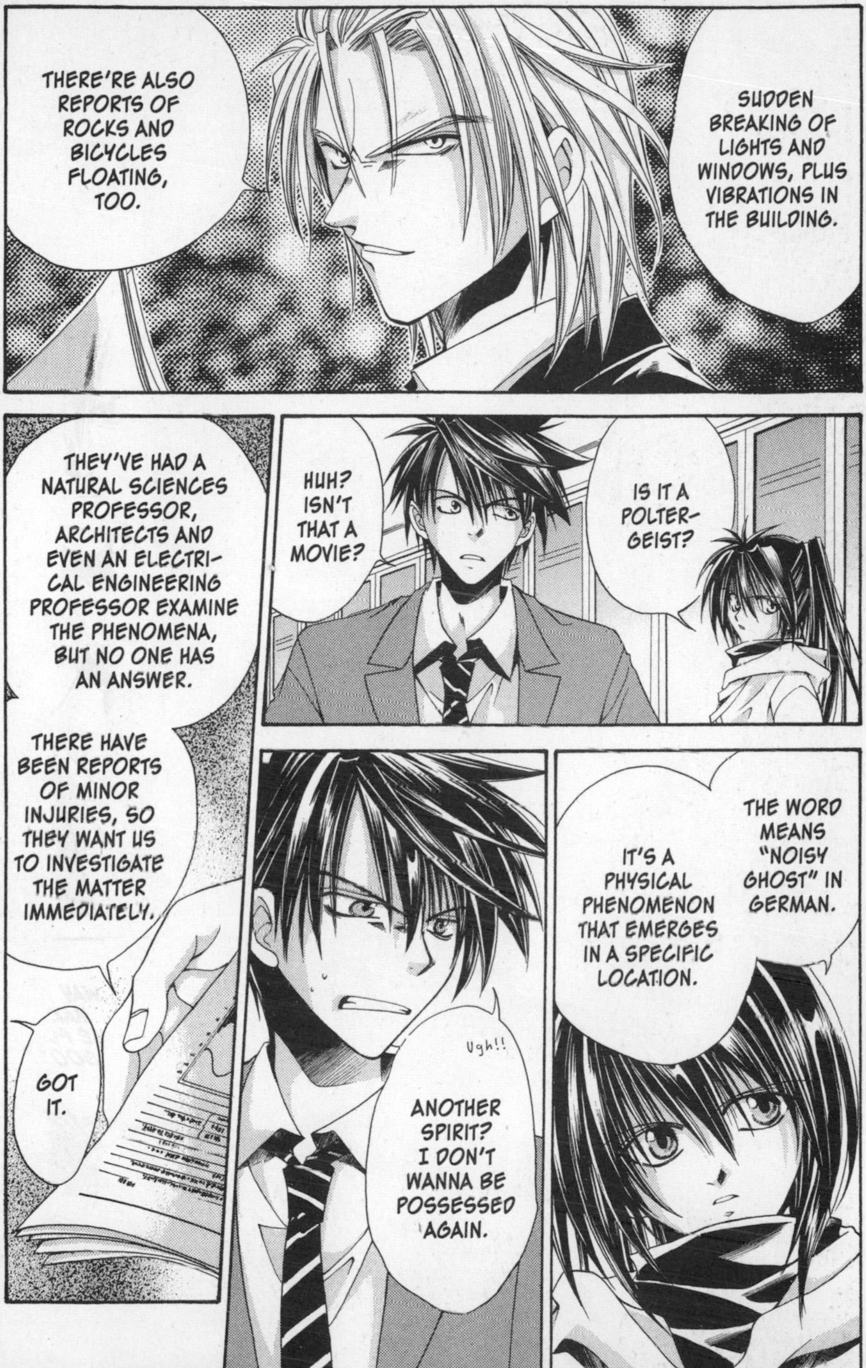
SUDDEN BREAKING OF LIGHTS AND WINDOWS, PLUS VIBRATIONS IN THE BUILDING.
THERE'RE ALSO REPORTS OF ROCKS AND BICYCLES FLOATING, TOO.
IS IT A POLTER-GEIST?
HUH? ISN'T THAT A MOVIE?
THE WORD MEANS "NOISY GHOST" IN GERMAN.
IT'S A PHYSICAL PHENOMENON THAT EMERGES IN A SPECIFIC LOCATION.
Ugh!!
ANOTHER SPIRIT? I DON'T WANNA BE POSSESSED AGAIN.
THEY'VE HAD A NATURAL SCIENCES PROFESSOR, ARCHITECTS AND EVEN AN ELECTRI-CAL ENGINEERING PROFESSOR EXAMINE THE PHENOMENA, BUT NO ONE HAS AN ANSWER.
THERE HAVE BEEN REPORTS OF MINOR INJURIES, SO THEY WANT US TO INVESTIGATE THE MATTER IMMEDIATELY.
GOT IT.

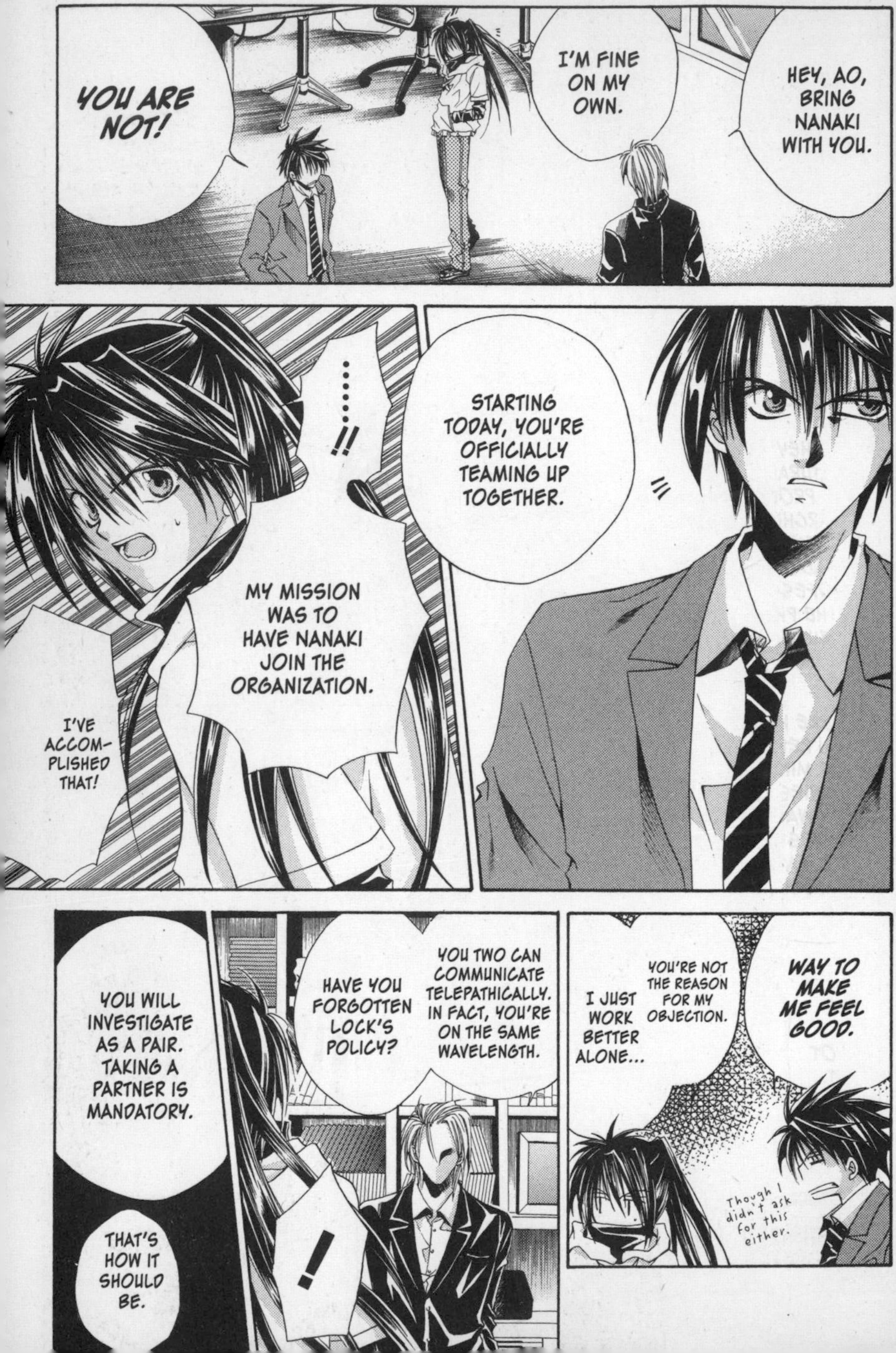
HEY, AO, BRING NANAKI WITH YOU.
I'M FINE ON MY OWN.
YOU ARE NOT!
STARTING TODAY, YOU'RE OFFICIALLY TEAMING UP TOGETHER.
......!!
MY MISSION WAS TO HAVE NANAKI JOIN THE ORGANIZATION.
I'VE ACCOMPLISHED THAT!
WAY TO MAKE ME FEEL GOOD.
YOU'RE NOT THE REASON FOR MY OBJECTION.
I JUST WORK BETTER ALONE...
Though I didn't ask for this either.
YOU TWO CAN COMMUNICATE TELEPATHICALLY. IN FACT, YOU'RE ON THE SAME WAVELENGTH.
HAVE YOU FORGOTTEN LOCK'S POLICY?
!
YOU WILL INVESTIGATE AS A PAIR. TAKING A PARTNER IS MANDATORY.
THAT'S HOW IT SHOULD BE.

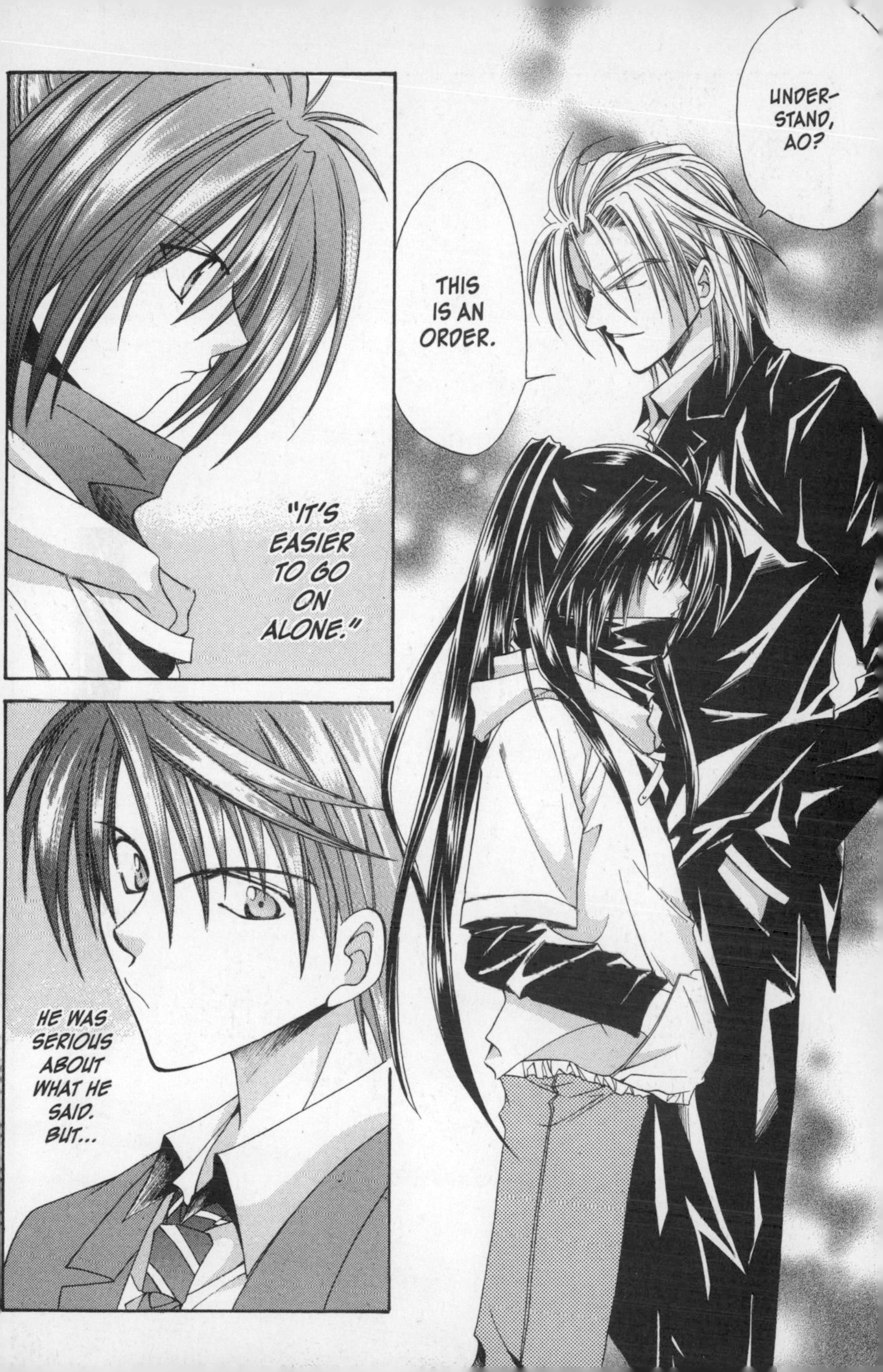
UNDER-STAND, AO?
THIS IS AN ORDER.
"IT'S EASIER TO GO ON ALONE."
HE WAS SERIOUS ABOUT WHAT HE SAID. BUT...

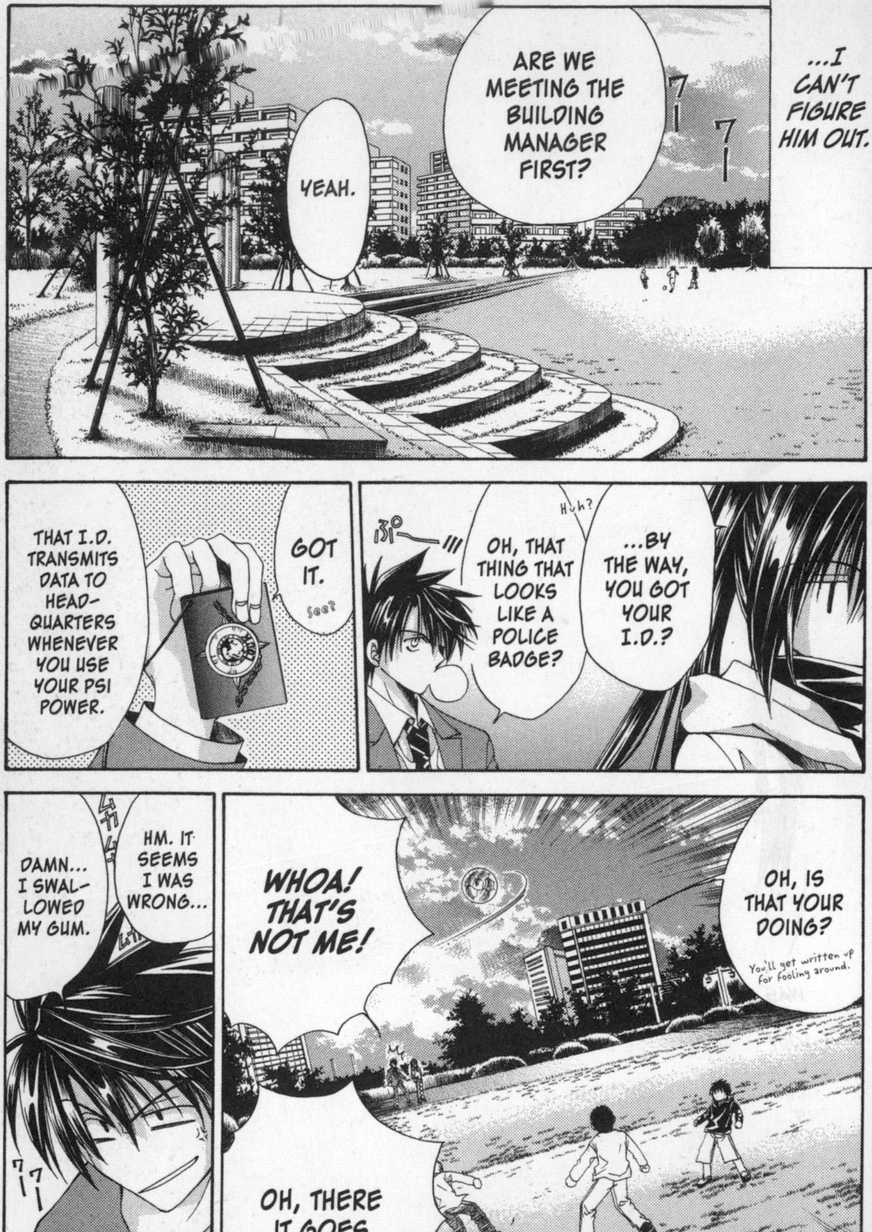
...I CAN'T FIGURE HIM OUT.
ARE WE MEETING THE BUILDING MANAGER FIRST?
YEAH.
...BY THE WAY, YOU GOT YOUR I.D.?
Huh?
OH, THAT THING THAT LOOKS LIKE A POLICE BADGE?
GOT IT.
See?
THAT I.D. TRANSMITS DATA TO HEAD-QUARTERS WHENEVER YOU USE YOUR PSI POWER.
OH, IS THAT YOUR DOING?
You'll get written up for fooling around.
WHOA! THAT'S NOT ME!
OH, THERE IT GOES AGAIN!!
HM. IT SEEMS I WAS WRONG...
DAMN... I SWAL-LOWED MY GUM.

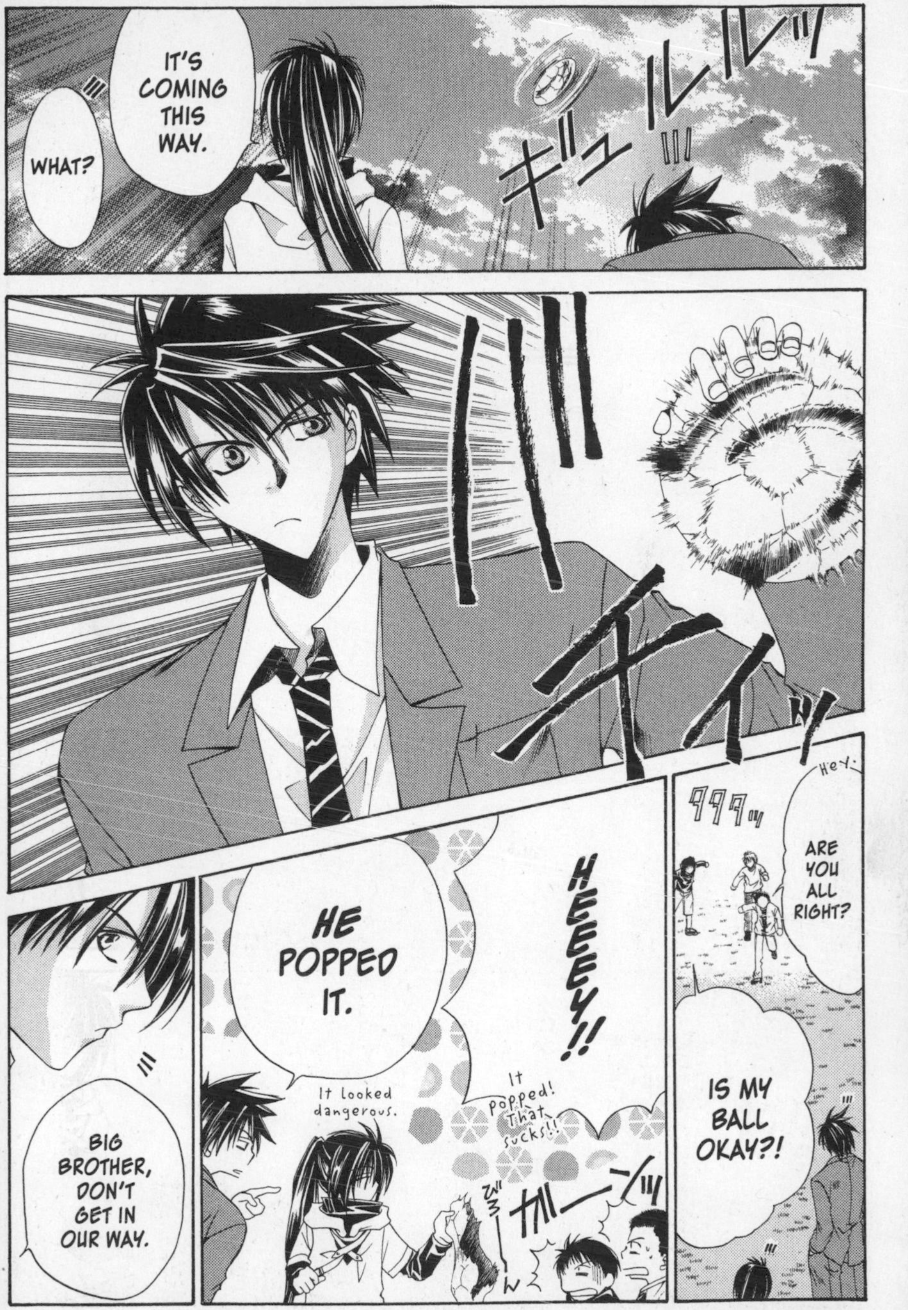
IT'S COMING THIS WAY.
WHAT?
ギュルルッ
Hey.
ARE YOU ALL RIGHT?
タタタッ
IS MY BALL OKAY?!
HEEEEY!!
HE POPPED IT.
It popped! That sucks!!
It looked dangerous.
BIG BROTHER, DON'T GET IN OUR WAY.

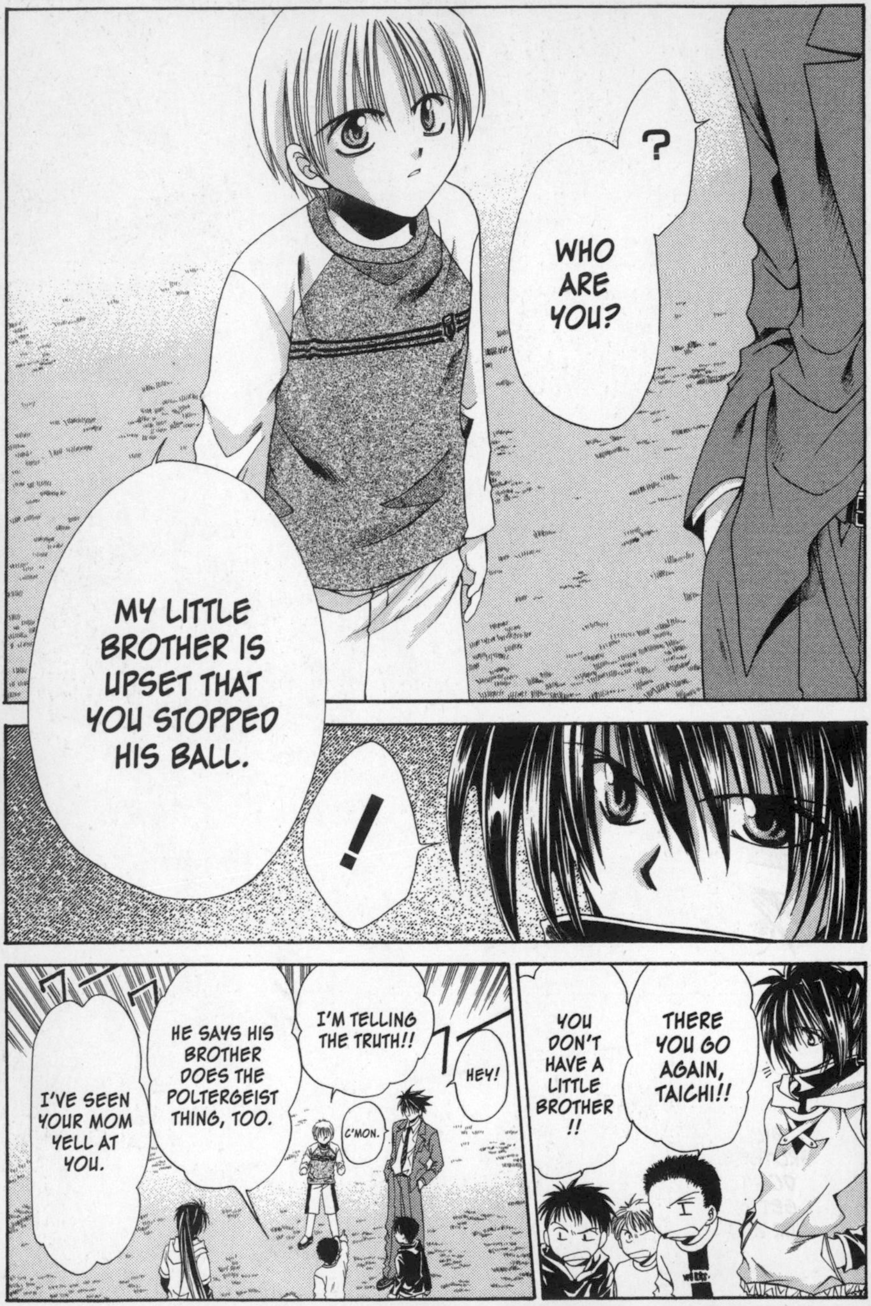
?
WHO ARE YOU?
MY LITTLE BROTHER IS UPSET THAT YOU STOPPED HIS BALL.
!
THERE YOU GO AGAIN, TAICHI!!
YOU DON'T HAVE A LITTLE BROTHER !!
I'M TELLING THE TRUTH!!
HEY!
C'MON.
HE SAYS HIS BROTHER DOES THE POLTERGEIST THING, TOO.
I'VE SEEN YOUR MOM YELL AT YOU.

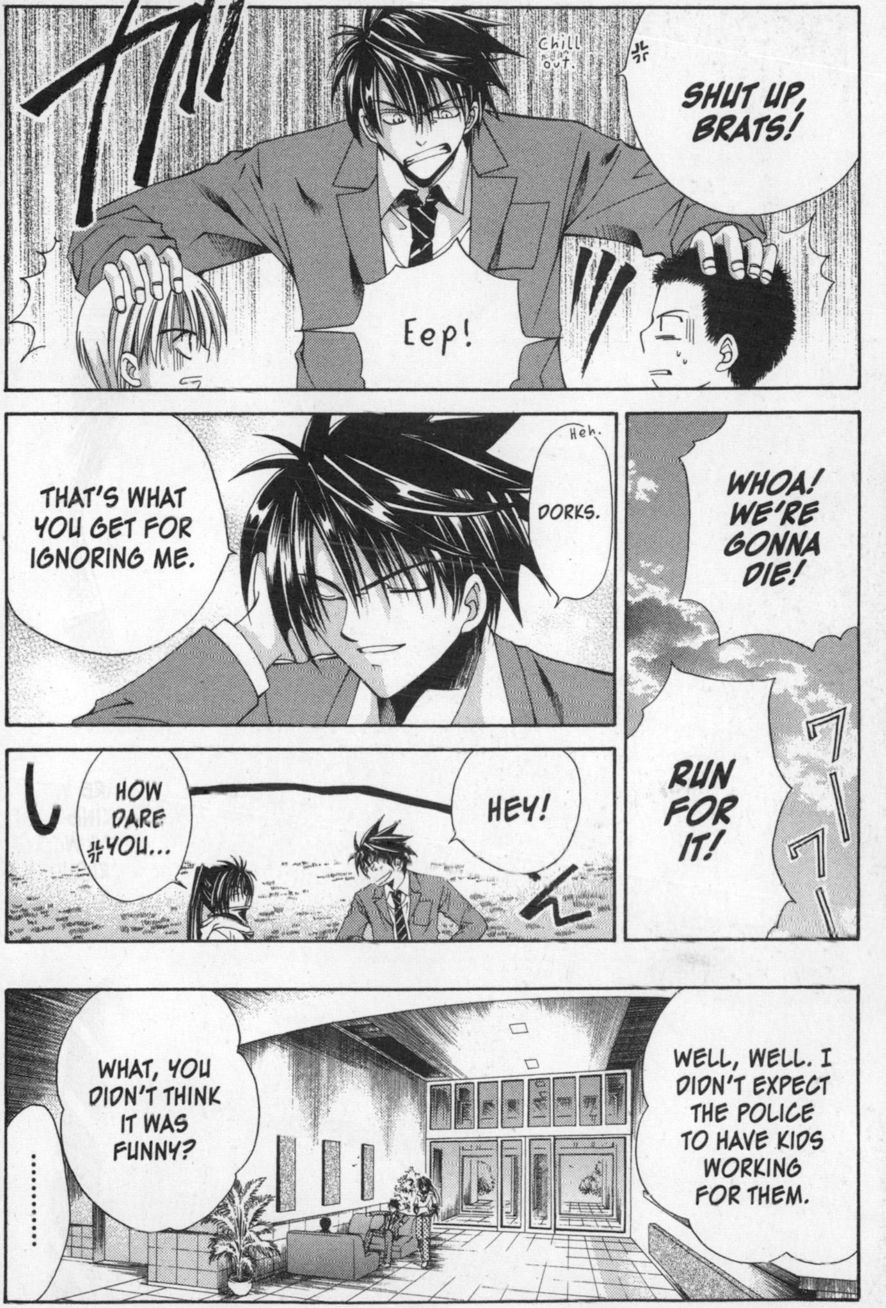
SHUT UP, BRATS!
Chill out.
Eep!
WHOA! WE'RE GONNA DIE!
RUN FOR IT!
Heh.
DORKS.
THAT'S WHAT YOU GET FOR IGNORING ME.
HEY!
HOW DARE YOU...
WELL, WELL. I DIDN'T EXPECT THE POLICE TO HAVE KIDS WORKING FOR THEM.
WHAT, YOU DIDN'T THINK IT WAS FUNNY?
....

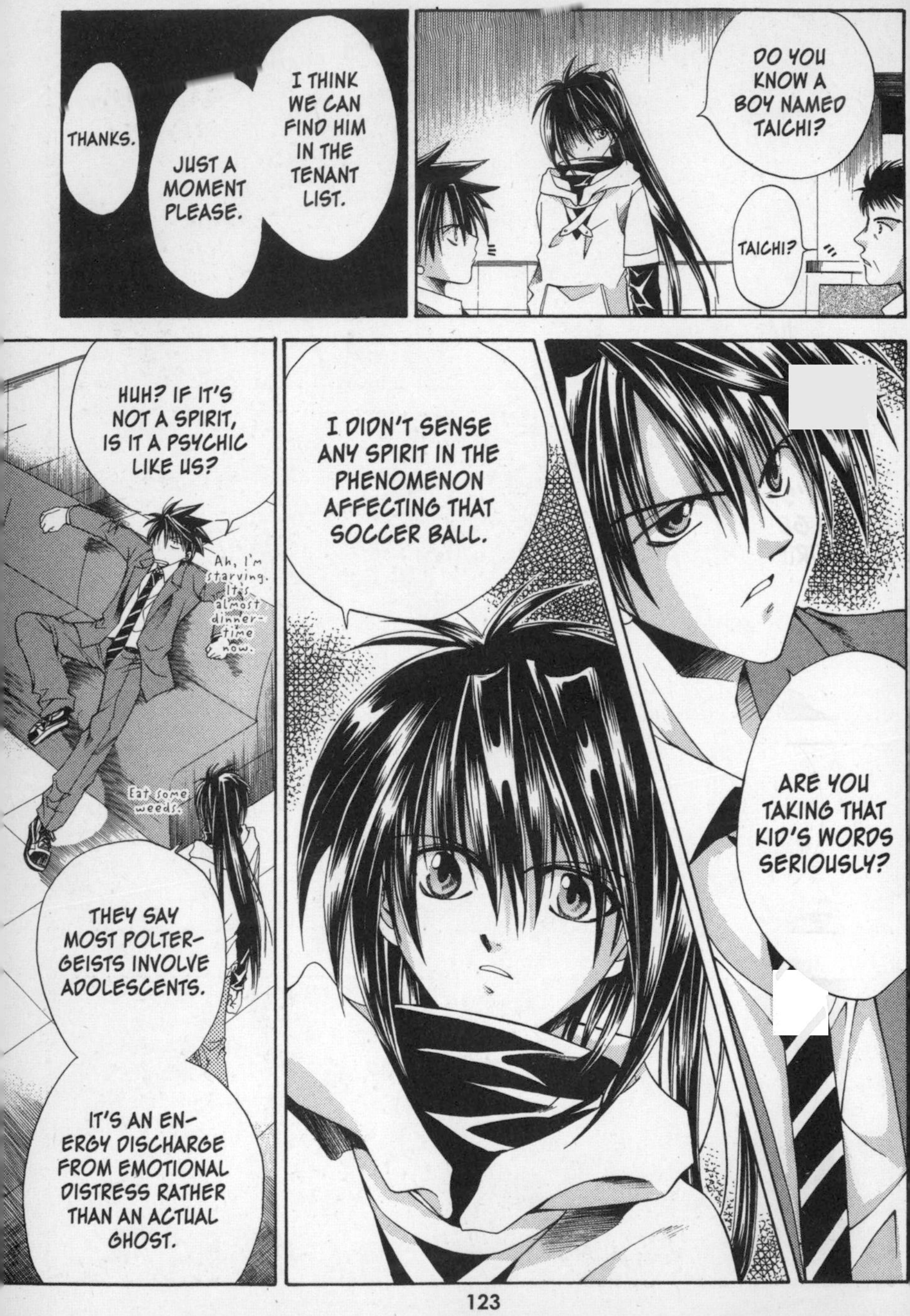
DO YOU KNOW A BOY NAMED TAICHI?
TAICHI?
I THINK WE CAN FIND HIM IN THE TENANT LIST.
JUST A MOMENT PLEASE.
THANKS.
ARE YOU TAKING THAT KID'S WORDS SERIOUSLY?
I DIDN'T SENSE ANY SPIRIT IN THE PHENOMENON AFFECTING THAT SOCCER BALL.
HUH? IF IT'S NOT A SPIRIT, IS IT A PSYCHIC LIKE US?
Ah, I'm starving. It's almost dinner-time now.
Eat some weeds.
THEY SAY MOST POLTER-GEISTS INVOLVE ADOLESCENTS.
IT'S AN EN-ERGY DISCHARGE FROM EMOTIONAL DISTRESS RATHER THAN AN ACTUAL GHOST.

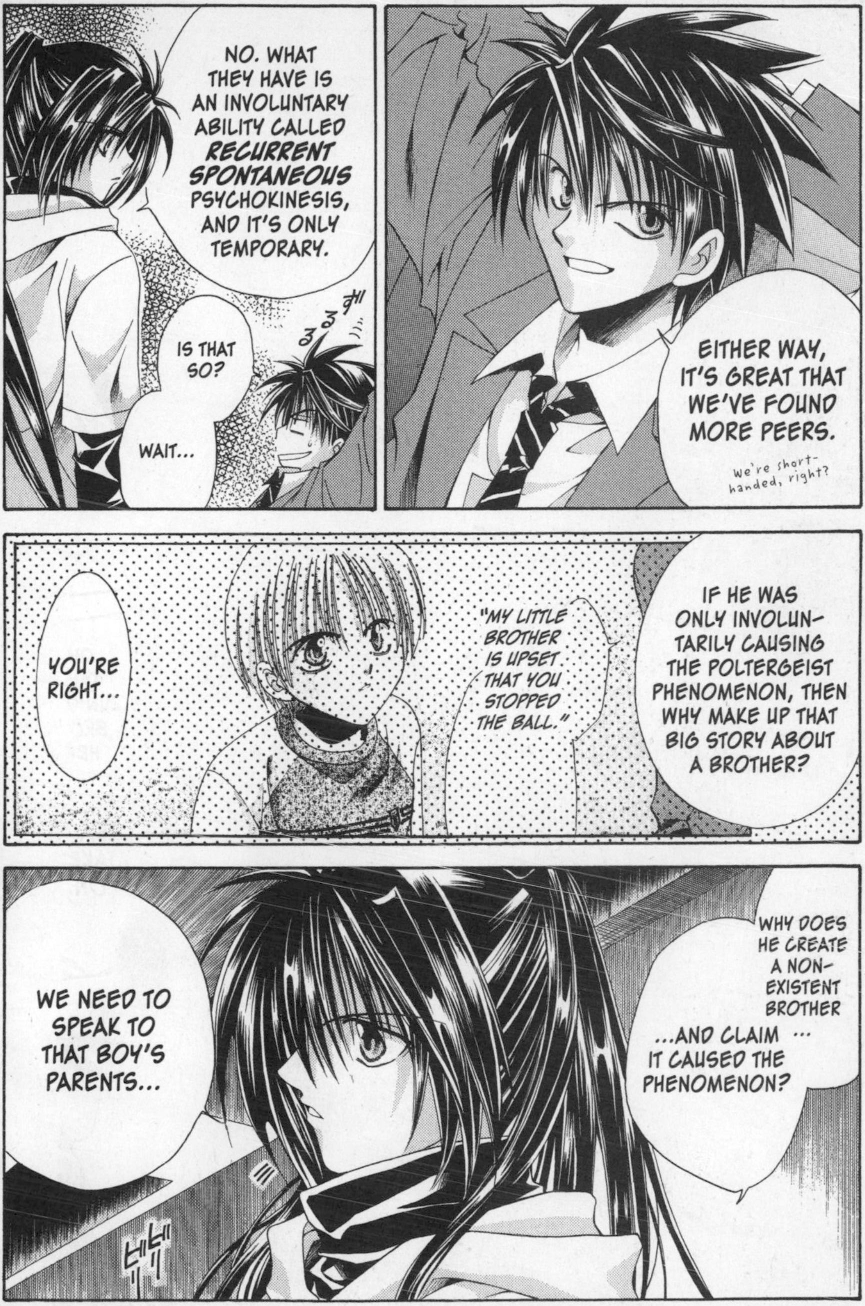
EITHER WAY, IT'S GREAT THAT WE'VE FOUND MORE PEERS.
We're short-handed, right?
NO. WHAT THEY HAVE IS AN INVOLUNTARY ABILITY CALLED ***RECURRENT SPONTANEOUS*** PSYCHOKINESIS, AND IT'S ONLY TEMPORARY.
IS THAT SO?
WAIT...
IF HE WAS ONLY INVOLUNTARILY CAUSING THE POLTERGEIST PHENOMENON, THEN WHY MAKE UP THAT BIG STORY ABOUT A BROTHER?
"MY LITTLE BROTHER IS UPSET THAT YOU STOPPED THE BALL."
YOU'RE RIGHT...
WHY DOES HE CREATE A NON-EXISTENT BROTHER ...
...AND CLAIM IT CAUSED THE PHENOMENON?
WE NEED TO SPEAK TO THAT BOY'S PARENTS...

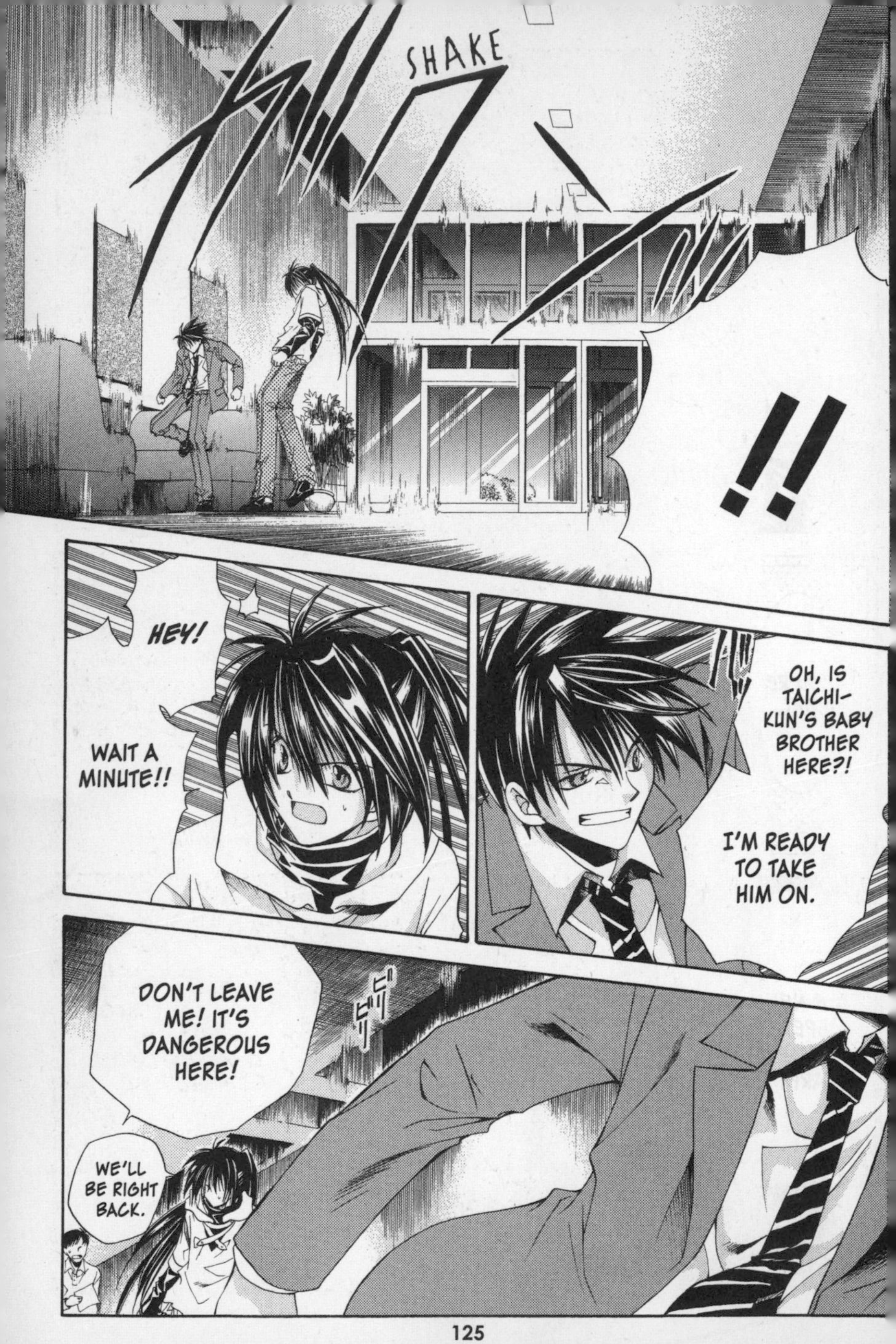
SHAKE
!!
OH, IS TAICHI-KUN'S BABY BROTHER HERE?!
I'M READY TO TAKE HIM ON.
HEY!
WAIT A MINUTE!!
DON'T LEAVE ME! IT'S DANGEROUS HERE!
WE'LL BE RIGHT BACK.

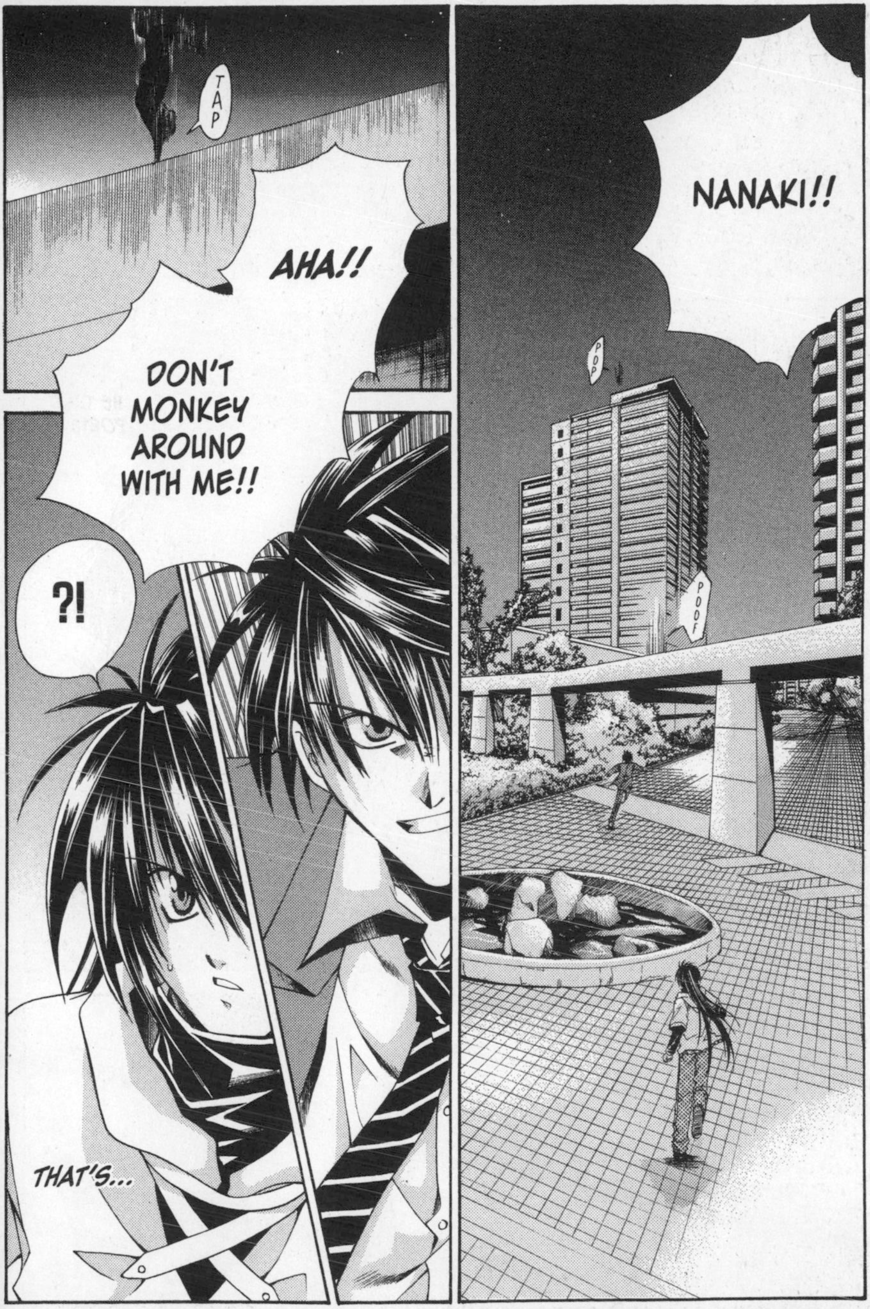

NANAKI!!
PDP
PDOF
TAP
AHA!!
DON'T MONKEY AROUND WITH ME!!
?!
THAT'S...

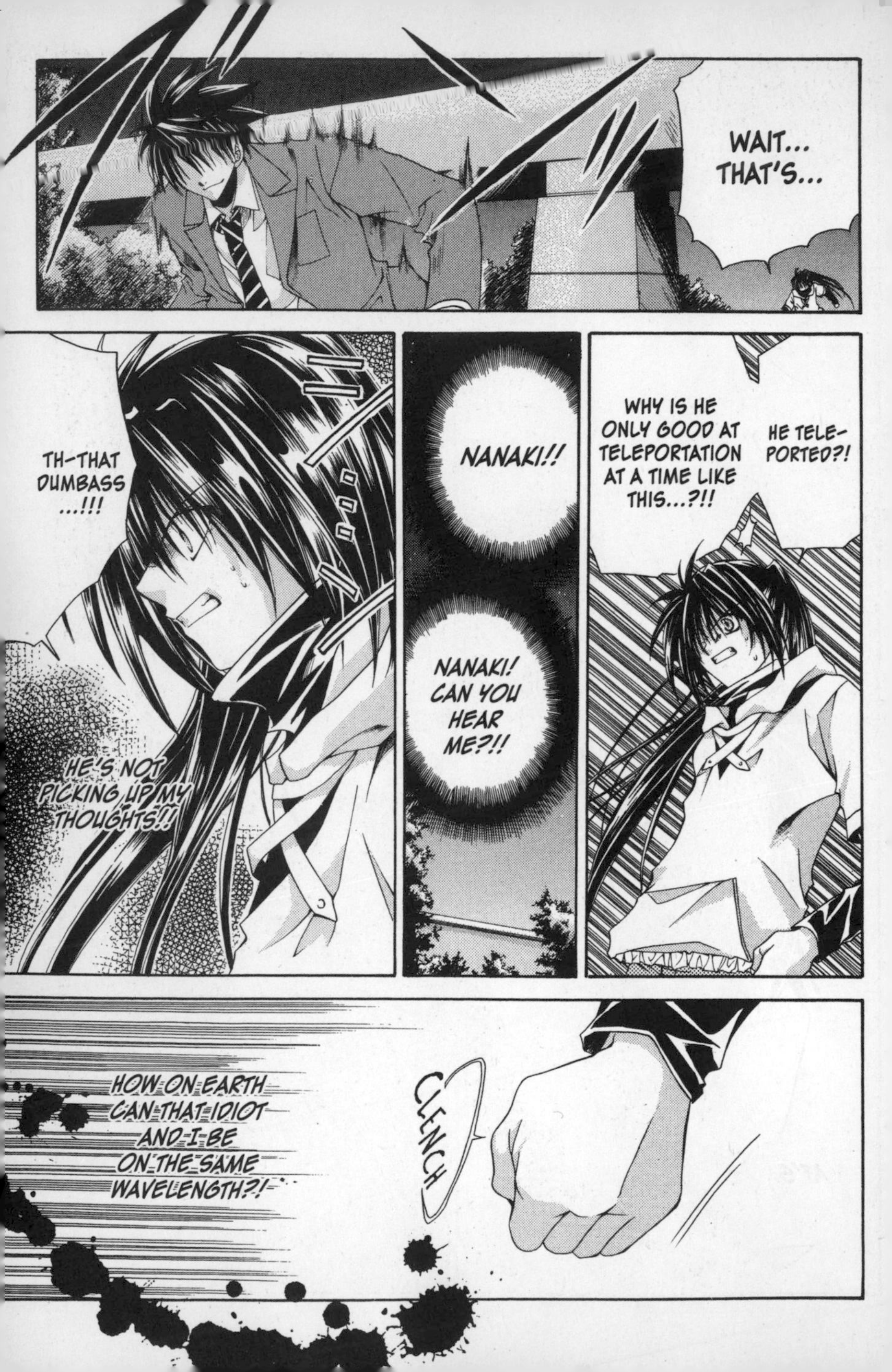
WAIT... THAT'S...
HE TELE-PORTED?!
WHY IS HE ONLY GOOD AT TELEPORTATION AT A TIME LIKE THIS...?!!
NANAKI!!
NANAKI! CAN YOU HEAR ME?!!
TH-THAT DUMBASS ...!!!
HE'S NOT PICKING UP MY THOUGHTS!!
CLENCH
HOW ON EARTH CAN THAT IDIOT AND I BE ON THE SAME WAVELENGTH?!

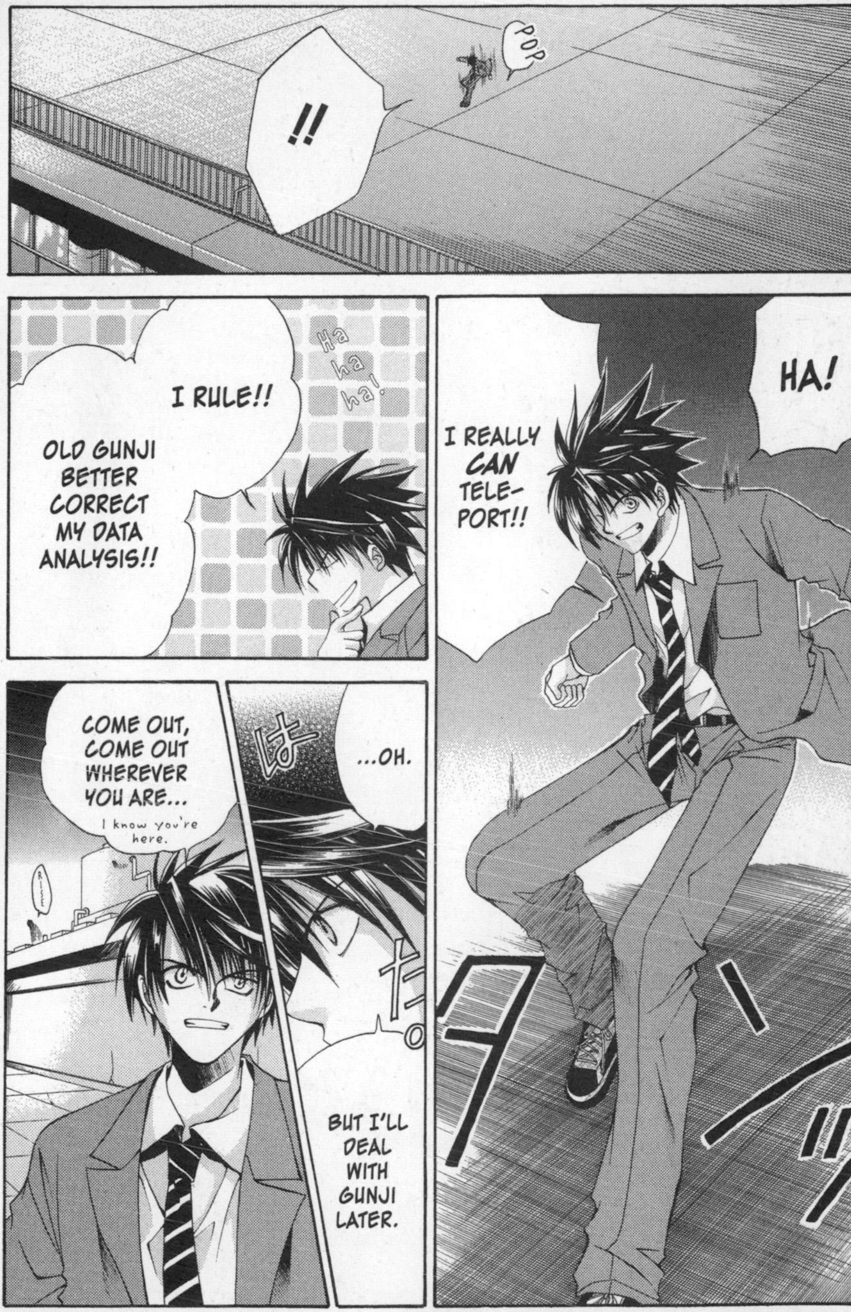

POP
!!
HA!
I REALLY CAN TELE-PORT!!
I RULE!!
Ha ha ha!
OLD GUNJI BETTER CORRECT MY DATA ANALYSIS!!
は
...OH.
BUT I'LL DEAL WITH GUNJI LATER.
COME OUT, COME OUT WHEREVER YOU ARE...
I know you're here.
RISE

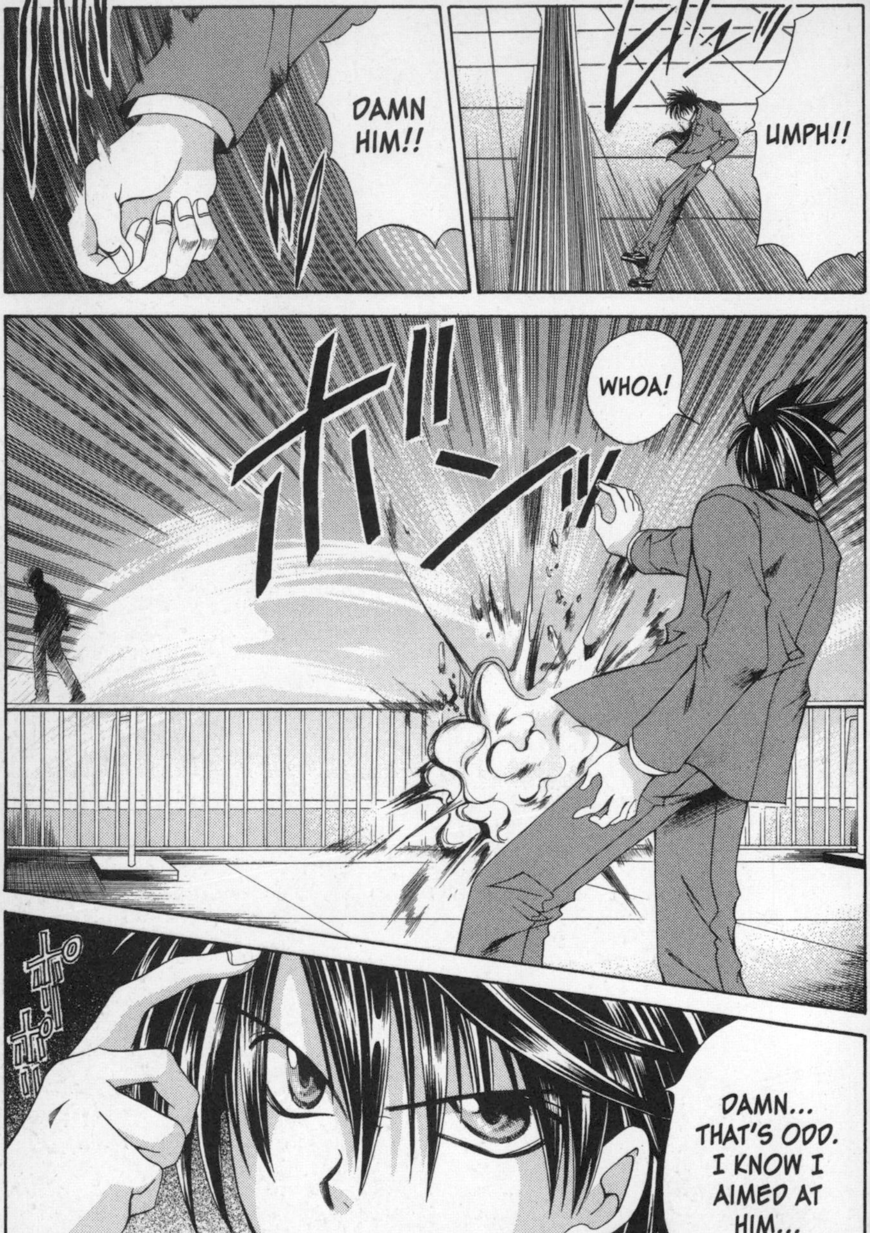
UMPH!!
DAMN HIM!!
WHOA!
DAMN... THAT'S ODD. I KNOW I AIMED AT HIM...

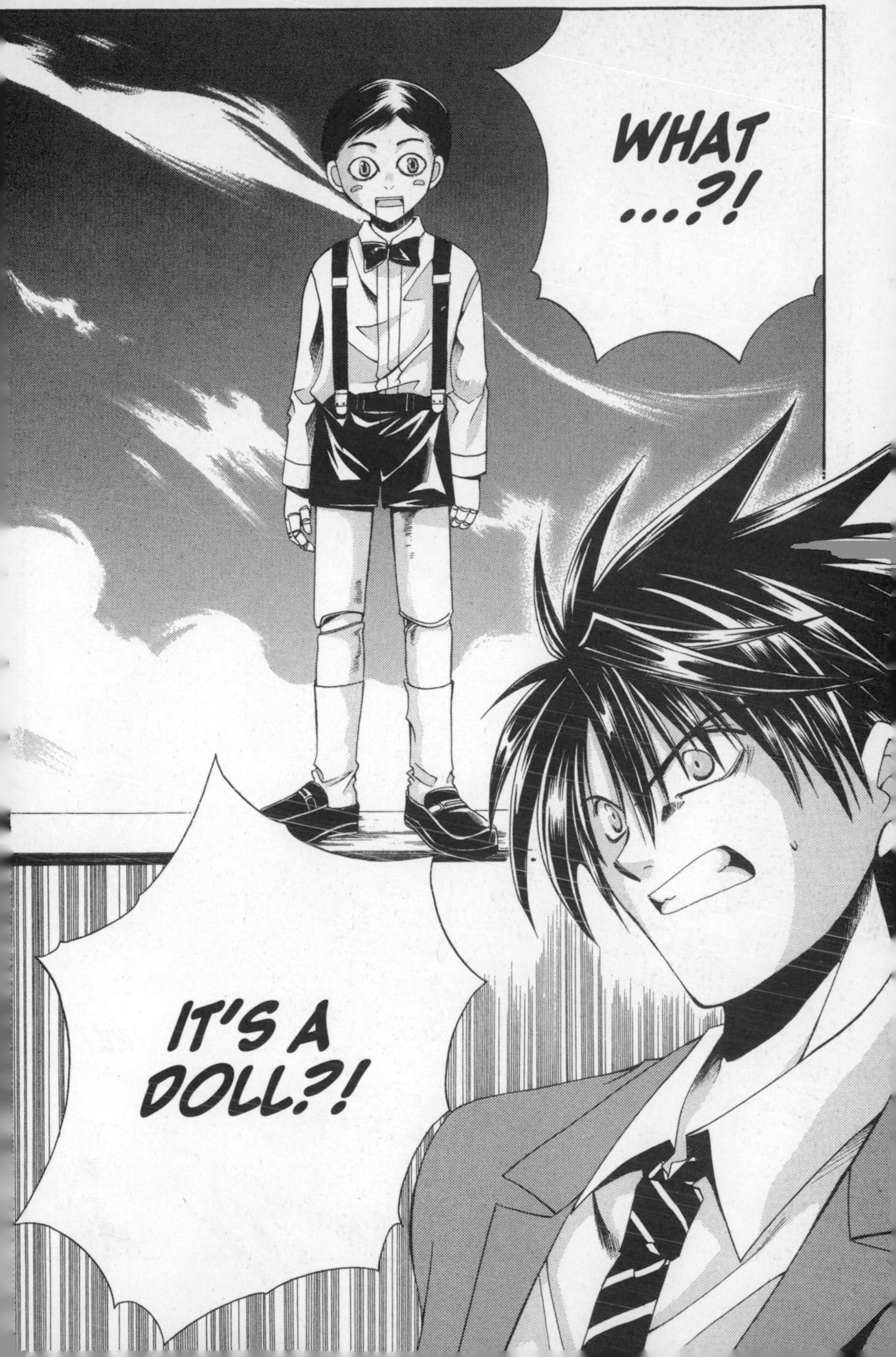
WHAT ...?!
IT'S A DOLL?!

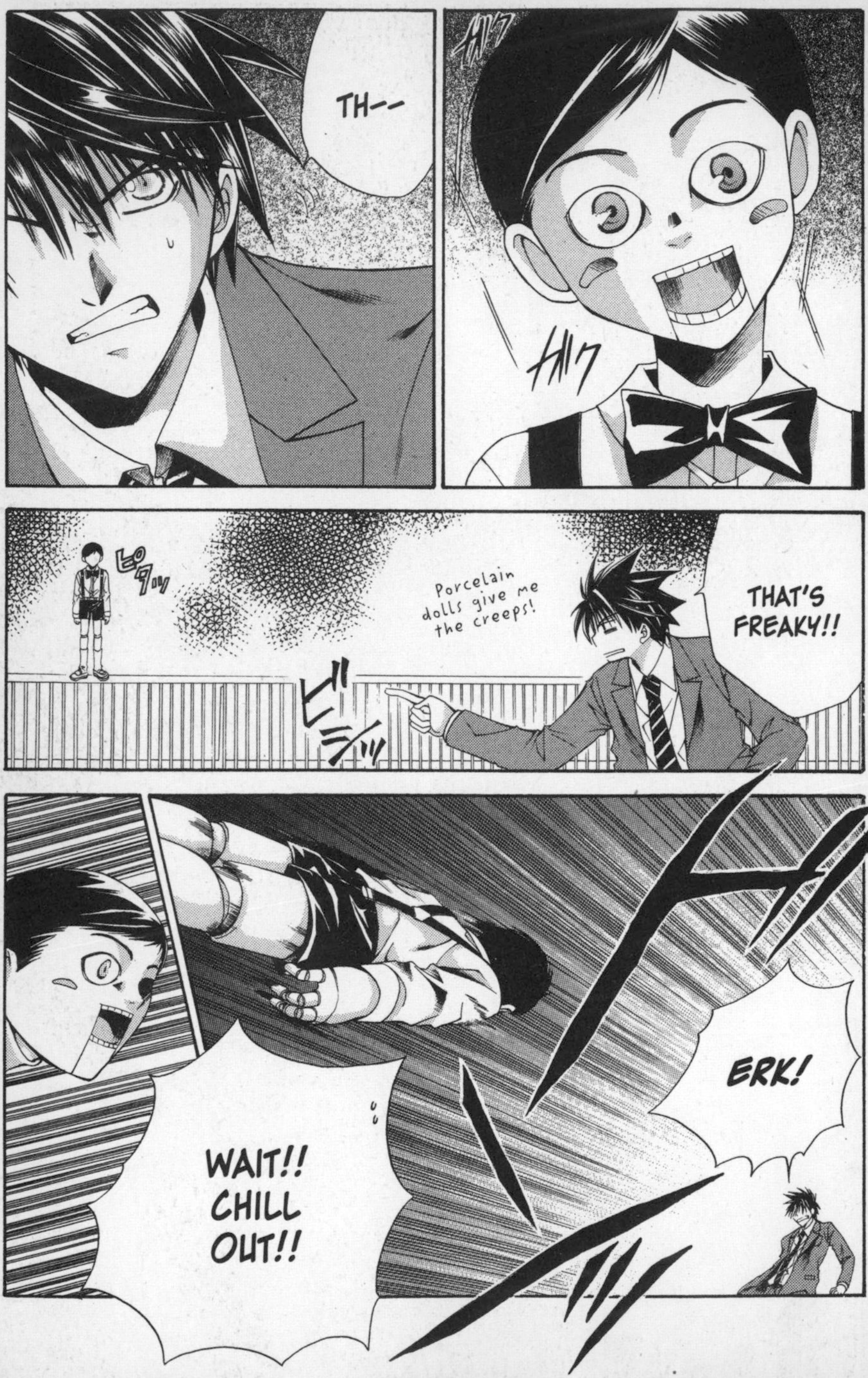
TH--
THAT'S FREAKY!!
Porcelain dolls give me the creeps!
ERK!
WAIT!! CHILL OUT!!

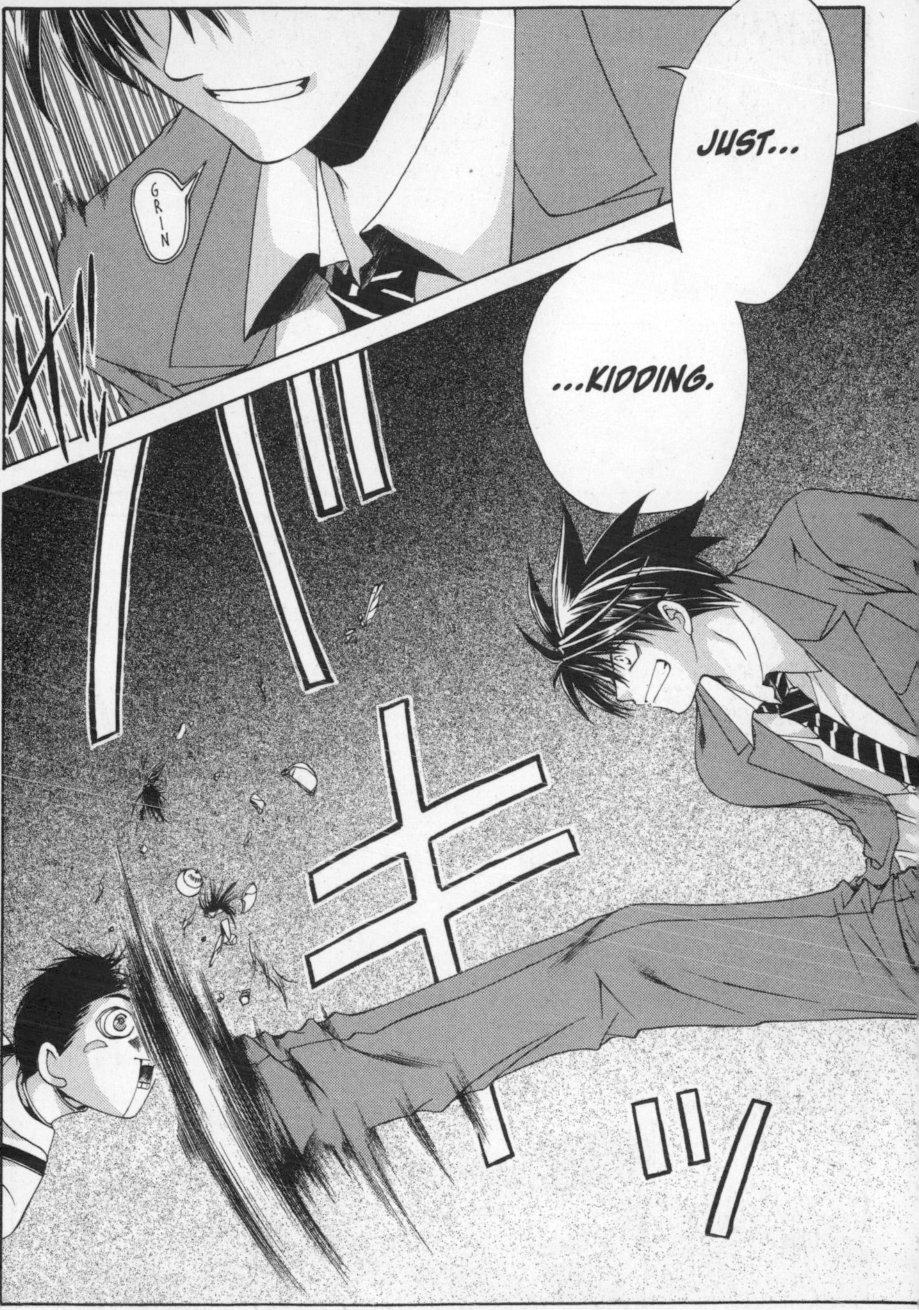
JUST...
GRIN
...KIDDING.

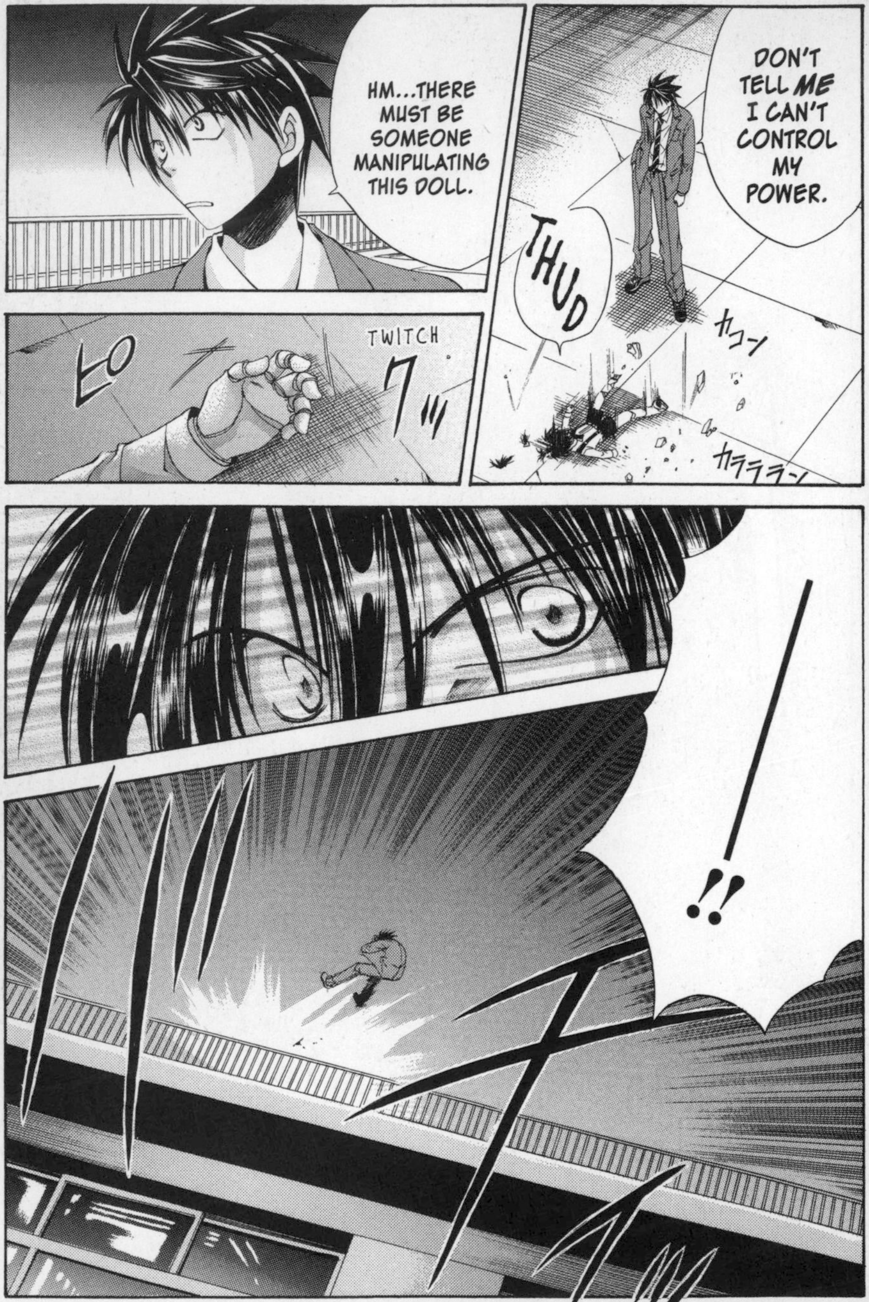
DON'T TELL *ME* I CAN'T CONTROL MY POWER.
THUD
カコーン
カラララーン
HM...THERE MUST BE SOMEONE MANIPULATING THIS DOLL.
TWITCH
ピクッ
!!

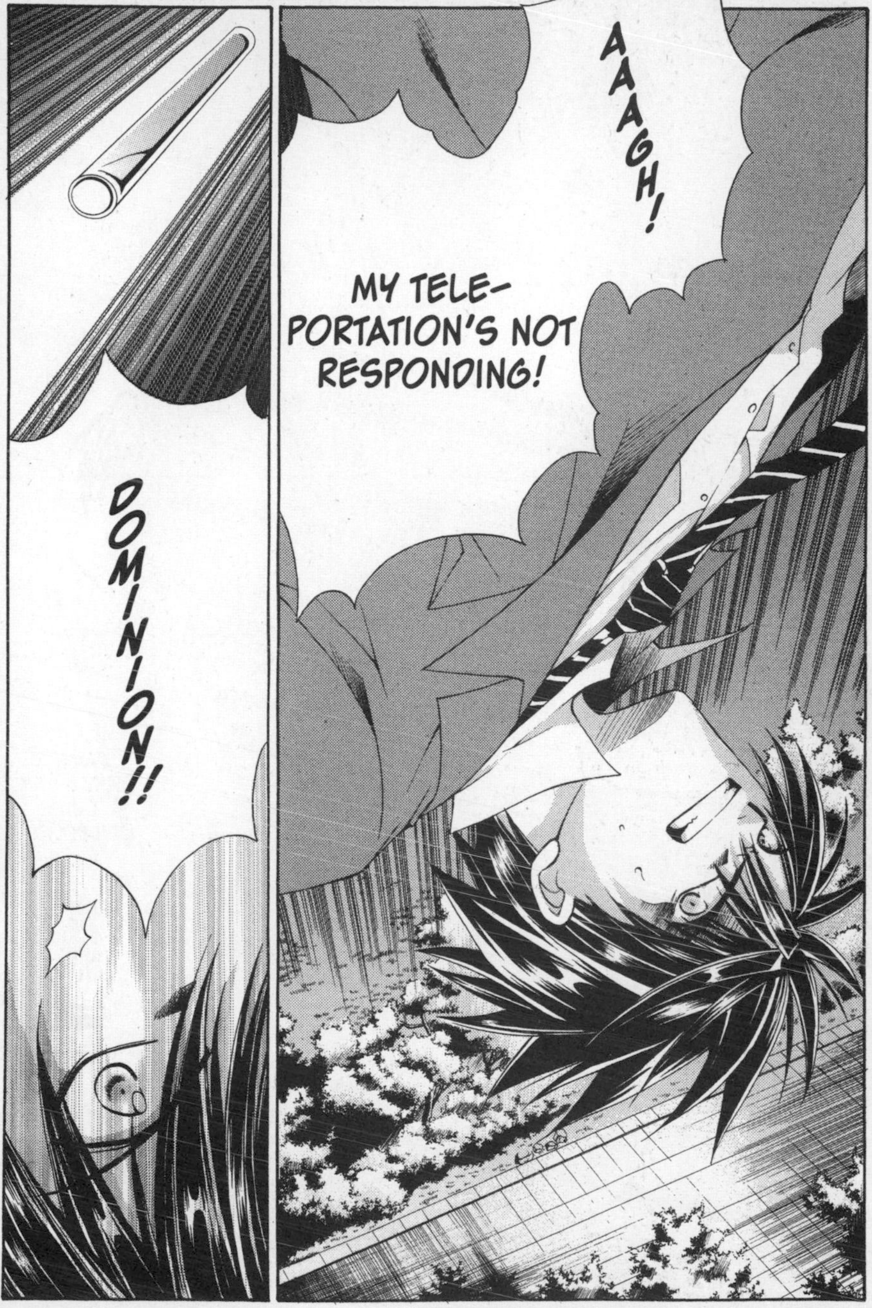
AAAGH!
MY TELE-PORTATION'S NOT RESPONDING!
DOMINION!!

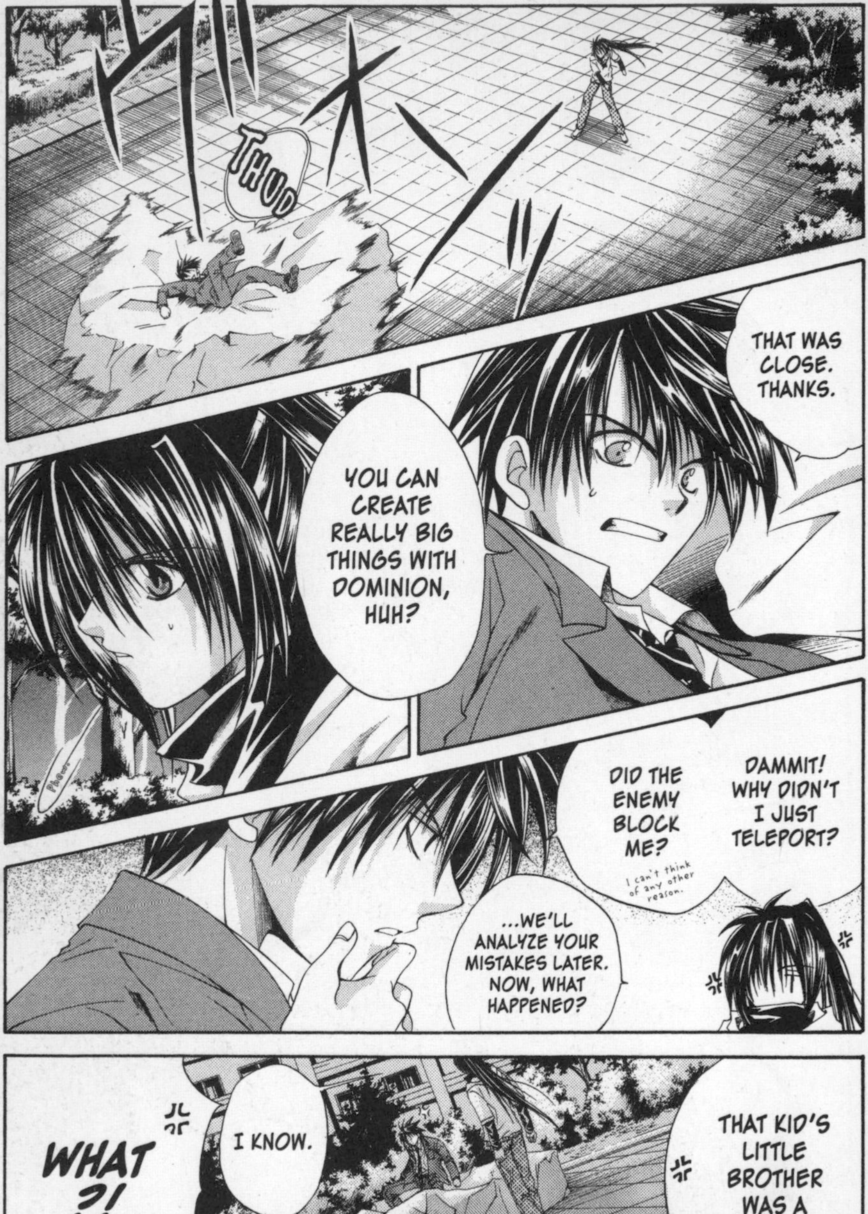
THUD
THAT WAS CLOSE. THANKS.
YOU CAN CREATE REALLY BIG THINGS WITH DOMINION, HUH?
Phew
DAMMIT! WHY DIDN'T I JUST TELEPORT?
DID THE ENEMY BLOCK ME?
I can't think of any other reason.
...WE'LL ANALYZE YOUR MISTAKES LATER. NOW, WHAT HAPPENED?
THAT KID'S LITTLE BROTHER WAS A DOLL.
I KNOW.
WHAT?!

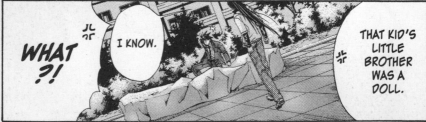

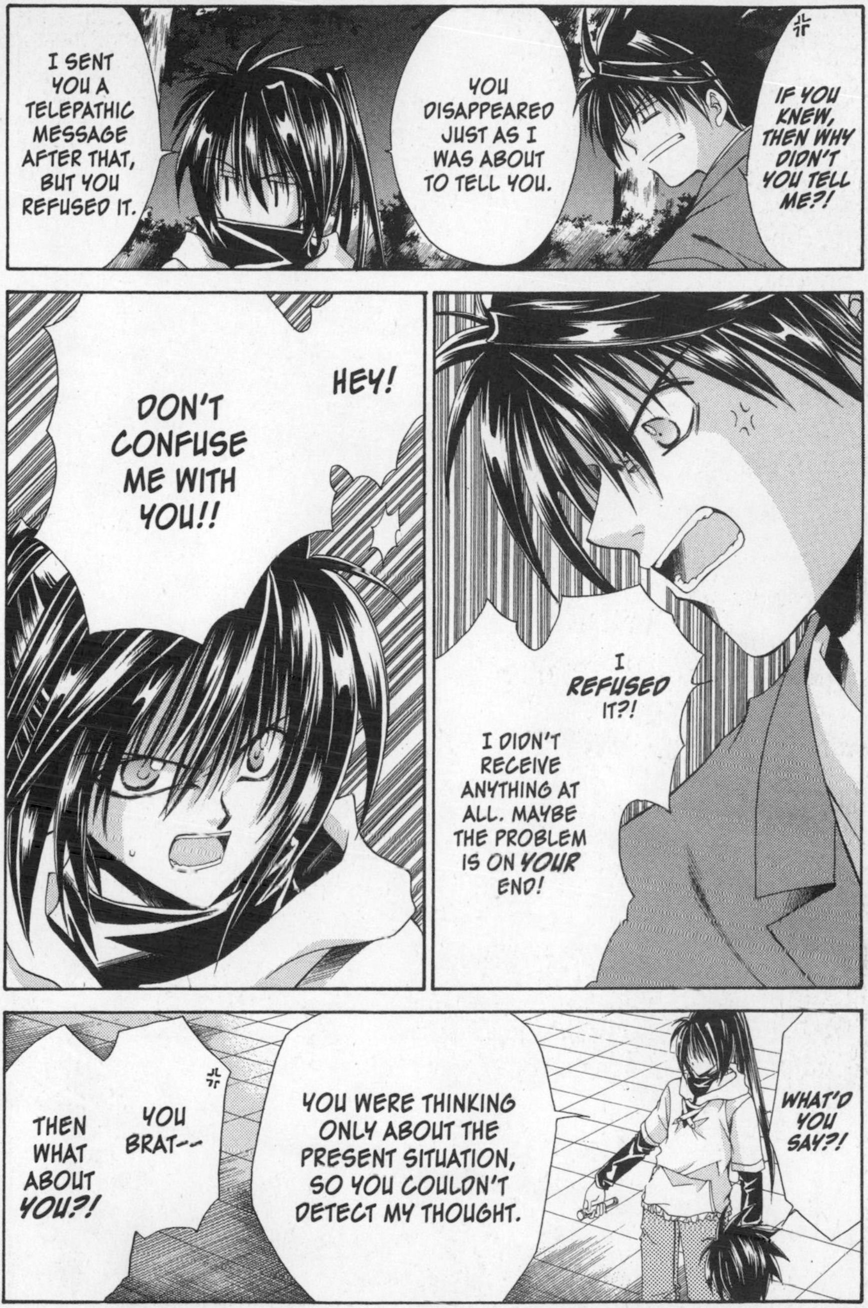
IF YOU KNEW, THEN WHY DIDN'T YOU TELL ME?!
YOU DISAPPEARED JUST AS I WAS ABOUT TO TELL YOU.
I SENT YOU A TELEPATHIC MESSAGE AFTER THAT, BUT YOU REFUSED IT.
I *REFUSED* IT?!
I DIDN'T RECEIVE ANYTHING AT ALL. MAYBE THE PROBLEM IS ON *YOUR* END!
HEY!
DON'T CONFUSE ME WITH YOU!!
WHAT'D YOU SAY?!
YOU WERE THINKING ONLY ABOUT THE PRESENT SITUATION, SO YOU COULDN'T DETECT MY THOUGHT.
YOU BRAT--
THEN WHAT ABOUT *YOU?!*

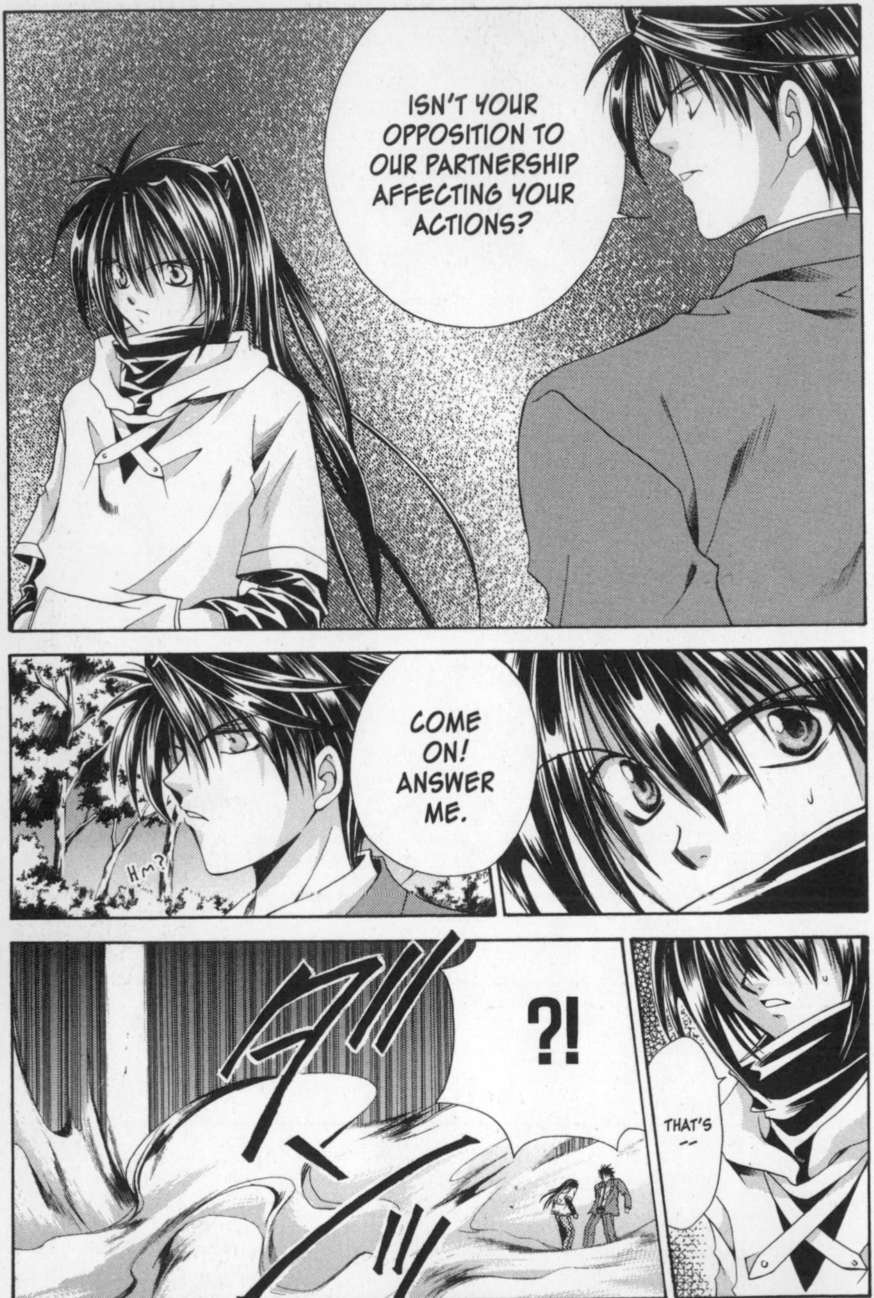
ISN'T YOUR OPPOSITION TO OUR PARTNERSHIP AFFECTING YOUR ACTIONS?
COME ON! ANSWER ME.
HM?
THAT'S --
?!

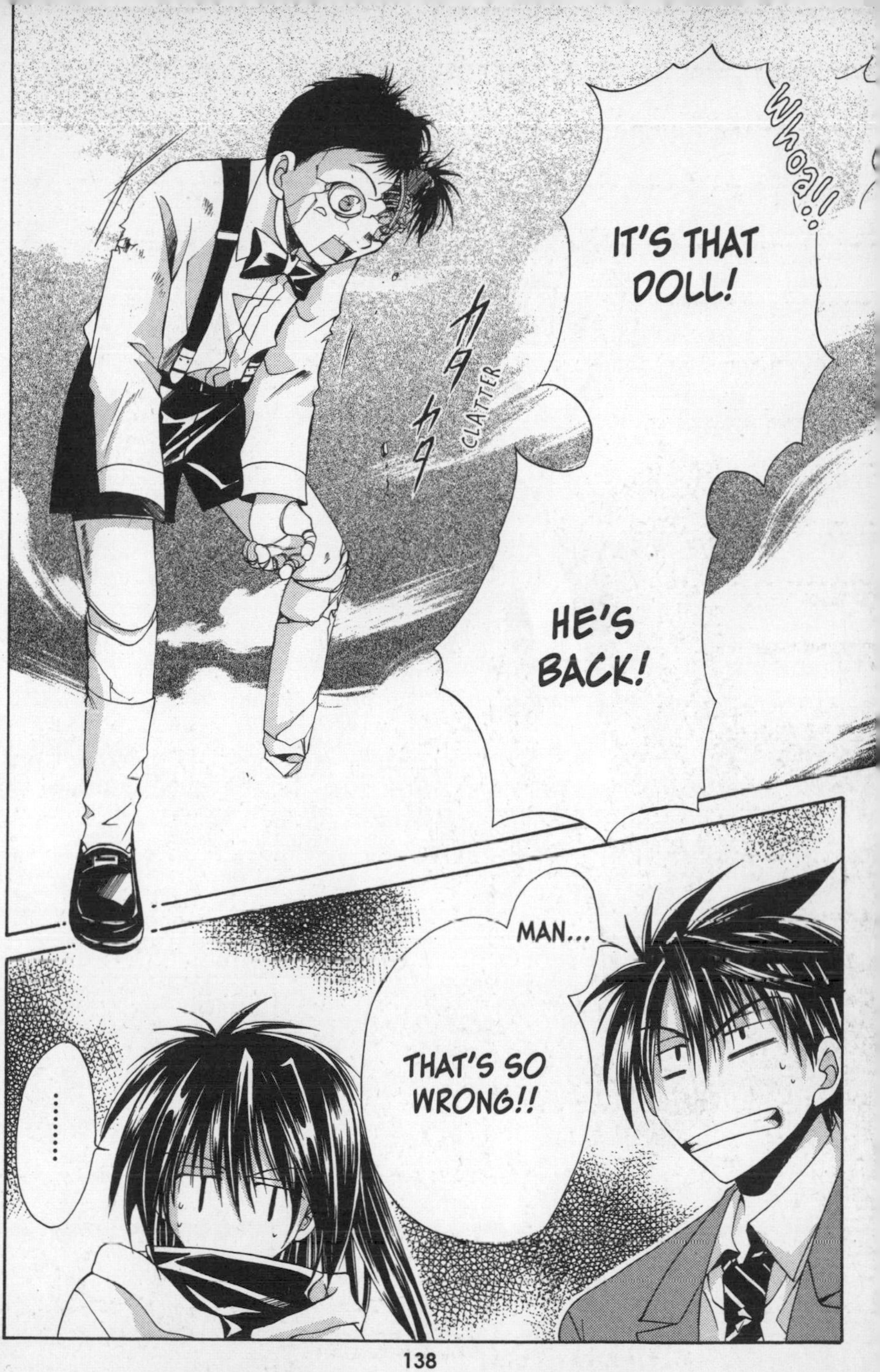
Whoa!!
IT'S THAT DOLL!
HE'S BACK!
カタカタ
CLATTER
MAN...
THAT'S SO WRONG!!
....

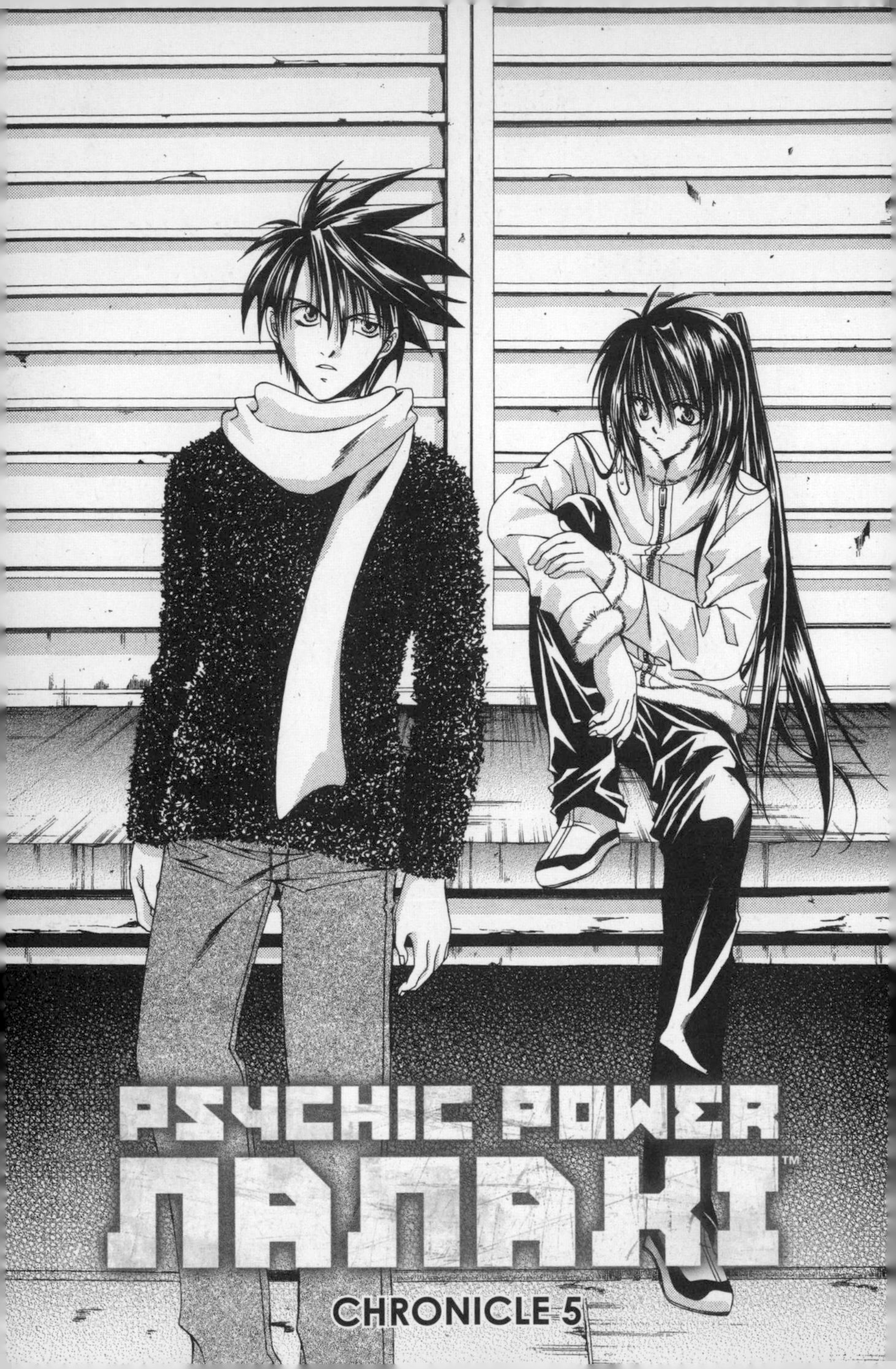
PSYCHIC POWER
NANAKI™
CHRONICLE 5

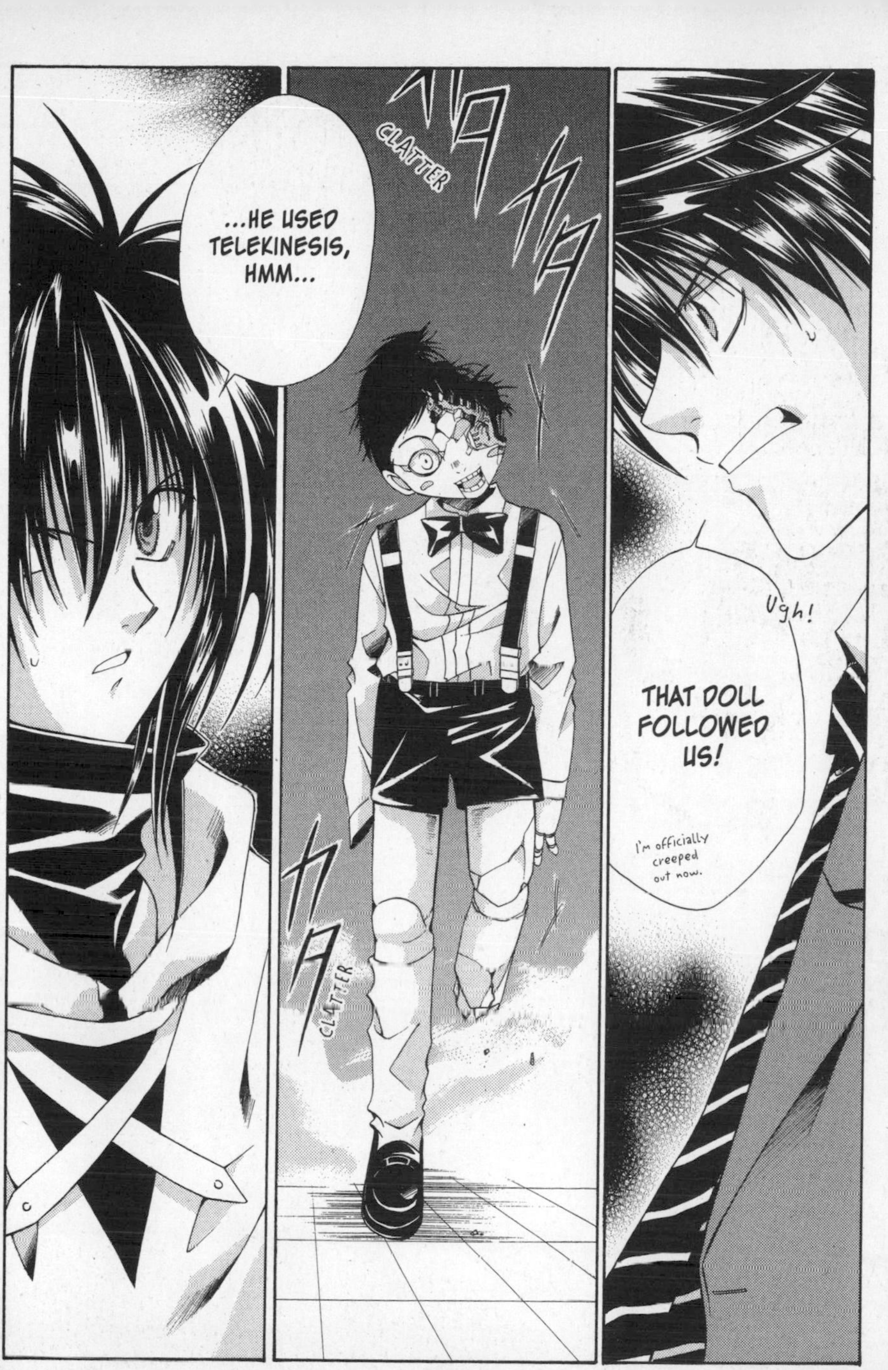
Ugh!
THAT DOLL FOLLOWED US!
I'm officially creeped out now.
CLATTER
CLATTER
...HE USED TELEKINESIS, HMM...

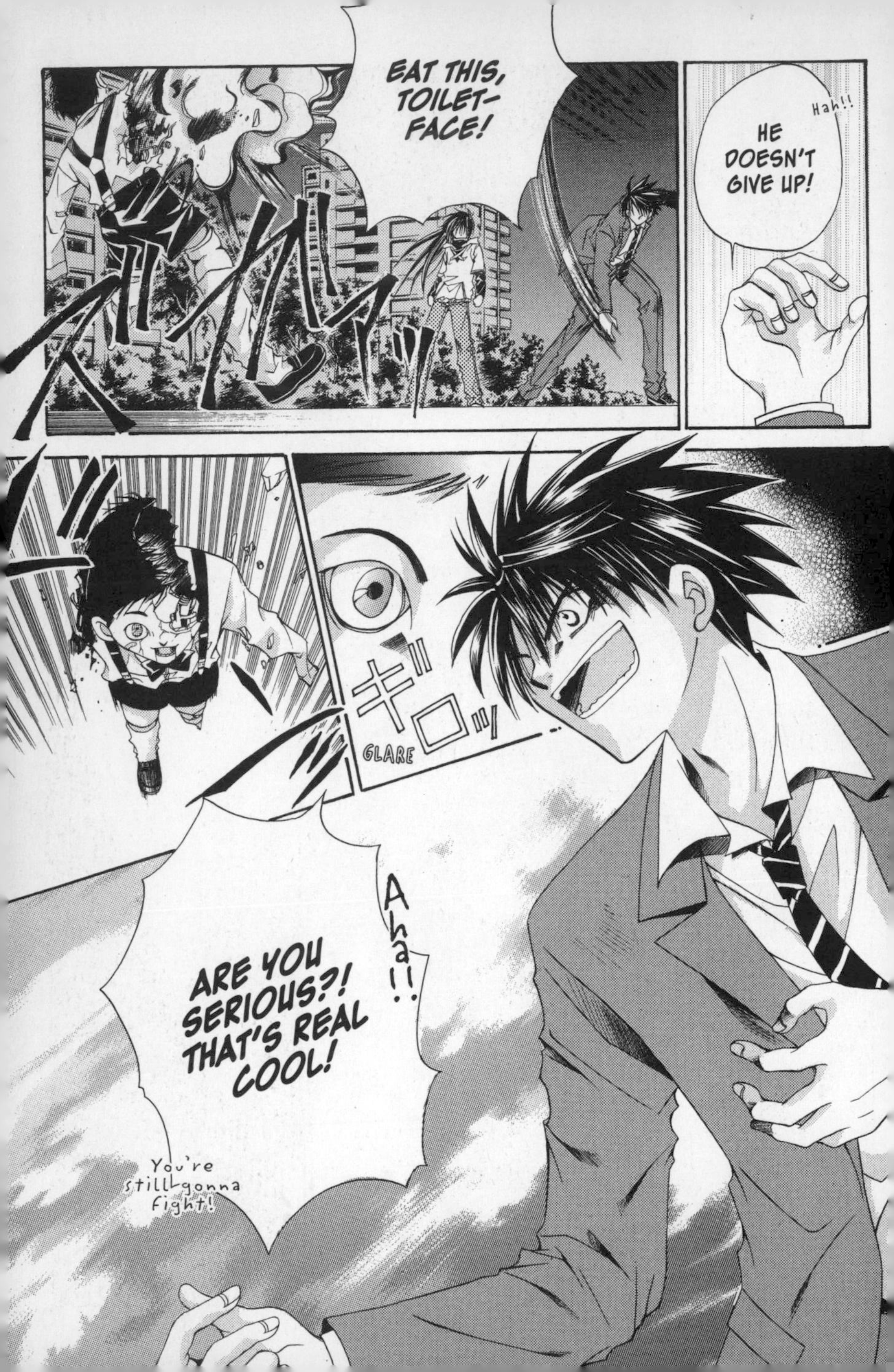
Hah!!
HE DOESN'T GIVE UP!
EAT THIS, TOILET-FACE!
ギロッ
GLARE
Aha!!
ARE YOU SERIOUS?! THAT'S REAL COOL!
You're still gonna fight!

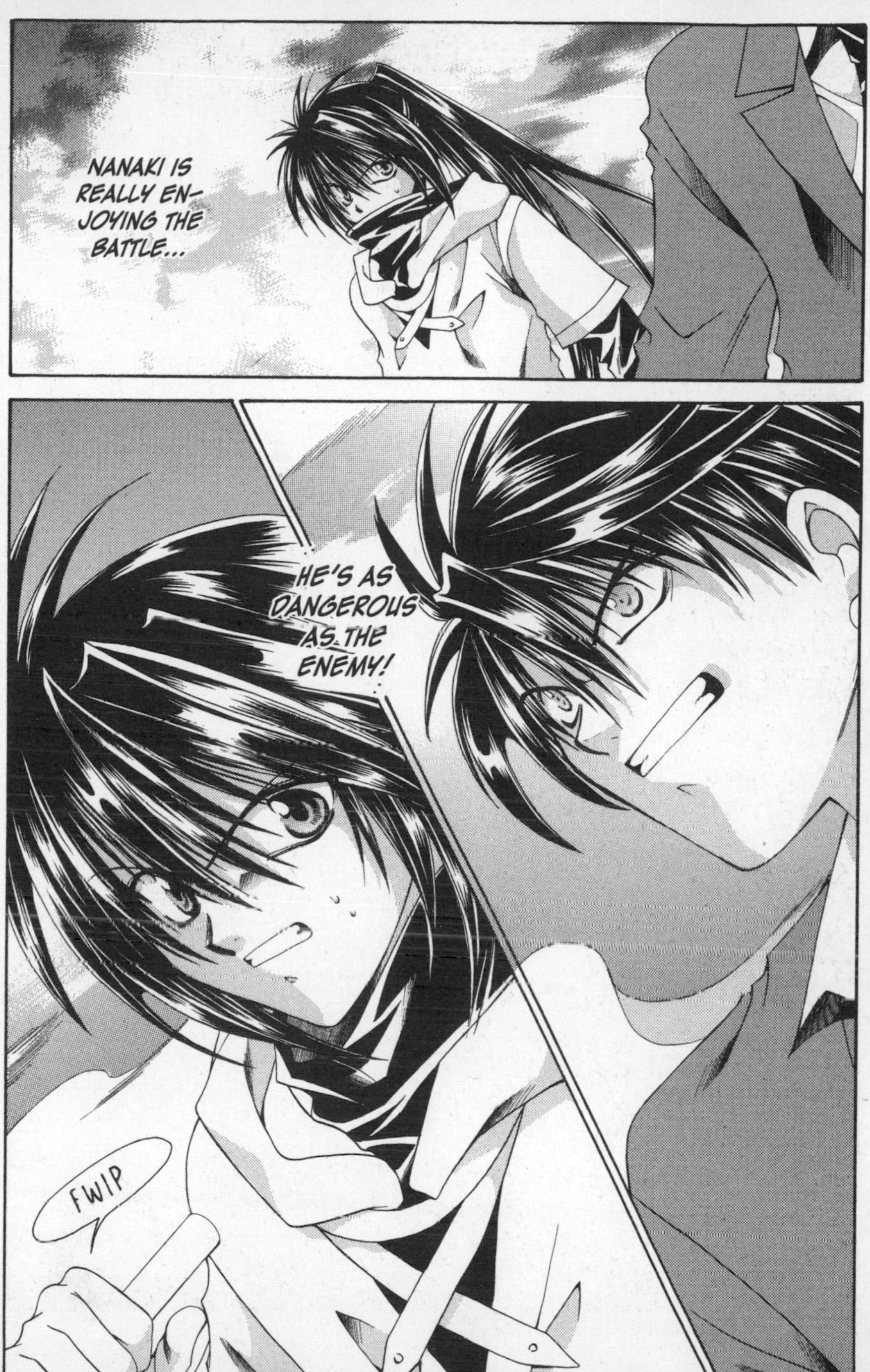
NANAKI IS REALLY EN-JOYING THE BATTLE...
HE'S AS DANGEROUS AS THE ENEMY!
FWIP

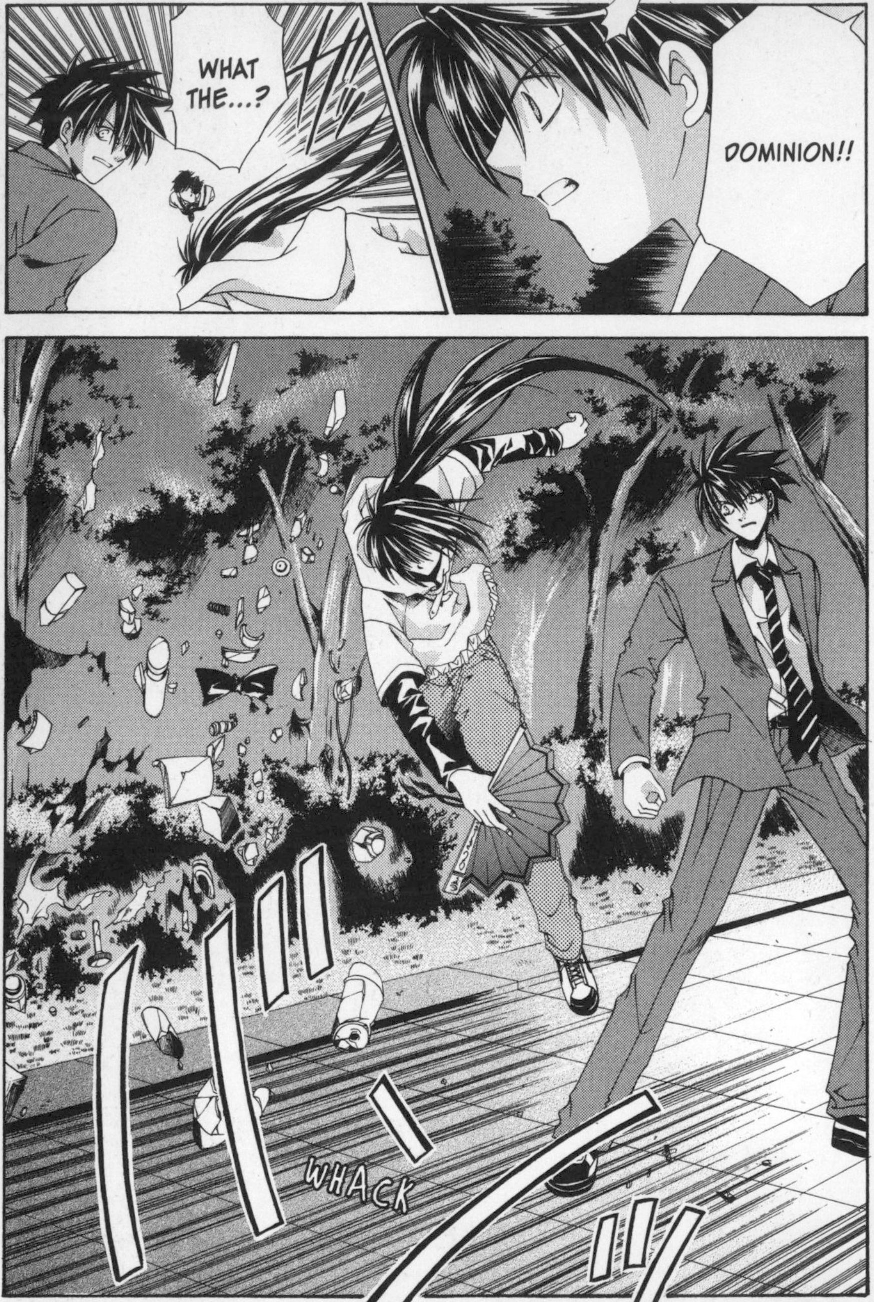
DOMINION!!
WHAT THE...?
WHACK

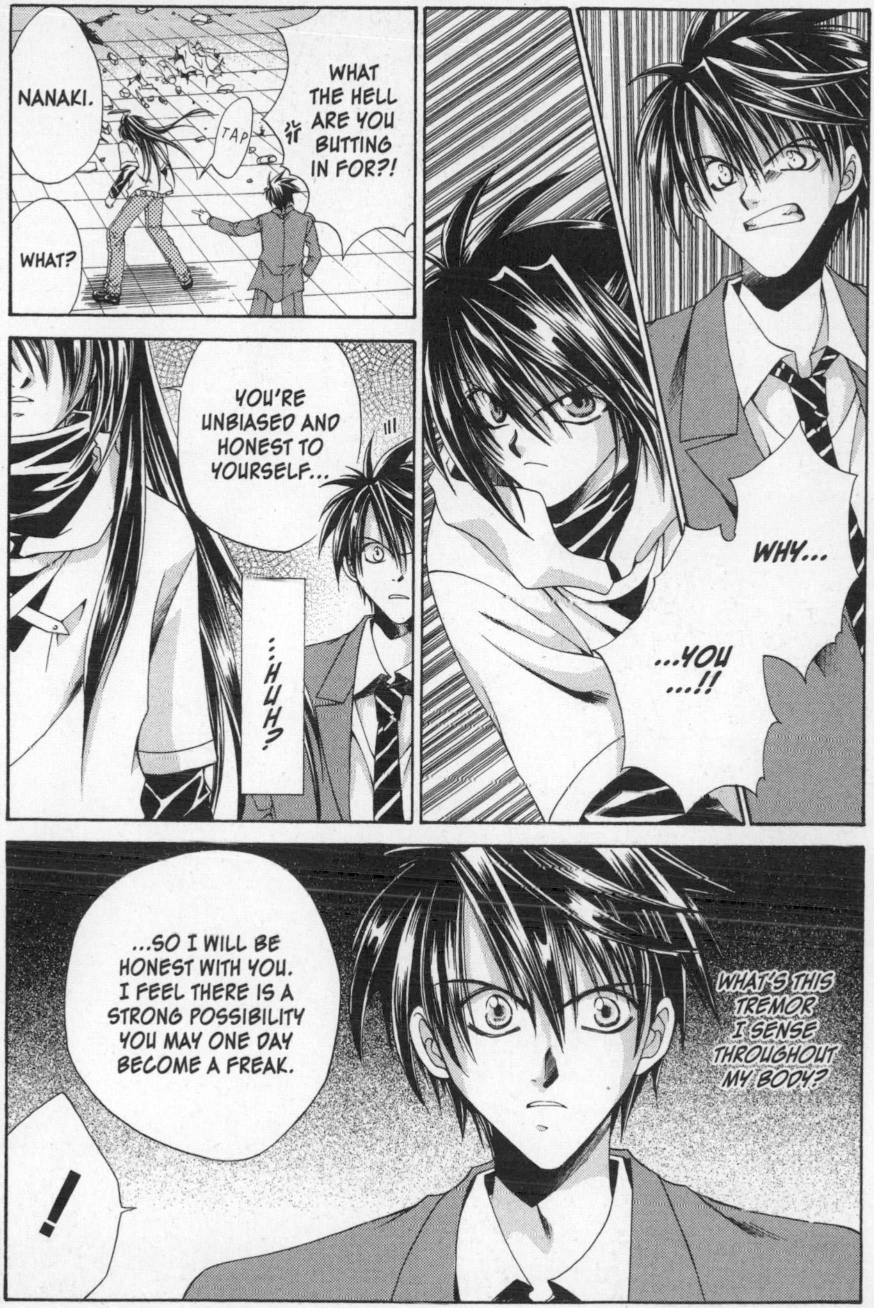
WHY...
...YOU ...!!
WHAT THE HELL ARE YOU BUTTING IN FOR?!
TAP
NANAKI.
WHAT?
YOU'RE UNBIASED AND HONEST TO YOURSELF...
...HUH?
WHAT'S THIS TREMOR I SENSE THROUGHOUT MY BODY?
...SO I WILL BE HONEST WITH YOU. I FEEL THERE IS A STRONG POSSIBILITY YOU MAY ONE DAY BECOME A FREAK.
!

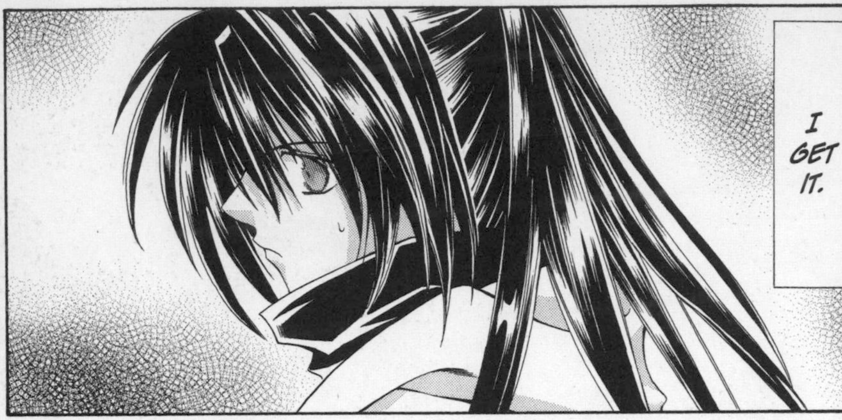
I GET IT.

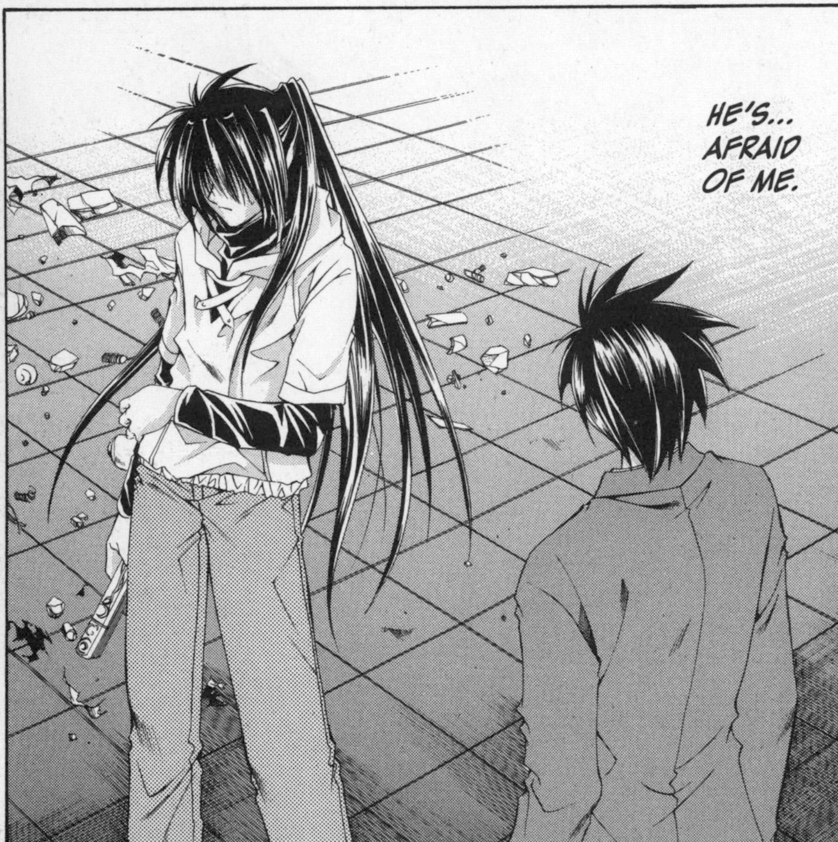
HE'S... AFRAID OF ME.

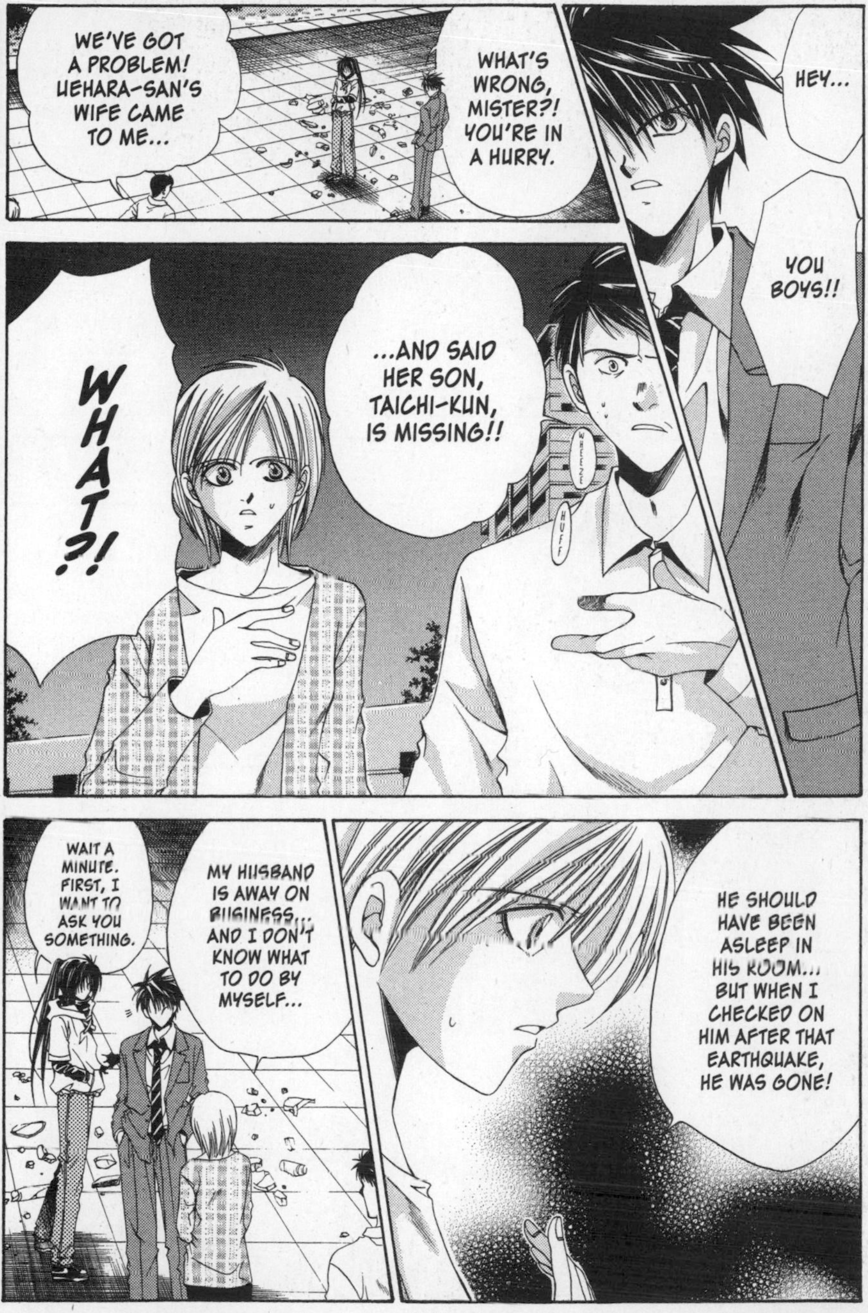
HEY...
YOU BOYS!!
WHAT'S WRONG, MISTER?! YOU'RE IN A HURRY.
WE'VE GOT A PROBLEM! UEHARA-SAN'S WIFE CAME TO ME...
...AND SAID HER SON, TAICHI-KUN, IS MISSING!!
WHEEZE
HUFF
WHAT?!
HE SHOULD HAVE BEEN ASLEEP IN HIS ROOM... BUT WHEN I CHECKED ON HIM AFTER THAT EARTHQUAKE, HE WAS GONE!
MY HUSBAND IS AWAY ON BUSINESS... AND I DON'T KNOW WHAT TO DO BY MYSELF...
WAIT A MINUTE. FIRST, I WANT TO ASK YOU SOMETHING.

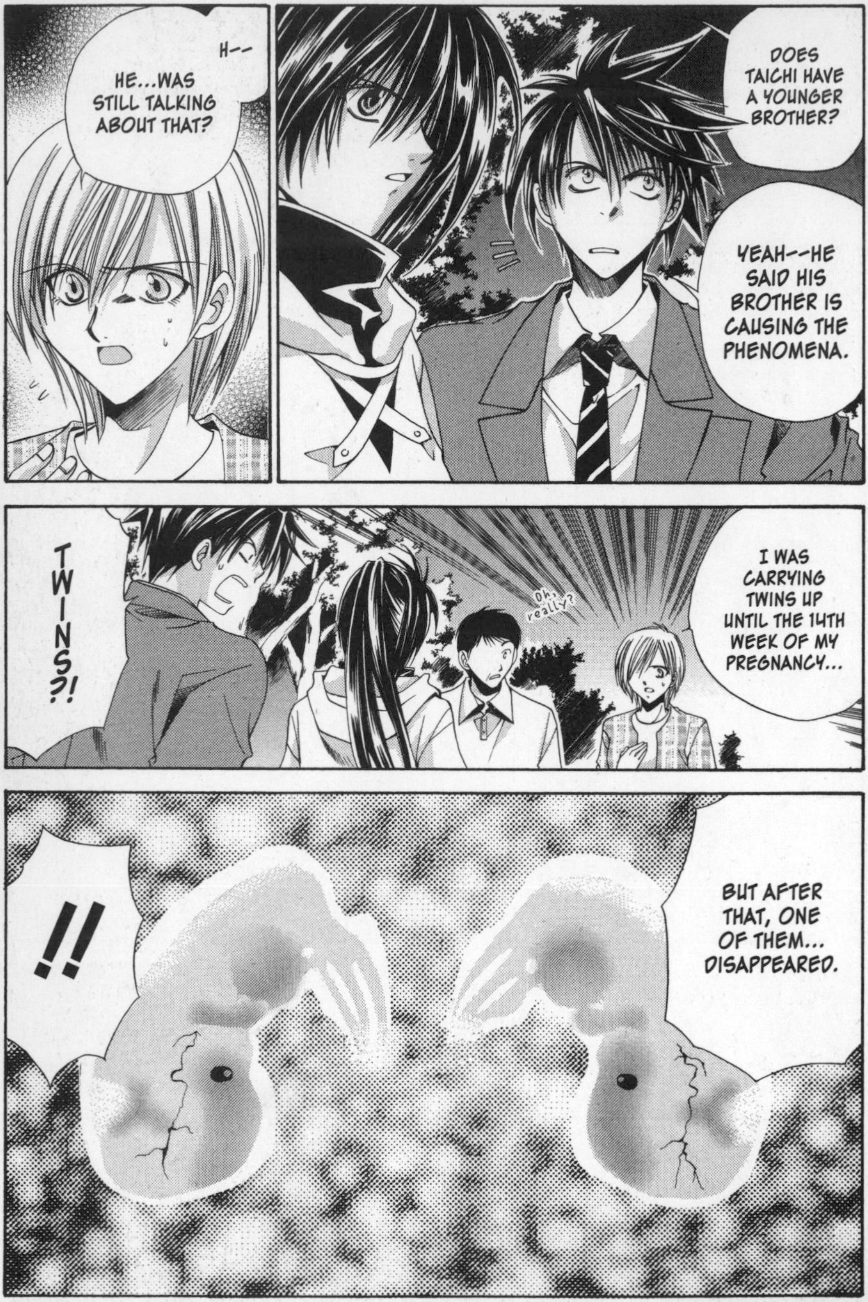
DOES TAICHI HAVE A YOUNGER BROTHER?
YEAH--HE SAID HIS BROTHER IS CAUSING THE PHENOMENA.
H--
HE...WAS STILL TALKING ABOUT THAT?
I WAS CARRYING TWINS UP UNTIL THE 14TH WEEK OF MY PREGNANCY...
Oh, really?
TWINS?!
BUT AFTER THAT, ONE OF THEM... DISAPPEARED.
!!

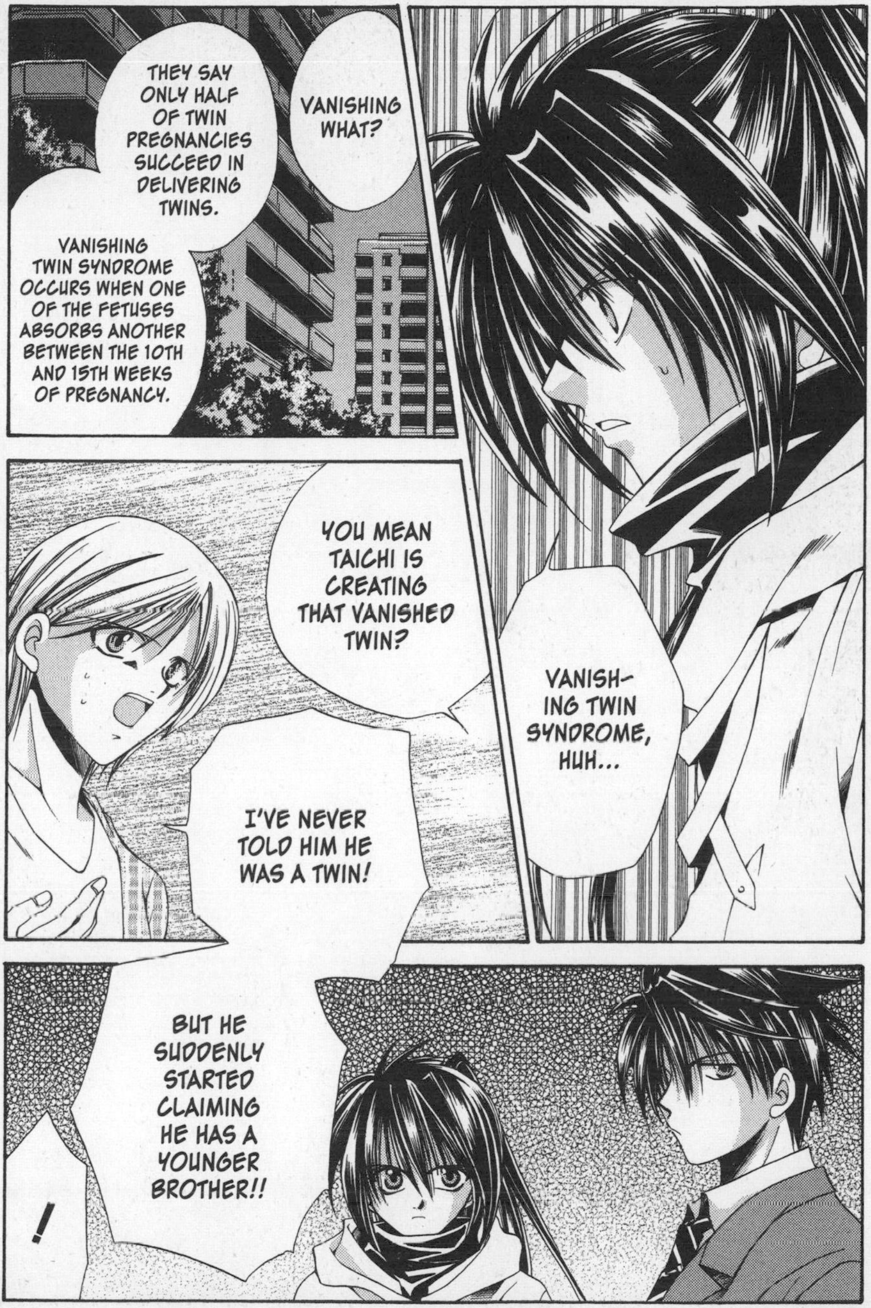

VANISH-ING TWIN SYNDROME, HUH...
VANISHING WHAT?
THEY SAY ONLY HALF OF TWIN PREGNANCIES SUCCEED IN DELIVERING TWINS.
VANISHING TWIN SYNDROME OCCURS WHEN ONE OF THE FETUSES ABSORBS ANOTHER BETWEEN THE 10TH AND 15TH WEEKS OF PREGNANCY.
YOU MEAN TAICHI IS CREATING THAT VANISHED TWIN?
I'VE NEVER TOLD HIM HE WAS A TWIN!
BUT HE SUDDENLY STARTED CLAIMING HE HAS A YOUNGER BROTHER!!
!

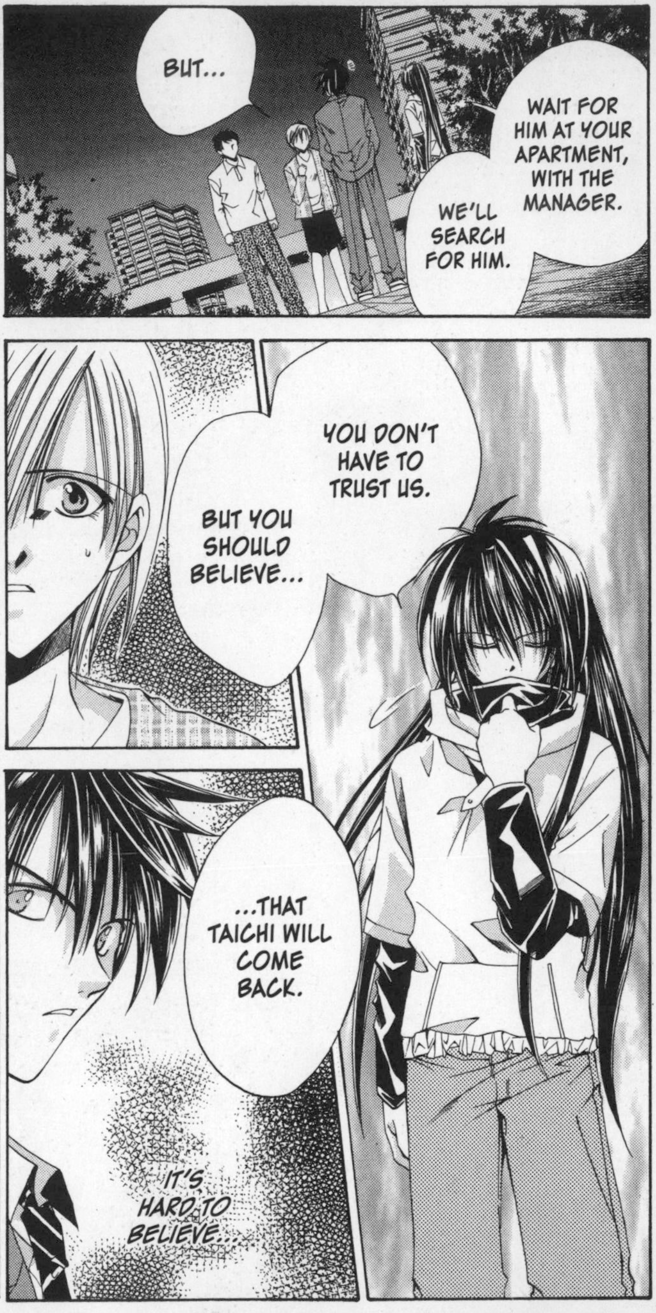
WAIT FOR HIM AT YOUR APARTMENT, WITH THE MANAGER.
WE'LL SEARCH FOR HIM.
BUT...
YOU DON'T HAVE TO TRUST US.
BUT YOU SHOULD BELIEVE...
...THAT TAICHI WILL COME BACK.
IT'S HARD TO BELIEVE...

久遠 青

KUDO, AO

- A member of the Paranormal Task Force (LOCK) First Division

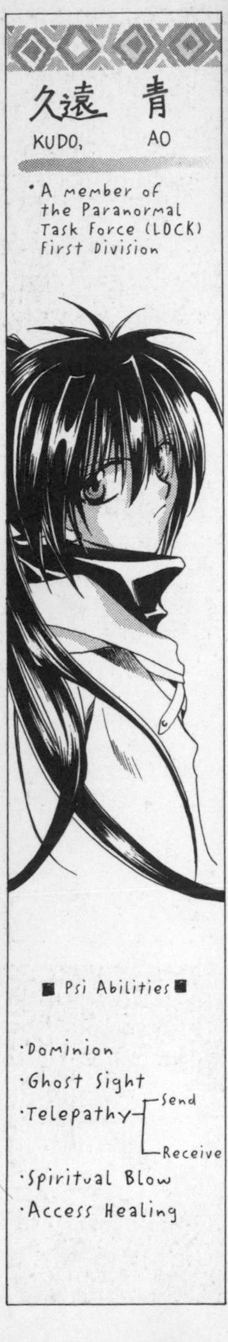

■ Psi Abilities ■

- Dominion
- Ghost Sight
- Telepathy — Send / Receive
- Spiritual Blow
- Access Healing

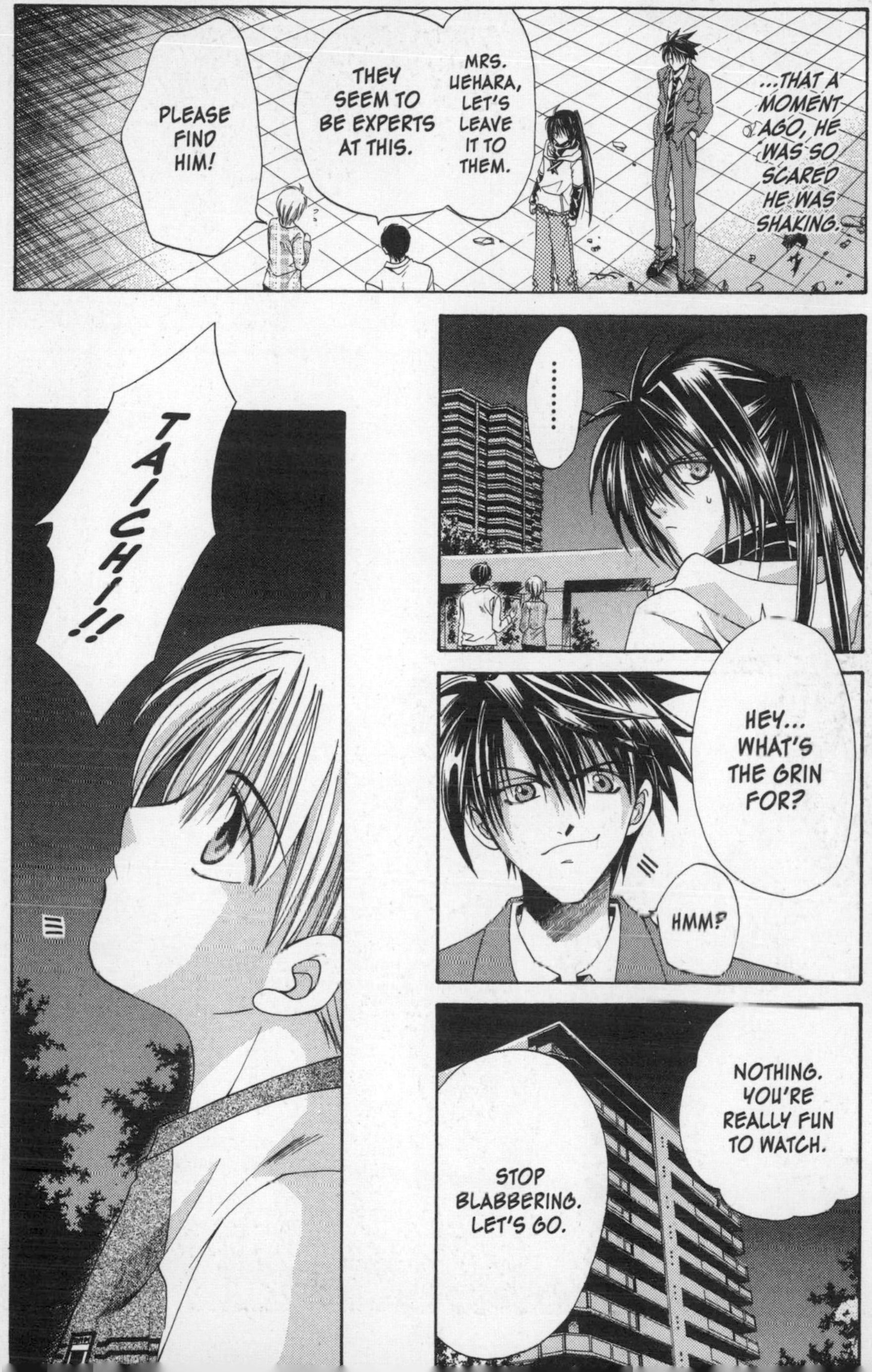
...THAT A MOMENT AGO, HE WAS SO SCARED HE WAS SHAKING.
MRS. UEHARA, LET'S LEAVE IT TO THEM.
THEY SEEM TO BE EXPERTS AT THIS.
PLEASE FIND HIM!
....
HEY... WHAT'S THE GRIN FOR?
HMM?
NOTHING. YOU'RE REALLY FUN TO WATCH.
STOP BLABBERING. LET'S GO.
TAICHI!!!

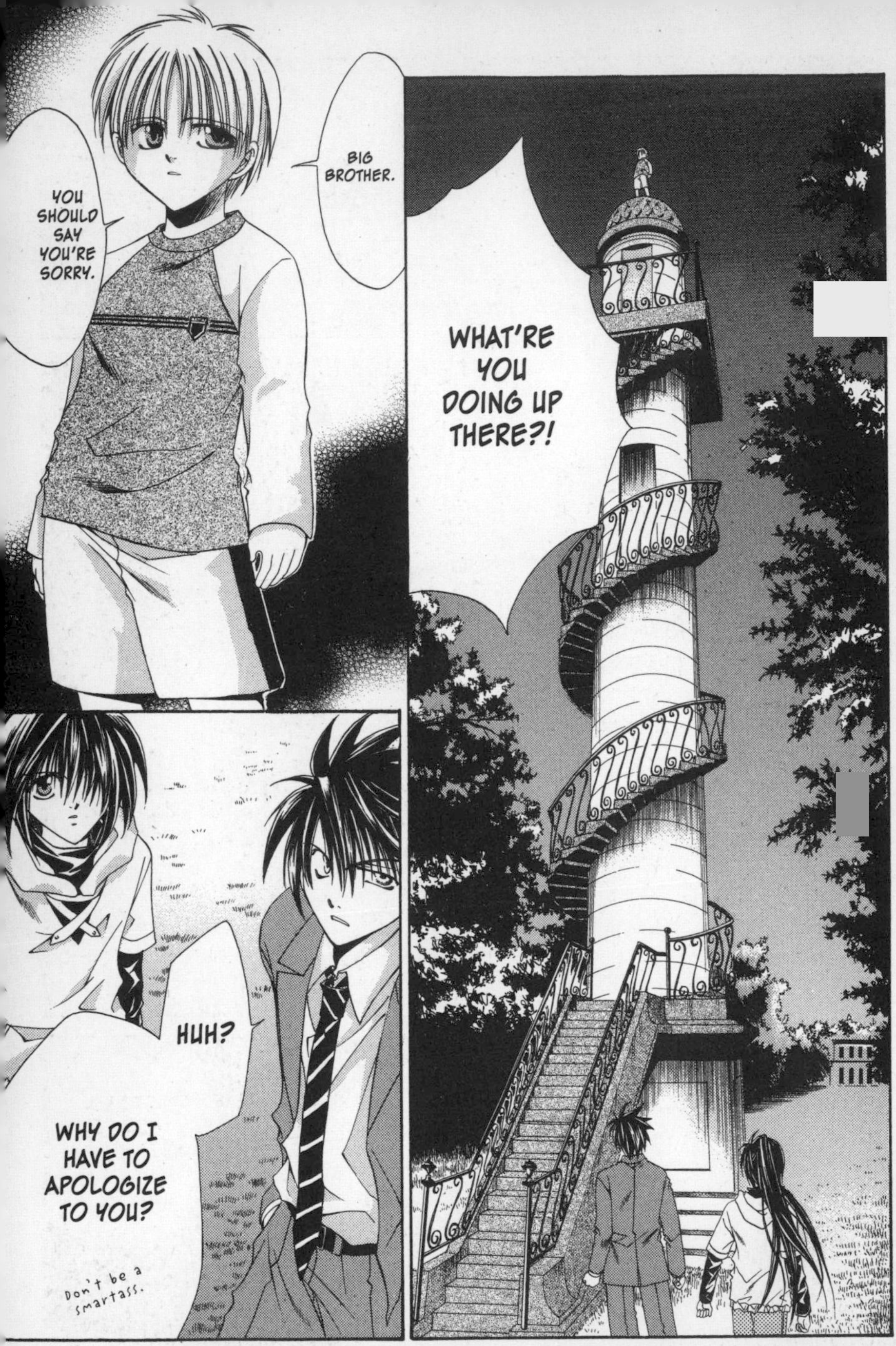
WHAT'RE YOU DOING UP THERE?!
BIG BROTHER.
YOU SHOULD SAY YOU'RE SORRY.
HUH?
WHY DO I HAVE TO APOLOGIZE TO YOU?
Don't be a smartass.

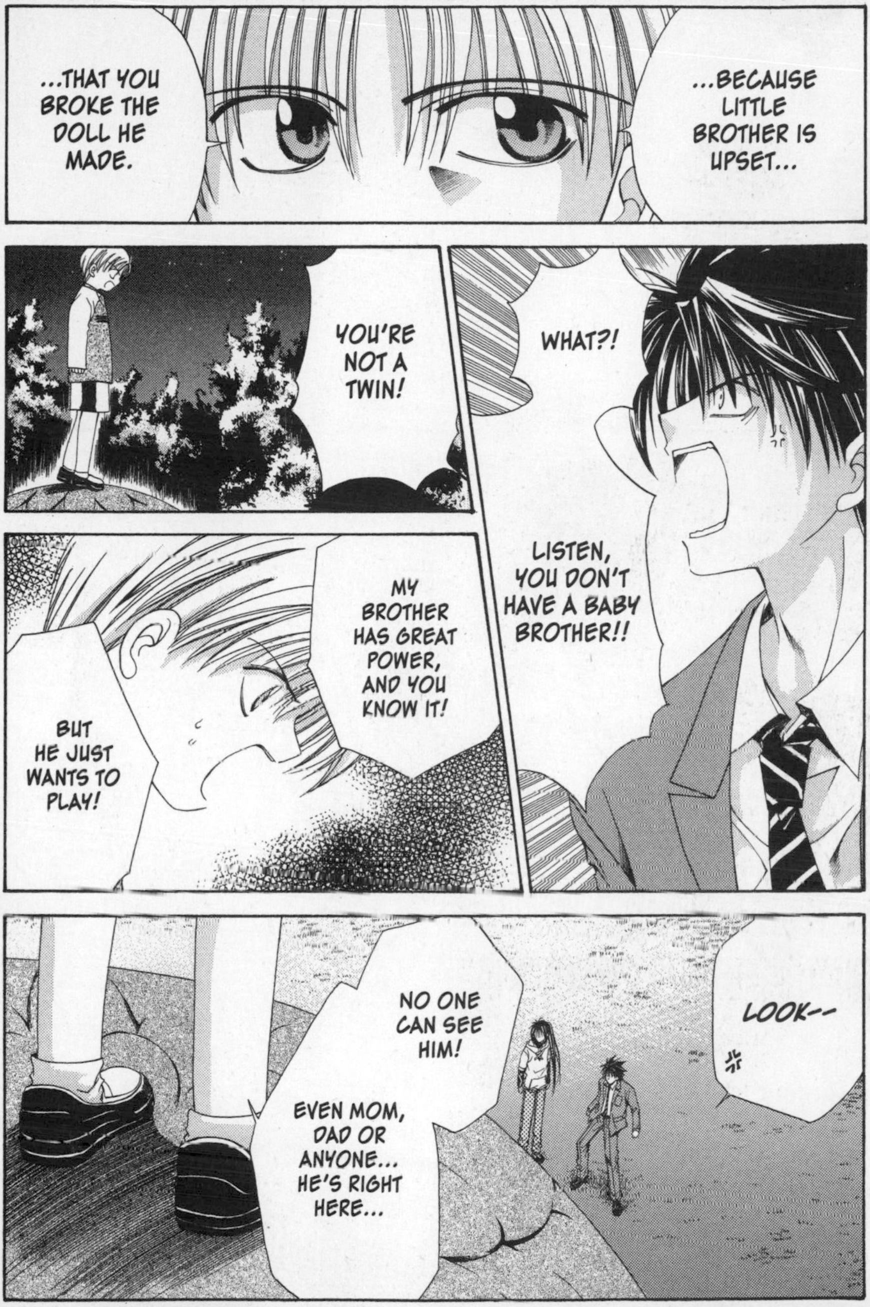
...BECAUSE LITTLE BROTHER IS UPSET...
...THAT YOU BROKE THE DOLL HE MADE.
WHAT?!
LISTEN, YOU DON'T HAVE A BABY BROTHER!!
YOU'RE NOT A TWIN!
MY BROTHER HAS GREAT POWER, AND YOU KNOW IT!
BUT HE JUST WANTS TO PLAY!
LOOK--
NO ONE CAN SEE HIM!
EVEN MOM, DAD OR ANYONE... HE'S RIGHT HERE...

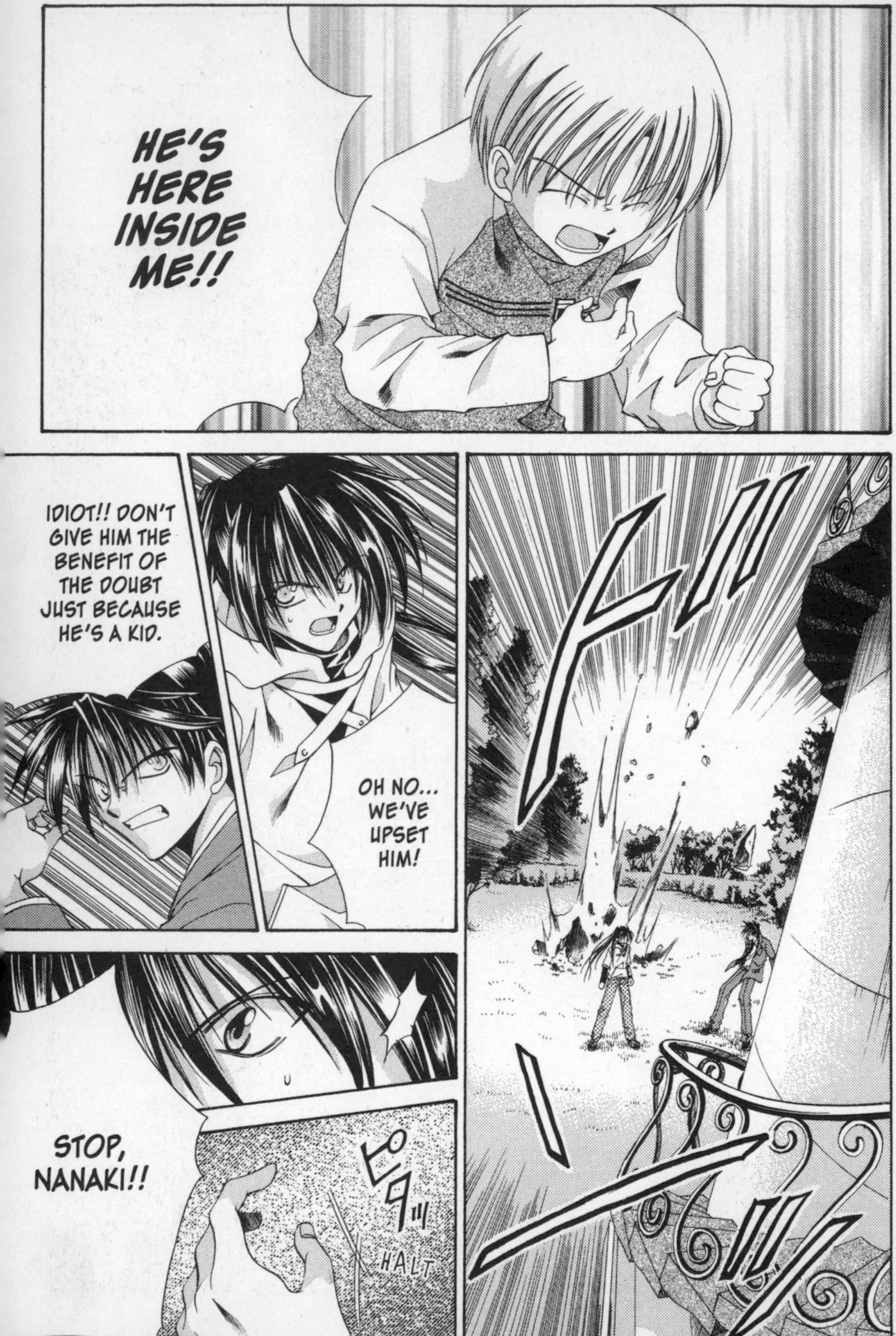
HE'S HERE INSIDE ME!!
OH NO... WE'VE UPSET HIM!
IDIOT!! DON'T GIVE HIM THE BENEFIT OF THE DOUBT JUST BECAUSE HE'S A KID.
STOP, NANAKI!!
HALT

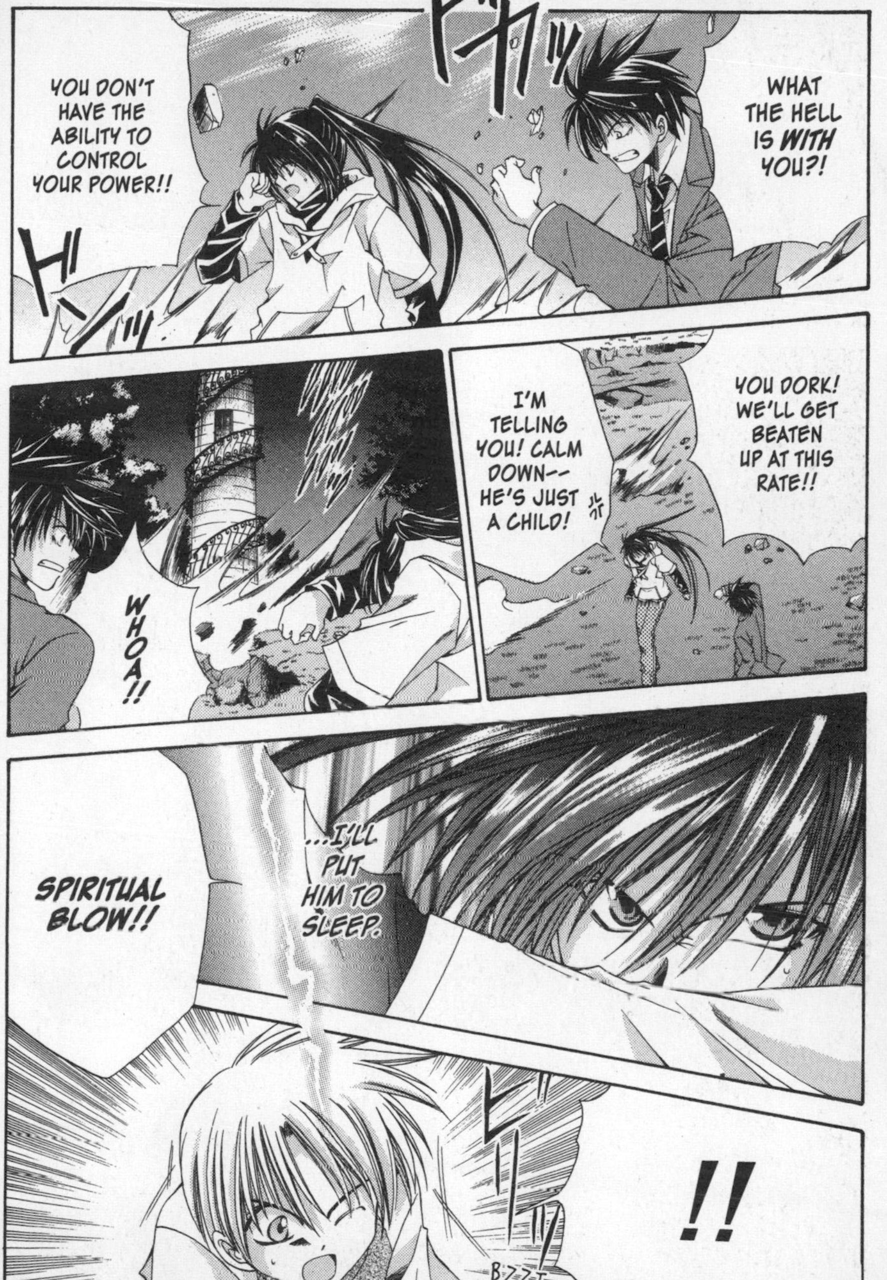
WHAT THE HELL IS WITH YOU?!
YOU DON'T HAVE THE ABILITY TO CONTROL YOUR POWER!!
YOU DORK! WE'LL GET BEATEN UP AT THIS RATE!!
I'M TELLING YOU! CALM DOWN-- HE'S JUST A CHILD!
WHOA!!
...I'LL PUT HIM TO SLEEP.
SPIRITUAL BLOW!!
!!
BZZT

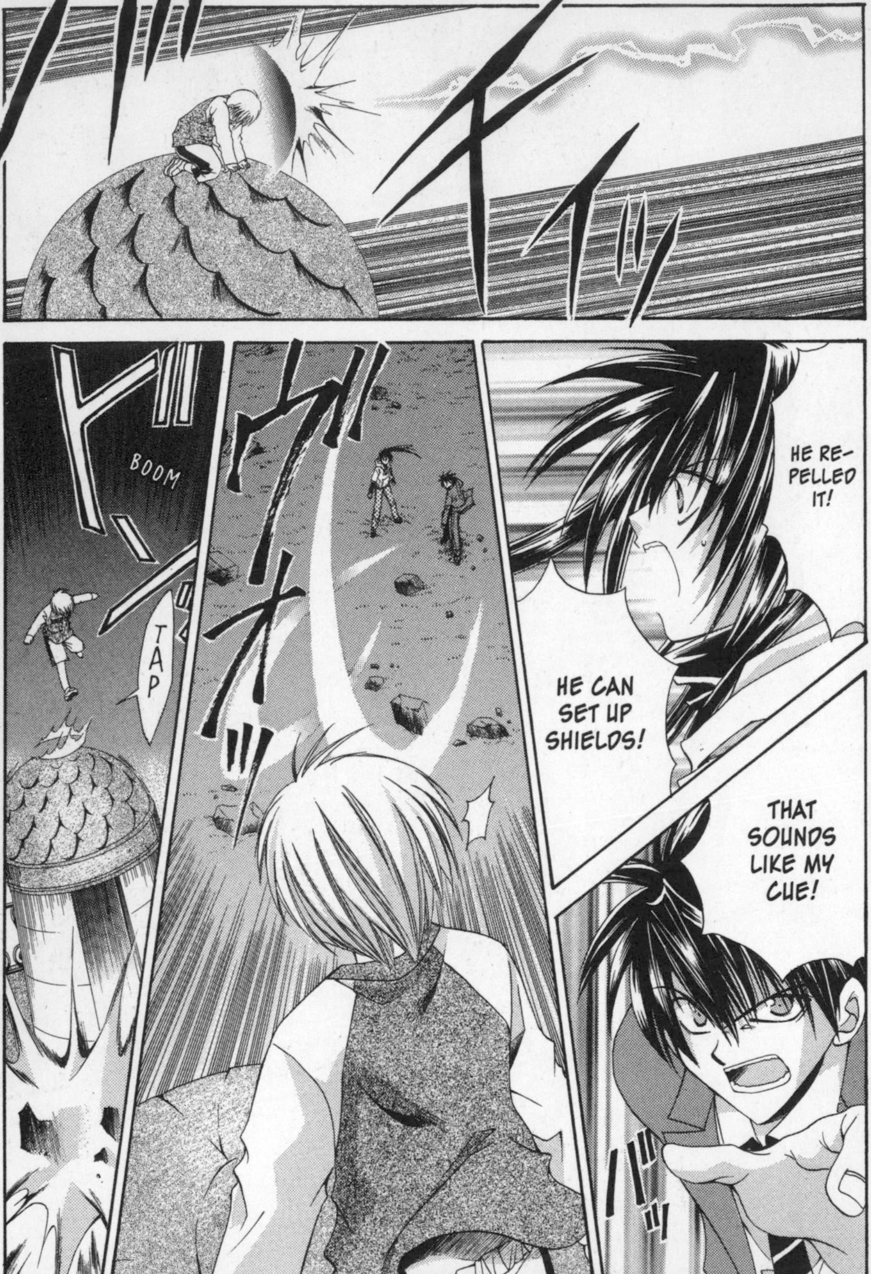
HE RE-PELLED IT!
HE CAN SET UP SHIELDS!
THAT SOUNDS LIKE MY CUE!
BOOM
TAP

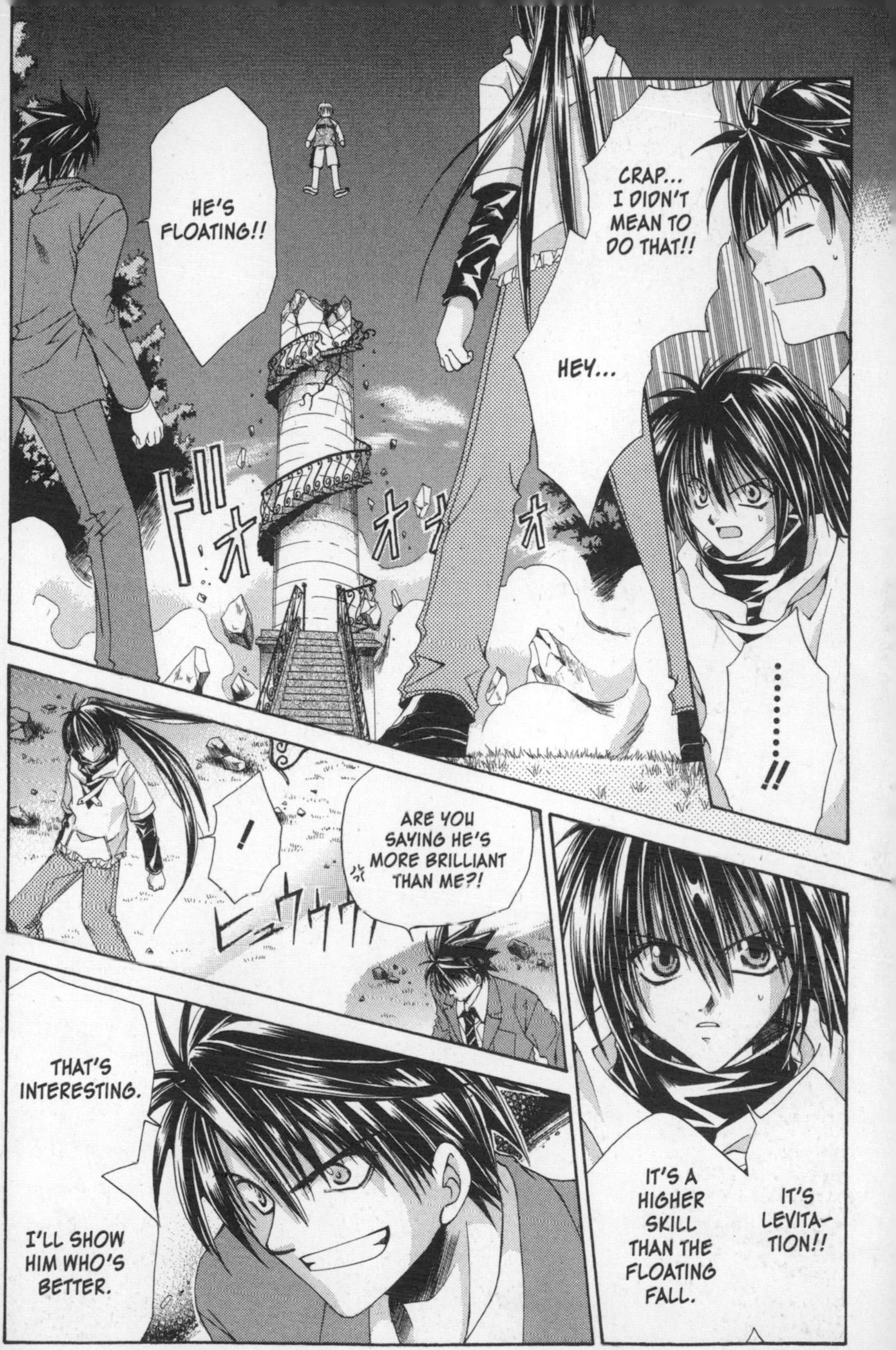
CRAP... I DIDN'T MEAN TO DO THAT!!
HEY...
......!!
HE'S FLOATING!!
IT'S LEVITATION!!
IT'S A HIGHER SKILL THAN THE FLOATING FALL.
ARE YOU SAYING HE'S MORE BRILLIANT THAN ME?!
!
THAT'S INTERESTING.
I'LL SHOW HIM WHO'S BETTER.

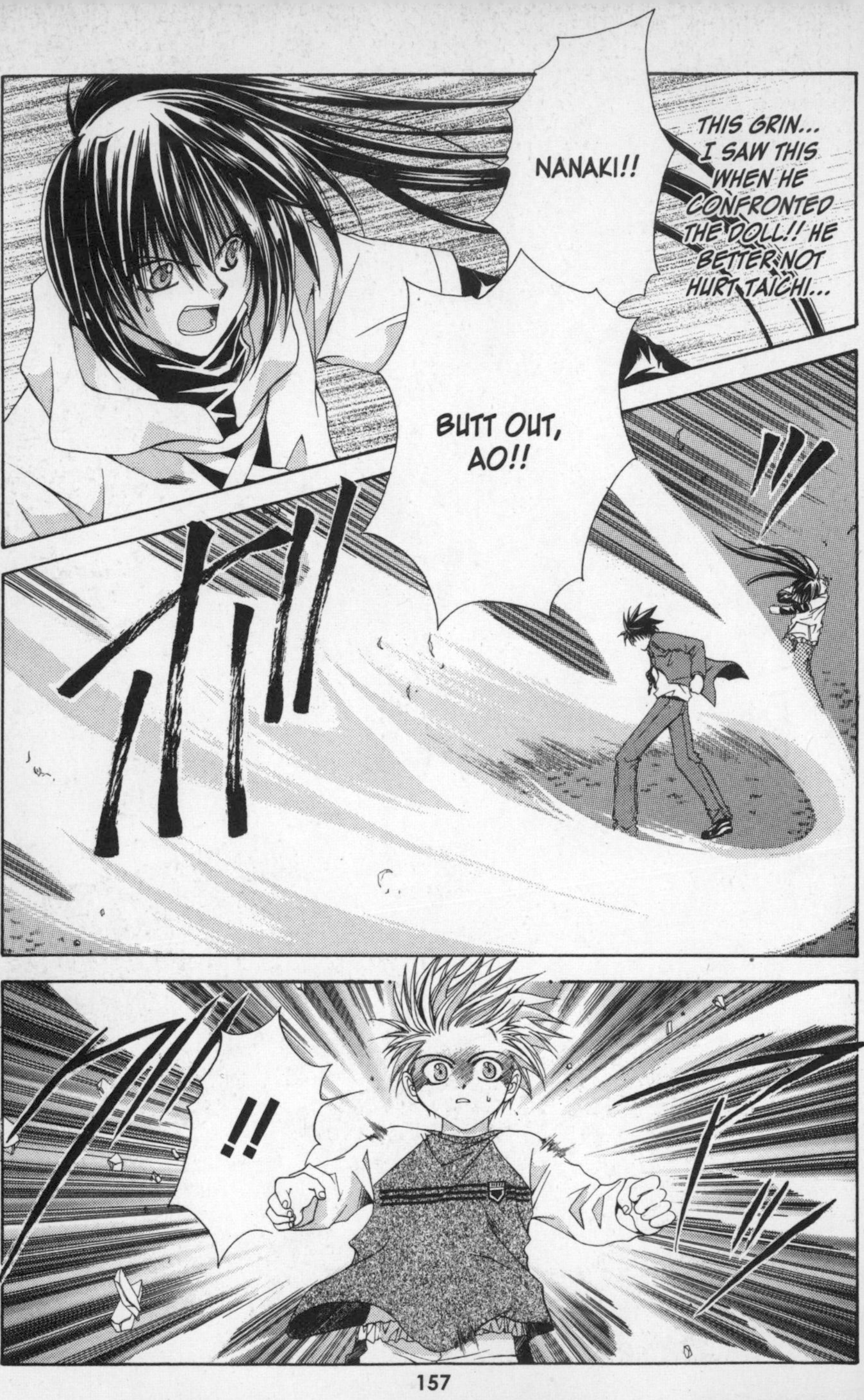
THIS GRIN... I SAW THIS WHEN HE CONFRONTED THE DOLL!! HE BETTER NOT HURT TAICHI...
NANAKI!!
BUTT OUT, AO!!
!!

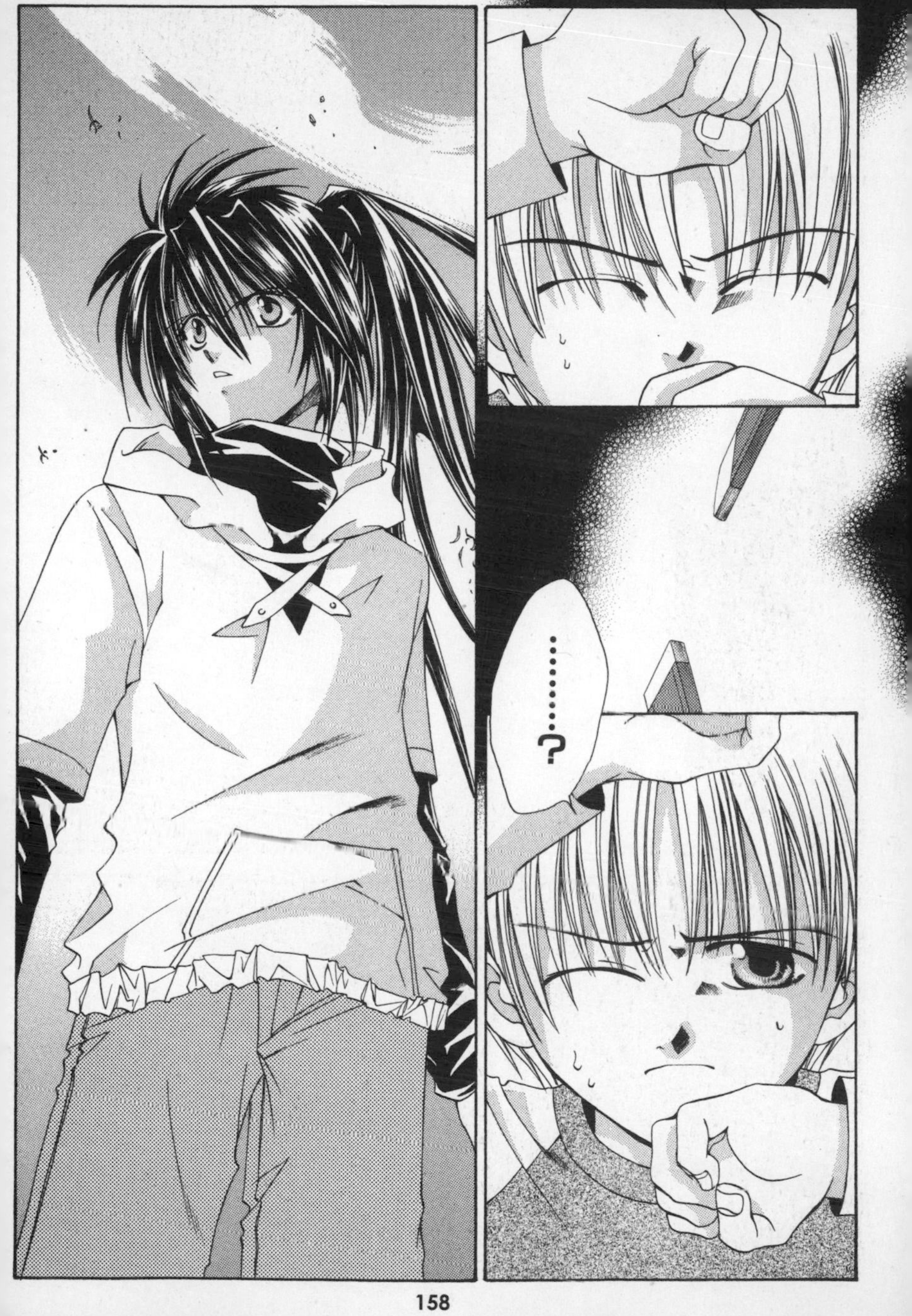
......?

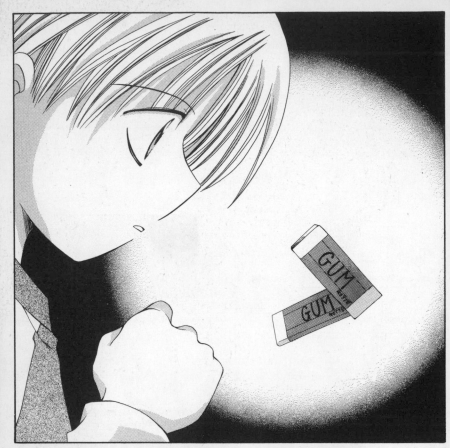

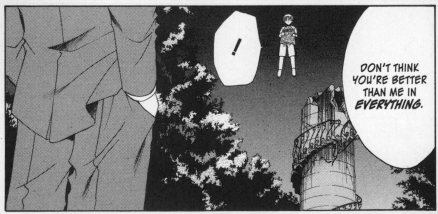

DON'T THINK YOU'RE BETTER THAN ME IN *EVERYTHING.*

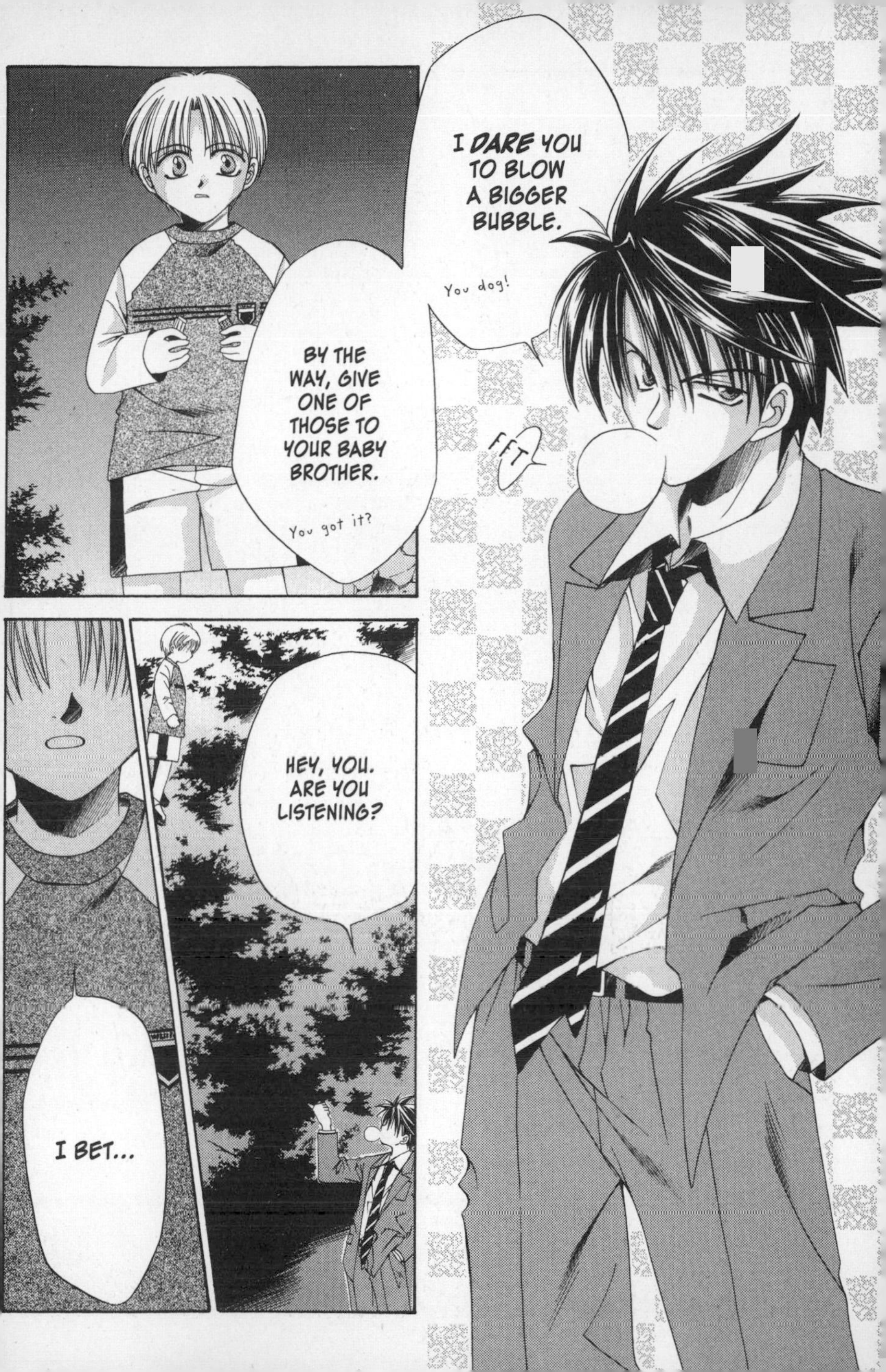
I DARE YOU TO BLOW A BIGGER BUBBLE.
You dog!
FFT
BY THE WAY, GIVE ONE OF THOSE TO YOUR BABY BROTHER.
You got it?
HEY, YOU. ARE YOU LISTENING?
I BET...

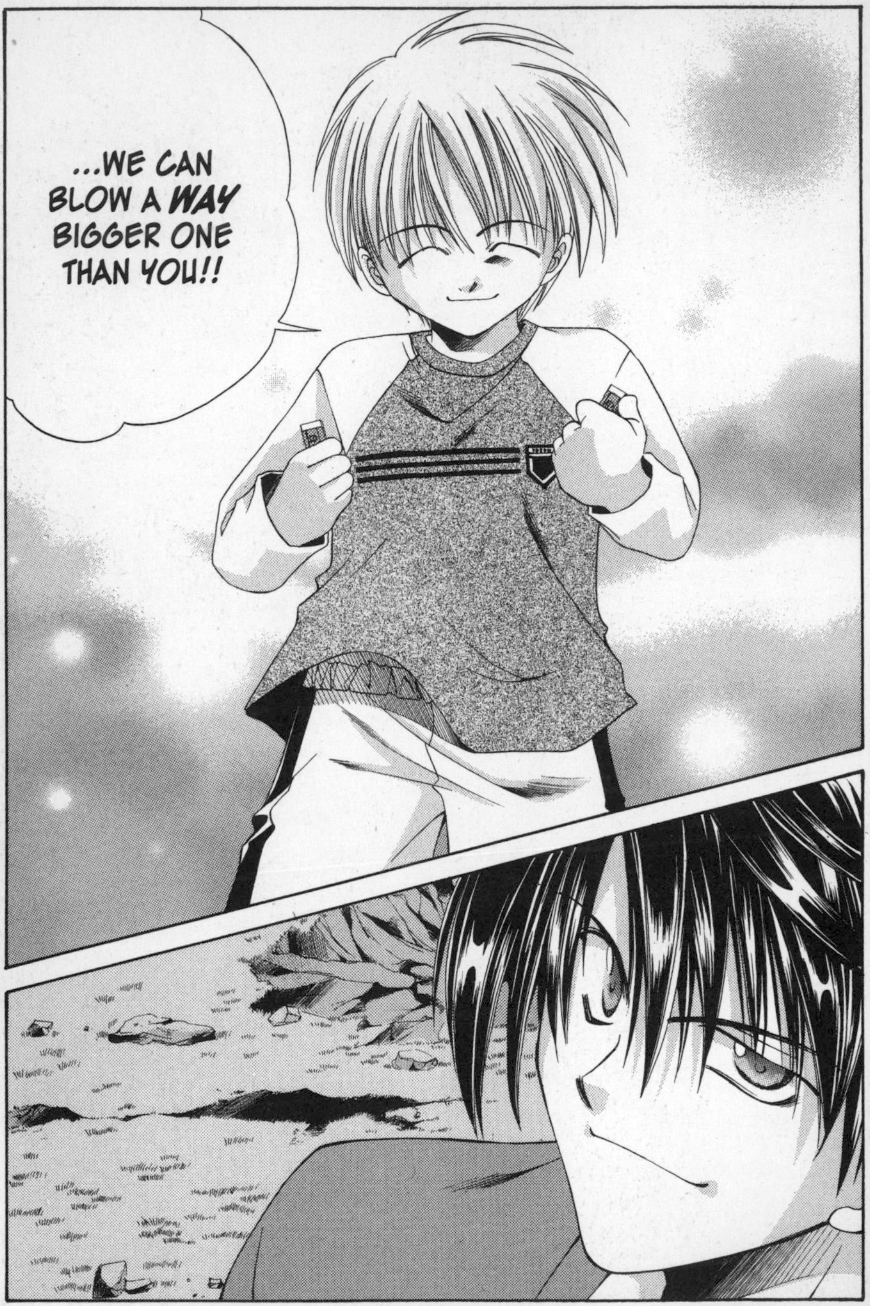
...WE CAN BLOW A WAY BIGGER ONE THAN YOU!!

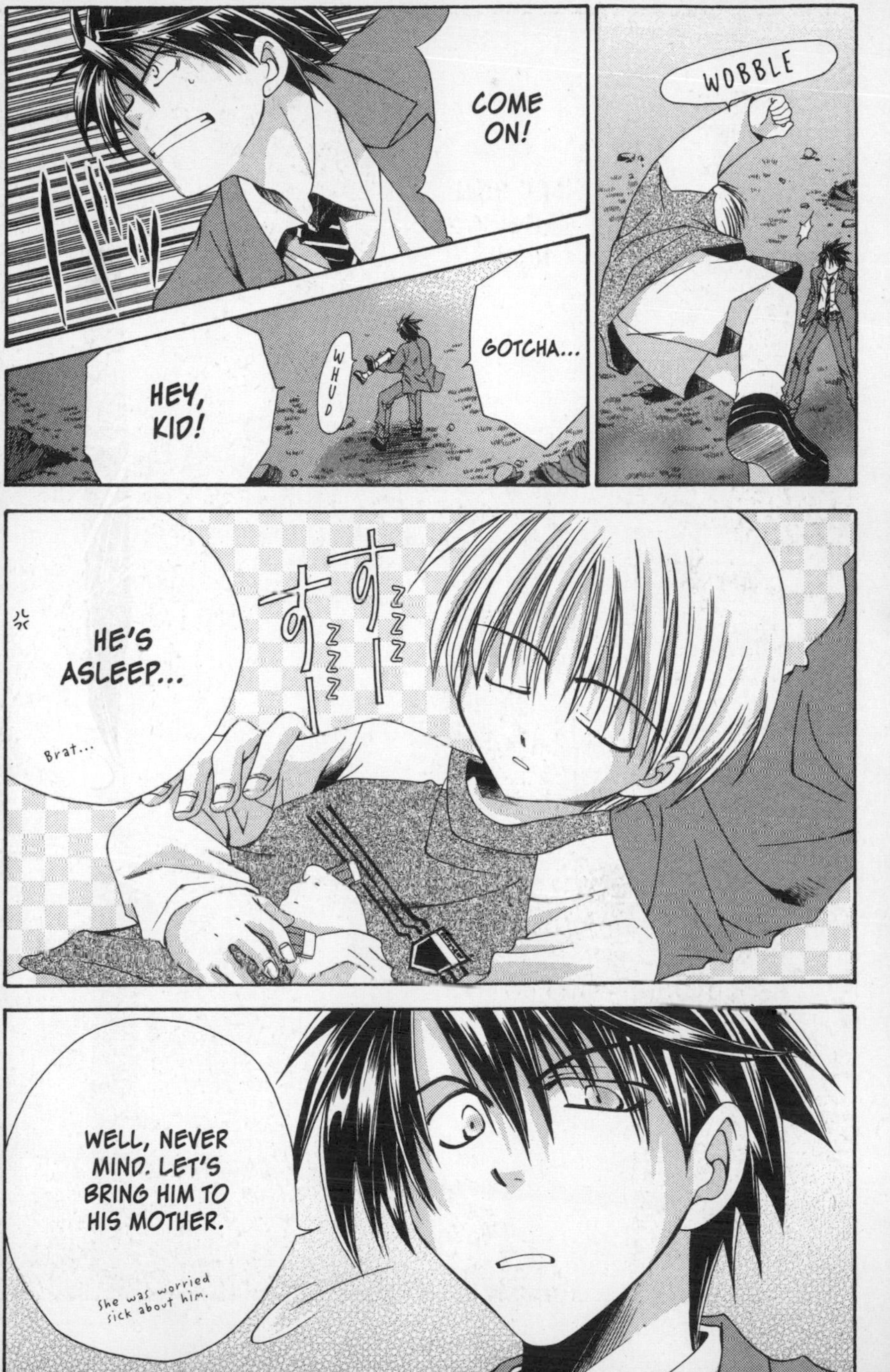
WOBBLE
COME ON!
GOTCHA...
WHUD
HEY, KID!
すーすー
ZZZ ZZZ
HE'S ASLEEP...
Brat...
WELL, NEVER MIND. LET'S BRING HIM TO HIS MOTHER.
She was worried sick about him.

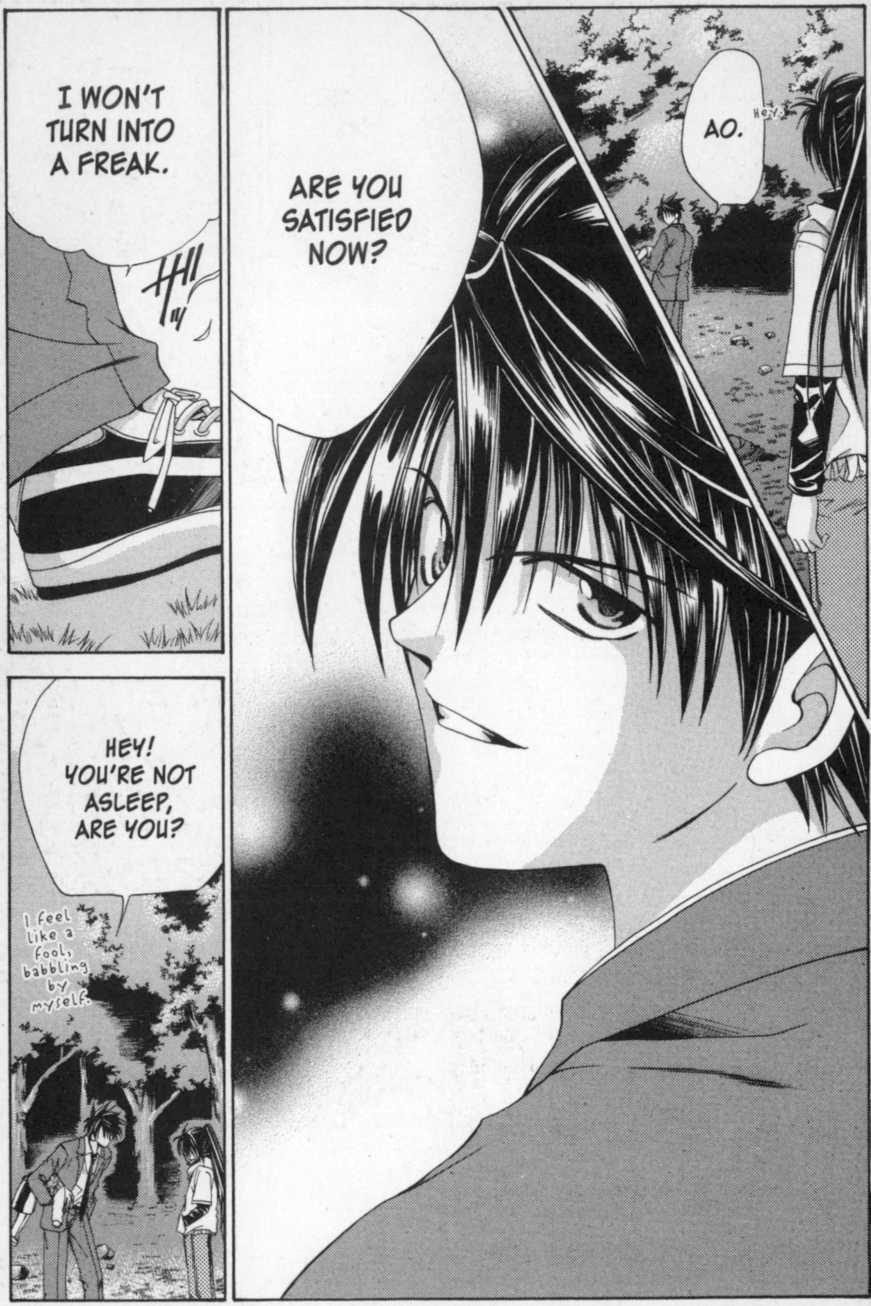
AO.
Hey.
ARE YOU SATISFIED NOW?
I WON'T TURN INTO A FREAK.
HEY! YOU'RE NOT ASLEEP, ARE YOU?
I feel like a fool, babbling by myself.

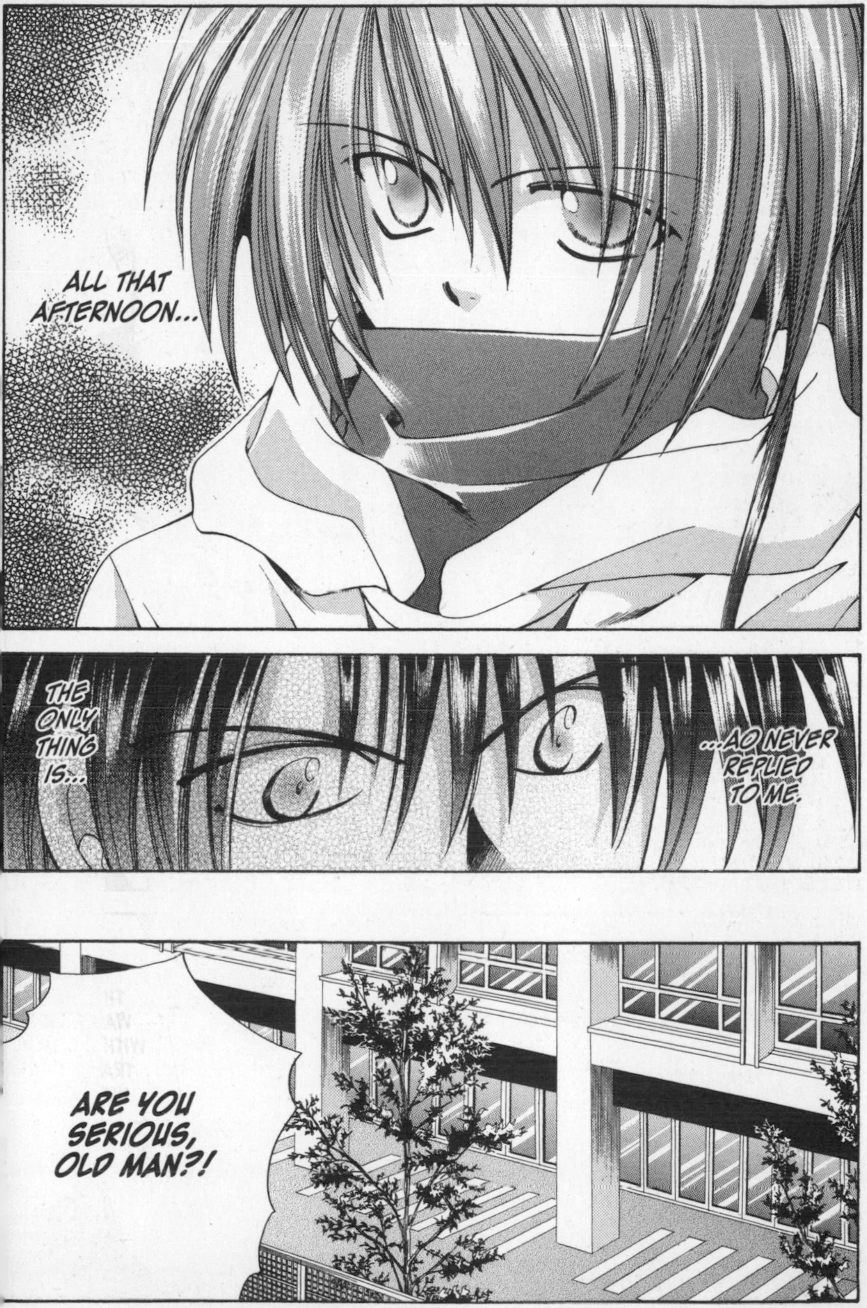
ALL THAT AFTERNOON...
THE ONLY THING IS...
...AO NEVER REPLIED TO ME.
ARE YOU SERIOUS, OLD MAN?!

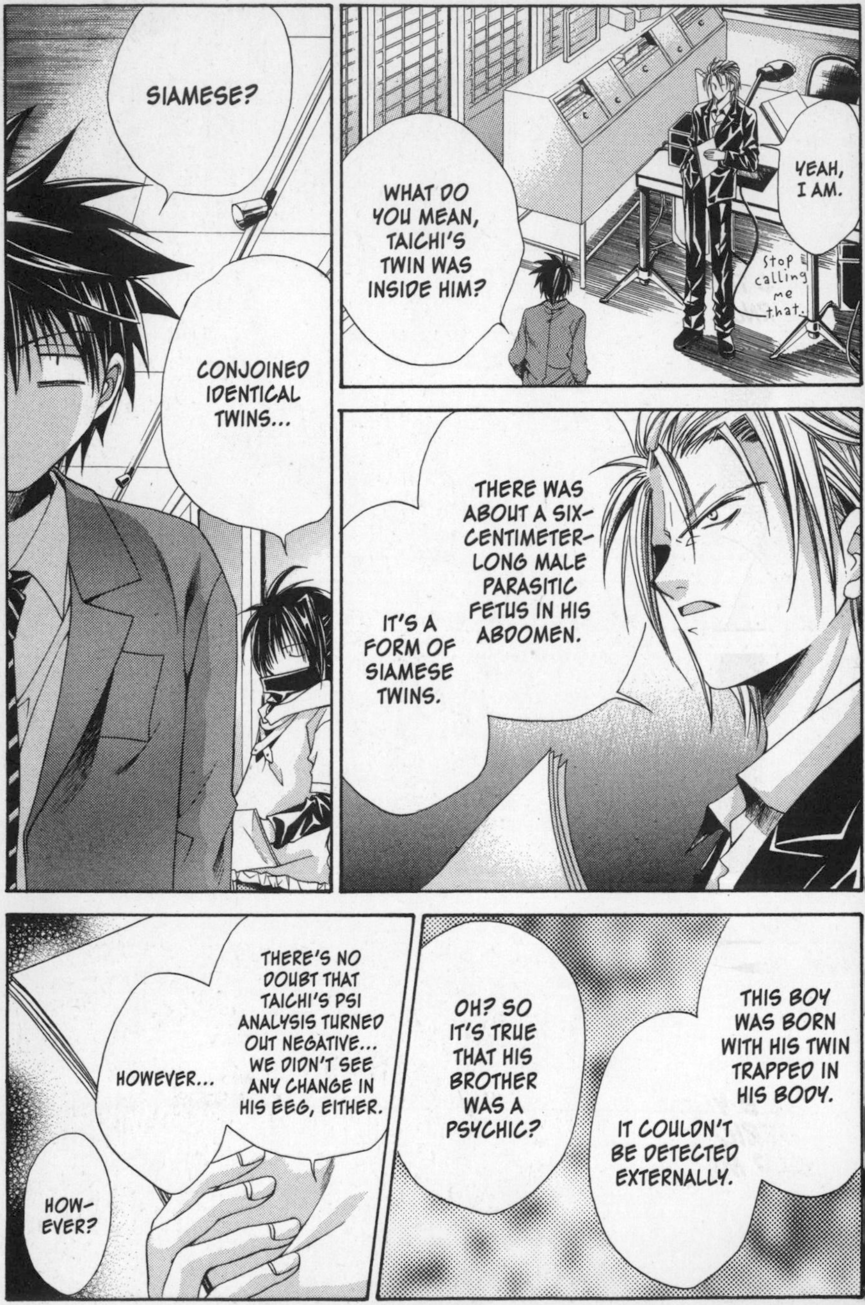
YEAH, I AM.
Stop calling me that.
WHAT DO YOU MEAN, TAICHI'S TWIN WAS INSIDE HIM?
THERE WAS ABOUT A SIX-CENTIMETER-LONG MALE PARASITIC FETUS IN HIS ABDOMEN.
IT'S A FORM OF SIAMESE TWINS.
SIAMESE?
CONJOINED IDENTICAL TWINS...
THIS BOY WAS BORN WITH HIS TWIN TRAPPED IN HIS BODY.
IT COULDN'T BE DETECTED EXTERNALLY.
OH? SO IT'S TRUE THAT HIS BROTHER WAS A PSYCHIC?
THERE'S NO DOUBT THAT TAICHI'S PSI ANALYSIS TURNED OUT NEGATIVE... WE DIDN'T SEE ANY CHANGE IN HIS EEG, EITHER.
HOWEVER...
HOW-EVER?

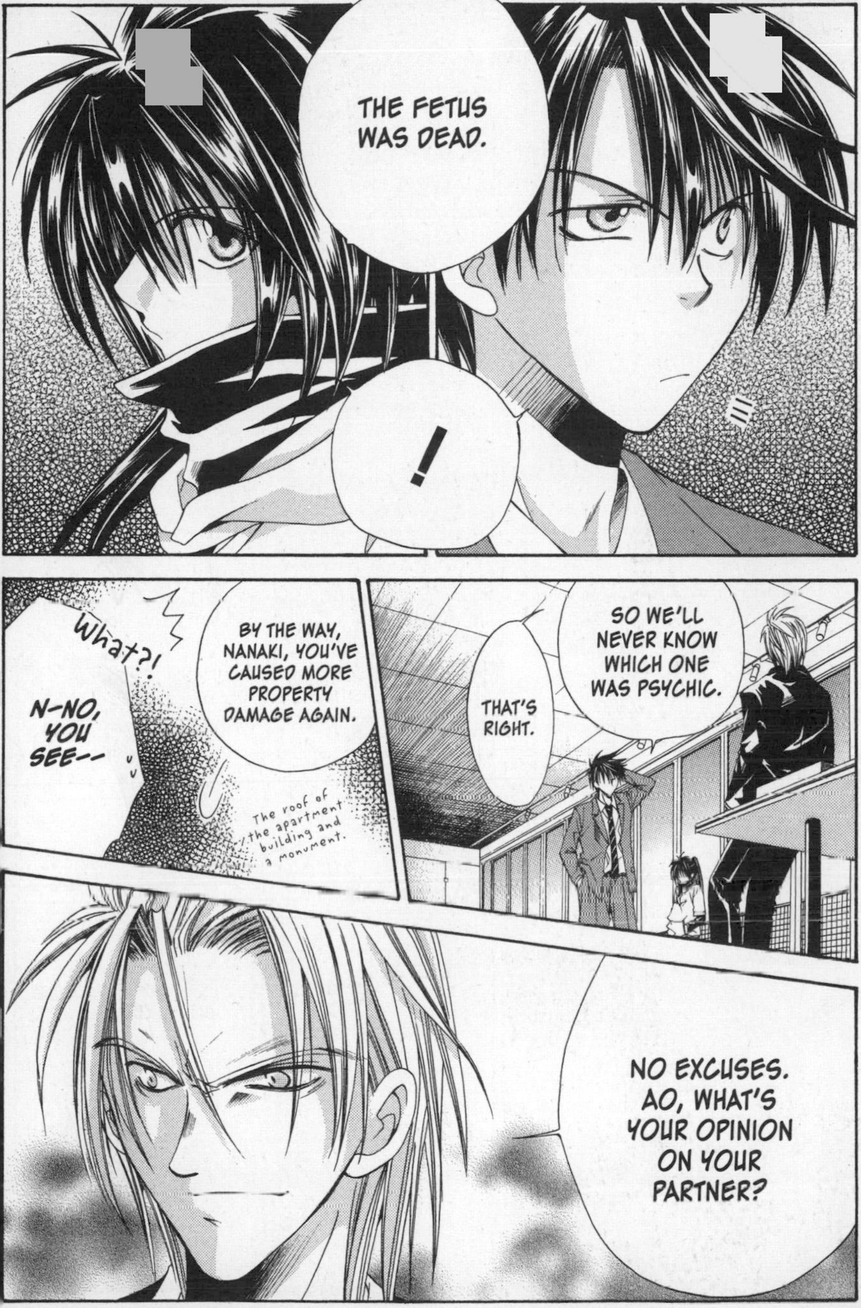
THE FETUS WAS DEAD.
!
SO WE'LL NEVER KNOW WHICH ONE WAS PSYCHIC.
THAT'S RIGHT.
BY THE WAY, NANAKI, YOU'VE CAUSED MORE PROPERTY DAMAGE AGAIN.
What?!
N-NO, YOU SEE--
The roof of the apartment building and a monument.
NO EXCUSES. AO, WHAT'S YOUR OPINION ON YOUR PARTNER?

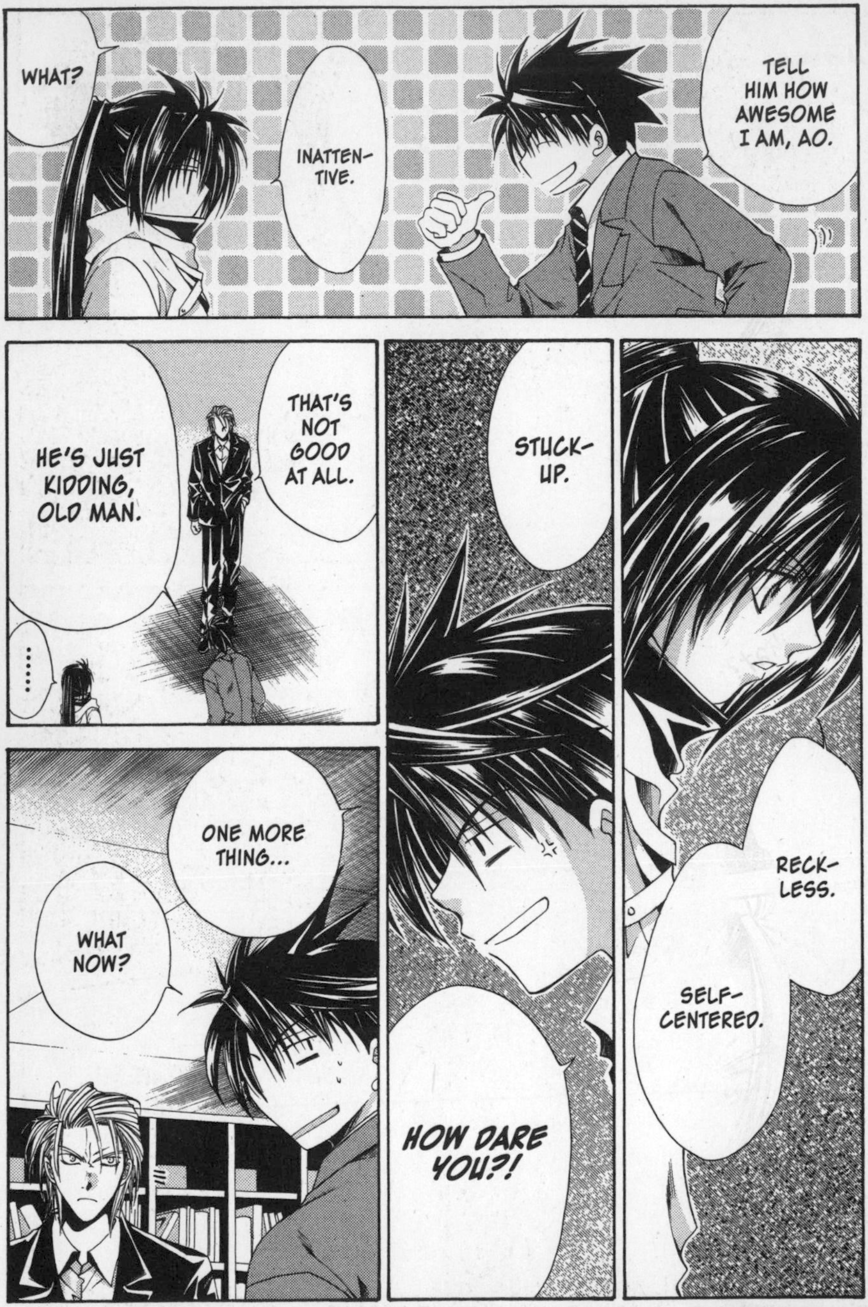
TELL HIM HOW AWESOME I AM, AO.
INATTEN-TIVE.
WHAT?
RECK-LESS.
SELF-CENTERED.
STUCK-UP.
HOW DARE YOU?!
THAT'S NOT GOOD AT ALL.
HE'S JUST KIDDING, OLD MAN.
......
ONE MORE THING...
WHAT NOW?

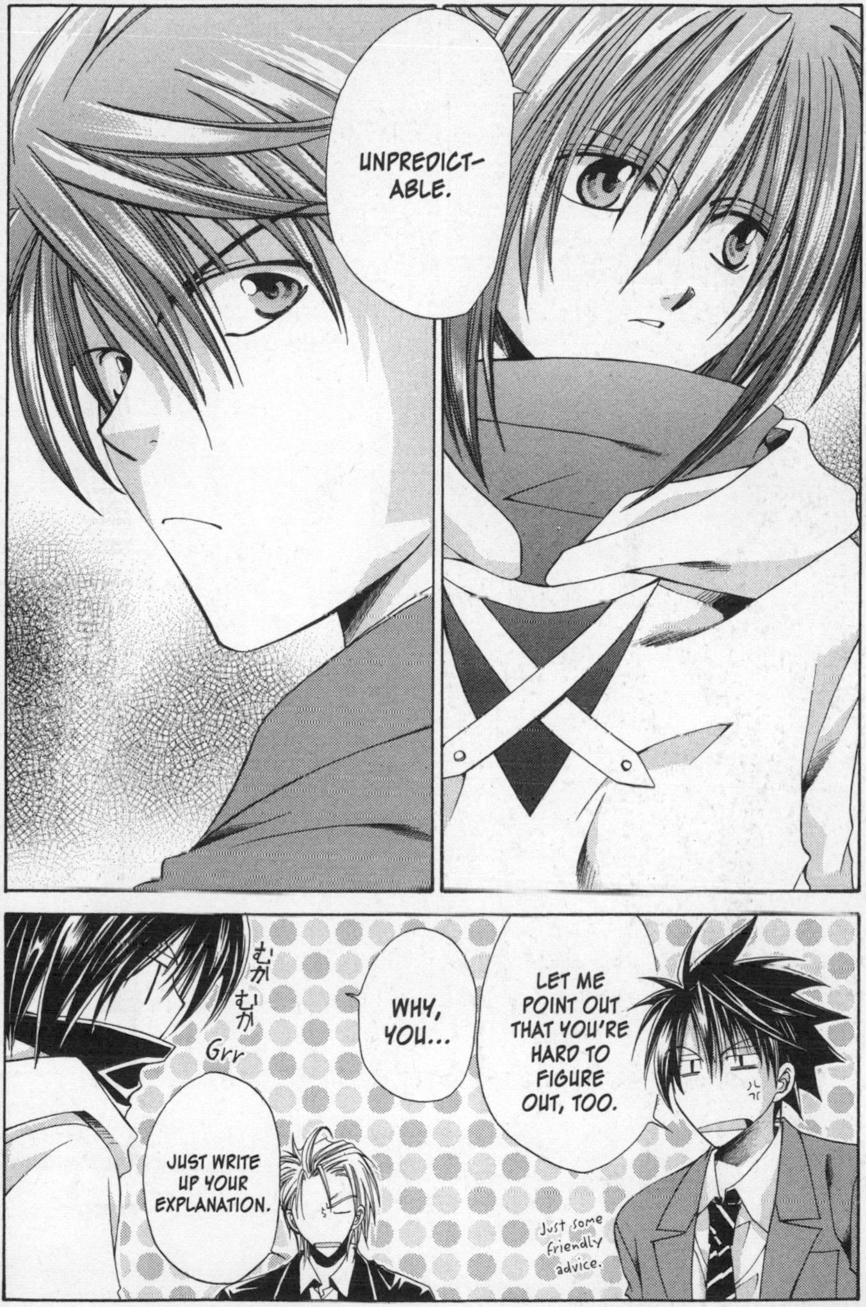
UNPREDICT-ABLE.
LET ME POINT OUT THAT YOU'RE HARD TO FIGURE OUT, TOO.
Just some friendly advice.
WHY, YOU...
むかむか
Grr
JUST WRITE UP YOUR EXPLANATION.

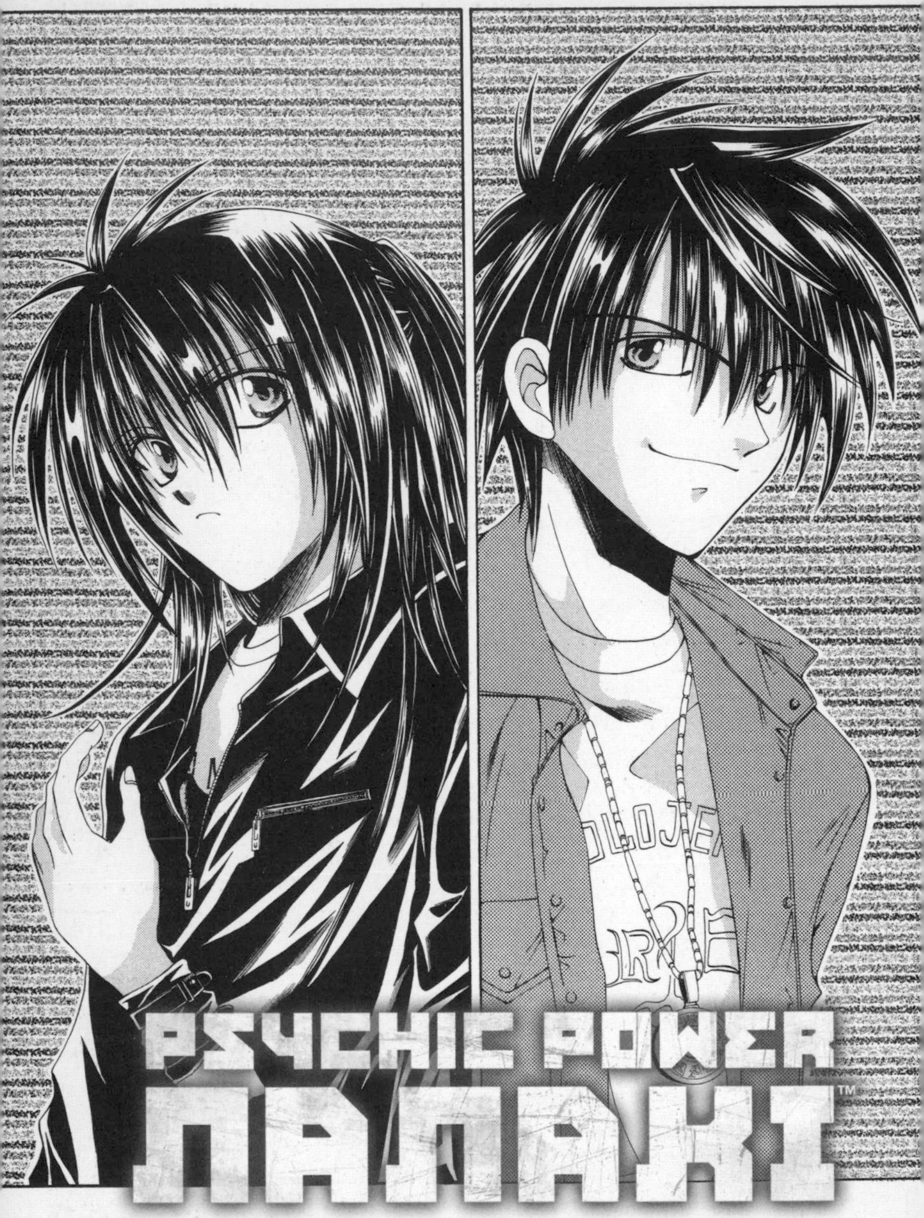
PSYCHIC POWER
NANAKI™

CHRONICLE 6

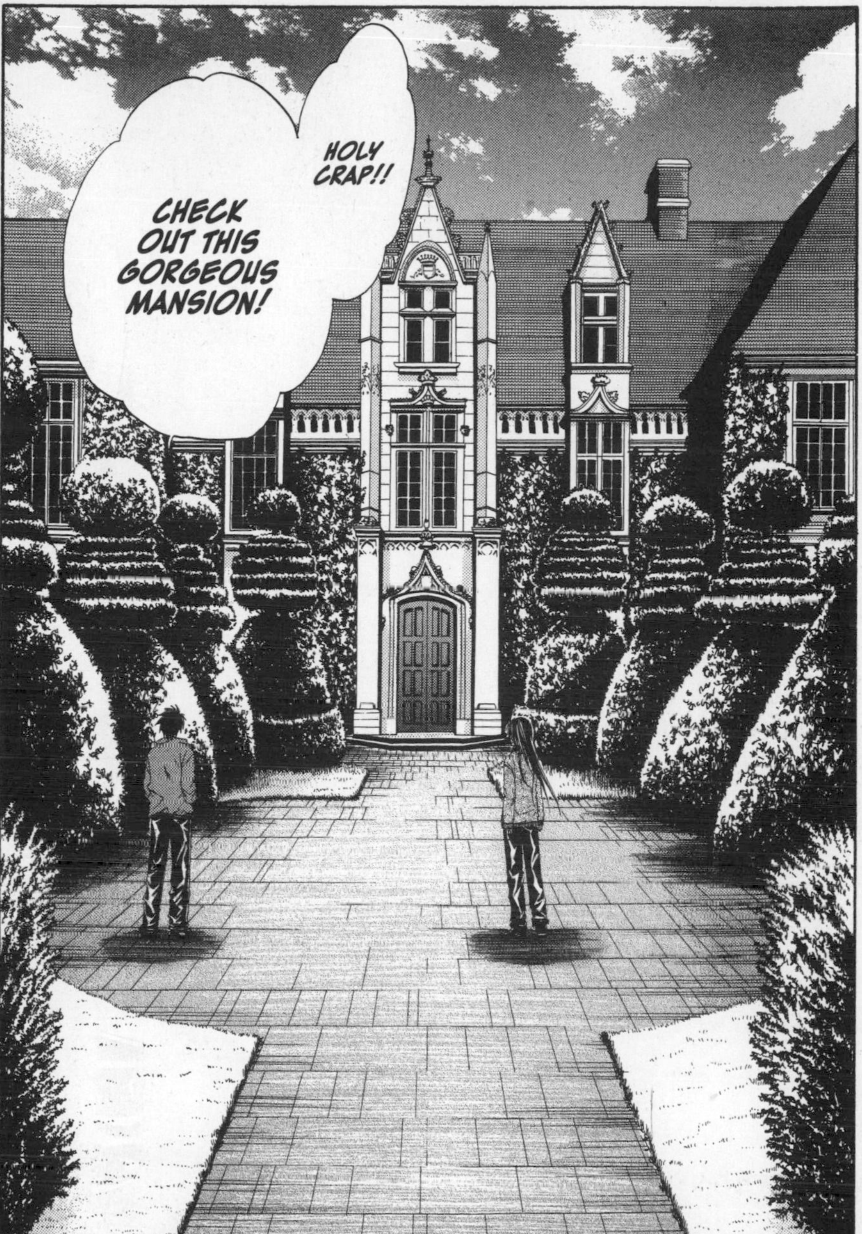
HOLY CRAP!!
CHECK OUT THIS GORGEOUS MANSION!

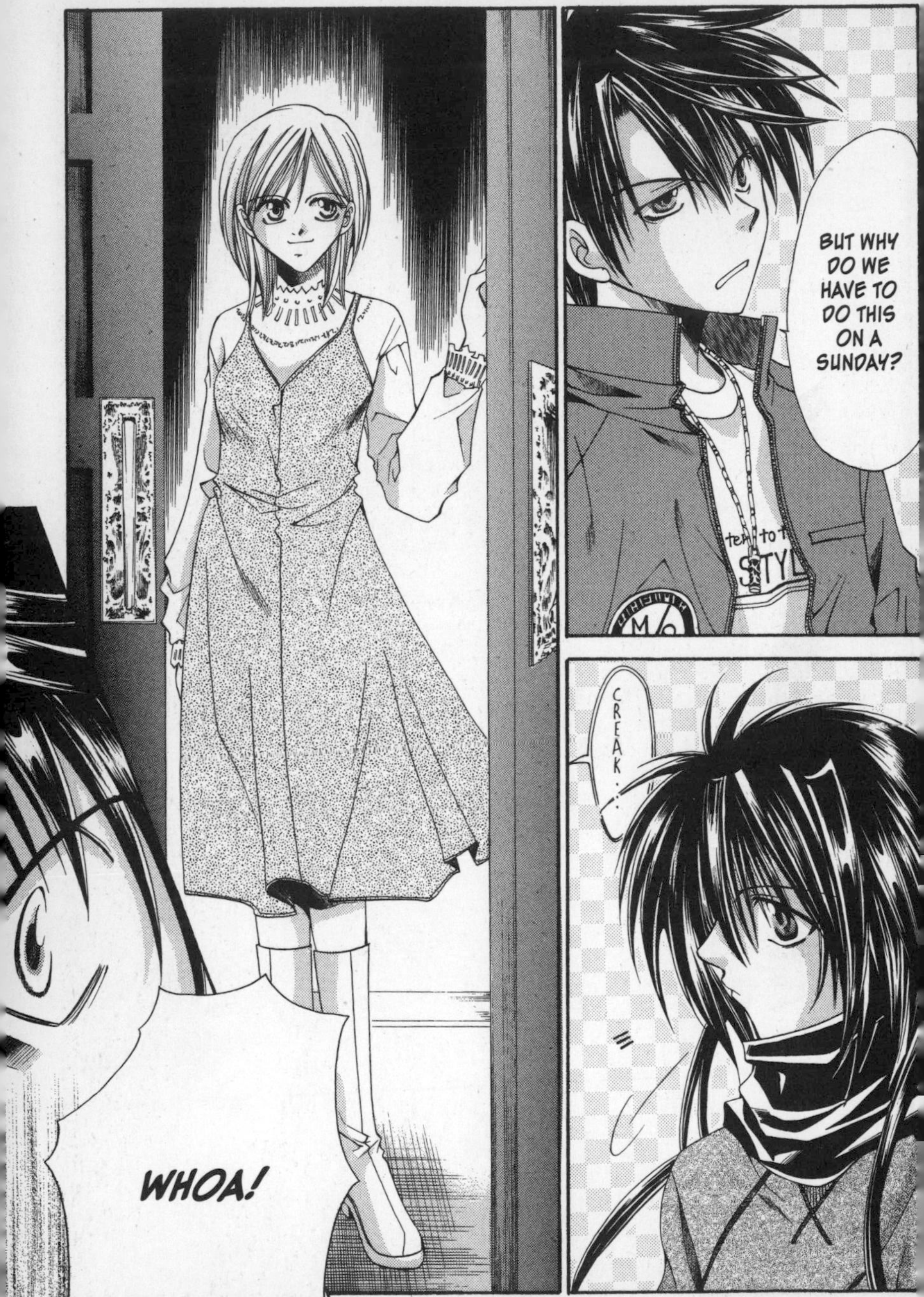
BUT WHY DO WE HAVE TO DO THIS ON A SUNDAY?
CREAK...
WHOA!

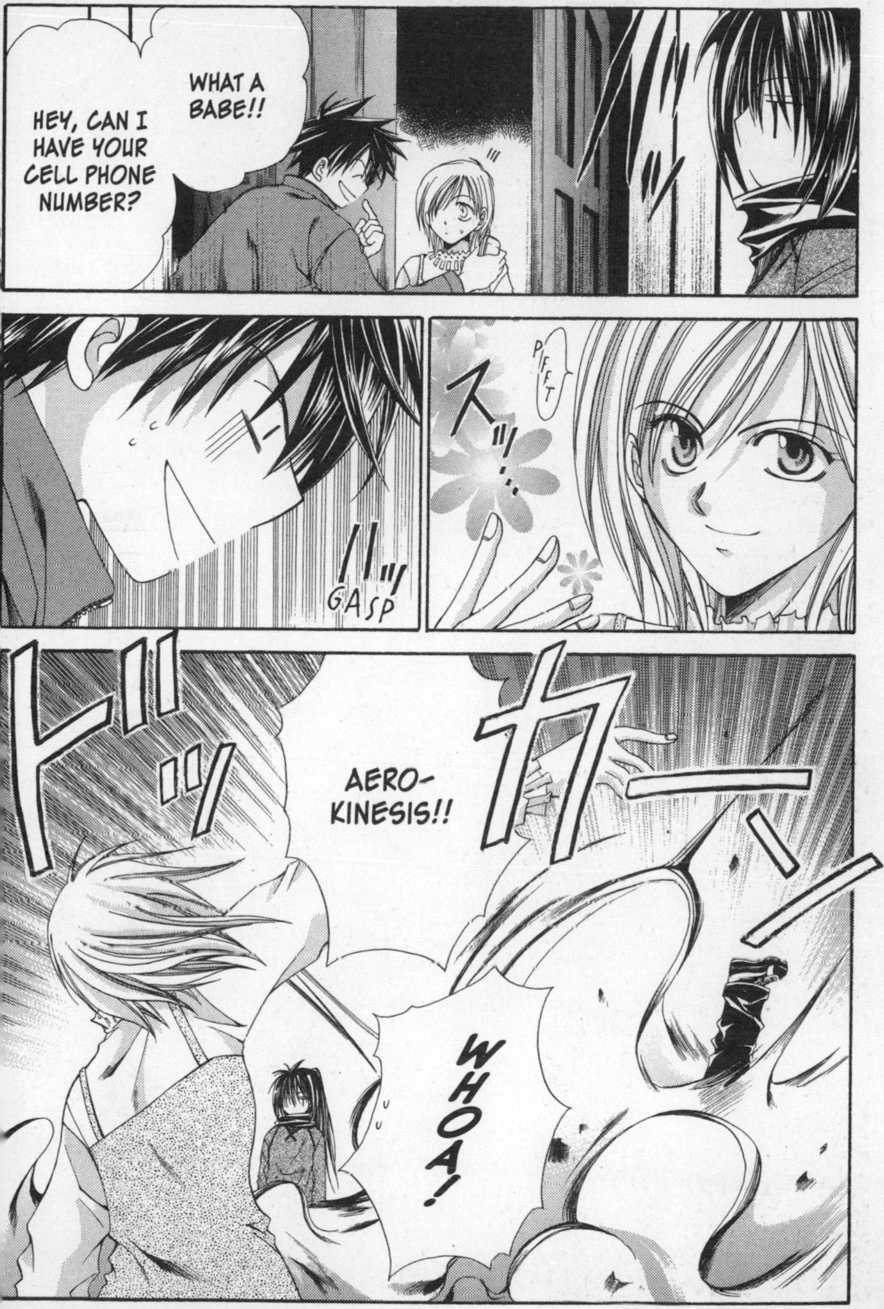
WHAT A BABE!!
HEY, CAN I HAVE YOUR CELL PHONE NUMBER?
PIFFT
GASP
AERO-KINESIS!!
WHOA!

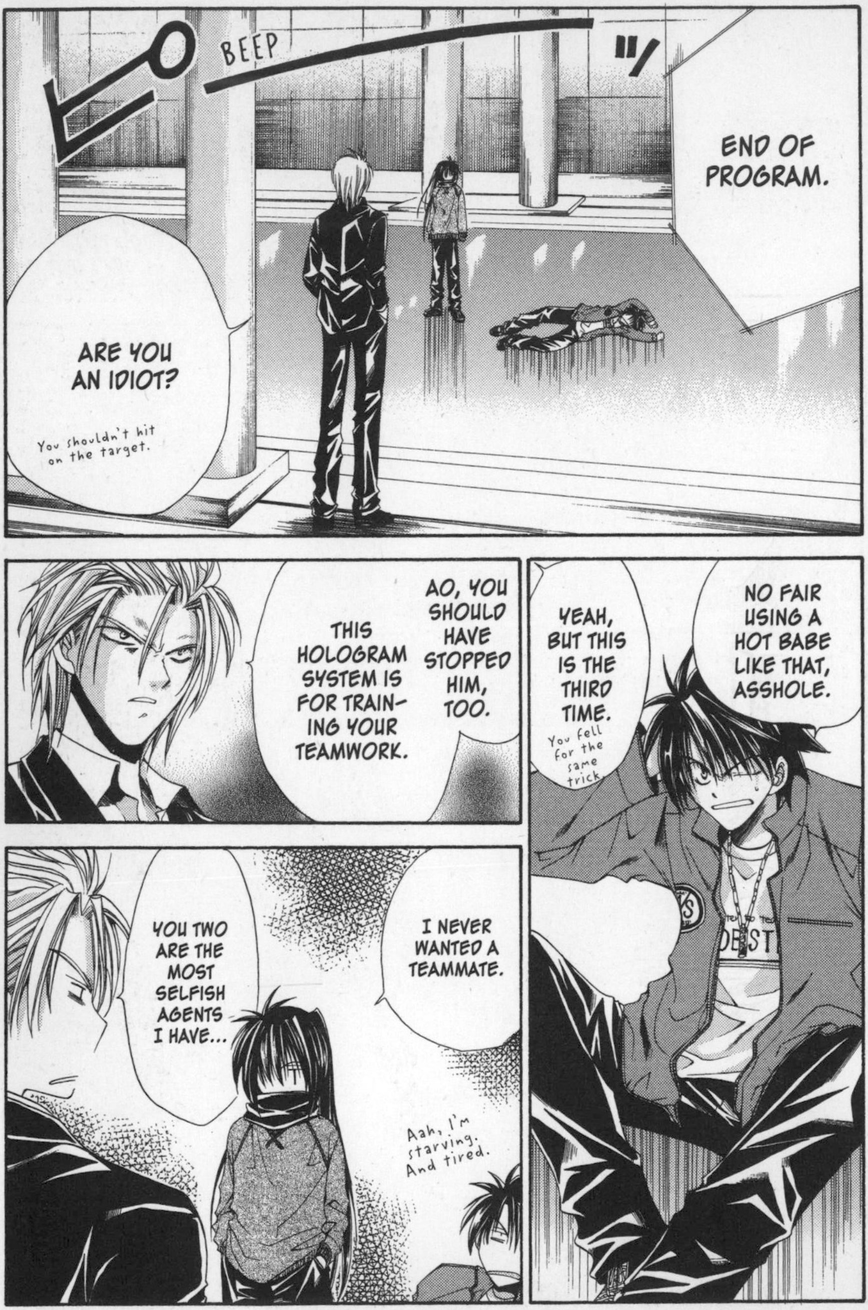
BEEP
END OF PROGRAM.
ARE YOU AN IDIOT?
You shouldn't hit on the target.
NO FAIR USING A HOT BABE LIKE THAT, ASSHOLE.
YEAH, BUT THIS IS THE THIRD TIME.
You fell for the same trick
AO, YOU SHOULD HAVE STOPPED HIM, TOO.
THIS HOLOGRAM SYSTEM IS FOR TRAINING YOUR TEAMWORK.
I NEVER WANTED A TEAMMATE.
YOU TWO ARE THE MOST SELFISH AGENTS I HAVE...
Aah, I'm starving. And tired.

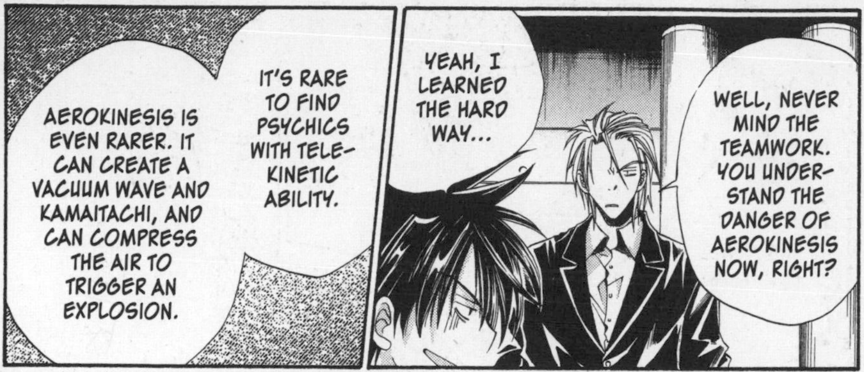
WELL, NEVER MIND THE TEAMWORK. YOU UNDERSTAND THE DANGER OF AEROKINESIS NOW, RIGHT?
YEAH, I LEARNED THE HARD WAY...
IT'S RARE TO FIND PSYCHICS WITH TELEKINETIC ABILITY.
AEROKINESIS IS EVEN RARER. IT CAN CREATE A VACUUM WAVE AND KAMAITACHI, AND CAN COMPRESS THE AIR TO TRIGGER AN EXPLOSION.

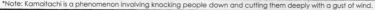

*Note: Kamaitachi is a phenomenon involving knocking people down and cutting them deeply with a gust of wind.

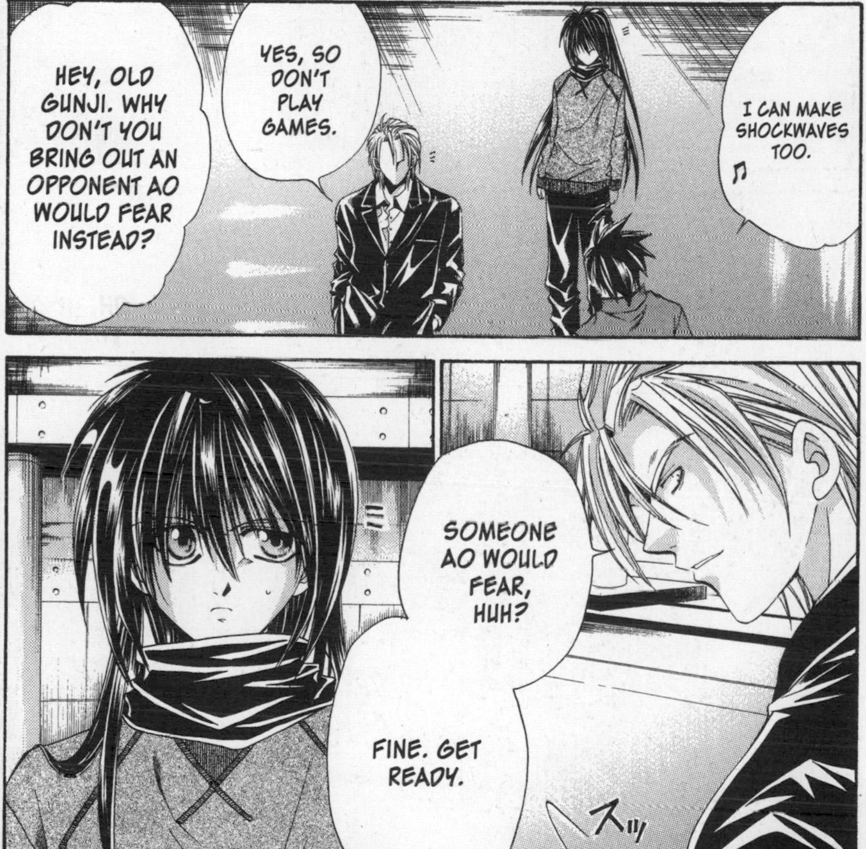
I CAN MAKE SHOCKWAVES TOO.
YES, SO DON'T PLAY GAMES.
HEY, OLD GUNJI. WHY DON'T YOU BRING OUT AN OPPONENT AO WOULD FEAR INSTEAD?
SOMEONE AO WOULD FEAR, HUH?
FINE. GET READY.
スッ

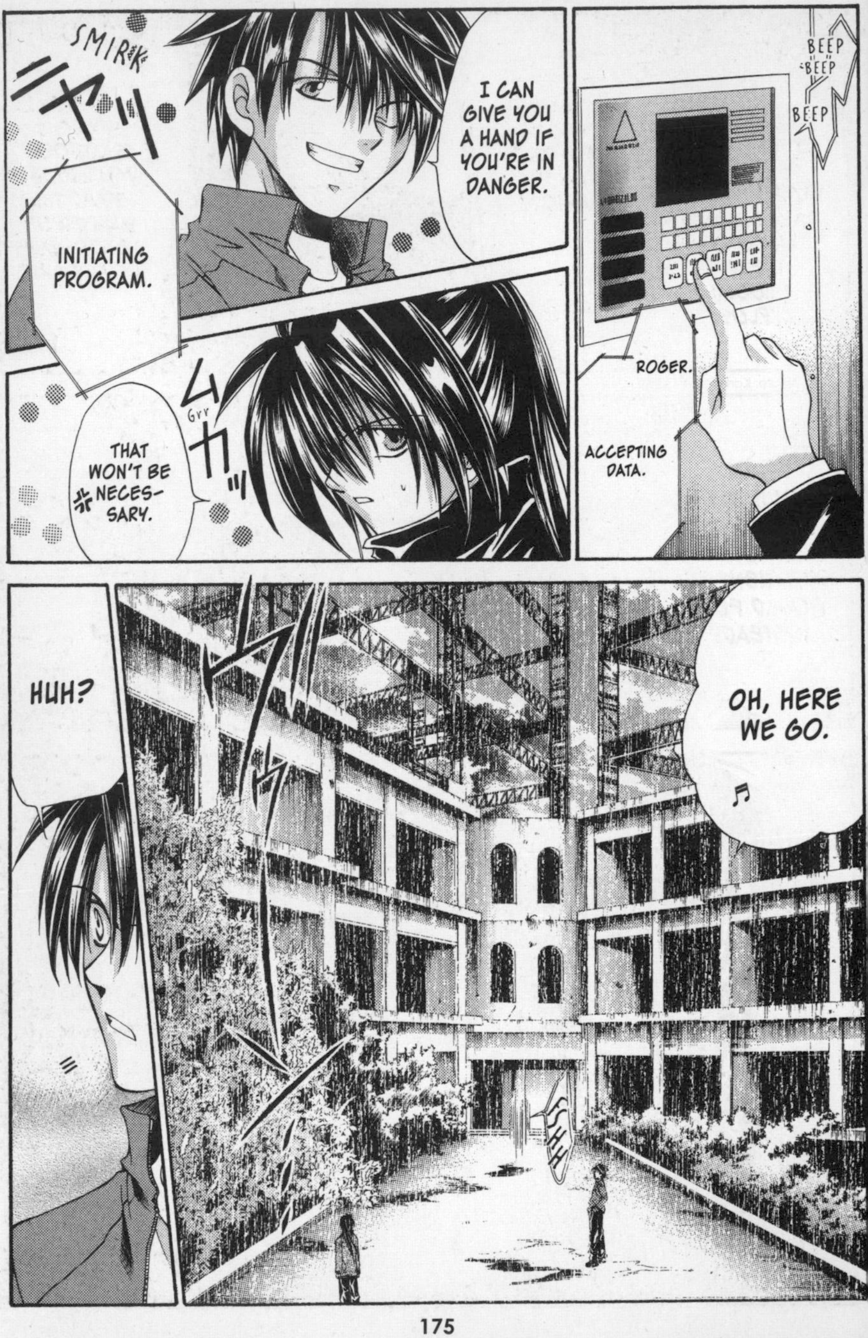
BEEP
BEEP
BEEP
ROGER.
ACCEPTING DATA.
SMIRK
ニヤッ
I CAN GIVE YOU A HAND IF YOU'RE IN DANGER.
INITIATING PROGRAM.
ムカッ
Grr
THAT WON'T BE NECES-SARY.
OH, HERE WE GO. ♪
FSHH
HUH?

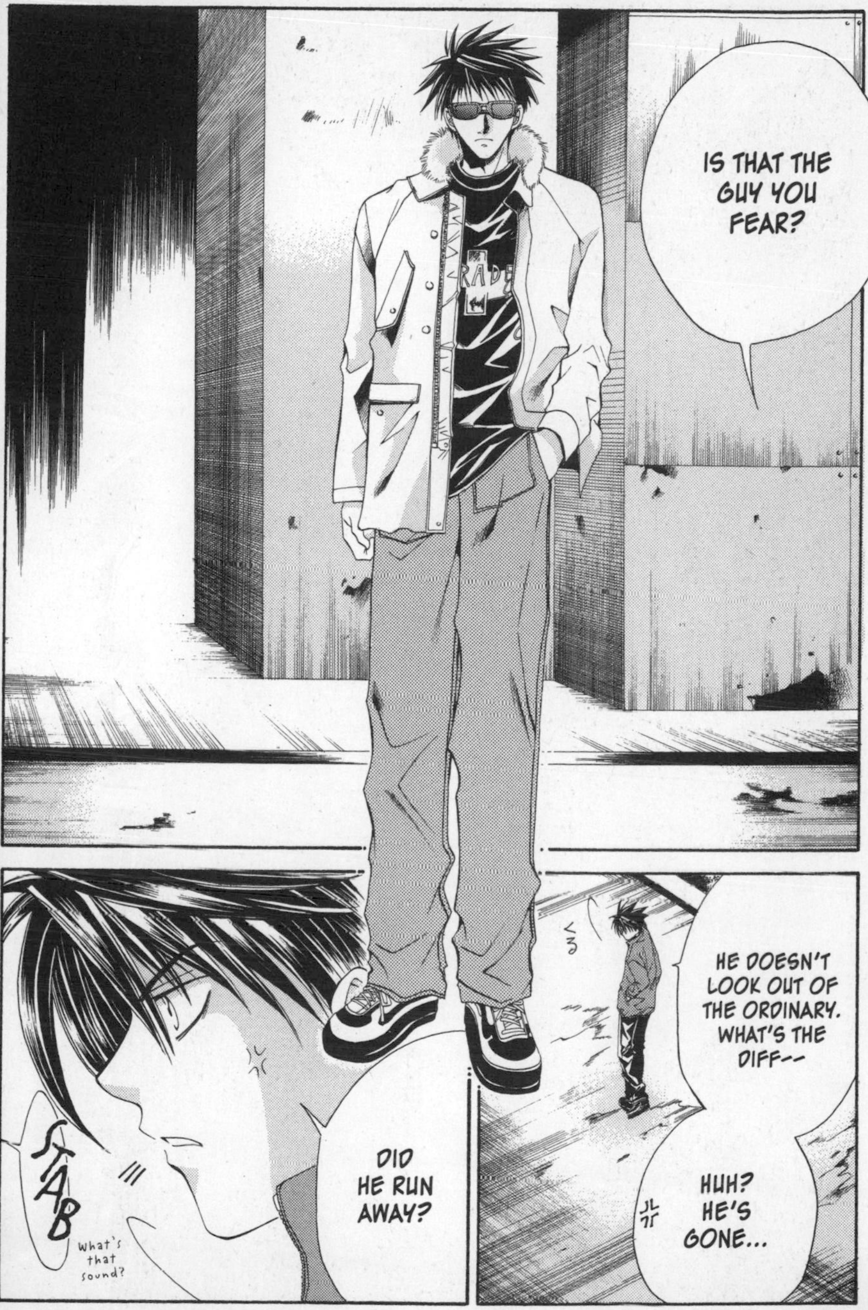
IS THAT THE GUY YOU FEAR?
HE DOESN'T LOOK OUT OF THE ORDINARY. WHAT'S THE DIFF--
HUH? HE'S GONE...
DID HE RUN AWAY?
STAB
What's that sound?

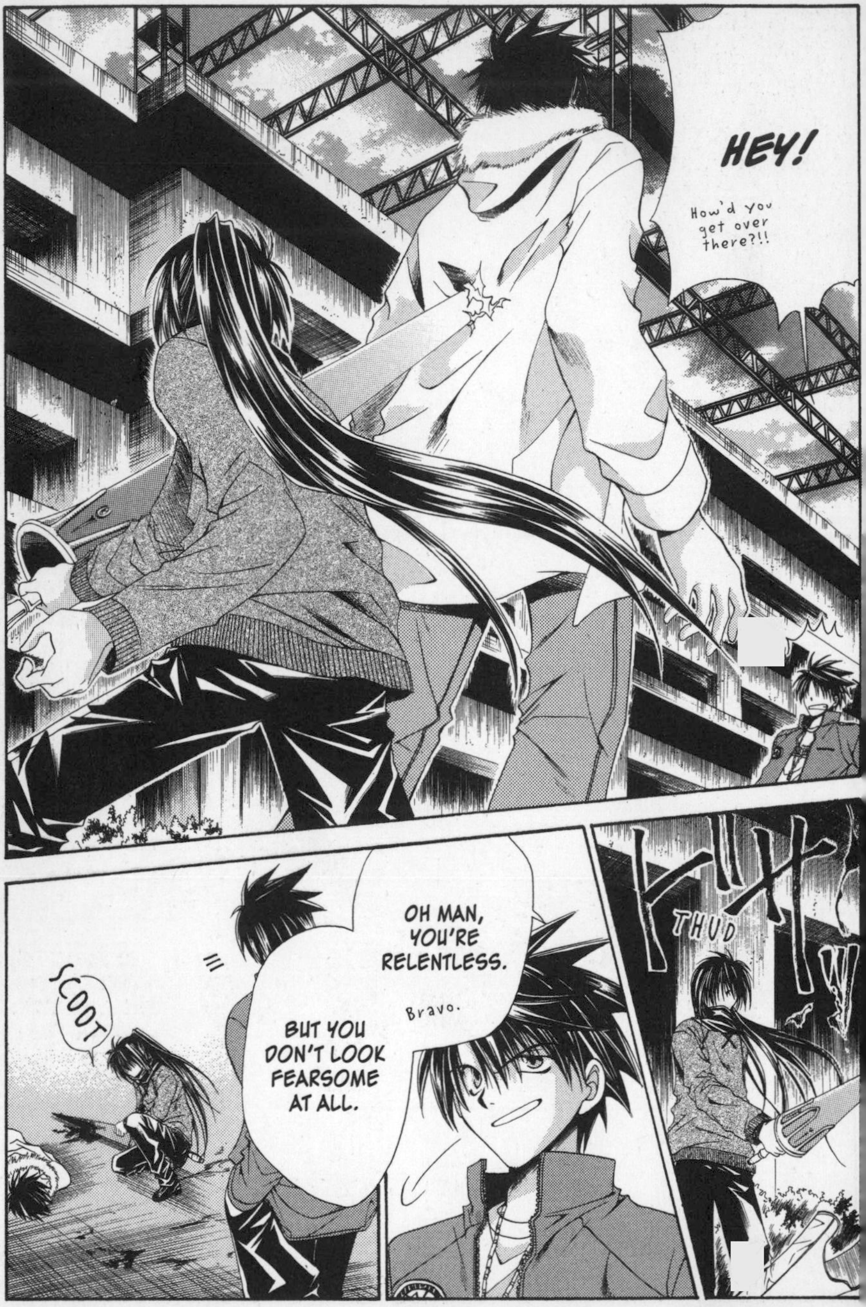
HEY!
How'd you get over there?!!
THUD
OH MAN, YOU'RE RELENTLESS.
Bravo.
BUT YOU DON'T LOOK FEARSOME AT ALL.
SCOOT

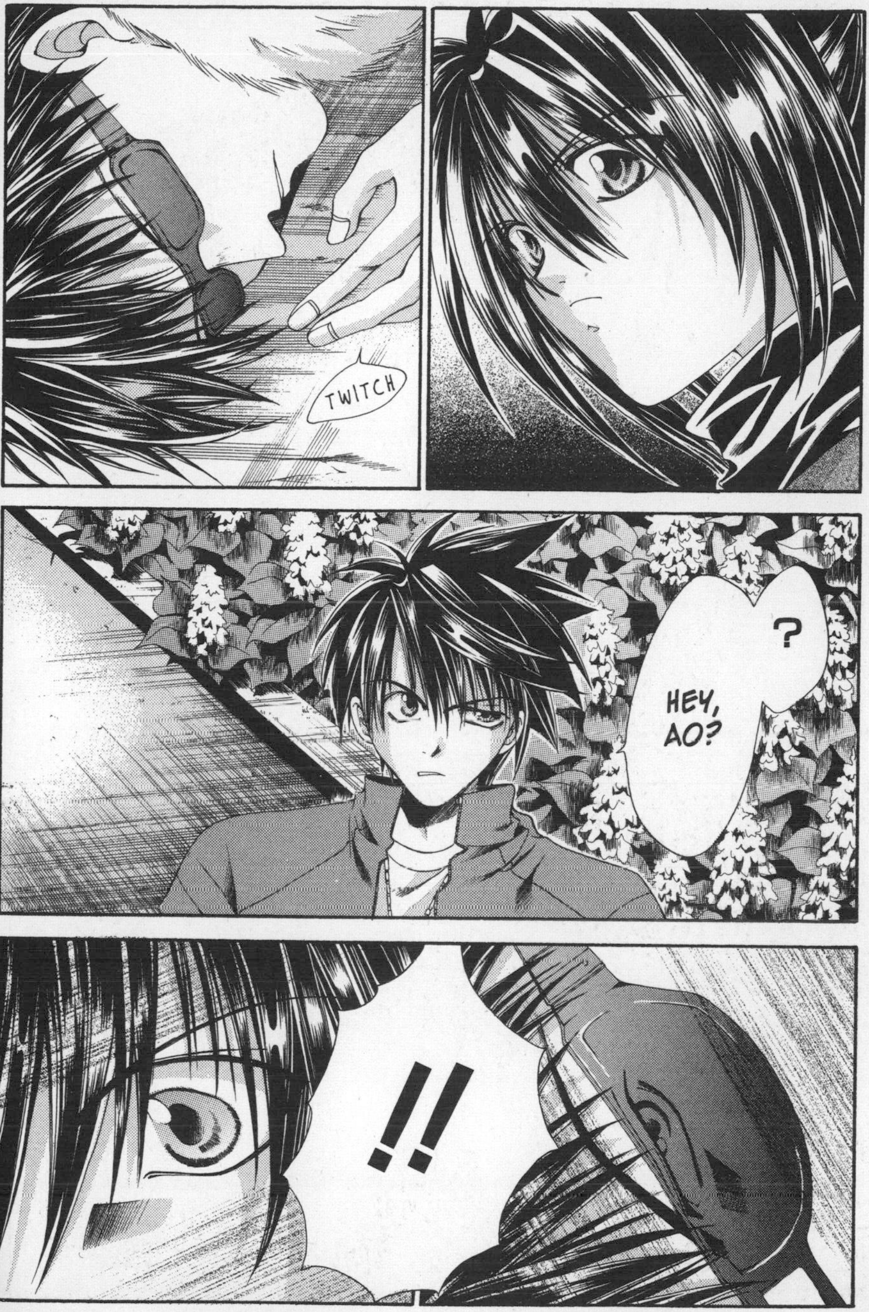
TWITCH
?
HEY, AO?
!!

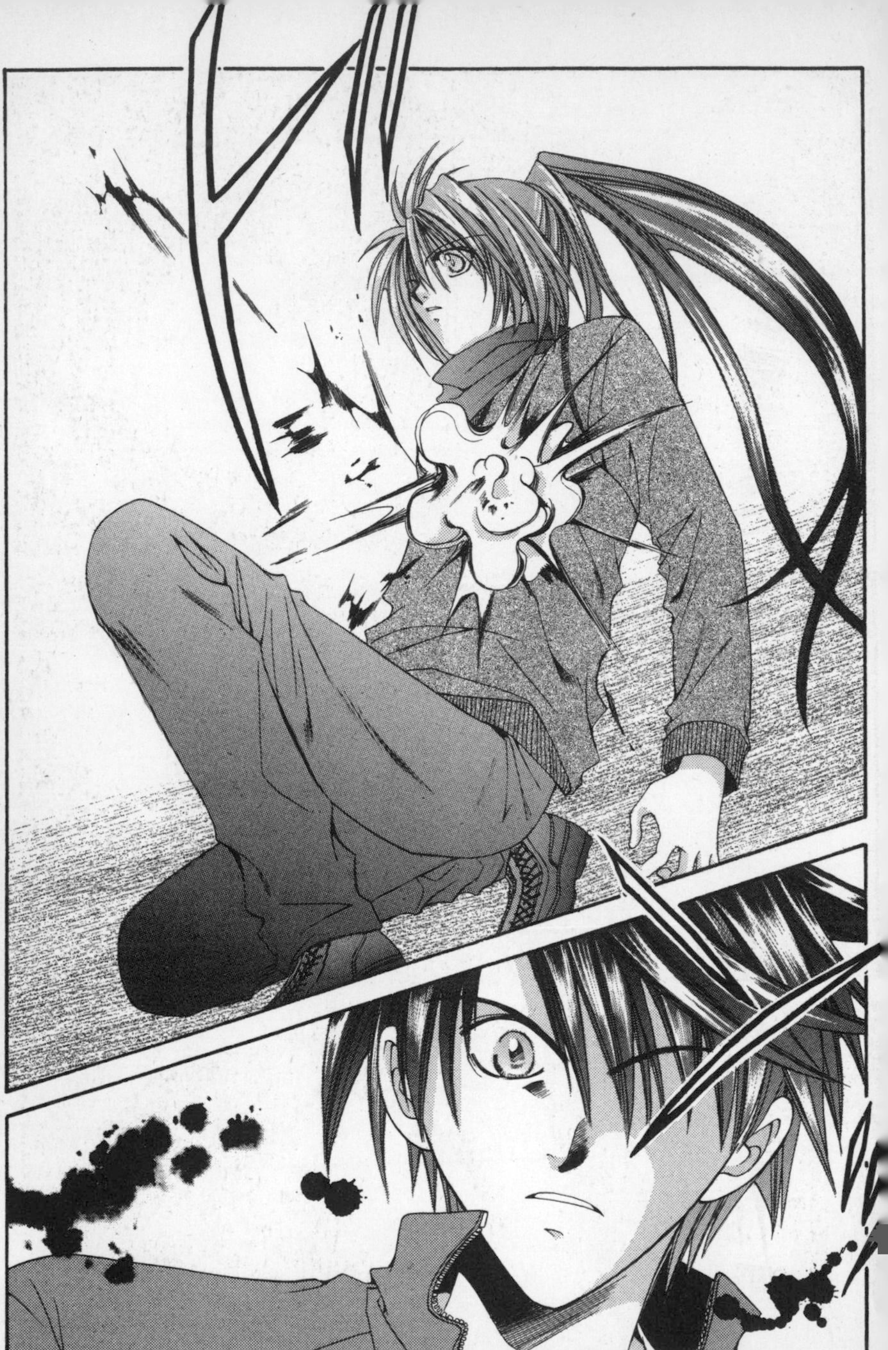

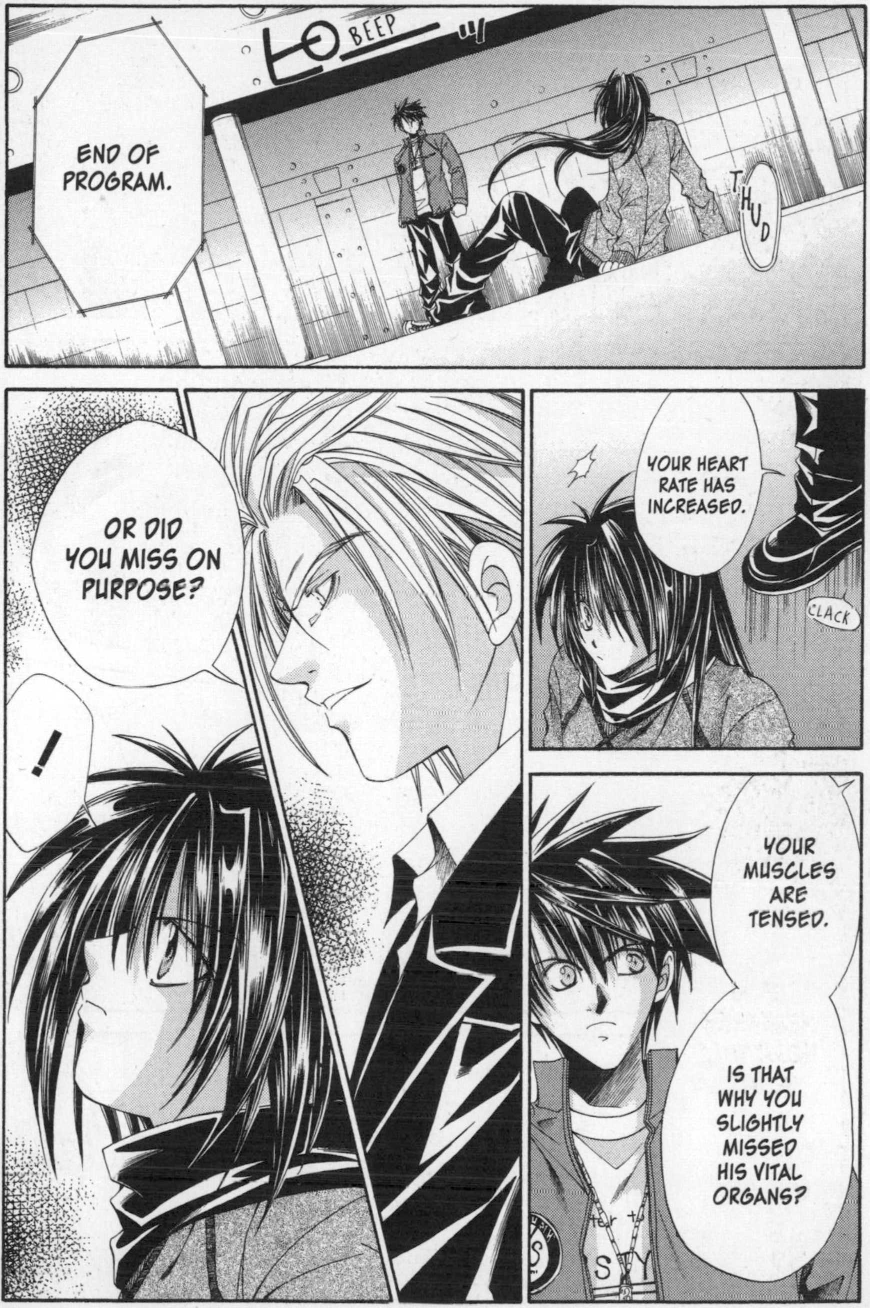
BEEP
END OF PROGRAM.
THUD
YOUR HEART RATE HAS INCREASED.
CLACK
YOUR MUSCLES ARE TENSED.
IS THAT WHY YOU SLIGHTLY MISSED HIS VITAL ORGANS?
OR DID YOU MISS ON PURPOSE?
!

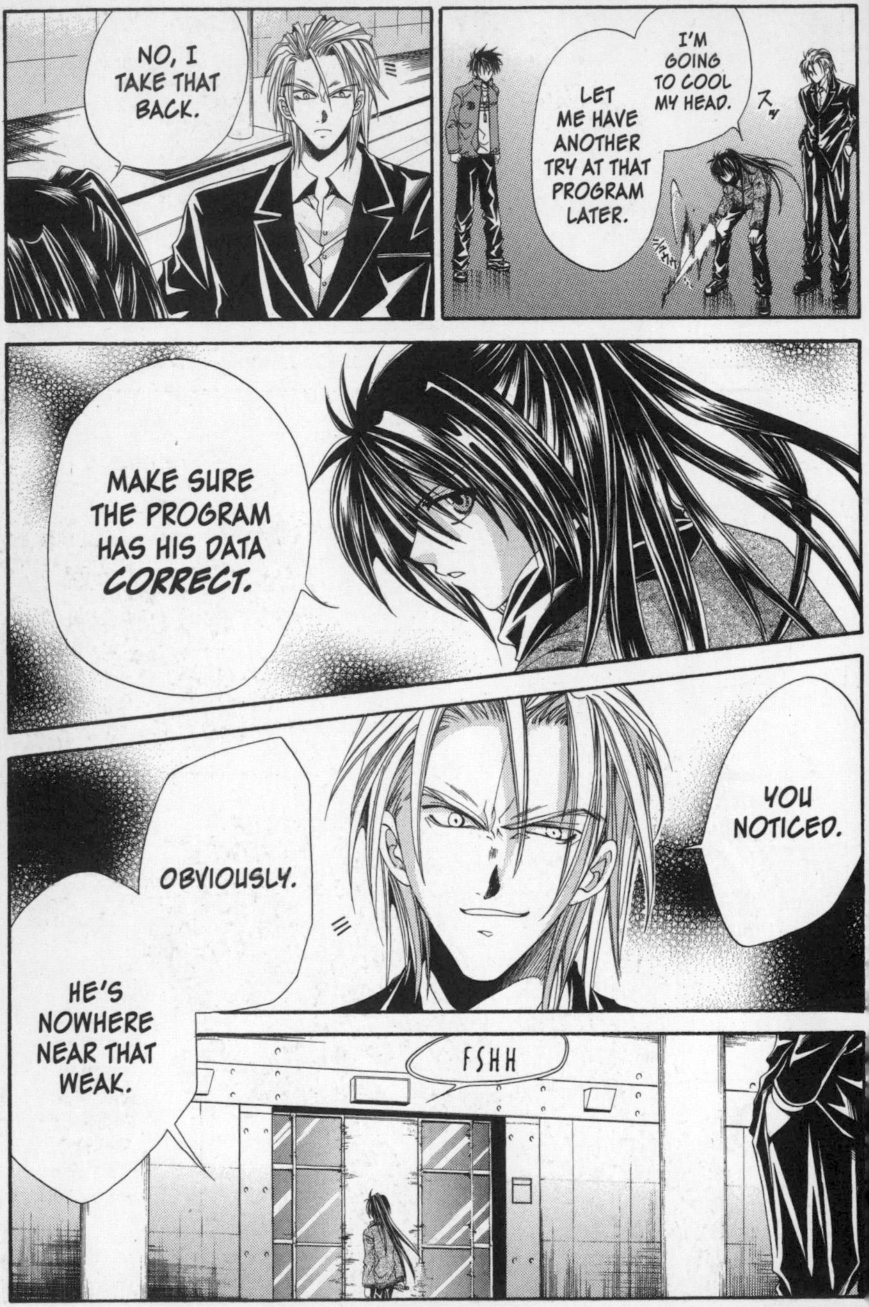
I'M GOING TO COOL MY HEAD.
LET ME HAVE ANOTHER TRY AT THAT PROGRAM LATER.
スッ
NO, I TAKE THAT BACK.
MAKE SURE THE PROGRAM HAS HIS DATA CORRECT.
YOU NOTICED.
OBVIOUSLY.
FSHH
HE'S NOWHERE NEAR THAT WEAK.

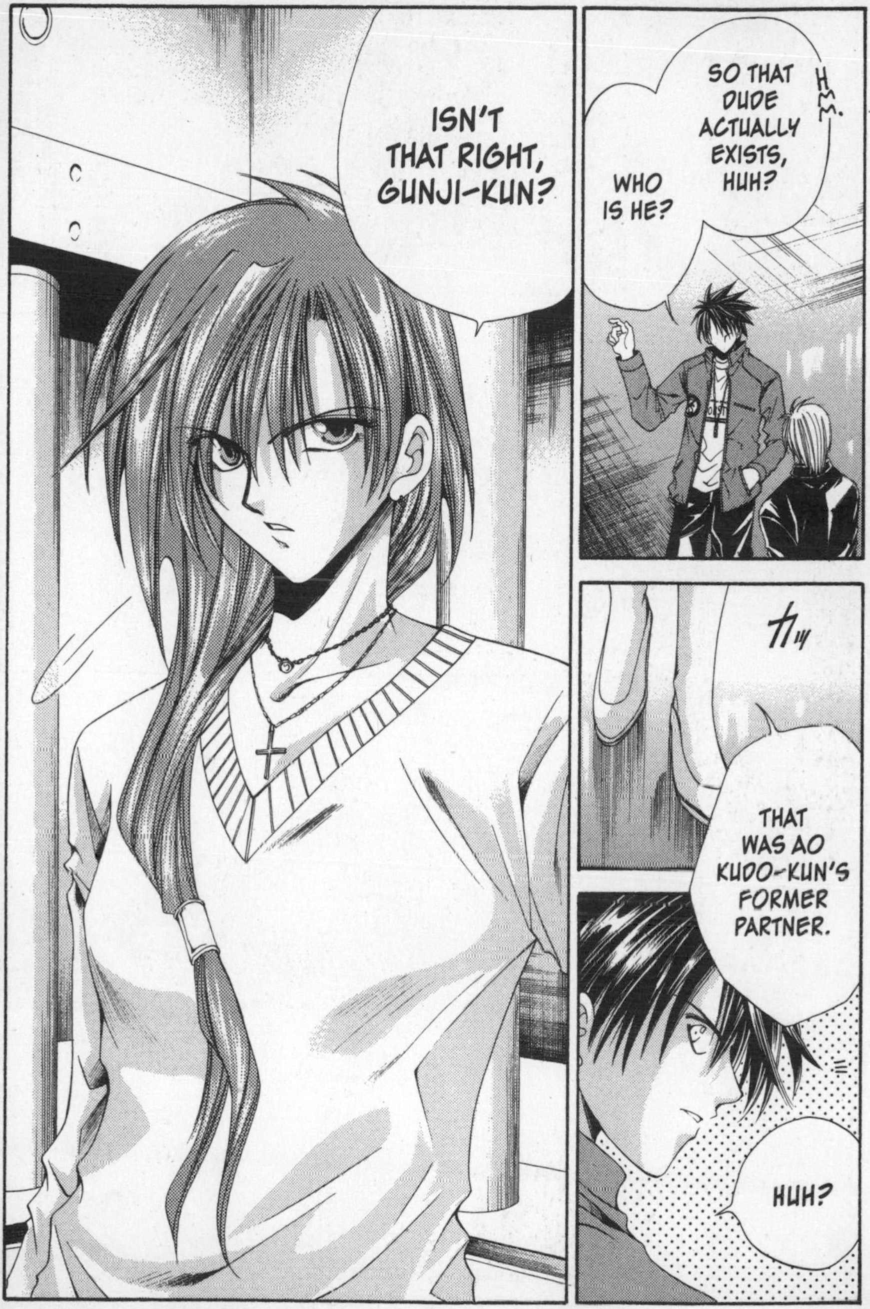
HMM.
SO THAT DUDE ACTUALLY EXISTS, HUH?
WHO IS HE?
カッ
THAT WAS AO KUDO-KUN'S FORMER PARTNER.
HUH?
ISN'T THAT RIGHT, GUNJI-KUN?

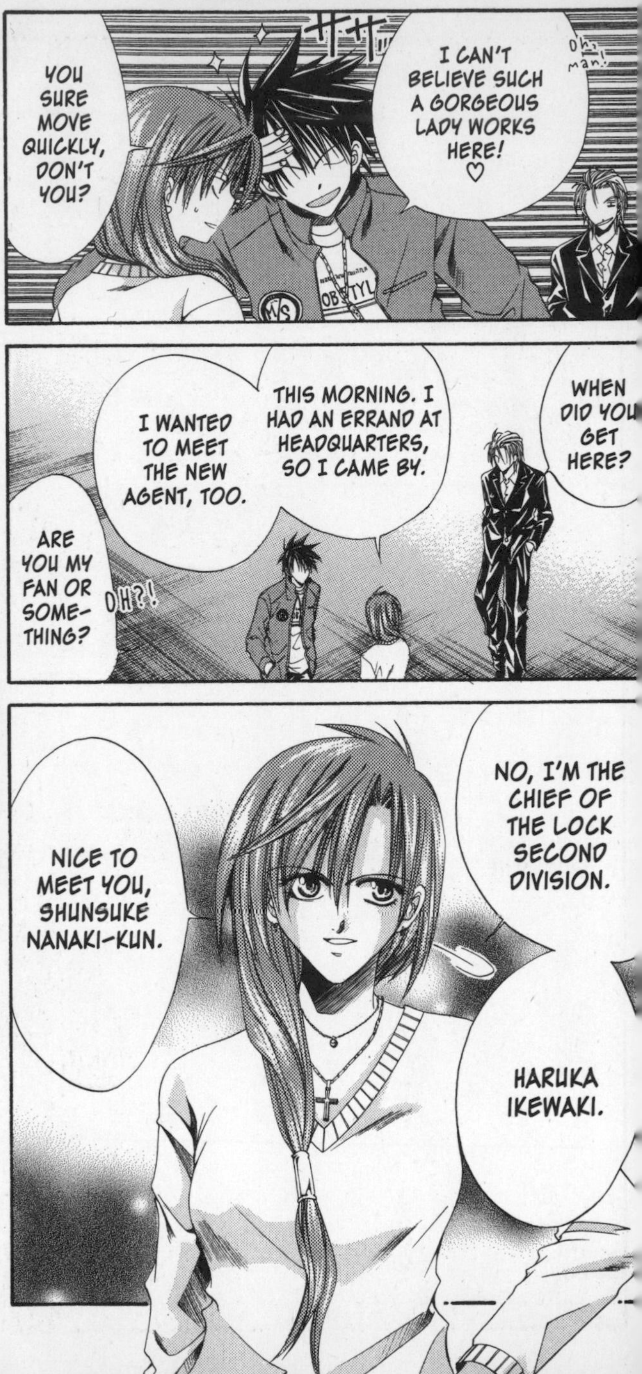
Oh, man!
I CAN'T BELIEVE SUCH A GORGEOUS LADY WORKS HERE! ♡
ササッ
YOU SURE MOVE QUICKLY, DON'T YOU?
WHEN DID YOU GET HERE?
THIS MORNING. I HAD AN ERRAND AT HEADQUARTERS, SO I CAME BY.
I WANTED TO MEET THE NEW AGENT, TOO.
OH?!
ARE YOU MY FAN OR SOMETHING?
NO, I'M THE CHIEF OF THE LOCK SECOND DIVISION.
HARUKA IKEWAKI.
NICE TO MEET YOU, SHUNSUKE NANAKI-KUN.

群寺 秀明

GUNJI, HIDEAKI

• Chief of the Paranormal Task Force (LOCK) First Division

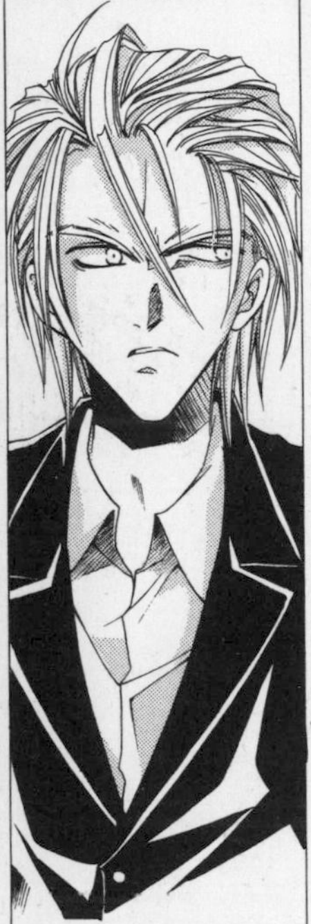

■ Psi Abilities ■

※ Since he hasn't fully shown his abilities in the story, they're still a secret. (Laughs.) I believe he'll exhibit them in a spectacular manner eventually.

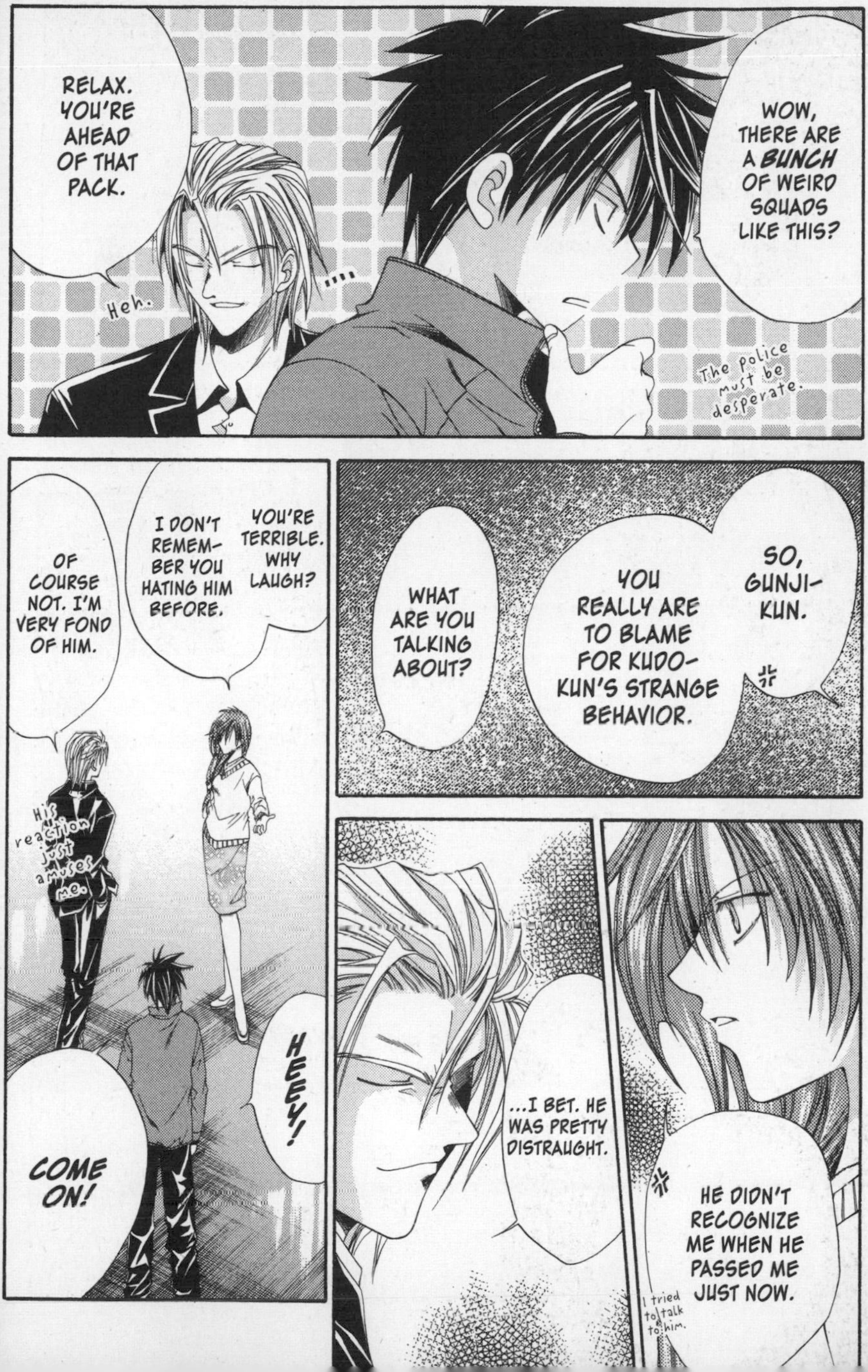
WOW, THERE ARE A *BUNCH* OF WEIRD SQUADS LIKE THIS?
The police must be desperate.
RELAX. YOU'RE AHEAD OF THAT PACK.
Heh.
....
SO, GUNJI-KUN.
YOU REALLY ARE TO BLAME FOR KUDO-KUN'S STRANGE BEHAVIOR.
WHAT ARE YOU TALKING ABOUT?
HE DIDN'T RECOGNIZE ME WHEN HE PASSED ME JUST NOW.
I tried to talk to him.
...I BET. HE WAS PRETTY DISTRAUGHT.
YOU'RE TERRIBLE. WHY LAUGH?
I DON'T REMEM-BER YOU HATING HIM BEFORE.
OF COURSE NOT. I'M VERY FOND OF HIM.
His reastion just amuses me.
HEEY!
COME ON!

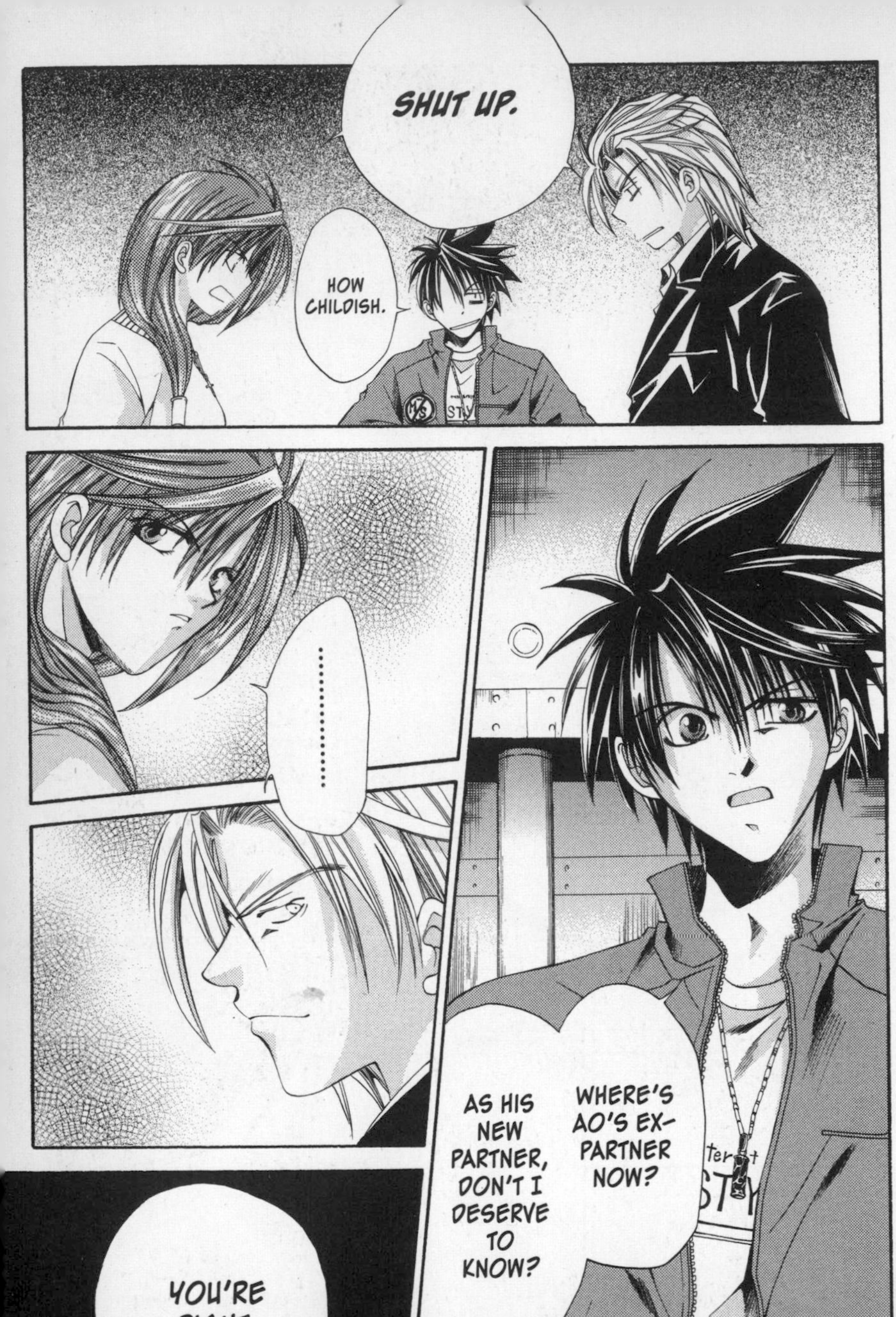

SHUT UP.
HOW CHILDISH.
WHERE'S AO'S EX-PARTNER NOW?
AS HIS NEW PARTNER, DON'T I DESERVE TO KNOW?
......
YOU'RE RIGHT.

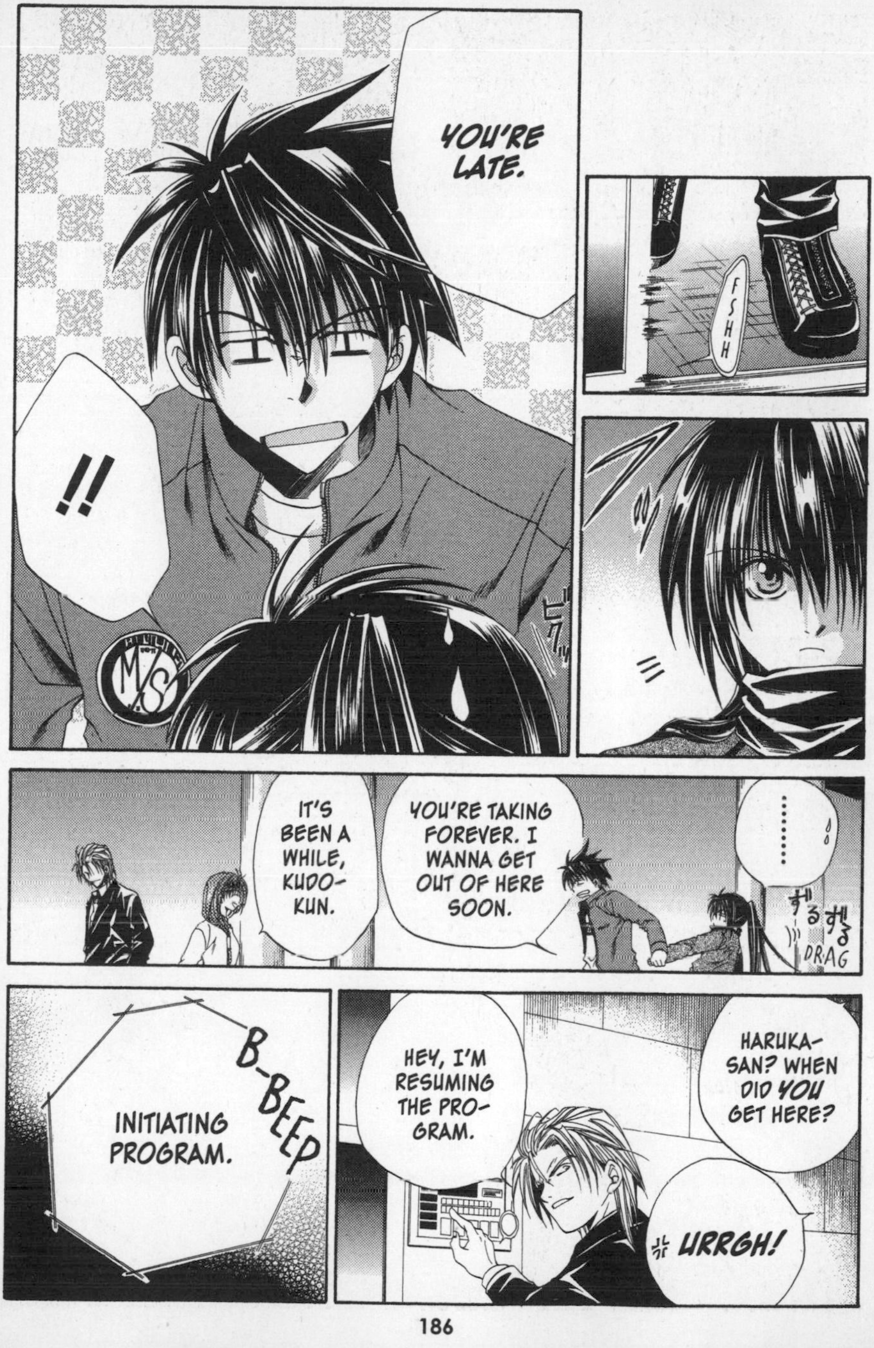
FSHH
YOU'RE LATE.
!!
……
ずるずる
DRAG
YOU'RE TAKING FOREVER. I WANNA GET OUT OF HERE SOON.
IT'S BEEN A WHILE, KUDO-KUN.
HARUKA-SAN? WHEN DID *YOU* GET HERE?
HEY, I'M RESUMING THE PRO-GRAM.
URRGH!
B-BEEP
INITIATING PROGRAM.

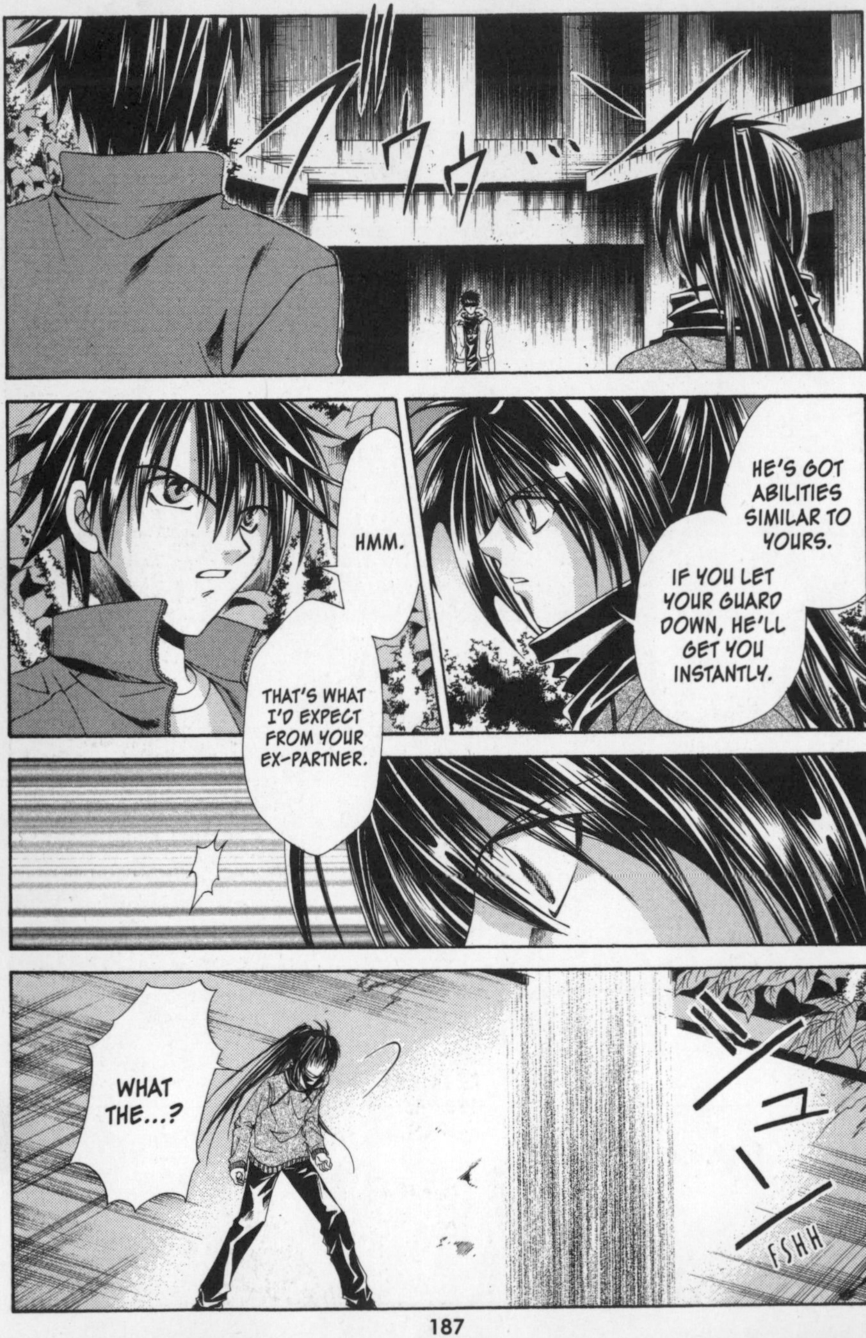
HE'S GOT ABILITIES SIMILAR TO YOURS.
IF YOU LET YOUR GUARD DOWN, HE'LL GET YOU INSTANTLY.
HMM.
THAT'S WHAT I'D EXPECT FROM YOUR EX-PARTNER.
FSHH
WHAT THE...?

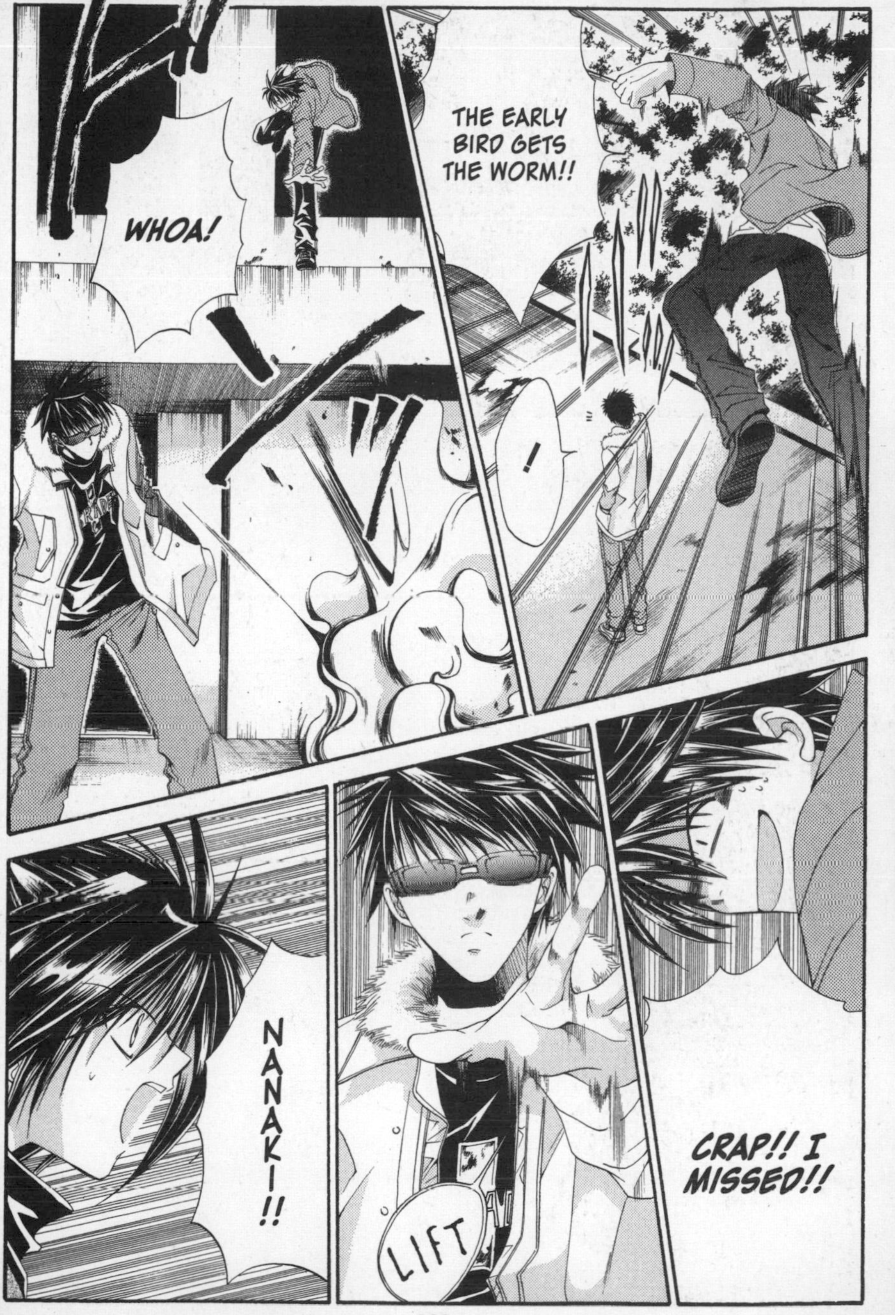
THE EARLY BIRD GETS THE WORM!!
!
WHOA!
CRAP!! I MISSED!!
LIFT
NANAKI!!

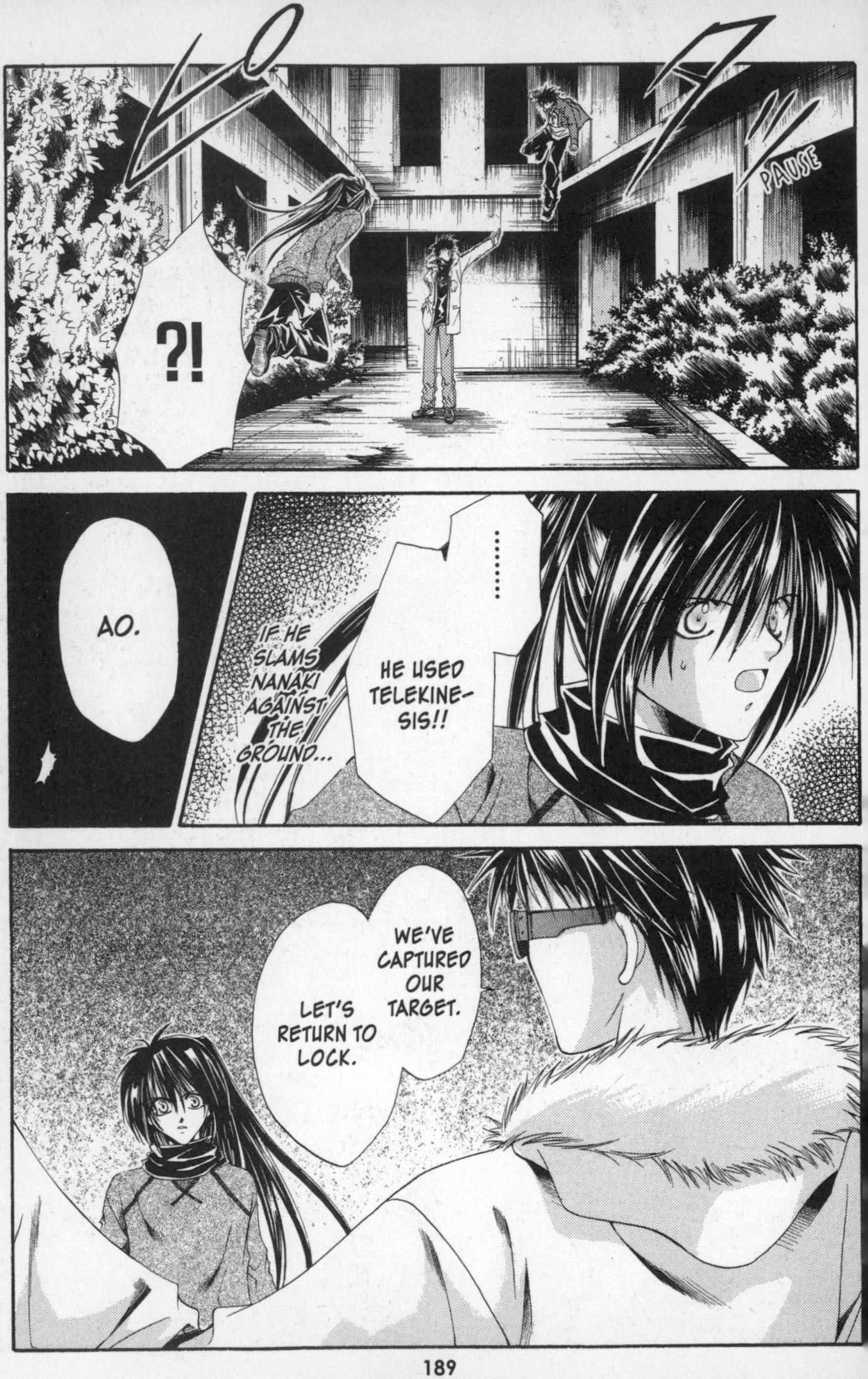
PAUSE
?!
......
HE USED TELEKINESIS!!
IF HE SLAMS NANAKI AGAINST THE GROUND...
AO.
WE'VE CAPTURED OUR TARGET.
LET'S RETURN TO LOCK.

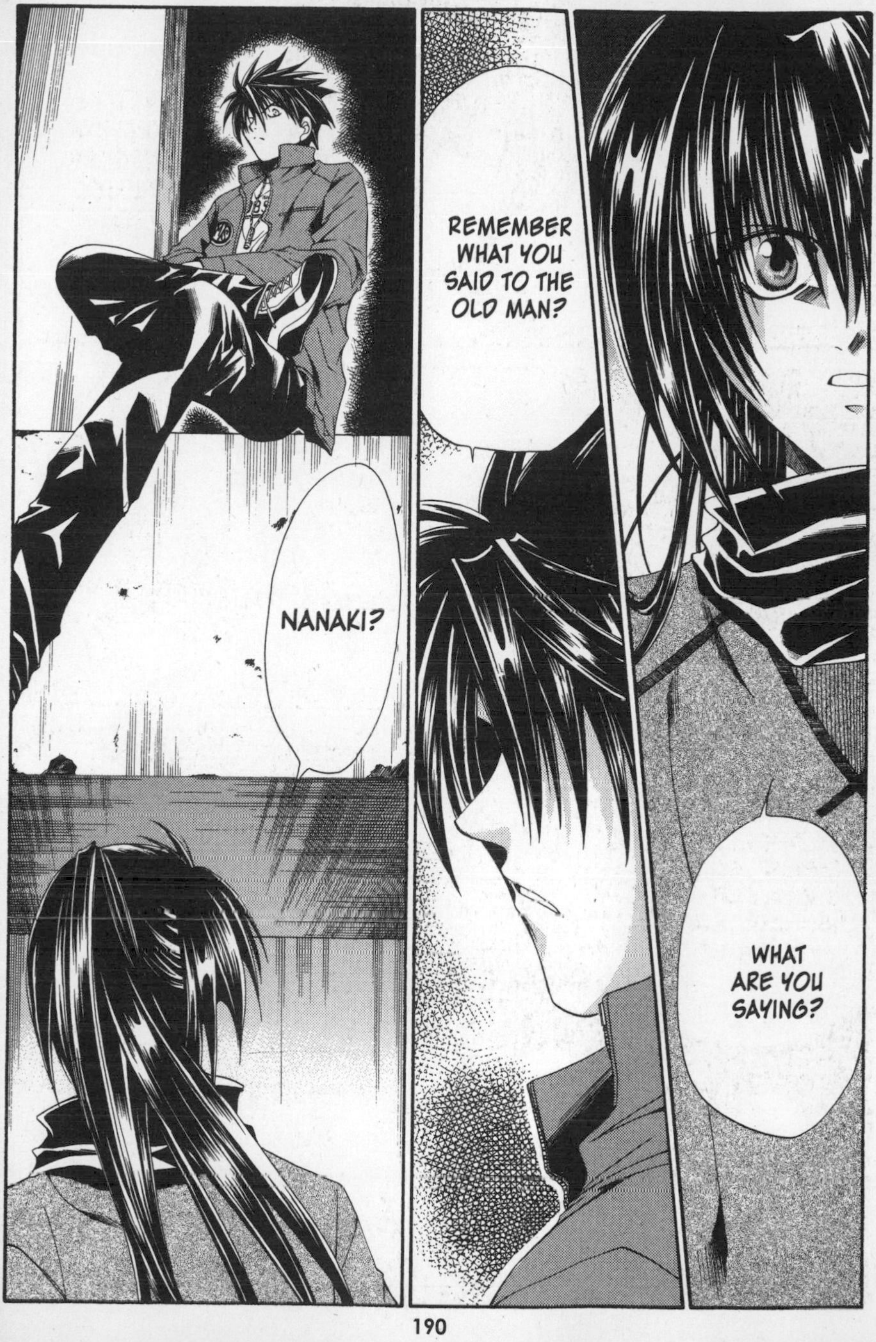
WHAT ARE YOU SAYING?
REMEMBER WHAT YOU SAID TO THE OLD MAN?
NANAKI?

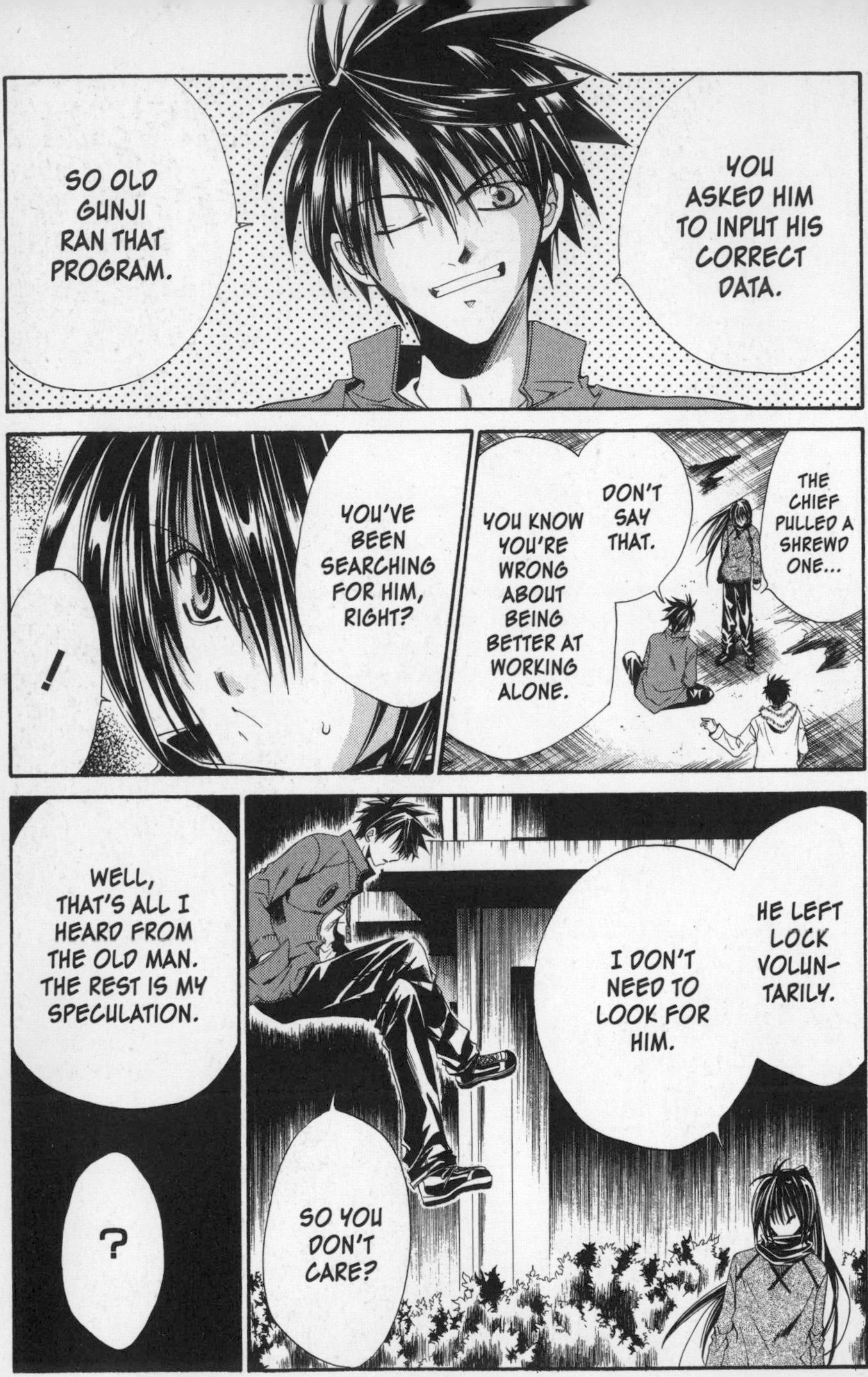
YOU ASKED HIM TO INPUT HIS CORRECT DATA.
SO OLD GUNJI RAN THAT PROGRAM.
THE CHIEF PULLED A SHREWD ONE...
DON'T SAY THAT.
YOU KNOW YOU'RE WRONG ABOUT BEING BETTER AT WORKING ALONE.
YOU'VE BEEN SEARCHING FOR HIM, RIGHT?
!
HE LEFT LOCK VOLUN-TARILY.
I DON'T NEED TO LOOK FOR HIM.
SO YOU DON'T CARE?
WELL, THAT'S ALL I HEARD FROM THE OLD MAN. THE REST IS MY SPECULATION.
?

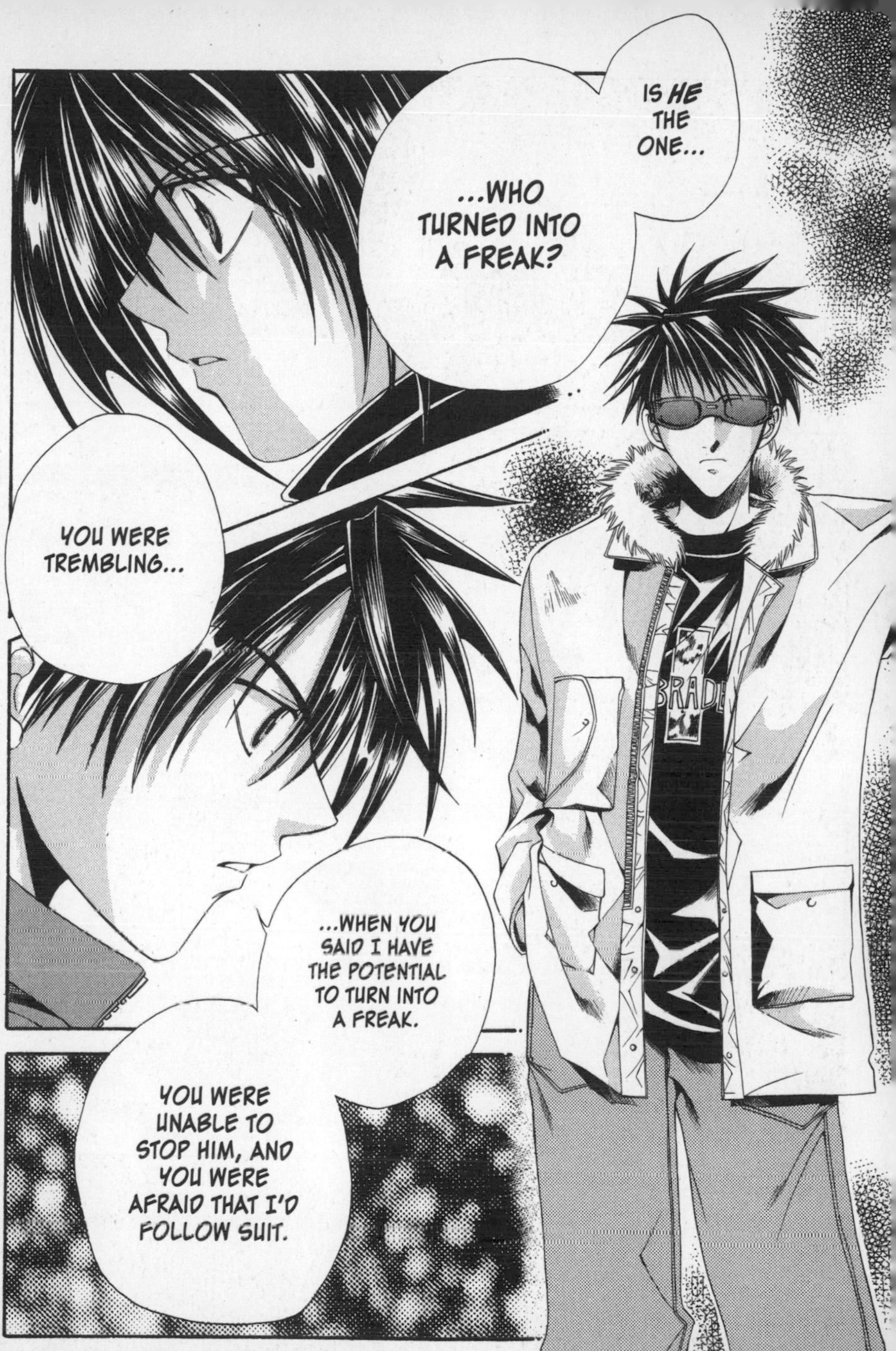
IS *HE* THE ONE...
...WHO TURNED INTO A FREAK?
YOU WERE TREMBLING...
...WHEN YOU SAID I HAVE THE POTENTIAL TO TURN INTO A FREAK.
YOU WERE UNABLE TO STOP HIM, AND YOU WERE AFRAID THAT I'D FOLLOW SUIT.

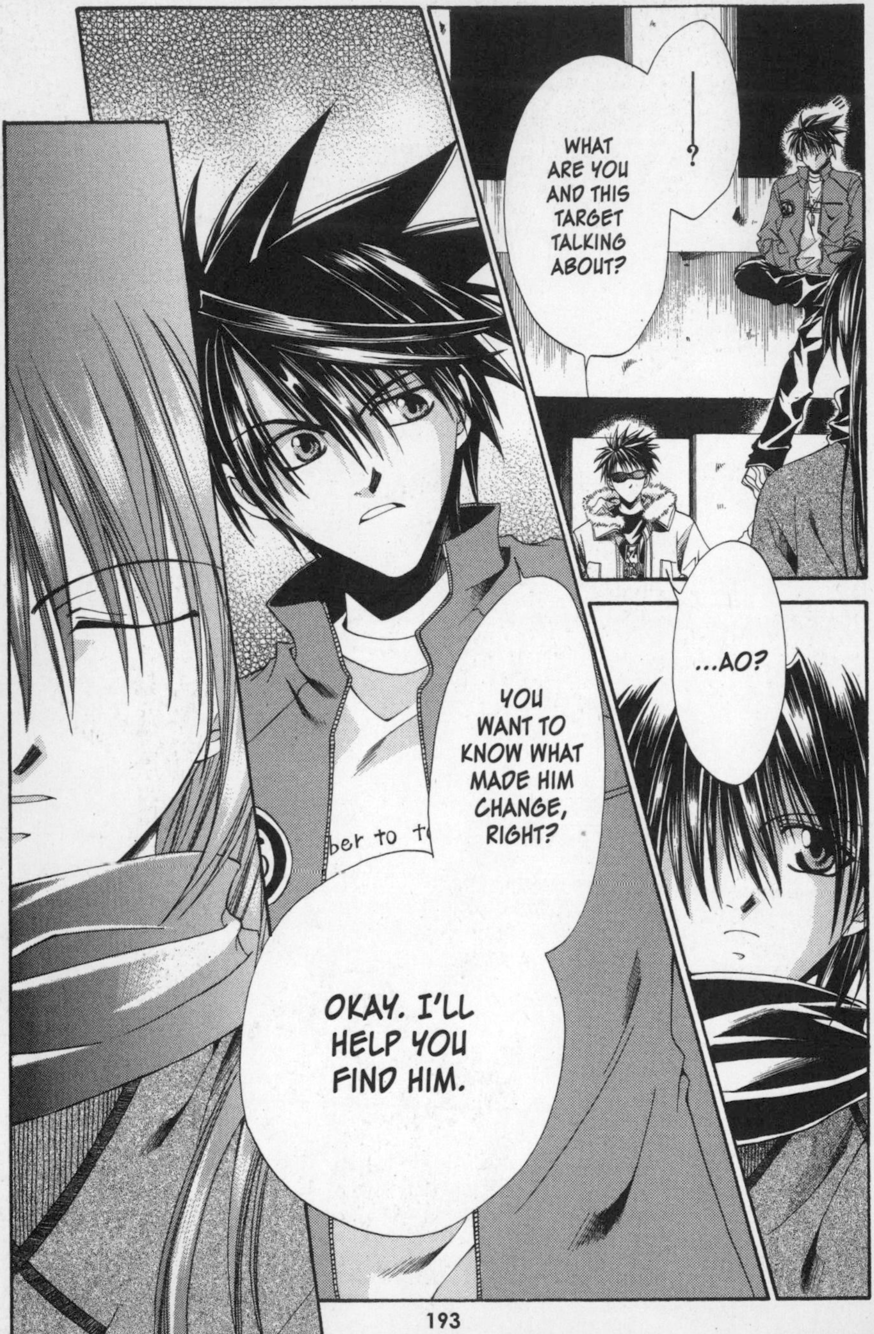
—?
WHAT ARE YOU AND THIS TARGET TALKING ABOUT?
...AO?
YOU WANT TO KNOW WHAT MADE HIM CHANGE, RIGHT?
OKAY. I'LL HELP YOU FIND HIM.

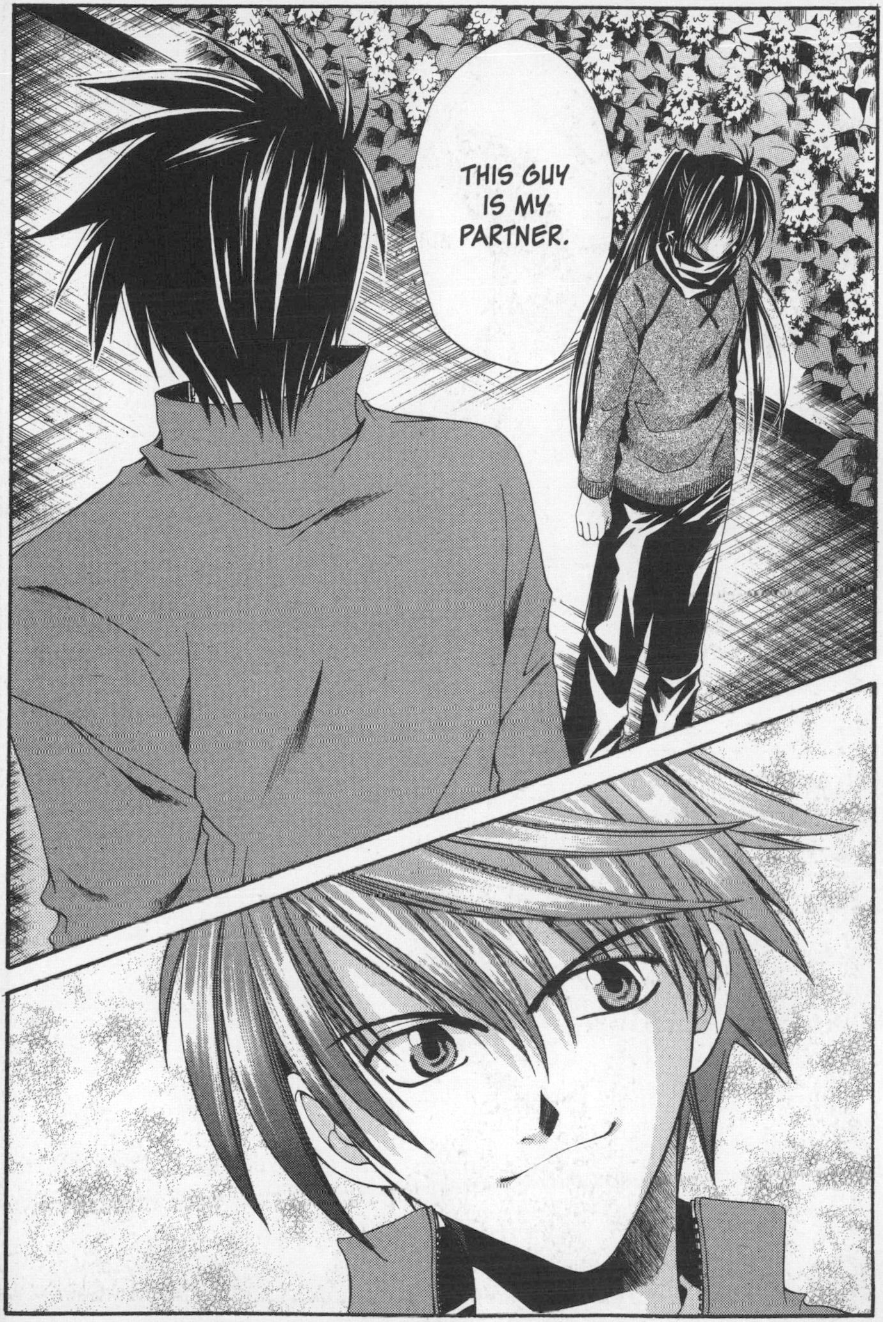
THIS GUY
IS MY
PARTNER.

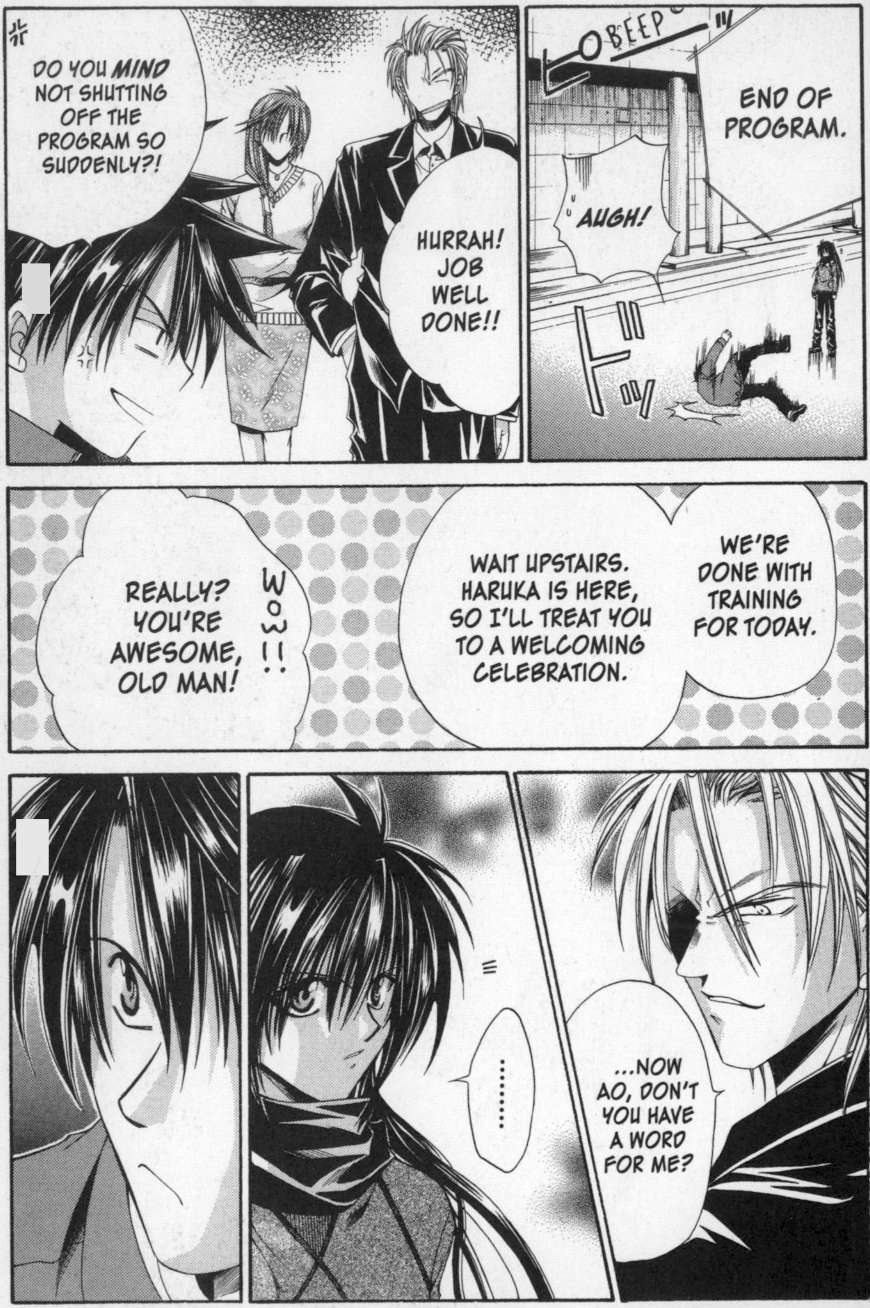
BEEP
END OF PROGRAM.
AUGH!
HURRAH! JOB WELL DONE!!
DO YOU MIND NOT SHUTTING OFF THE PROGRAM SO SUDDENLY?!
WE'RE DONE WITH TRAINING FOR TODAY.
WAIT UPSTAIRS. HARUKA IS HERE, SO I'LL TREAT YOU TO A WELCOMING CELEBRATION.
WOW!!
REALLY? YOU'RE AWESOME, OLD MAN!
...NOW AO, DON'T YOU HAVE A WORD FOR ME?
....

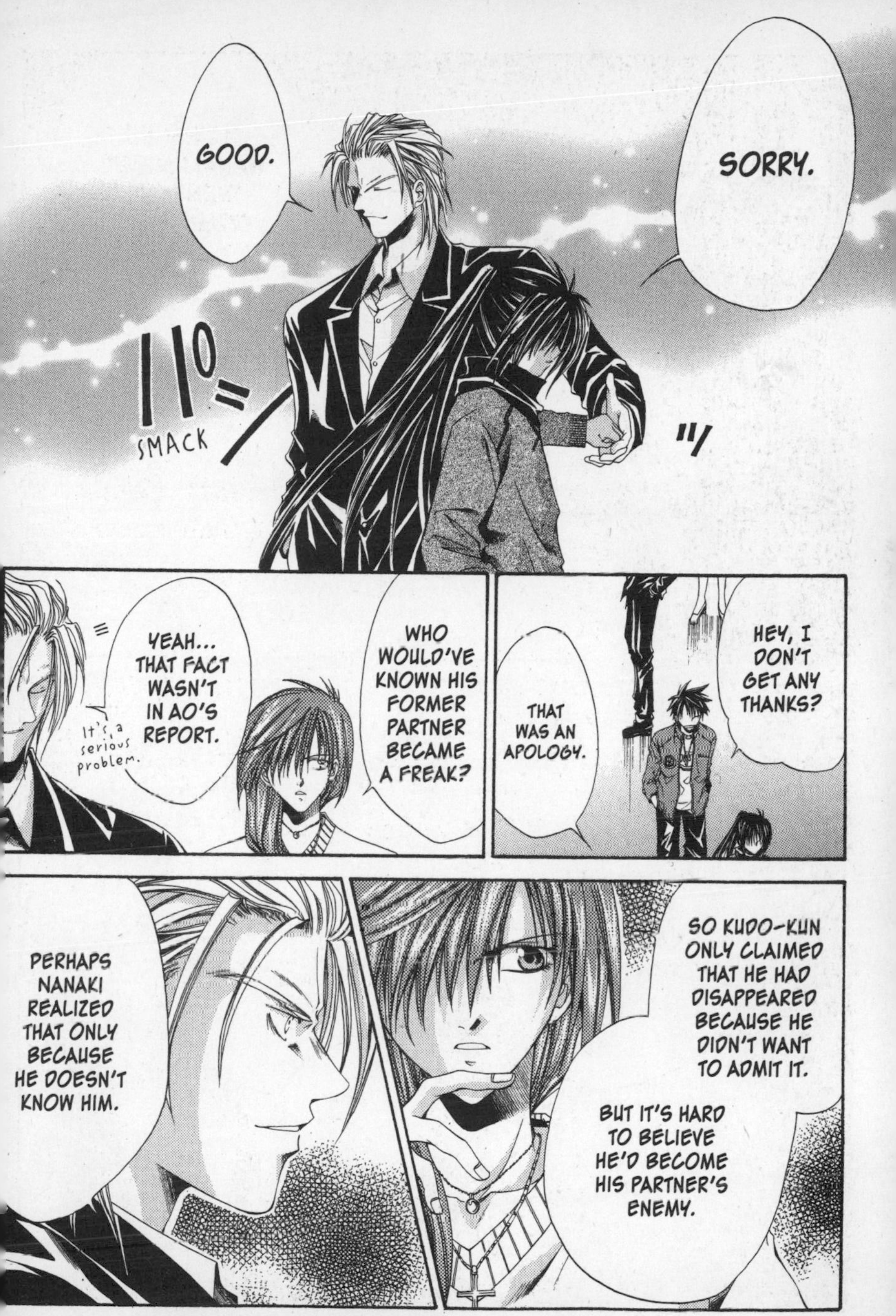
SORRY.
GOOD.
SMACK
HEY, I DON'T GET ANY THANKS?
THAT WAS AN APOLOGY.
WHO WOULD'VE KNOWN HIS FORMER PARTNER BECAME A FREAK?
YEAH... THAT FACT WASN'T IN AO'S REPORT.
It's a serious problem.
SO KUDO-KUN ONLY CLAIMED THAT HE HAD DISAPPEARED BECAUSE HE DIDN'T WANT TO ADMIT IT.
BUT IT'S HARD TO BELIEVE HE'D BECOME HIS PARTNER'S ENEMY.
PERHAPS NANAKI REALIZED THAT ONLY BECAUSE HE DOESN'T KNOW HIM.

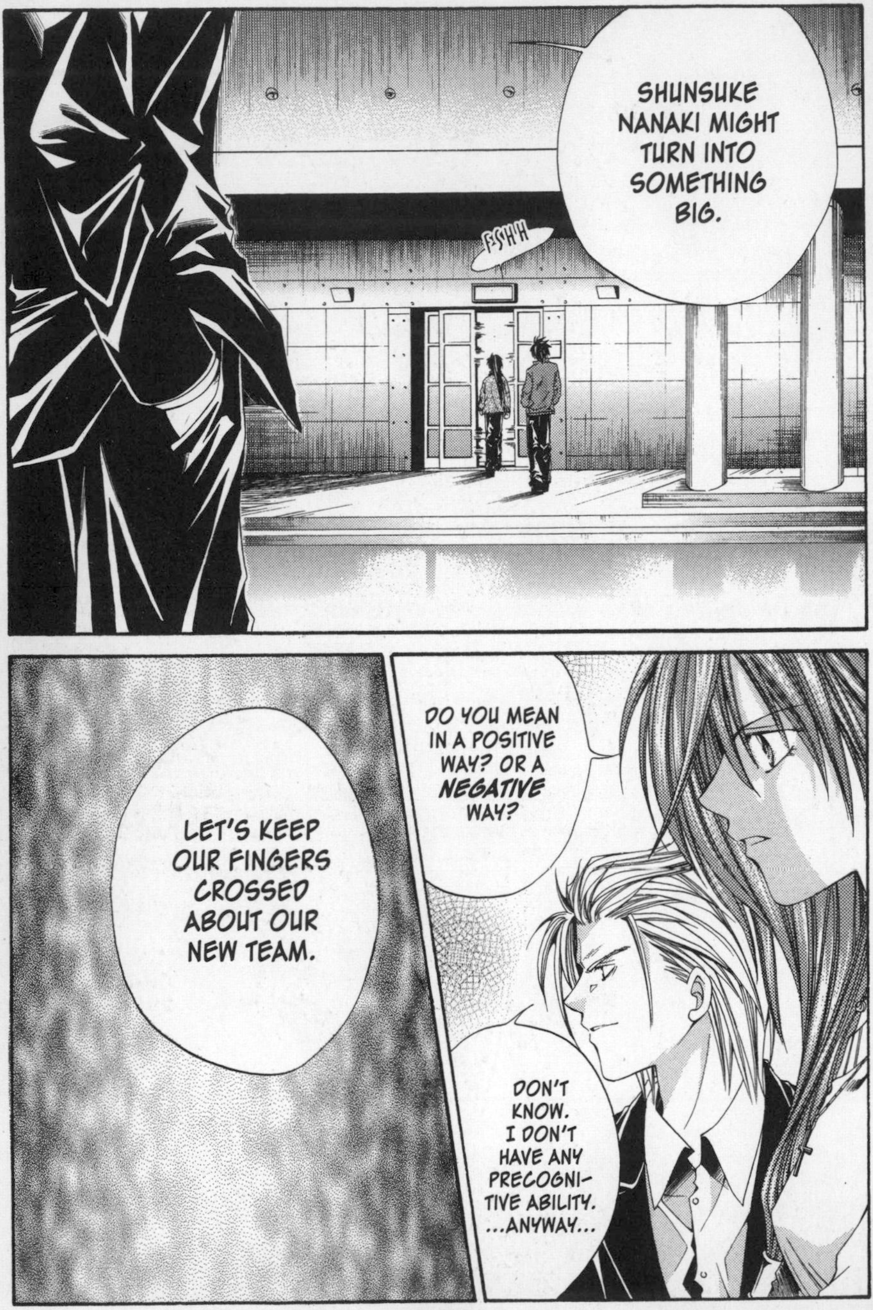
SHUNSUKE NANAKI MIGHT TURN INTO SOMETHING BIG.
FSH'H
DO YOU MEAN IN A POSITIVE WAY? OR A *NEGATIVE* WAY?
DON'T KNOW. I DON'T HAVE ANY PRECOGNI-TIVE ABILITY. ...ANYWAY...
LET'S KEEP OUR FINGERS CROSSED ABOUT OUR NEW TEAM.

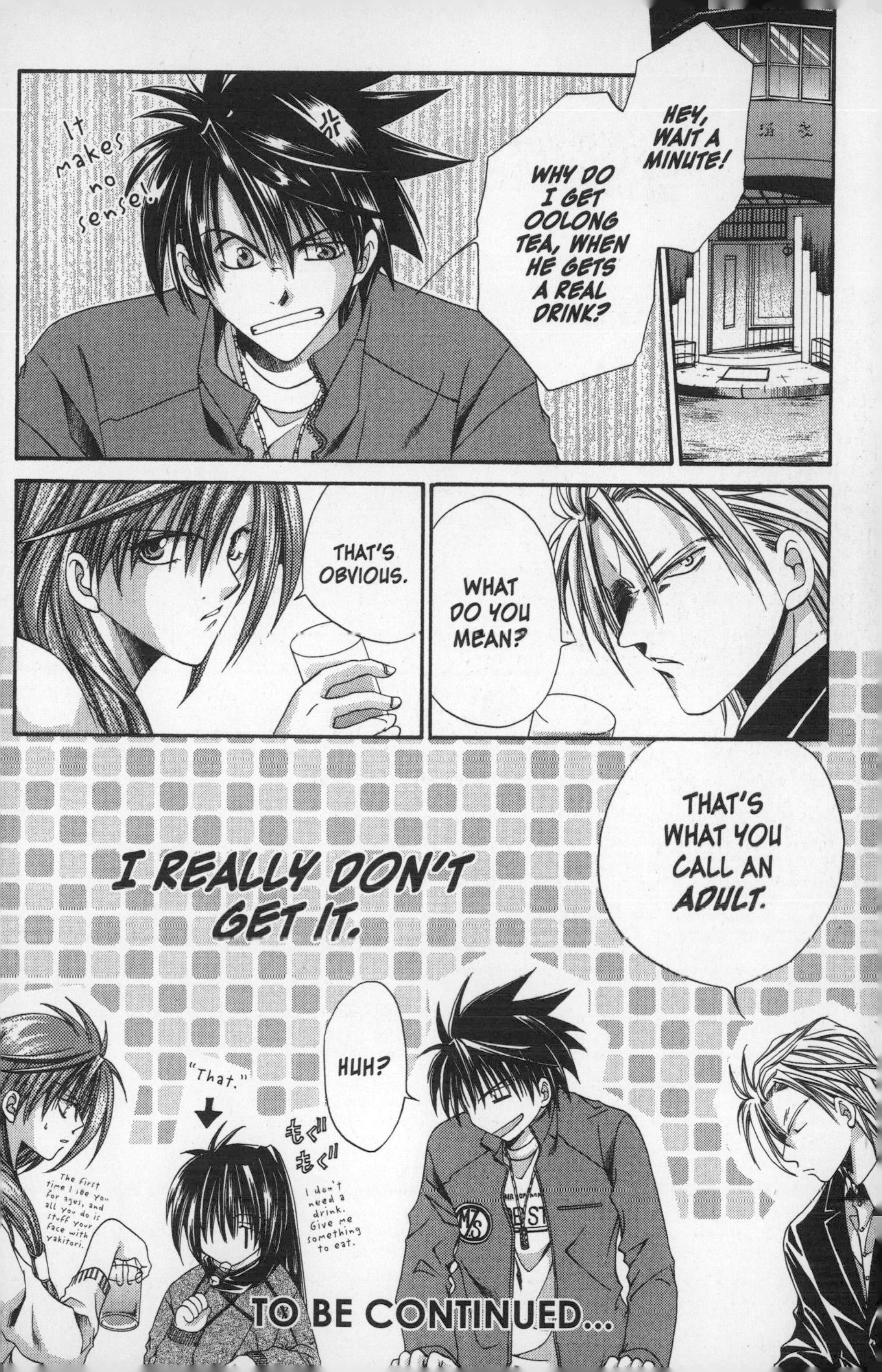
HEY, WAIT A MINUTE!
WHY DO I GET OOLONG TEA, WHEN HE GETS A REAL DRINK?
It makes no sense!
WHAT DO YOU MEAN?
THAT'S OBVIOUS.
THAT'S WHAT YOU CALL AN ADULT.
I REALLY DON'T GET IT.
HUH?
"That."
もぐもぐ
I don't need a drink. Give me something to eat.
The first time I see you for ages, and all you do is stuff your face with yakitori.
TO BE CONTINUED...

POST SCRIPT

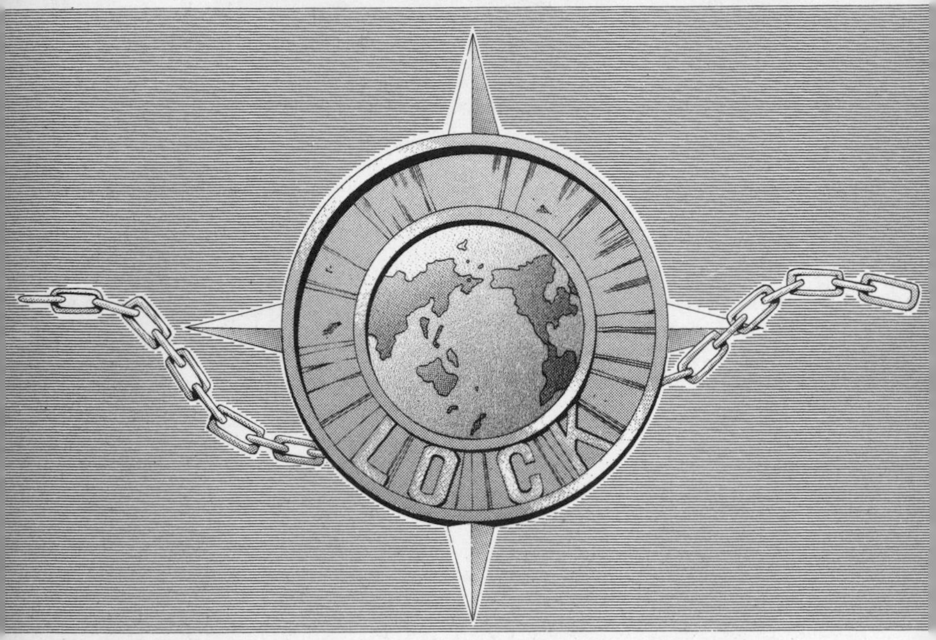
LOCK

Welcome to the postscript! Let's have a chat now, for a change. (Laughs). I'll say a bit more about the characters I introduced earlier. Nanaki, Ao and Gunji all act without me having to think, so they're very easy to draw. I wanted to use a number and a color for names, and that's how I came up with Nanaki [seven] and Ao [blue]. Gunji's name was one my friend requested.

I couldn't decide on Nanaki's and Ao's designs until the last minute. Originally, Nanaki had a subtle hairdo based on a certain father. (Who's that father? (Laughs.)) But I felt he didn't seem strong enough, so I decided to give him spiky hair.

In Ao's case, I wasn't sure what to do with his hair. I had initially planned it to be the same length as the twins' mother's hair in chronicles 4 and 5. When I showed Ao with short and long hair to my friend, she chose the latter. That was simply the way I made that decision.

Originally, Gunji was going to have a real attitude. But I changed my mind, since Nanaki already behaves like that.

...So this is the manga in which these characters make their debut. Thank you for reading all the way to the end. I also appreciate those who sent me letters and gifts. Please continue to support me (laughs).

I give thanks to my friends, acquaintances, the people who help me with my manga, my editor, and my family. See you later!

—Ryo Saenagi

NEXT TIME IN

PSYCHIC POWER
NANAKI™
TOKYOPOP®
2
RYO SAENAGI

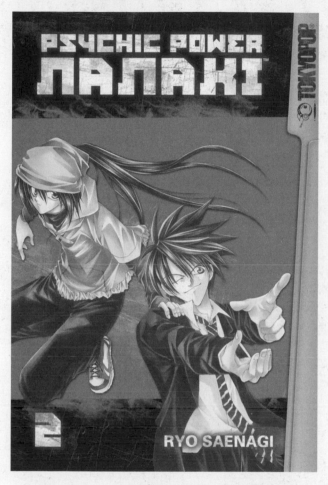

Trouble seems to follow Nanaki wherever he goes! First he has a female stalker trying to prove his psychic ability, and then his partner Ao is kidnapped by a crystal gazer! Will Nanaki be able to save him in time?

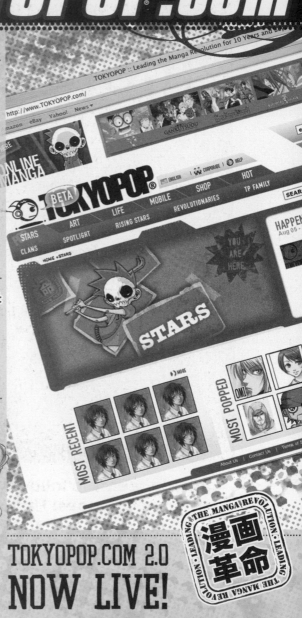
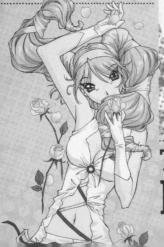

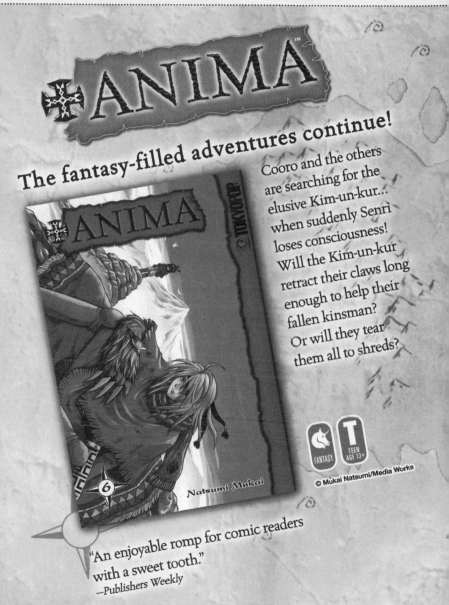

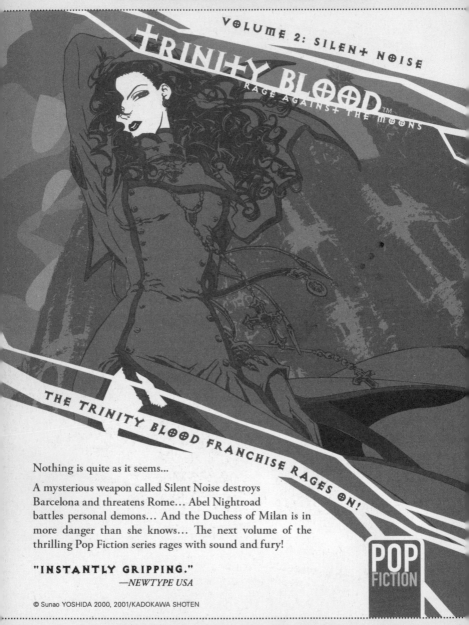

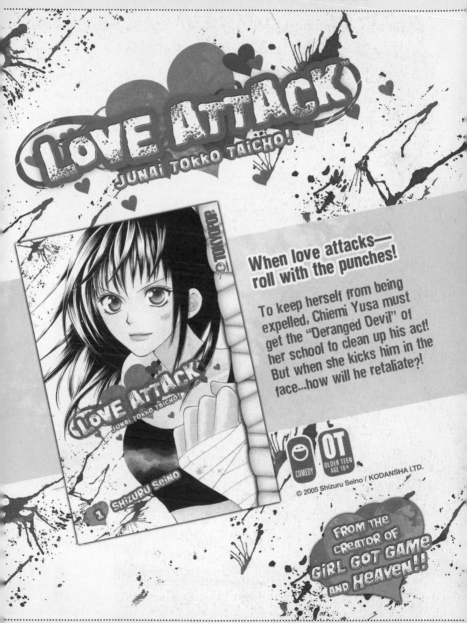

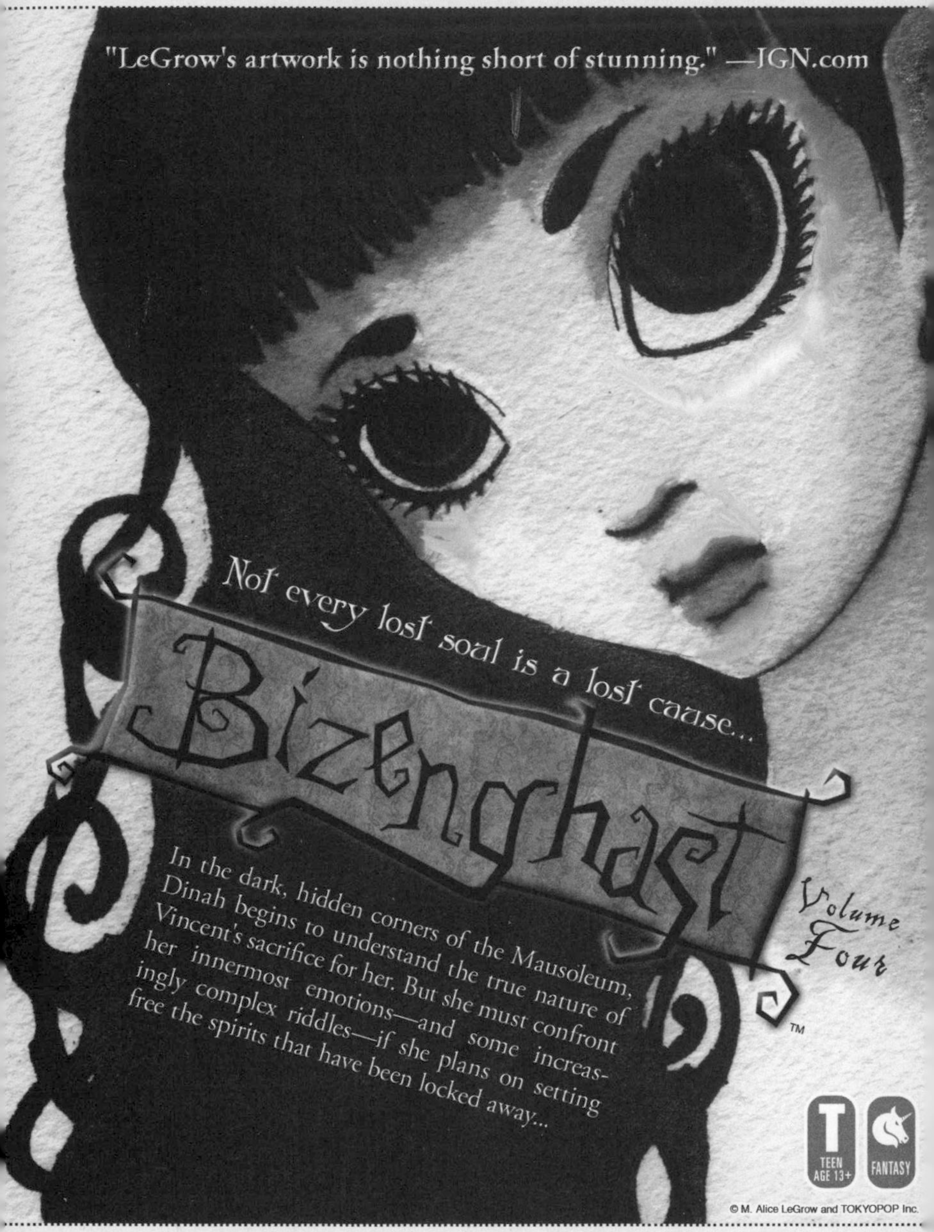
"LeGrow's artwork is nothing short of stunning." —IGN.com
Not every lost soul is a lost cause...
Bizenghast™
Volume Four
In the dark, hidden corners of the Mausoleum, Dinah begins to understand the true nature of Vincent's sacrifice for her. But she must confront her innermost emotions—and some increasingly complex riddles—if she plans on setting free the spirits that have been locked away...
TEEN AGE 13+
FANTASY
© M. Alice LeGrow and TOKYOPOP Inc.

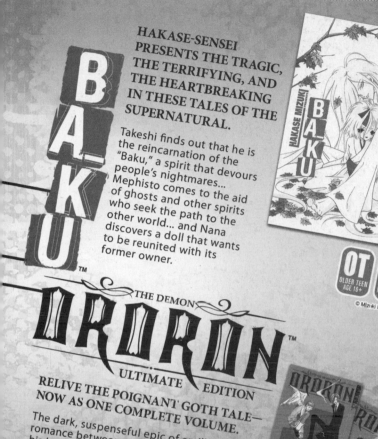
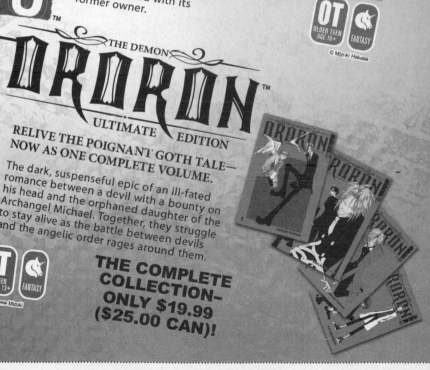

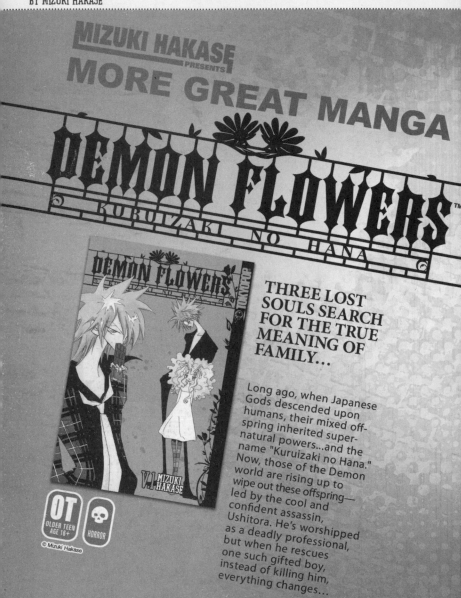

STOP!

This is the back of the book.
You wouldn't want to spoil a great ending!

This book is printed "manga-style," in the authentic Japanese right-to-left format. Since none of the artwork has been flipped or altered, readers get to experience the story just as the creator intended. You've been asking for it, so TOKYOPOP® delivered: authentic, hot-off-the-press, and far more fun!

DIRECTIONS

If this is your first time reading manga-style, here's a quick guide to help you understand how it works.

It's easy... just start in the top right panel and follow the numbers. Have fun, and look for more 100% authentic manga from TOKYOPOP®!

1
2
3
4
5
6
7
8
9
10

漫画革命
THE MANGA REVOLUTION · LEADING

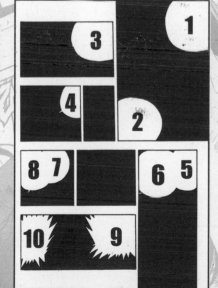

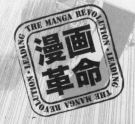